PENGUIN

CHARLES J

L. G. Mitchell is Fellow and Tutor in Modern History at University College, Oxford. He is also the author of *Lord Melbourne*.

Charles James Fox

L. G. MITCHELL

PENGUIN BOOKS

PENGUIN BOOKS

Published by the Penguin Group
Penguin Books Ltd, 27 Wrights Lane, London W8 5TZ, England
Penguin Putnam Inc., 375 Hudson Street, New York, New York 10014, USA
Penguin Books Australia Ltd, Ringwood, Victoria, Australia
Penguin Books Canada Ltd, 10 Alcorn Avenue, Toronto, Ontario, Canada M4V 3B2
Penguin Books (NZ) Ltd, 182–190 Wairau Road, Auckland 10, New Zealand

Penguin Books Ltd, Registered Offices: Harmondsworth, Middlesex, England

First published in the USA by Oxford University Press 1992
First published in Great Britain in Penguin Books 1997
1 3 5 7 9 10 8 6 4 2

Printed in England by Clays Ltd, St Ives plc

Contents

Contents

To Nieuil

Preface

My debts are many. I acknowledge with gratitude the kindness of the following owners of manuscript collections in allowing me access to their materials: His Grace the Duke of Devonshire, the Marquess of Lansdowne, the Earl of Halifax, the Earl Fitzwilliam, the Hon. Mrs Anne Brooke, the Hon. Simon Howard, K. Adam, Esq. of Blair Adam, Coutts Bank, the Provost and Fellows of Eton College, Brooks's Club, the Principal and Fellows of Hertford College, Oxford, and the Warden and Fellows of Merton College, Oxford. I would also like to recognize the generosity of the British Academy in funding part of the research on which this study is based.

Inevitably, my friends find themselves subjected to pressing requests for help. Penny Hatfield, Arlene Shy, Andrew Duncan, Paul Langford, and Mark Hewitson have shown themselves all kindness and encouragement. I can only hope that they, in particular, will be amused by what they now read.

L.G.M.

University College, Oxford
1991

Short Titles

In referring to published sources, the following short titles have been used:

Auckland	*Journal and Correspondence of William Eden, First Lord Auckland*; (London 1861).
Burke	*The Correspondence of Edmund Burke*, ed. T. Copeland; (Cambridge 1958–70).
HMC	*Historical Manuscripts Commission.*
Holland	*Henry Fox, First Lord Holland*, ed. Lord Ilchester; (London 1920).
Fox	*Memorials and Correspondence of C. J. Fox*, ed. Lord J. Russell; (London 1853–7).
Lennox	*Life and Letters of Lady Sarah Lennox*, ed. Lady Ilchester and Lord Stavordale; (London 1901).
Malmesbury	*Diaries and Correspondence of Lord Malmesbury*, ed. Earl of Malmesbury; (London 1844).
Minto	*Life and Letters of Sir Gilbert Elliot, First Earl of Minto*, ed. Lady Minto; (London 1874).
Parl. Hist.	*The Parliamentary History.*
Prince of Wales	*Correspondence of George, Prince of Wales*, ed. A. Aspinall; (London 1963–71).
Rogers	Rev. A. Dyce, *Reminiscences and Table Talk of Samuel Rogers* (Edinburgh 1903).
Sheridan	*The Letters of R. B. Sheridan*, ed. C. Price; (Oxford 1966).
Speeches	*The Speeches of the Rt. Hon. C. J. Fox in the House of Commons*, ed. J. Wright; (London 1815).
Trotter	[J. Trotter], *Circumstantial Details of the Long Illness and last Moments of the Right Hon. Charles James Fox* (London 1806).
Walpole	*Horace Walpole's Correspondence*, ed. W. S. Lewis; (New Haven, Conn. 1937–80).
Windham	L. S. Benjamin, *The Windham Papers* (London 1913).
Wraxall	*The Historical and Posthumous Memoirs of Sir Nathaniel Wraxall*, ed. H. B. Wheatley; (London 1884).

Author's Note

All quotations retain the original spelling and accents.

I

A Father's Son,
1749–1774

FEW fairies seem to have attended the birth and baptism of Charles James
Fox. Born on 24 January 1749, in Conduit St in London, he was unflatteringly described by his father as 'weakly, but likely to live. His skin hangs all
shrivell'd about him, his eyes stare, he has a black head of hair, and 'tis
incredible how like a monkey he look'd before he was dressed.'[1] Dark
features, a heavy beard, and a rather hirsute appearance became the caricaturist's stock-in-trade in their depiction of the man in later life. His nickname became 'the Eyebrow' in recognition of their magnificent luxuriance.
On top of all this, the child was given the names Charles and James. These
were Stuart names, redolent with the conflicts of the seventeenth century,
and Fox acquired them only four years after Bonnie Prince Charlie had
invaded England. With the snuffing out of his invasion, the Stuart cause was
truly dead, but even so prudent parents might have chosen names, in 1749,
that were a little more Hanoverian or politically neutral. Throughout his
life, Fox was known as Charles James, not simply Charles. It seemed that
both Christian names were intoned to emphasize the controversial inheritance of a man whose whole life would be spent in controversy.

The Fox family, in fact, had the strongest Stuart connections. Charles
Fox's grandfather, Sir Stephen Fox, had been a page-boy to Charles I on the
scaffold in 1649.[2] His father, Henry Fox, first Baron Holland, had learnt to
love the Hanoverians, but the allegiance had not been his birthright. All of
this had been reinforced by the distaff·side of the family. Fox's mother,
Caroline, as a daughter of the second Duke of Richmond, was a direct
descendant of Charles II. Charles James Fox was a great-great-grandson of
the Merry Monarch, whom, according to some writers, he strongly resembled. Little wonder then that, when discussing his own nephew's new
baby, Fox should admit that 'you are right about the Baby's having from

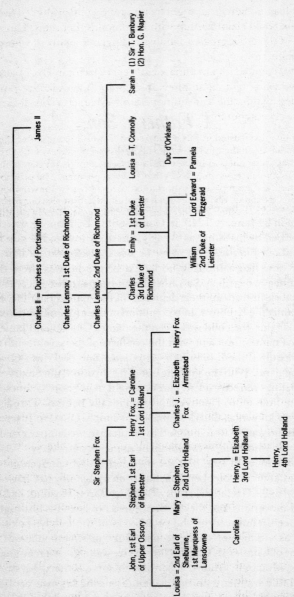

FIG. 1. The immediate family of Charles James Fox

one side at least an hereditary right to admiration of Royalty.'[3] Through his mother, Fox could claim kinship with Richmonds, Leinsters, Lansdownes, and many of the other greatest families in England, many of whom shared his Stuart inheritance.[4]

If ancestry counted for anything, nearly every factor in Fox's background should have made him an admirer of kings and the executive power that they wielded within the constitution. Sir Nathaniel Wraxall and many others were clear about this:

If ever an individual existed in this country who from his natural bias would have inclined to maintain in their fullest extent all the just prerogatives of the Crown, and who would have restrained within due limits every attempt on the part of the people to diminish its influence, we may assert that Fox was the man. The principles of his early education, the example and exhortations of his father — for whom he always preserved an affectionate reverence which constituted a most pleasing feature of his character — his first political connections, all led him to the foot of the throne.[5]

The fact that virtually the whole of Fox's political life was spent attacking the incompetence and malevolence of kings was incongruous. The sight of Fox and his friends attacking the exercise of executive power was so odd that Horace Walpole found it comic: 'On a motion for expunging thanks to Dr. Nowell for a sermon vindicating Charles I, which was carried by 151–42, General Keppel, General Fitzroy, and Charles Fox, all descendants of Charles I, voted against the sermon.'[6] To many contemporaries, the prevarications and changes of front that marked Fox's career were to be accounted for by the fact that he was playing a role that was unnatural to him. He was a natural royalist who had somehow been re-routed into the most determined opposition to George III. His often expressed disgust for the profession of politics was thought to be a cry of desperation on the part of a man who was acting against his own inclinations. It was one answer to the many incongruities of Fox's career.

In spite of an unpromising physical appearance, the Hollands were quickly delighted with their second son. Their eldest boy, Stephen, was amiable but slow-witted. Their youngest, Henry, was also amiable but definitely more suited to the army than to any of the more demanding professions. Charles, by contrast, was quick, intelligent, and appallingly precocious. Famously, Charles Fox enjoyed one of the most indulged childhoods in English history. The only restraint exercised on the boy came from his mother. She could be 'peevish' with the child.[7] She could compare him unfavourably with the infant William Pitt, who, she predicted, 'will be a thorn in Charles's side as long as he lives'.[8] She could even remonstrate with her husband over his indulgence of Charles's whims and fancies.[9] Not surprisingly, perhaps, at the age of 7, Fox informed his father that he much preferred him to his mother.[10] On the night before his mother's death, Fox was seen sitting up all night at White's, discussing plans on how to make a killing during the new racing season.[11]

Lady Caroline, in fact, had very little influence on her son's development. Frequent illnesses and long absences in Bath made her a rather remote figure in Fox's life. Further, even she fell victim to the extraordinary charm that the boy could exert. As she informed her sister:

You can have no idea how companionable a child he is, nor how infinitely engaging to us he is. If Mr Fox and I are alone, either of us, or only us two, he never leaves one; enters into any conversation going forwards; takes his book if we are reading; is vastly amused with any work going on out of doors, as indoors—furniture or anything that's going forwards; will set [*sic*] and read by me when my stomach is bad and I lye down between sleeping and waking; and is in every respect the most agreeable companion. I know you'd make allowances for my partiality, for these same qualities, so pleasing to us, often make him troublesome to other people. He will know everything, watches one if one wants to speak to any body, and is too apt to give his opinion about everything; which, tho' generally a very sensible one, makes him appear pert to other people.[12]

No mother was ever more prophetic. For those who were to know and like him, Fox's personality was utterly compelling. For those who did not, 'pert' would have been too mild an adjective to describe his behaviour. Lady Caroline's feeble attempt to set terms to the boy's conduct came to nothing.[13]

Without doubt, the dominant influence on Fox was his father. It was Henry Fox who decreed that his children 'were to receive no contradiction'.[14] When the boy was barely 3, Henry Fox enjoyed breakfasting with him, and found him 'as civil & as good & as lively as could be; very brisk indeed'.[15] A few years later, the father was irritated that a summons to the House of Commons prevented him from dining '*tête à tête* with Charles,' who was 'infinitely engaging & clever & pretty'.[16] Although Fox was nominally in the charge of a nurse called Nelly, Henry Fox took time off from a busy parliamentary career to record the smallest detail of the boy's progress. Nothing was too insignificant. On 11 March 1752, he solemnly informed his wife that the boy had made 'no Stool', and then began to worry about the likelihood of piles.[17] Kingsgate, the family's mansion in Kent, was always intended for the favoured second son,[18] and such signs of parental favour did nothing to harm Fox in the eyes of his brothers. Stephen and Henry Fox admired their brother almost as much as their father, and relations between the three brothers were cordial throughout their lives. Charles Fox was the Joseph of his family, but, unlike his biblical counterpart, had no penalties to pay.

Very soon, stories began to circulate in London about Henry Fox's indulgence of his precocious son. Allegedly, he stood by while his watch was smashed. Having promised that a wall should be demolished in the boy's presence, and having forgotten his promise, Henry Fox ordered the wall to be rebuilt, so that Charles could witness the second demolition. There seemed to be no limits set to the boy's behaviour, and foreigners began to take up the tales about the indulgent father:

un soir qu'il avoit à préparer des dépêches de grande importance, comme il falloit qu'elles partissent le lendemain matin, il les apporta chez lui, afin d'y travailler avec plus de soin. Fox, qui n'avoit pas plus de dix ans, entra comme de coutume, dans le cabinet de son père, dont la porte n'étoit jamais fermée pour lui: il s'avisa de prendre un papier tout prêt à sceller, et après avoir fait semblant de le lire avec beaucoup d'attention, il le jetta au feu, disant que cela ne lui plaisoit pas. Tout autre que son père eût été irrité d'une telle étouderie; mais au lieu d'en paroître fâché, il retourna tranquillement à son bureau en chercher une copie, et se mit à le recommencer.[19]

This French writer used this story and similar ones to explain the irregularities, moral and financial, of Fox's later life. Many English contemporaries did the same. Henry Fox's deep love for his son made it impossible for him to restrain the boy's exuberance or hobble his personality.

In return, Fox adored his father. As he assured his mother, the only aspect of his monumental gambling losses that gave him pain was the thought that they embarrassed his parents:

In regard to what you say of my father's feelings *a mon sujet* I am sure if you could have known how very miserable you have made me you would not have said it. To be loved by you & him has always been (indeed I am not Hypocrite whatever I may be) the first desire of my life. The reflection that I have behaved in many respects ill to you is almost the only painful one I have ever experienced. That my extreme imprudence & dissipation has given you both uneasiness is what I have long Known, & I am sure I may call those who really know me to witness how much that thought has embittered my life . . . Indeed, indeed my dear Mother no son ever loved a father & mother as I do.[20]

In the same letter, Fox promised to prove his affection by mending his ways. But the letter was written from Newmarket, an ominous sign, and no improvement was forthcoming. Sarcastically, the far-seeing eyes of Mme de Geoffrin led her to 'demande a tout le monde si ce charles fait un meilleur usage de son esprit, de ses talents, et de son tems, que de l'employer a ruiner son père'.[21] This was unduly cynical. There was no reason to doubt Fox's protestations of affection or his inability to fulfil them.

In one crucial respect, Fox repaid his father in full measure. For the whole of his career, Fox defended his father's political reputation. This was no easy brief. Henry Fox, as Paymaster during the Seven Years War, was widely believed to have embezzled huge sums of public money. His accounts were not accepted by Parliament until well after his retirement from office. For the whole of his life, Charles Fox was repeatedly called upon to defend his father's memory, and this was a filial duty that he piously fulfilled. Indeed, it may have been one of the reasons he remained in politics so long, when virtually every other impulse was prompting him to think of retirement. Fox's upbringing may have been unconventional, but it gave him fierce family loyalties. This was Henry Fox's reward for his indulgence of 'the Boys, who together shall ever govern me'.[22]

*

As in all other matters, Fox followed his own inclinations on the question of education. When the boy was 7, Holland simply informed his wife that 'Charles determines to go to Wandsworth.'[23] His choice was a school kept by a certain Frenchman called Pampellone. His Ilchester and Leinster cousins already attended the school, and competition between the families was formidable. Writing to his brother, Holland reported 'a great vying between Lord Stavordale and Charles. Your son intends, if possible, to recover the place he has lost as to making Latin in which mine has got before him; and mine is determined he shall not.'[24] The progression to Eton was more predictable. He entered Dame Milward's House on 22 June 1758. His father's letters record the usual schoolboy rites of passage. Charles was often ill,[25] not immune from accidents,[26] and ordered to 'moderate his Eating'.[27] Dr Barnard, the headmaster, recorded with pride many years later that Fox had been the last boy he had flogged, in a long and distinguished career. The offence had been attendance at a theatrical performance in Windsor.[28] As he grew into adolescence, his heavy, swarthy features became confirmed. According to one story, a bargeman, seeing the naked Fox clambering on to the bank after a dip in the Thames, was so struck by his 'excessive hairiness' that he cried out, 'Damn my eyes, Jack, but I believe there's Nebuchadnezzar just come up from grass.'[29] Gibbon, more sedately, called Pitt a 'pleasure boat' and Fox a 'black collier'.[30]

 More seriously, he acquired at Eton a love of classical languages that became a source of comfort and pleasure for the rest of his life. Latin had many uses. At the age of 12, he employed it to send love verses to his cousin, Lady Susan Fox Strangways, a lady who was coincidentally, and perhaps importantly, also much esteemed by the young George III: 'Charles Fox has made some lattin [*sic*] verses that were sent up for good; the purport of them is to desire a pigeon to fly to his love Susan, & carry her a letter from him, & that if it makes haste it will please both Venus its mistress & him. There now, are you not proud to have your name wrote in a scholar's exercise?'[31] A few years later, his aunt, Lady Sarah Bunbury, received the same compliment.[32] Fox described himself and his two pretty relations as 'three Persons of the most approved wisdom and conduct'.[33] Latin and puppy love went nicely together, and gave the schoolboy status. In 1761, Fox asked his elder brother to use the following address when sending him books: 'Eton Bucks near Windsor Bucks, ha ha ha ha.'[34] Whatever its purpose, Eton thought fit to publish Fox's efforts in Latin and to hold them up to public approbation.[35]

If Etonian Latin proved the quality of the gentleman, Etonian friendships were even more sustaining in the long run. As will be seen, Foxite politics could later be defined as the manipulation of friendship. Men followed Fox, not because they necessarily agreed with his views, but because they found his character utterly compelling. Burke, long after the termination of his political association with Fox, admitted that he was a 'man made to be loved'.[36] Fox adored being '*much'd* by his friends'.[37] Fox's company was so sought after that a new verb, 'to Charley',[38] was coined to describe the pleasure of being invited for the weekend. His approbation conferred status on those who sought it, dignified views, and confirmed talent. Twenty years after his death, the sheer power of Fox's personality was sharp in the memory: 'his presence gave more éclat to the assemblies even of a Royal Duchess, than that of the Heir Apparent. To be honoured with praise, or even with recognition, by Mr Fox, stamped the young aspirants after distinction with a value which nothing else could confer, and at once gave them currency, in the society to which they were ambitious of rising.'[39]

Fox revelled in the company of friends. Among the nicknames that he and his friends invented for themselves were 'the Gang' and 'the Confederates of the Bank'.[40] They were to borrow each other's houses and mistresses.[41] They were to die in each other's presence.[42] One of the few regrets Fox ever expressed about his public life was 'that though I have been twice a Minister, with the single exception of the Bishop of Downe . . . not one of my friends is the better for my power.'[43] His circle of friends formed a cocoon of warmth and uncritical admiration. There were dangers in the exclusivity of these friendships, notably that Fox could, from time to time, be properly accused of being reluctant 'to invite the knowledge of what is said out of his own circle',[44] but the benefits were also enormous. His friends formed his principal capital. Brooks's Club, where the 'gang' congregated, was rightly described as the 'liaison qu'entraine le jeu'.[45]

In a sense, the concept of Foxite was formed at Eton. Dr Barnard's Entrance Book covering the years 1756–61 is a roll-call of names that appear endlessly through Fox's career. Joining Fox in Dame Milward's House were the second Duke of Leinster, the first Marquess of Cholmondeley, two

Waldegrave brothers, the future Lord Walsingham, the second Earl of
Ilchester, Viscount Galway, the second Marquess Townshend, and his brother John. In other Houses were to be found James Hare, Thomas Poole,
the future Lord Salisbury, Uvedale Price, William A'Court, the future Earl
of Carlisle and the future Earl Fitzwilliam, the Duke of Buccleuch, William
Windham, and the future Duke of Northumberland.[46] Some of these men
went on to become Fox's closest friends and political associates, like Fitzwilliam and Carlisle. Some, like Buccleuch, saw more of Fox at Newmarket
than in Parliament. More retiring peers like Salisbury merely helped financially. Whether names appear on future division lists or subscription lists
matters little, however. What is clear is that Etonian friendships stuck.
Reviewing Fox's school career in 1787, *The World* concluded that his 'companions were then the same as they are now'.[47] When Fox left Eton, 'as too
witty to live there—and a little too wicked',[48] he had learnt the power of
friendship and the potential of his own personality. His leaving portrait,
which now hangs in the Provost's Lodgings, was given by him to a school for
which he always expressed great regard and gratitude.

By contrast, Oxford was never held in much affection. Fox was entered
for Hart Hall, now Hertford College, in the autumn of 1764. It was a good
choice. Under the Principalship of Richard Newton, Hart Hall was one of
the more demanding colleges in a university that was not renowned for
stretching aristocratic undergraduates unduly, and initially Fox responded.
As he explained to a friend, 'I did not expect my life here to be so pleasant as
I find it, but I really think to a Man who reads a great deal there cannot be a
more agreeable place.'[49] He read yet more classical authors and enjoyed
dabbling in mathematics. He was sufficiently fond of one of his tutors to
solicit preferment for him many years later.[50] But, overall, Oxford had not
moved him spiritually or intellectually. On going down, he reflected that he
was 'totally ignorant in every part of usefull knowledge. I am more convinced every day how little advantage there is in being what at School and
the University is called a good Scholar.'[51] Late in life, he detested Oxford as
'the capital of Toryism', advised his nephew not to bother with 'so foolish a
thing as a degree', and commiserated with him for being 'obliged to be at
Oxford for your various nonsenses'.[52] No doubt Fox's natural indolence
made him a poor scholar, but the sleepy qualities of eighteenth-century
Oxford offered few new stimuli. It could hardly improve on Eton's training
in the classics; and there was little else. To understand the development of
Fox's personality, one must look elsewhere.

In a broad sense, France was Fox's university, not Oxford. In early
adolescence, he was taken by his father for an introductory encounter with

Paris. As his great schoolfriend, Carlisle, recorded, it was a profoundly exciting experience:

It pleased too indulgent a father to carry him at 15 to Paris, when he ought to have been at Eton School. He talked French admirably, & employd [*sic*] it in declaiming against Religion with a fashionable grace that wd. have charmed Voltaire himself. He gamed deep; had an arranged intrigue with a certain Mad.ᶜ de Quallens, of high fashion, came back to Eton, & was whipped with me for stealing out of Church, to play at Tennis.[53]

Turning down the offer of another visit for Christmas 1763, Fox tried to use this as proof that 'the petit maître de Paris is converted into an Oxford pedant',[54] but he was not convincing. Paris now had 'great charms' for him. He returned to Eton in the autumn of 1763 having lost a great deal of money and probably his virginity. The schoolboy could be seen swaggering round Windsor 'with his hatt [*sic*] & feather very french & very much improved'.[55] His Parisian experience became the terms of reference by which he judged the politeness of any society he later found himself in.

In April–May 1765, Fox again visited the French capital, in the company of his brother Stephen and his mother.[56] His Oxford tutor, William New-come, encouraged the excursion, expressing the hope, in a rather unworldly manner, that 'you will return with much keenness for Greek and for lines and angles.'[57] He would be disappointed. According to his father, Fox 'relished' Paris 'as much as ever', and called the city 'such a nurture in Education [as] was never seen'.[58] Fox certainly met and conversed with Hume while abroad, but the philosopher both accurately judged the talent which confronted him and the dangers which encompassed it:

David is extremely surpriz'd at his knowledge, force of mind, and manly ways of thinking at his age. At the same time he has insinuated his fears to me, that the dissipation of this kind of Parisian life might check his ardor after useful knowledge, and lose in all appearance a very great acquisition to the publick. I told Charles this conversation between me and Hume, and that I was obliged to own that the risk would be very great, 99 times in a hundred, but that I trusted to a noble and worthy ambition, which I thought I saw very strong in him, and which gave me the strongest assurance that he would neither disappoint the public nor his friends. Tho' Charles won't promise anything positively upon this subject, yet he acknowledges himself to be entirely of my opinion.[59]

If there is a hint of arrogance in Fox's remark, this is not accidental. Even in Paris, the most sophisticated city in the world, the 16-year-old had no notion of humility. When one of the most intelligent and renowned hostesses in Paris refused to receive him, the boy wrote to his father, asking 'Do not you think Mme Geoffrin a very silly Woman, not to cultivate more so agreeable an acquaintance as I am.'[60]

Further visits in 1769 and 1771 confirmed Fox's view that Paris was everything a young man could wish for, the chance of conversing with clever people and sexual licence. At 20, Fox was the accomplished man of the world writing naïvely about love. He listed among the great qualities of the French that they treated

> l'amour d'une manière si legere, si agréable. Apres tout les
> grandes passions sont de dernier ridicule, & avec le temps je
> t'en ferai convenir.
> Pour guerir de la maladie
> Qu'amour on nomme, deux beaux yeux
> Reussiront mille fois mieux
> Que l'austère Philosophie
> S'amuser avec deux tetons
> D'une jeune & jolie filette
> Vaut mieux que les doctes leçons
> Des Senecas et des Platons
> Et la petite Henriette
> Seroit un meilleur medecin
> En ces cas que le grand Tronchin.[61]

Gasconade and swagger fill Fox's letters from France. His closest friends were treated to such useful tips on gallantry as never 'courir apres une femme c'est bourgeois cela'.[62] Little wonder that Parisians were slow to accept Fox's pretensions. Mme du Deffand told Horace Walpole that, 'toute réflexion faite', Fox 'me plaît médiocrement; il a de l'esprit, mais c'est un esprit précoce, il ne mûrira jamais, il est sans goût, sans saveur, il est âpre et vert; son imagination, son feu, le mèneront loin, mais il croit trouver tout en lui et il négligera toujours l'instruction et l'étude dont il n'aura pas besoin pour la circonstance du moment . . . Il y a du Jean-Jacques.'[63] The image of Fox as the eternal adolescent, never willing to shoulder the full responsibility of either love or politics, was to become an enduring one.

In September 1766, Fox left England on the Grand Tour, and did not return until 2 August 1768.[64] After spending the winter of 1766–7 with his family in Italy, he seems to have been left largely to his own devices. While in his company, Lord Holland was delighted that all this travelling was turning Charles into the 'petit maître achevè [*sic*]', and found his son 'beyond Measure kind and attentive to me, he has a good heart & more to be admired for that than for his head which you know is is [*sic*] no bad one.'[65] Italy in fact had an enduring influence on Fox. He acquired its language, and its literature was read and re-read throughout his life. He commanded Fitzpatrick to 'learn Italian as fast as you can, if it be only to read Ariosto. There is more good poetry in Italian than in all other languages that I understand put together . . . I do not believe there is any book in the world has so much entertainment in it as Bocace. Make haste and read all these things that you may be fit to talk to Christians.'[66] An audience with the Pope was amusing in retrospect, though 'Fox put on so rueful a countenance, looked so like a disarmed Culprit that it was impossible to resist laughing, which his Holiness was too good-natured to be offended with.'[67] What Fox liked in Italy was not its religion, but its associations with the classical world and the power of its poetry. He would always cite Ariosto, Boccaccio and Metastasio among his favourite authors.

For much of 1767 and 1768, Fox was at large in or near France. For travelling companions he had his Etonian circle of Fitzwilliam, Carlisle, and Uvedale Price. Their adventures were predictably picaresque. Voltaire was too preoccupied to offer dinner, but he did allow them a short interview, after which he provided a list of books that, in his opinion, would protect the young men from all religious prejudices. Gibbon in Lausanne was more hospitable and more free with his time.[68] Travelling confirmed the dandy in Fox. He affected fashionable red heels for his shoes and on his head carried a 'little odd French hat'.[69] Allegedly, he made a special journey from Paris to Lyons to buy waistcoats.[70] His French acquaintance was, of course, much broadened. He became friends with the Duc de Lauzun and attended the levée of the Duc d'Orléans. Men who were to play leading roles in the great Revolution had come within Fox's compass at a very early stage of his life.[71] His tour abroad provisioned him with all the philosophy, friendships, and fashion that would mark him out, on his return to London, as a man of the world.

France and Italy also underlined that element in Fox's character that revelled in sexual licence. To describe his escapades in this context, Fox invented a *doppelgänger* called 'Carlino', as if to offload guilt. The adventures of Charles or 'Carlino' were certainly vivid. He was late for a rendezvous in Genoa with Carlisle for reasons that Don Giovanni would have understood:

He told me He had nearly broken his appointment, for you must know since we parted I have been in a sort of scrape. I have run away with a Jeweller's wife. & where the Devil did you run to? Into the Mountains, with the design of conveying her to England, I was so much in love. And how soon were you out of love?—in a few days. Made it up with the husband, bought off Assassination, & here I am.[72]

A full account of Fox's intrigues was published in Geneva in 1785; according to the author, the lady's name had been Clementine, and Fox had actually killed her husband.[73] Few English politicians can have had their private life catalogued in this way for the perusal of a European audience. For much of his career, Fox would be accused of operating a morality

peculiar to himself or no morality at all. His reputation for what contemporaries pleasantly called 'gallantry' was established before he entered
public life.

Cities and towns were defined, in letters to schoolfriends, by the extent to
which they offered sexual possibilities. Turin was dull because 'I do not
know any thing I can tell you from this place that will divert you, only that
there has been a woman of fashion put in prison lately for f——g (I suppose
rather too publicly) a piece of unexampled tyranny! & such as could happen
in no place but this . . . Kitty & Angelina are as charming as ever; I believe
they will be my principal company while I am here.'[74] Nice was worse
because the town had 'no whores'. Eventually, matters improved:

> There is a Mrs Holmes here an Irish woman more beautiful than words can express
> . . . Now it so happens that tho' this woman is exquisite entertainment for Charles,
> yet, as she is chaste as she is pure, she does not altogether do for Carlino so well.
> There is also at that same Nice a silversmith's wife, who is almost as fair as Mrs
> Holmes, but not near so chaste, & she attracts me thither as regularly in the evening,
> as the other does in the morning. Ask Fitz. whether he remembers a certain Mad.ᵉ
> de Castelinard a silversmith's wife. She is the woman who at present receives
> Carlino, who never desired, much less had better lodging. I was a long time here
> before I could get a f—— but in recompense for my sufferings, I have got a most
> excellent piece that must be allowed.[75]

The same letters cheerfully and philosophically record 'poxes and claps' as
the price to be paid for entertainment. The pain could be alleviated by turning out Latin verses on venereal disease for the amusement of his friends.[76]

Until the middle 1780s, when he took up with Mrs Armistead, Fox's private life was publicly conducted on rules learnt in France, and predictably
attracted much comment. Back in England, Fox, at 20, reflected on his Grand
Tour, and his conclusions would not have pleased the moralist. Parisian
women were the most delightful and accomplished in the world. Brothel life
'est un sujet si noble, que ce seroit l'avilir que de le celebrer en prose.'[77]
Marriage was an absurdity. He assured Richard Fitzpatrick that he had
'nulle inclination pour le mariage, que c'était même mon aversion, & que
rien ne m'y pourroit engager.'[78] He would not enter into a stable relationship until he was 35 and would not marry until he was 46. For the
moment, the young man was clear that 'friendship was the only real happiness in the world.'[79] France had totally confirmed Fox's reliance on mistresses
and Etonian friendships.

*

Complementing the influence of France was the influence of London. At a
very early age, Fox plunged happily into the vigorous social life of clubs,

dinner-parties, and dances that filled the London Season. By the time he was 25, he was a member of the Literary Club,[80] the Dilettanti Society,[81] and, most prestigiously, the Club itself.[82] At meetings of these societies, Fox encountered Burke and could converse with Goldsmith, Dr Johnson, and the other literary giants of the day. Boswell recorded that, in Johnson's presence, even Fox could be shy.[83] Less seriously, in the early 1770s, Fox was one of London's leading Macaronis, dandies in tight-fitting and often bizarrely cut clothes, who strutted around London to the scandal of many and to the delight of the cartoonist. The scruffy and unkempt Fox that is so often represented in the cartoons of the 1780s and 1790s had little in common with the rather elegant young man, whose clothes yet again marked him out as thoroughly Frenchified.[84] The young Fox, in terms of fashion or social and intellectual companionship, had all the status that London society could afford.

Fox was fashionable too in not allowing religion to influence him unduly. Voltaire would have been proud of his pupil when he told the House of Commons in 1773 that 'Religion was best understood when least talked of.'[85] There were to be no external constraints on the conduct of Fox, who, at the astonishingly early age of 15, seems to have been living an independent existence in London, and drawing freely on his father's banker.[86] In London and in Oxford, gambling losses became a regular feature of his letters to his parents, mingled with pious resolutions to abandon the habit. The boy assured his father that he had 'a most fixed Resolution never again to play', but he also had the self-knowledge to be not 'sure enough of my strength to give an absolute promise'.[87] Just as an addiction to gambling was an ingrained element in Fox's character before he was out of his teens, so was the experience of being pursued by irate tradesmen brandishing unpaid bills. He complained to Fitzpatrick of every day being 'Pelted with a letter' from some 'hound' of a shopkeeper demanding payment.[88] Here was a pattern that would be repeated over and over again for the rest of his life.

Gambling losses and money shortages led the young Fox into many scrapes and lapses of judgement. For example, in 1773, a certain matchmaker called Mrs Grieve paid Fox £300 for allowing his coach to be seen outside her house, thereby endowing the building with a certain éclat. The same lady then persuaded him that all his financial problems would be at an end if he were to marry a certain 'Miss Phipps', an heiress from the West Indies. In the event, the lady in question turned out to be a penniless 'Blackamoor', and the trick played on Fox was so comic that Samuel Foote immediately incorporated it into his next play, *The Cozeners*. Fox, whose peccadilloes were rarely private, now had the pleasure of seeing his latest escapade played out on the London stage before appreciative audiences.[89] None of this moved Fox at all. Even when he was a young man, it was one of Fox's greatest strengths or greatest weaknesses that he was absolutely impervious to opinion at large. Carlisle was very clear about this:

He was incapable of assuming virtues he had not, & equally of any restraint when the gratifications of his appetites were concerned. Feeling that by gaming, wine, women, loss of fortune, pressure of debt . . . the respect of the world was not easily retrievable, he became so callous to what was said of him, as never to repress a single thought, or even temper a single expression when he was before the public.[90]

His London circle was self-sufficient and self-supporting.[91]

By contrast, the countryside held few attractions. In the same letter to Fitzpatrick, life at Kingsgate in Kent is described in terms of 'je me promens a cheval & a pied, je mange, je bois, je dors', and contrasted to a recent visit to London where 'We had a pleasant Gourmand dinner at Vernon's, low Quinze & Piquet, I was struck for about 60. This with fucking in cundums frigging etc. was my chief employment in Town.'[92] Taking refuge in the worldly language of French, Fox wrote verses on the advantages of town-living over life in the countryside. Addressing friends with nicknames like 'Vice' and 'Bully', Fox rhymed as follows:

> Ces messieurs nous repetent sans cesse
> que dans ce sejour enchanteur
> on trouve la paix, et le bonheur,
> la volupté et l'allegresse,
> Sous l'humble toit du laboureur,
> des Palais fuyant la tristesse.
> Croira qui voudra, mais pour moi
> ces radoteurs ont beau precher,
> je choisirois l'état de Roi,
> plutôt que celui de Berger.[93]

Such views are a far cry from those expressed by Fox in middle age, when leaving the quiet of St Anne's Hill for the capital was barely tolerable. For the young man, London and its dissipations were everything.

There was a price to be paid for these preferences. Fox's self-indulgence was no secret, and writers quickly began to bemoan wasted talents, a theme that would re-echo throughout his career. It was thought tragic that so talented a man 'should have rendered himself so useless to his country'.[94] Anything could be believed about Fox, and where truth gave out, rumour was just as credible. In 1783, for example, in the middle of a constitutional crisis, a pamphlet appeared in London on the art of breaking wind, which was allegedly written by Fox for a wager.[95] It was a type of publicity that would follow Fox throughout his political career.

Criticism was mitigated by two factors. First, Fox's behaviour took place within a context which made it unusual, but not exceptional. As his cousin recorded, conventional religion and morality were at a discount in the 1760s and 1770s:

His birth was at an unfortunate period for him—It was just when the *New Philosophy* was broach'd wch. has since broke down all the dikes of Religion & Morality . . . When he grew up it was in its full vigour & fashion—& certainly had as was natural great influence on a mind like his, young & fervent in his inclinations, with sharp passions & confident in his powers—& his Education had nothing in it that cd. at all counteract any of those principles & doctrines.[96]

As Carlisle remembered, Fox spent his youth in a London presided over by '37 Ladies . . . who would have all been affronted, had you supposed their [*sic*] had been a grain of conjugal fidelity among them.' Interestingly, Carlisle goes on to identify France as the source of these manners, and the French Revolution as marking a watershed in moral values, when the 'great Academy of refined profligacy perished with its Professors'.[97] Certainly moral values are never constant, and those that Fox learnt and refined in his youth would look out of place thirty years later. For the moment, they had a certain currency.

Secondly, Fox's indiscretions were overlaid by a charm of personality that made forgiving him one of his friends' greatest and most irresistible pleasures. His vices were artless. There was no hypocrisy in them and a naïvety that was astonishing in so intelligent a man. One of his closest friends saw 'so little cunning or suspicion in his nature, that he was ever the prey of Knaves, even to fools'.[98] In his enthusiasms and his robust responsiveness to life, Fox was almost childlike. Above all, he was absolutely free of ambition: 'For pleasure, ambition has been perpetually sacrificed, & for sensual indulgence he has himself helped to choke up all the avenues that led to those situations.'[99] Fox was totally unconcerned 'that the public too frequently felt itself insulted by the bare-faced exhibition of weakness'.[100] For much of Fox's career, private life held more attractions than public. He was a friend, drinking partner, and, finally, husband, before he was a politician. It was endearing that a man of such abilities should be content never to be 'anything but a lounging fellow'.[101]

*

If Paris and London were the two factors that encouraged a natural disinclination in Fox to busy himself with the tedium of politics, a third pushed him inexorably in the opposite direction. It might simply be termed family obligation. Fox belonged to a family which believed that English

politicians had not accorded it the status that it deserved. Indeed, part of
Fox's preference for France lay in his suspicions of England. Aged 14, he
assured his father that 'Je suis toujours Français dans le cœur, et en vérité ce
n'est pas merveilleux que je les donne la preference avant un peuple ingrat,
comme nous autres.'[102] Family demands and experience set the agenda for
Fox's politics. He had to enter Parliament to defend ancestral decisions and
to continue old vendettas.

The most pressing was that concerning his father's career. Hamlet-like,
Fox, by duty and affection, was bound to defend the behaviour of his father.
As a young MP in 1771, Fox denied that his father had been responsible for
the Massacre of the Pelhamite Innocents, and added that, even if he had, 'it
was right to break the power of the aristocracy that had governed in the
name of the late King.'[103] When he insisted that his father had not been a
corrupt manipulator of electoral campaigns, he drew on himself the charge
that he wished to exercise 'an hereditary right of managing elections'.[104]
The difficulty was that, after long years in politics, Henry Fox's hands were
notoriously unclean, and all the brave words of a talented son could not
repair the damage. In particular, there was the problem of Henry Fox's
accounts during his term of office as Paymaster-General. It was widely believed that he had embezzled huge sums of public money, and, as has been
said earlier, his accounts were not accepted by Parliament until long after
his death. Every mention of the matter brought Fox to his feet. A speech of 8
April 1794 is typical. On that occasion, Fox offered the following lame
excuse:

The fact was certainly true that his father had made a large fortune—great fortunes
were made by the predecessors of his father in that office—great fortunes were also
made by his successors. It was as true that great and unaccounted deficiencies
existed in his office; but it was equally true that such deficiencies were as great and as
unsettled under former paymasters as him, and with as little personal blame.[105]

A correlation could always be made in the public mind between the Fox
family and peculation, and it was an association that would often harm Fox
in his career.

Inevitably, Charles Fox inherited his father's enemies. Henry Fox's dismissal from politics in May 1765 was ascribed to great Whig aristocrats
punishing him for his loyalty to Bute. Certainly, Bute was long seen as the
family's patron. An application for an earldom in 1772 was made through
the former favourite.[106] The young Fox was 'angry' at the way his father had
been treated, but Henry Fox philosophically reflected that 'He may be the
more egg'd on by it. May not I build on him for many hours of Comfort?'[107]
He was not disappointed. The boy produced a poem passionate in its defence

of Bute and Henry Fox and contemptuous of those who had contributed to their downfall:

> Longtems du peuple Pitt favori adoré
> Les meprisant toujours, en fut toujours aimé
> Estimant leur amour, il prodigua leur vie
> Et cherchoit la gloire au depens de sa patrie.
> Le peuple malheureux, ebloui de succés
> Voyoit bien ses victoires sans voir leurs effets.
> Dedaignant de la Paix la douceur plus tranquille,
> Il suivit volontiers une Guerre inutile;
> Loua de ses projets le detestable Auteur,
> Content d'être perdu, pourvu qu'il fut vainqueur,
> Et chantant de leur Pitt la vertu si vantée,
> De la Chine au Perou etend son renommée.
> Tandis que de son Prince veritable ami
> Bute vivoit, toujours, vertueux et hai;
> En vain, il terminoit, par une Paix heureuse,
> Une Guerre, à la fois, funeste & glorieuse.
> Nous Lui refusâmes l'amour qui fut dû,
> Il perdit cet amour en suivant la vertu.
> Nous sommes des ingrats, qui rendant nos hommages
> A un fourbe orateur, refusons nos suffrages,
> Au digne Citoyen, qui nous aime, a ce point.
> Qu'il nous veut conserver, quand nous n'en voudrons point.
> Preserver ce portrait, cher Nicall, d'une terre,
> Que je rougis, en effet, de nommer ma mère.[108]

The Fox family subscribed to a very clear demonology. As this poem suggests, the Elder Pitt was a central figure in it, and the fact Fox spent so much of his political life attacking his son must have been particularly sweet for him. Also among the perceived villains of politics were the aristocratic families of the Whig Old Corps. Fox was delighted when, with regard to the Rockingham government, he found 'everybody laughing at them & holding them cheap'.[109] As for the political connection of the Duke of Bedford, he confessed himself 'ill-natured enough to be very sorry whenever there is a chance of the Bedfords' being pleased'.[110] He always wanted them to be 'ill used',[111] and he always spoke of them 'in his old Strain of dislike'.[112] In a sense, this distaste for the great Whig families maintained an even older family tradition. Dukes of Bedford and Devonshire, carrying the surnames Russell and Cavendish, had contributed to the overthrow of Charles I and the difficulties of Charles II, Fox's ancestors. Their attack on Henry Fox was therefore par for the course. Fox believed that a wicked, grasping aristocracy had held George I and George II in thrall, while oligarchy was established in England. When George III tried to break their power, using the honest services of Bute and Henry Fox, aristocracy fought back and was exposed for the corrupt phenomenon it was. Even Etonian friendships could not overcome this aversion. Fox told Fitzwilliam[113] that nothing could 'balance the obligations our family has to Lord Bute, and the shocking ingratitude it has met with from the Bedfords'.[114]

Later generations were to find these adolescent views astounding. Fox was to spend most of his political life defending the Whig aristocracy and its historical record. He was to number Russells and Cavendishes among his closest friends. George III was to become, in his mind, an unredeemably awful thing. It was therefore almost comic that the young Fox should denounce 'the factious opposition of many of the Nobles', and should wish to 'put a stop to an aristocratic party that had been gaining ground for some years, and which should it succeed, is worse even than the absolute despotism'.[115] He very much wanted, in 1771, 'to break the power of the aristocracy'.[116] The violent change of direction between the early and later years was endlessly commented upon, and was usually taken as a further sign of Fox's instability. This was unfair. The discrepancy lies in a young man initially adopting, without thought or question, the prejudices of an adored father. Later experience, the influence of other men, and his own intelligence would take him in a different direction. Fox would be a better Whig for being a convert to Whiggery.

*

Charles Fox was elected to Parliament on 10 May 1768, when at the age of 19 he was technically ineligible to stand. The borough of Midhurst had been secured for him by his father. He made his first speech on 9 March 1769.[117] Few men were better prepared for politics. Paris, London, and Eton had equipped him with all necessary attainments, and his childhood had been spent in the centre of politics. He had been attending debates in the two Houses of Parliament since he was 14.[118] Few débutants were busier or made a name more quickly. Between 1769 and 1774, he spoke 254 times.[119] Only eight MPs spoke more. The speeches were often made without the benefit of notes or a decent night's sleep.[120] A great talent was immediately recognized. Fox in his early speeches took on Burke, Wedderburn, and Savile with a precocity that astounded. Nor was this ability tempered by any trace of modesty. Horace Walpole noted that 'Charles Fox, with infinite superiority in parts, was not inferior to his brother in insolence.'[121] He had 'no Modesty'.[122] Nevertheless, his father was delighted that his infant Samuel should be hailed as a wonder. Referring to one of Fox's speeches that had been 'all off-hand, all argumentative', he told a friend that, 'I hear of it spoken of by everybody as a most extraordinary thing, and I am, you see, not a little pleased with it.'[123]

The issue on which Fox chose to make his mark was John Wilkes and the metropolitan radicalism that he represented. In this, he was simply following a family line. Wilkes had viciously attacked Bute and George III. That fact alone would have made him an enemy of the Fox tribe. Even as a boy, Fox had detested him,[124] and now a full vendetta was set in motion. The Fox brothers insisted on no quarter in the House of Commons, and Stephen Fox proposed the candidature of Wilkes's opponent in the Middlesex elections. As a result, Holland House was surrounded by a Wilkite mob demanding blood.[125] Fox's contempt for Wilkes and London low-life would later seem strange in a politician who was to glory in the title 'Man of the People'. In 1769–70, such contempt was the stock-in-trade of the Fox family. It also recommended the young politician to the attention of Lord North and George III. Early in 1770, he was appointed to the Admiralty Board. *Plus royaliste que le roi*, he was hailed by Horace Walpole as 'the meteor of these days'.[126]

The period between February 1770 and March 1774 was that in which Fox was in office for the longest period in his whole career. In these years, he was twice appointed to government office, to the Admiralty Board in February 1770 and to the Treasury Board in December 1772,[127] and twice he resigned. By the age of 25, Fox's two controversial resignations had exasperated George III, irritated Lord North, and bewildered the political world generally. He seemed intent on demanding that the whole of politics should be run on his terms. When checked, his intemperance seemed to threaten his whole career with ruin. He was still 'the phenomenon of the age',[128] but established politicians would not be pushed too far. Chatham, no stranger to immoderate behaviour, accounted for Fox's theatrical politics by attributing it to inexperience. He told his protégé, Shelburne, that 'the part of Mr Fox must naturally beget speculations; it may, however, be all resolved without going deeper, into youth and warm blood.'[129] This was only partly true. The period 1770–4 was in fact marked by a steady adherence to lines of politics determined by family considerations. The young man was not his own master, but his father's creature. Therein lies his consistency and his motive for two astonishing resignations.

Throughout these years there is a steady and determined effort on Fox's part to destroy Wilkes and the London authorities who protected him. In March 1771 Fox, calling Wilkes 'a profligate libeller', expatiated on how little regard he had for the popular politics that London and Middlesex represented:

What acquaintance have the people at large with the arcana of political rectitude, with the connections of kingdoms, the resources of national strength, the abilities of ministers, or even with their own dispositions? . . . Sir, I pay no regard whatever to the voice of the people: it is our duty to do what is proper, without considering what may be agreeable; their business is to chuse us; it is ours to act constitutionally, and to maintain the independency of Parliament.[130]

Fox strongly advocated the severest penalties against Wilkes himself, printers who libelled the House, and London Aldermen who encouraged them. He was seen to be 'at the head of these strong measures'.[131] On 28 and 29 March, Fox was assaulted by a mob.[132] Shrewdly, Horace Walpole noted the family connection: 'Charles Fox, as if impatient to inherit his father's unpopularity, abused the City as his father used to do.'[133]

In his strident campaign against London, Fox also irritated Lord North. The Prime Minister had hoped to pursue more moderate courses, but felt himself being pushed by a young man's intemperance into policies he disliked. In return, Fox was contemptuous of North's caution, which he took for cowardice. Relations between the two men deteriorated sharply and became competitive. According to some, Fox 'seemed to assume the direction of the House'.[134] An MP could cheekily ask Lord North if Fox had succeeded him as 'the minister'.[135] Horace Walpole was clear about the dangers that the young man was creating for himself: 'at twenty-two he acted and was hated as a leader of a party; his arrogance, loquacity and intemperance raising him the enemies of a Minister before he had acquired the power of one.'[136] Ever the gambler, Fox was playing for the highest stakes in politics, in defence of a family obligation.

That same sense of obligation accounts for his first resignation, on 15 February 1772. Ostensibly, his action was in response to the introduction of the Royal Marriages Act. This measure, requiring all the descendants of George II to acquire the monarch's consent before marrying, was taken by the Fox family as a personal slight. Henry Fox after all would not have been allowed to marry his own wife had such a measure been in operation earlier.[137] As early as 6 January, Fox announced his intention to bring in amendments, and, after resigning, he vigorously opposed it as being 'big with Mischief'.[138] From the start, however, there were sceptics on the question of whether the bill alone could account for Fox's actions. Walpole noted that, when Fox announced his intention of opposing the bill, he had not yet read it,[139] and that, when his own counter-proposals came before the House, he was at Newmarket races.[140] Fox himself later confessed that 'the Bill alone (if I had no reason to complain of Lord North) would not have made me resign.'[141] The bill was taken as a final insult by an aggrieved family nursing a long memory of grievance.

Rightly or wrongly, in his first two years in office, North had offered no patronage to the Fox family. There was no recompense for their sufferings in the 1760s. Fox could not advance the fortunes of his schoolfriends, nor could he help his cousin's husband. These facts alone seemed, to some, to explain his resignation.[142] Even worse, Holland's advancement to an earldom never came. North seemed to go out of his way to snub the family. As Lady Holland complained to her youngest son:

Ld. North has treated both your brothers with much slight. They have not obtained of him the smallest favor they have asked for Salisbury people or others whom they have apply'd for, and Ste. says Ld. Radnor has got things he has been refused. What has most hurt Charles was Ld. North never acquainting him, nor sending to him at a meeting of Commoners that he had about this bill . . . a most unpardonable neglect.[143]

Not being consulted on the Royal Marriages Bill, a measure which so nearly touched his own family, merely convinced Fox that 'Ld. North did not treat him with the confidence & attention he used to do', and that therefore, although 'he had not any one particular reason for this step', resignation was in order.[144] North, allegedly, was dismayed by Fox's decision and was very ready 'to take all blame upon himself'. On the other hand, he may have reflected that so young a man had no right to be especially consulted on government measures, or that his avaricious relations should be particularly regarded in the distribution of spoil.

Certainly, Fox's resignation over the Royal Marriages Act may be attributed to collective family grievance. 'It is very complicated', wrote Fox, '& arises from so many different circumstances.'[145] It was so clearly a family decision that some contemporaries believed that Henry Fox had actually ordered his son to resign,[146] and that therefore it would be 'the opposition of half an hour'.[147] Gibbon, too, saw no principle in Fox's behaviour and found it difficult to believe that he would go into active opposition. It was amusing to watch him trying 'to pronounce the words *Country, Liberty, Corruption*'.[148] Neither was surprised when Fox re-entered government ten months later. Fox had no disagreement with North over America, India, or the great issues of the day. Indeed, he went out of his way to call North 'a minister whose general conduct he so much approved'.[149] Fox went out of office because he felt he could not rehabilitate his father, help his cousins, or advance his friends.

An almost identical game was played out in 1774, and led to Fox's second resignation in February of that year. It was as sudden and bewildering as the first. For fifteen months, Fox had toiled with unusual application at the Treasury Board.[150] True, he still occasionally broke ranks, notably on issues involving religious toleration,[151] but, for the most part, he had proved himself to be a loyal and useful member of North's government. Suddenly, all this changed. This time the issue concerned a pamphlet, written by Horne Tooke, that impugned the impartiality of the Speaker of the House of Commons. On 14 February, its printer, Woodfall, was summoned before the House, where he apologized submissively. North was inclined to let the matter rest there. To his astonishment, Charles Fox insisted on having Woodfall committed to Newgate: 'Charles Fox, with the most indecent arrogance, stuck to his point, and declared that he would take the sense of the House, and Lord North was so weak as to vote with him . . . Lord North's conduct was irresolute, Charles Fox's presumptuous, and every step he made added to his unpopularity.'[152] North's public humiliation by Fox 'incensed' the King, who now took the view that Fox had 'so thoroughly cast off every principle of common honour and honesty, that he must become as contemptible as he is odious'.[153] Fox was completely unrepentant. When asked at Almack's if North had dismissed him, Fox replied, 'No; but if he does, I will write a letter to congratulate him and tell him that, if he had always acted with the same spirit, I should not have differed with him.'[154]

Five days later, Tooke himself appeared before the House, having been named by Woodfall as the author of the offending pamphlet. Fox took the opportunity of berating North 'for his imprudence in promising Woodfall indemnity for betraying Horne',[155] and such was his manner that the King was clear that 'his conduct is not to be attributed to conscience, but to his aversion to all restraints.'[156] There seemed to be a lack of all perspective in his behaviour. The prosecution of Woodfall and Tooke was small beer, but the young man 'talked as if the fate of Caesar and Rome depended upon his conduct'.[157] Directly accusing Lord North of surrendering the rights and privileges of the Commons,[158] he was scathing about the Prime Minister's indecision and unwillingness to act. As a friend noted: 'He defies, corrects, and drives Ministers into minorities, in order to uphold Government.'[159] Contemporaries, searching for a plausible motive for Fox's behaviour, believed they had found it in Lord North's refusing to give him and Burke land concessions in America. Walpole thought that the whole incident proved that Fox had become 'the dupe of Burke'.[160] Certainly by that date Fox's personal animus against the Prime Minister was intense. Principle still played little part in his actions. It was the politics of personality, hot and unremitting.

Whatever his motives, Fox's conduct was too much for the King. Under his direction, Lord North sent Fox the famous, ironically worded note of dismissal: 'Sir, his Majesty has thought proper to order a new commission of the Treasury to be made out, in which I do not perceive your name.'[161] Fox was so unconscious of his own situation that, when he received this note, he believed that it was a practical joke perpetrated by George Selwyn or John Crauford.[162] In fact, there was no joke. Fox was out of office for the second time in four years. He was to remain in that condition until 1782. His friends, recalling his royal ancestor, began calling him Charles the Martyr.[163] Others were less charitable. Fox himself had no doubts about who had engineered his dismissal. In his view, Lord North was a weak, good-natured puppet. It was George III who had brought his career to a halt: 'He was at Court today determined the King should speak to him, who only asked him if he was out today. I think he might have returned a good answer, which he failed—"No, but I was yesterday thanks to your Majesty"—or somewhat like it.'[164] Henceforward, the poisonous relationship of mutual suspicion and hostility between George III and Fox was to become an enduring theme of politics. It had far-reaching consequences.

*

Finding himself once again out of government in February 1774, Fox was still in the happy position of having many political options. No great matter of principle had been involved in either the resignation of 1772 or the dismissal of 1774. His opinion of Lord North's public performance was unflattering, but he always liked the man's private qualities. His secretary later noted:

It always appeared to me that Mr Fox had a very lively regard for Lord North, as he never mentioned him but in a strain of eulogy. He said that he was the most accomplished wit he had ever known; and in domestic life, in the circle of friends and followers, when collected at his table, had all the candour of Walpole without the grossness.[165]

His later association with Fox in the Coalition of 1783 was not as surprising or incongruous as many contemporaries saw it, if their earlier political alliance is taken into account. In retrospect, some of Fox's friends believed that North could have done more to manage Fox. Carlisle thought that

North did nothing to heal the wound, & consequence was the converting a most powerful & attached friend into a bitter enemy, & driving him into the arms of a faction, the principles of which he adopted not from inclination but resentment. Five days before that event He was held by the opposition in execration, & in return those who composed that faction in contempt by him . . . [North withdrew his trust in Fox] at the suggestion of some . . . who persuaded [him] he risked too much in trusting one so young & whose private life excited such severe, & such general animadversion. Upon this hinge has turned what has been of such moment to Fox.[166]

The idea that Lord North made a present of Charles Fox to the Rockingham Whigs is probably unjust, however. George III could more properly face such an accusation. Nothing had happened that prevented Fox resuming cordial relations with North. With the King, however, that was already almost out of the question.

His freedom of action was also enlarged by the death of his father on 1 July 1774. Fox would continue to have regard to his father's battles in the 1740s and 1750s, and to note family friends and enemies, but obviously their impact was lessened as their physical symbol was removed. With the Elder Pitt, the fourth Duke of Bedford, and Bute all being withdrawn from politics as well, family ghosts, though never laid, were less in evidence. With the death of his elder brother, Stephen, in November 1774, Charles became the undisputed guardian of the Fox family tradition in politics.[167] It was a burden he would have to carry until his nephew came of age, and beyond. In March 1774, one month after leaving office, Fox 'without heat left himself at liberty to take what part he should please.'[168] There was no set of principles to dictate a direction.

By the end of 1774, contemporaries found it hard to decide whether the gothic quality of Fox's private life was more to be wondered at than the extraordinary quality of his forays into politics. He was clearly a prodigy. He knew Paris and London. He was the club-friend of the leading writers and artists of the day. He had twice been in government and had twice left it. He was one of the most amusing men in London and one of the most dissolute. He had earned the undying enmity of his king. He was still only 25.

2

The Making of a Whig,
1774–1782

BETWEEN 1774 and 1782, Fox, on some interpretations, finally managed to slough off the prejudices of his family to emerge as a Rockingham Whig. If so, the transformation was astonishing. The descendant of Charles II had allegedly become a leading figure in the Whig party, whose central point of faith was a distrust of kings. The process began with Fox's resentment over his treatment by North and George III between 1770 and 1774. The intellectual influence of Burke capitalized on the young man's sense of grievance to convince him of Whiggery's value. Above all, the American War of Independence finally divorced Fox from his former associates. This, cumulatively, constitutes a strong case, and one which contains many points of interest and some truth. It is not, however, the whole truth. In 1782, Fox was not a Whig in the sense that he had foreclosed on all other options. True, he now had more Whig friends, but he also differed from those new friends on many issues. The lack of firm principle, which had marked his early years, still gave him total flexibility.

Central to the argument that Fox achieved Whiggery, or had it thrust upon him, between 1774 and 1782 is America and its claims to independence. Certainly it was the issue that held centre stage in these years, and it is equally the issue which is omnipresent in Fox's speeches. He claimed to be an expert on the subject. George Washington he described as 'my illustrious friend'. Washington's 'talents and virtues' were 'the best possible apology for this freedom'.[1] Buff and blue, the colours of Washington's army, were adopted as 'uniform of the Fox club, and the cover of the *Edinburgh Review* . . . and . . . became, during the war with the colonies, the badge of the entire Whig party'.[2] Fox and the Whigs supported the Americans, because they believed that if George III succeeded in imposing a despotism in America, he would surely follow up that success by doing the same in England.[3] In his lifetime, the association of Fox with America was strong in the minds of contemporaries. Augustus Foster confessed that 'I always have Mr Fox in my mind when I think of the United States. I know that he has a strong prejudice in favor of this country.'[4] After his death, his nephew reflected with pleasure on 'the predilection it is so gratifying to think that the Americans have for our name'.[5]

While in Paris yet again, between November 1776 and January 1777, Fox took the opportunity to meet rebel American diplomats,[6] and recorded later that during the same visit Benjamin Franklin 'honoured me with his intimacy'. To Fox, Franklin likened the War of Independence 'to the ancient crusades'.[7] On returning home, he warned the Commons against suspending Habeas Corpus in America, because such a move would confirm a Franco-American alliance. Referring repeatedly to his 'own knowledge', he asserted that England was 'on the verge of a war with France'.[8] Further information about America reached Fox directly from his friend John Burgoyne, who had incongruously been lured away from the gaming table to lead one of the British armies, and from Richard Fitzpatrick.[9] In such letters, Lafayette was reported as wishing to be remembered to Fox.[10] By contrast, Lord North's information from America was much less deep or varied. As a result, Fox exultantly accused the Ministry of acting 'under the dominion of the grossest and dullest ignorance'.[11] There can be no doubt that Fox took great pride in his American connections, largely forged in Paris, and quite possibly these friendships did separate him to some extent from his old associates around Lord North.

Within a month or so of leaving office, Fox began to attack North's American policies. The suddenness and virulence of his defence of the Americans must be a little suspect. He had said little or nothing on the issue before his dismissal. Now, it became his major preoccupation. In the public eye, Fox was early identified as an opponent of the American War, of which he roundly accused Lord North of being the instigator. In April 1774, both Fox brothers voted to repeal the duty on tea.[12] Fox argued that, whatever the theoretical argument about whether a British government did or did not have the right to tax America, experience showed that attempts to tax America were ineffective and fraught with danger. He 'imputed all the present disturbances to the persisting in taxation, and said the Americans had now discovered that taxation was used as punishment, and that it was bad policy to use power to punish with, nor was it prudent to risk more in the contest than was necessary'.[13] In pursuing this vendetta, Lord North invaded chartered rights, as in Massachusetts: 'If taxation be intended, their charters must be annihilated.'[14] An inept attempt to tax had produced no revenue, and had disastrously broadened the dispute into a discussion about the constitutional relationship between Britain and the colonies, all of which was essentially unnecessary.

As Fox took up America in 1774 and 1775, his remarks were often deeply personal. He associated the collapse of British authority in the colonies with what he saw as the incapacity of Lord North. As a junior minister, he had been impatient with North's caution. Now the contempt became public. In supporting a motion for peace proposals to be offered to the colonies, Fox 'pledged himself to join Mr Burke, in pursuing the noble lord, and bringing him to answer for the mischiefs occasioned by his negligence, his inconsistency, and his incapacity: he said not this from resentment, but from a conviction of the destructive proceedings of a bad minister.'[15] He also assured the House that 'the greatest folly of his life was in having supported Lord North, with which his lordship was always upbraiding him.'[16] As these remarks indicate, Fox had to dispel a doubt in the minds of contemporaries as to whether his new loathing of North and his policies owed more to an intellectual conversion or to the painful experience of being thrown out of office. Quite possibly, Fox took up the obvious issue at hand and gradually talked himself into a new role. His objections to North's American policies were as much practical as theoretical. Expediency was involved as much as principle, and the extent to which Fox had any emotional investment in the American issue was always open to question. Bad news from America was simply 'a great cause of amusement to Charles'.[17]

Uppermost in Fox's mind were belief that the war would be a protracted one, and that there was a good chance that the Americans would win. Neither of these practical thoughts were widely shared in 1775 or 1776. The betting book at Brooks's Club makes gloomy reading. On 11 March 1776, Fox wagered against the idea that the war would be over within two years. As late as November 1780, Fox backed the notion that in 1785 England would still be at war and that Lord North would still be prime minister.[18] Faced with unending hostilities, Fox saw himself confronted with a no-win situation. If the Americans gained their independence, the economic consequences for England would be terrible. If George succeeded in bringing the colonies to heel by force, royal tyranny would then be extended to England.

I am still convinced the Americans will finally succeed whether by Victories or Defeats; and if they do not, I am sure . . . that it will check all future enterprize to such a degree as to give the completest triumph to Toryism that it ever had . . . Whatever happens for God's sake let us all resolve to stick by them as handsomely (or more so) in their adversity as we have done in their glory, & still maintain the Whig cause . . . to be the only true principle of Politicks'.[19]

So pessimistic was Fox that, as early as 1776, he had confronted the independence issue, and had decided that, if the alternatives were reconquering America or granting independence, the latter option was infinitely preferable. He opposed the raising of taxation for 'so ignoble a purpose, as the carrying on a war commenced unjustly, and supported with no other view than to the extirpation of freedom'.[20] In discussing America's Declaration of Independence, Fox argued that 'the Americans had done no more than the English had done against James the Second.'[21] By 1778, there was the additional argument for allowing independence that America could by then not be reconquered without war with Spain and France as well. This early acknowledgement that America might win, and perhaps deserved to win, did nothing to enhance Fox's popularity. His views seemed dangerously unpatriotic at the beginning of a war that few believed the Americans could win. A cartoon of 1776, entitled *A Sketch of Modern Patriotism*, shows America as an Indian attacking Britannia with a tomahawk, while Fox and his friends look on approvingly.[22] Throughout his career, Fox would be accused of loving foreigners better than Englishmen, and the charge did much to damage his political character.

As the war unfolded, Fox's contempt for the North administration publicly deepened. They seemed incapable of going either backwards or forwards. As he ironically informed Fitzpatrick: 'What the Ministers intend doing besides keeping their places, upon which they are very decided, I cannot even guess. They know as little how to make peace as war. In short, they are as completely at a non plus as people can be.'[23] Cheerfully admitting that 'We are, and ever shall be, as much proscribed as ever the Jacobites were formerly,'[24] hunting ministers through the disasters in America became a kind of sport for Fox and his friends. News of fresh defeats provoked an avalanche of oratory that North, Germain, and Sandwich simply and literally could not answer.[25] Ministers with direct responsibility for the war came to dread Fox. For example, Lord George Germain, the Army Minister, was badly bruised when news of Burgoyne's defeat at Saratoga reached England. 'With great violence,'[26] Fox 'charged Lord George with the whole badness of the plan'.[27] Theatrically, he likened the unfortunate minister to a certain doctor, 'who would persist in drawing blood because he had written a book on bleeding'.[28] From the tone of Fox's letters and speeches, it is clear that he enjoyed lacerating incompetents as much as vindicating his views on the American question.

Spectacular benefits could be derived from this kind of pursuit, most notably in the spring of 1779. Lord Sandwich, the Navy Minister, had been unwise enough to order the court martial of Admiral Keppel on a charge of

not doing his duty, in refusing to engage a French fleet in the Channel.
Keppel came from one of the great Whig families, which believed that
Sandwich had only acted out of spite. He 'wished ill to Keppel'.[29] Accordingly, Fox, Rockingham, and other leading Whigs took lodgings in Portsmouth, where the trial was to be held, in order to give their friend moral
support.[30] On receiving news of Keppel's acquittal, Fox thought it appropriate to organize a riot by way of celebration, and encouraged a mob to
break Lord George's windows. 'The mischief pleasing the juvenile leaders,
they marched to the Admiralty, forced the gates, and demolished Palliser's
and Lord Lisburne's[31] windows. Lord Sandwich, exceedingly terrified,
escaped through the garden, with his mistress Miss Ray, to the Horse Guards,
and there betrayed most manifest panic.'[32] A pamphlet, appearing a few
days after the riot, accused Fox of planning the whole event in advance in
Betty's, a coffee house in St James's. He and his friends had 'terrified into fits
and miscarriages several women, by the rude barbarity of their behaviour'.[33]
Unrepentantly, Fox pleaded in the House of Commons for the rioters to be
pardoned.[34] This cheeky response was complemented by his contributions
to a newspaper called *The Englishman*, which was entirely devoted to the Keppel
case.[35]

The sound of breaking glass was not unknown in eighteenth-century
London. Nor was it unusual for mob behaviour to be sponsored by figures
from the political élite. So pointed were Fox's castigations of ministers, however, that the climate of politics became positively poisonous. In November
1779, Fox labelled a certain supporter of Lord North named William Adam
'a Beast of Nature', a 'Pest of Society', and a 'Libeller of Mankind'.[36] Unfortunately, these words were recorded in the press, and Adam accused Fox
of putting them there. Fox denied this and a duel ensued. The two men met
in Hyde Park at eight in the morning of 29 November.[37] Both men fired
twice, and Fox was hit 'in the belly, but only slightly'.[38] Fox jokingly
dismissed the incident with the quip that he would certainly have been killed
if Adam's pistol had not been charged with government powder, which by
definition was ineffective. It was lucky for the Whigs that Fox survived. It
was lucky for Fox that Adam survived. In later life, Adam was to take charge
of Fox's shaky finances and become a close family friend.

If Fox was inclined to pass the duel off as a nonsense, others were not. His
cousin reported that 'it is by every body, & ought to be, considerd [*sic*] as a
determined plan'd assassination to get rid of an adversary they cant answer
and who they look on as their Perdition . . . it was a scheme to kill him most
undoubtedly.'[39] As cynical a man as Shelburne thought the same. When
Fitzpatrick reported the duel to him, Shelburne annotated the letter with the

remark that 'the infamous Scotch rascal must certainly have been set on.'[40] Whigs remembered that, a year earlier, Fox had almost been provoked into a duel with another government supporter,[41] and Burke began to feel that a general pogrom had been unleashed against the Whigs.[42] In retrospect, these opinions could be thought hysterical. Their importance lies in the fact that the climate of politics was such that intelligent men and women could believe that Fox was to be murdered at the instigation of government.

What is true is that, as the American crisis deepened, Fox became the man whom the government would most have liked to see murdered, had such action been in their acknowledged repertoire. It was Fox who harried Germain and Sandwich with the greatest pleasure. It was Fox who opposed all thought of secession from Parliament among the Whigs. In defeat or victory, the absurdity of trying to bring America back to allegiance by force had to be emphasized and re-emphasized:

A secession at present would be seen as running away from the conquerors, and we should be thought to give up a cause which we think no longer tenable . . . it is become still more necessary . . . to express openly and fairly . . . the well-grounded apprehensions every man must entertain from the power of the Crown, in case his Majesty should be able to subdue the American continent by the force of his arms. Above all, my dear Lord, I hope it will be a point of honour among us all to support the American pretensions in adversity as much as we did in their prosperity, and that we shall never desert those who have acted unsuccessfully upon Whig principles, while we continue to express our admiration of those who succeeded in the same principles in the year 1688.[43]

When in 1777 Rockingham and Burke opted for a secession from Parliament, Fox refused to follow.[44] Their secession confirmed him as one of the leading opponents of the American War in the public eye. It was a reputation he was to retain until peace was secured in 1783.

*

The argument that the American War converted Fox from Northite politics to Rockingham Whiggery depends to some extent on how far the issues raised by that experience became profoundly personal. It could be claimed that Fox would never again be able to work happily with George III and Lord North. Certainly, evidence for vitriolic exchanges between the three men is not hard to find. For the whole period 1774 to 1782, Fox flung words of opprobrium at North. So public and unremitting was his contempt that when he formed the famous Coalition with North in 1783, it created a national scandal. In the election of 1784, a pamphlet was produced by Fox's opponents, entitled *The Beauties and Deformities of Fox, North and Burke*. This was effective propaganda, in that it simply reproduced the expressions that these men had used to describe each other over the previous ten years. Fox accused North of 'every species of falsehood and treachery'.[45] The Prime Minister was 'the blundering pilot who has lost a whole continent'.[46] All the rhetorical arts could barely do justice to the awfulness of Lord North: 'not Lord Chatham, not the Duke of Marlborough, no, not Alexander, nor Caesar, had ever conquered so much territory as Lord North had lost, in one campaign.'[47] The whole adminstration was 'held in the most universal contempt both by friends and enemies'.[48]

Quotations of this kind could be multiplied almost indefinitely. As the war drew to close, Fox, referring a friend to a speech given by Shakespeare to Richard Plantagenet in *Henry VI* on the loss of English territories in France, went on, 'Good God what is this! Indeed it is intolerable to think that it should be in the power of *one* Blockhead to do so much mischief.'[49] The state of the country was 'enough to make one sick; how ruinous everything done by Tories is always destined to be'.[50] As far as Fox could see, the resignation of North was an essential precondition to either a successful prosecution of the war or the securing of an honourable peace: 'Lord North has talked much of the confusion his resigning would occasion. He did not see how; he did see what confusion his staying would make.'[51] Such sustained abuse led many people to conclude that the American issue had irrevocably transformed North, in Fox's eyes, from patron to implacable foe. They believed that, since it was inconceivable that the two men should ever work together again, Fox had no choice but to work with the Rockingham Opposition. Whether Fox ever became a Whig by conviction could remain a matter of debate. What was clear was that he had to be a Whig, because he had repeatedly asserted in public that Lord North was politically unspeakable.

The same argument applied with even more force to Fox's relations with George III. Not unreasonably, as the war dragged on, Fox saw the King as instigator of English policy towards America. Unfortunate comparisons could be drawn with his grandfather, George II:

His late majesty was not one of those princes whom history dignifies with the title of hero; yet this country never was at a higher pitch of glory than during the latter part of his reign; because it was governed by a ministry so formed as to have in its constitution the principles of success; a ministry who knew the interests of their country . . . What a melancholy contrast does the situation of the empire under that ministry form with the present![52]

George III, banking too much on the claims of hereditary right, was misusing the powers invested in the Crown with disastrous results: 'For, had the present king any hereditary right? Parliament, indeed, had made him the successor to the throne, but hereditary right he had none. He was . . . the

mere creature of the people's instituting, and held nothing but what he held
in trust for the people, for their use and benefit.'[53] All actions and expend-
itures of the Crown should be open to public scrutiny.[54]

As Fox himself admitted, these were 'warm' words. They betoken the
gradual formation in his mind of the great fear that was to influence the
whole of his political career. The American War and its disasters led him to
think that George III might be intent on undermining parliamentary life, in
order to establish a despotism on the fashionable, European model. Burke
had been hinting at this possibility in the 1760s. The events of the 1770s
made such notions more plausible. At best, George III seemed to be acting
as 'his own unadvised Minister'.[55] Nonentities like North, Germain, and
Sandwich were merely puppets. At worst, the King's behaviour could be
compared to that of James II, whose name, in the eighteenth century, was
synonymous with tyranny.[56] Property and its defence was the central preoccupation of eighteenth-century politics. It gave men status and a claim to
a voice in politics. The great Whig families of Rockingham, Bedford, and
Devonshire, by right of great property, had great status. George's refusal or
inability to work with these men gave rise to the notion that he was opposed
to the fundamental claims of property itself. The grand Whiggery of aristocrats, who had been condemned as his father's enemies by the young Fox,
were now hailed as the defenders of English liberties against a would-be despot.

The American War was the central feature of the King's strategy. It
created a huge vested interest, which looked only to the King, and which
would unquestioningly do his bidding. Army and navy men in need of promotion forgot their principles, as did contractors and investors in government loans: 'The American war begot extraordinaries; extraordinaries begot
loans; loans begot douceurs; and douceurs begot members of parliament;
and members of parliament again begot all these things. There was a
mutual dependence among them absolutely inseparable. Thus the power
and security of ministers were generated by that war which was the ruin of
the country.'[57] National considerations made it abundantly clear that a war
between England and her colonies was a nonsense. It could only benefit
England's enemies in Europe. The continuation of hostilities was therefore
the work of selfish, sectional interests, led by the King. Fox warned the
Commons that 'Corruption sweeps every thing before it,'[58] and with its
assistance the King could buy the loyalty of Parliament:

It was the trained bands under the well-known command of the muster-master-
general, to borrow a term from his lordship, who carried every question in that
House; it was those who were in the possession of great emoluments, of pensions and
inefficient places: it was the contractors, whose profits within a single year amounted

to almost a princely fortune; it was the subscribers to the loan . . . it was these men who in the midst of national misfortune and of public calamity . . . were amassing fortunes by their servility.[59]

Those who resisted corruption could hope for little in politics.[60]

When, in April 1780, Dunning brought forward his famous Resolution, claiming that the influence of the Crown had increased, was increasing, and ought to be diminished, Fox predictably supported him. The Resolution was 'glorious'.[61] It sharply and simply raised the fundamental point at issue: 'the question now was . . . whether that beautiful fabric [the English Constitution] . . . was to be maintained in that freedom, in that purity, in that perfection . . . for which blood had been spilt; or whether we were to submit to that system of despotism, which had so many advocates in this country.'[62] Speaking a month later in favour of shorter Parliaments, he candidly told the House that, 'if any of his constituents were to ask him what our present misfortunes were ascribeable to? he should say, the first cause was the influence of the Crown, the second, the influence of the Crown, and the third, the influence of the Crown.'[63] By the end of the American War, it appeared that Fox's politics had been transformed. The young apologist for monarchy in the 1760s had become its sternest critic. Fox, apparently, had come to Whiggery because he had come to suspect the intentions of George III. It was no secret that the King, holding Fox responsible for debauching his sons, returned that antipathy in full measure.[64]

*

Any account of Fox's supposed conversion to Rockingham Whiggery between 1774 and 1782 must concern itself with the influence of Edmund Burke. American debates brought Fox and Burke together in the most fruitful of associations. The two men had known each other since 1764, and, although the setting for their meetings was more often literary than political, they had developed a deep respect for each other's talents. In 1777, Fox went on a tour of Ireland, and Burke advertised his qualities to his Irish connections: 'Dont [*sic*] you like Charles Fox? If you were not pleased on that short acquaintance you would on a further; for he is one of the pleasant-est men in the world, as well as the greatest Genius that perhaps this country has ever produced. If he is not extraordinary, I assure you the British domin-ions cannot furnish any thing beyond him.'[65] The planes on which Fox and Burke met were necessarily restricted. Burke was not a clubman, a gambler, or a rake. Even so, their great talents deferred, one to the other.

After Fox's resignation from North's government, Burke tried hard to secure that talent for the Whig party. In letters which sound more like

tutorials in Whiggery, he endeavoured to convince Fox that the Rockingham party must henceforth be his home:

Though (as you are sensible) I have never given you the least hint of advice about
joining yourself in a declared connexion with our party nor do I now—yet . . . I love
that party very well, and am clear that you are better able to serve them than any
man I know . . . For I much doubt, whether, with all your parts, you are the man
formed for acquiring real interior favour in this Court or in any. I therefore wish you
a firm ground in the Country; and I do not know so firm and sound a bottom to
build on as our party.[66]

In later life, Burke's affection for Fox resembled that of tutor for pupil. He
regarded him as a protégé. In the 1780s and 1790s, when Burke felt challenged for the intellectual leadership of Whiggery, his resentment against
the pretensions of Sheridan was never extended to Fox. When he broke with
Fox over the French Revolution, there was as much sorrow as anger in his
words. In return, Fox always admired Burke, honoured his debts to his intelligence, and was bitterly upset by the loss of his friendship after 1791.
Whatever steps Fox took towards Whiggery, the progress was eased by Burke's
authority and concern.

*

One other factor seemed to allow Fox to drift further and further away from
his early political loyalties. By 1779–80, Fox was emerging as a populist. In
1780, Fox became Member of Parliament for Westminster, one of the
largest and most prestigious constituencies in the country. It was to be his
base in politics for the rest of his life. Geography allowed Westminster to
press on the nerve of politics. When defeated in the Commons, Fox not
infrequently adjourned to a meeting of Westminster electors, where the
speech was repeated to cheers that could be heard in the House. A pamphlet
rehearsing the speech duly followed. Greatly enjoying his title of 'Man of the
People', Fox now began to argue that so corrupt was government, that
popular meetings and the popular opinion they represented were justified,
in order to pressurize government. In retrospect, Fox was clear that meetings 'tended to hasten the conclusion of that war'.[67] All of this is a far cry
from the beliefs of the young Fox, who had harried Wilkes and Woodfall for
allegedly doing the same thing. Once Fox had been the champion of the
idea that a Parliament, once elected, should never be coerced. Now, he was
not so sure.

On a number of issues, the necessity of keeping up his popularity led him
to patronize radical notions. In a high-profile manner, he began, for example, to defend the Irish Volunteer Movement, which had been formed in

1779 to demand redress of Irish grievances in trade and taxation. To many Englishmen, these demands sounded uncannily like those recently heard in America. Grievances in arms could easily be termed rebellion. Fox did not agree. He told the Commons that 'The Irish Associations had been called illegal: legal or illegal, he declared he entirely approved of them. He approved of that manly determination which, in the dernier ressort, flew to arms in order to obtain deliverance.' There was a parallel to be drawn with England, where there too 'The first men of rank, fortune, and character, in both Houses, had firmly and virtuously resolved to set their faces against this increasing, this alarming influence of the crown.'[68] No doubt he was influenced in these views by the fact that his uncle, the Duke of Leinster, figured among the leaders of the Volunteers. Irish dukes and English dukes found political conversation easy. They, with the Americans were all victims of a malevolent king. Publicly, he asserted that the Irish 'had not a friend . . . more warmly attached to their interests'.[69] He assured his uncle that he had 'never missed any opportunity of declaring in public as well as in private, how much I wished you success in all the points you were likely to push.'[70] The granting of legislative independence to Ireland in 1782 by a government of which Fox was a part gave him enormous satisfaction.

Even more surprising than the spectacle of Fox hobnobbing with Irish radicals was the appearance of Fox in the rowdy company of their English equivalents. Feeling that he had been 'shamefully remiss with respect to attempts out of Parliament',[71] Fox now seemed anxious to make up for lost time. On 2 February 1780, Fox, at a meeting of, allegedly, 3,000 people, was proposed as Member for Westminster. Seeing Fox on the same platform as such radicals as Wilkes, Sawbridge, and Jebb convinced Horace Walpole that Fox's conversion from Northite to Rockingham Whig was complete:

Last Wednesday a meeting was summoned in Westminster Hall. Charles Fox harangued the people finely and warmly; and not only a petition was voted, but he was proposed for candidate for that city at the next general election, and was accepted joyfully. Wilkes was his zealous advocate—how few years since a public breakfast was given at Holland House to support Colonel Lutterel against Wilkes! Charles Fox and his brother rode thence at the head of their friends to Brentford. Ovid's *Metamorphoses* contains not stranger transformations than what party can work.[72]

The macaroni cavalier had now become the Man of the People.

In the autumn of 1780, Fox was duly elected Member for Westminster. So great was royal animosity to Fox assumed to be, that everyone expected a sharp contest. As early as March, Lady Susan Lennox had written, 'I know the influence of the Spirit of freedom, but yet I own I fear the still greater influence of the Crown, & you may be sure that they would lose twenty

Elections rather than not disappoint him of a seat.'[73] Her fears were well founded. Fox had to work hard to secure the seat,[74] and when the contest was over, he was reported to be 'pretty much knocked up'.[75] As custom demanded, he was 'carried triumphantly through the whole town',[76] but Court influence had been exerted to the maximum against him, and with good reason. Westminster gave Fox a national platform. It had enormous potential. In December 1781, for example, Fox could call a meeting of 9,000 people in Westminster Hall to consider 'the present alarming crisis of public affairs'. Fox denounced the American War because it 'had originated in delusion; it had been conducted, and was continued in delusion', and concluded that the King 'would not persevere in the war against the declared voice of the people of England'.[77] The 'people' referred to were the electors of Westminster. Government fears on these occasions were real and troops were put on standby.[78] As Member for Midhurst or Orkney and Shetland, Fox's career rested on privilege and patronage. As Member for Westminster, he moved outside the world of rotten boroughs into the bright light of popularity. It must have been a heady experience.

The most immediate consequence of Fox's association with Westminster was a new-found interest in parliamentary reform. This important topic is more fully dealt with elsewhere,[79] but it is crucial to underline the fact that Fox's control of Westminster was conditional upon his support for reform. It is this issue which first brings Fox into the company of men like John Jebb and Thomas Cartwright, who by 1780 were demanding nothing less than universal male suffrage. It is as a member of the Westminster committee for reform that Fox first writes to Christopher Wyvill, perhaps the leading parliamentary reformer of the day, to invite 'a free and unreserved Communication of sentiments either by letter or conference or both'.[80] The types of parliamentary reform advocated by these men varied considerably, but they all had a common starting-point in a fear of Crown influence. One strong argument for all of them was that reform was necessary to stop the establishment of a royal despotism. In Fox's case, it was the overwhelming argument. Sending a petition for reform to Shelburne, Fox noted that

The great and respectable Names which have appeared upon this occasion, cannot fail of giving great Satisfaction to every true lover of his Country; but when we see such Names upon an occasion in a Minority, we cannot help thinking that we have an additional proof that in complaining of the exhorbitant Influence of the Crown, we do not complain of an imaginary Grievance.[81]

Fox's fear of the executive influence of the Crown had made him a reformer. His prize for seemingly taking that step were new friendships among the radicals and the representation of one of the most prestigious constituencies in the country. In November 1780, Westminster congratulated him on exposing 'the pernicious principles and the destructive measures of an abandoned administration', and offered him a bodyguard. William Adam called him 'the King of Westminster'.[82]

Apparently, his radicalism knew few bounds. He publicly supported the notion of 'a more equal, and consequently new mode of representation', though the details of what that might be were vague. He publicly supported the idea of more frequent parliaments, though he spoke against it in private. Wyvill's favourite hobby horse of introducing one hundred new MPs for county constituencies could be ridden by Fox, who 'declared loudly' for it.[83] The turmoil of the Gordon Riots, in the summer of 1780, did nothing to moderate Fox's enthusiasm. He deplored the rioters and their works, but insisted that there was no connection between them and the respectable reformers of Westminster and Yorkshire. Describing the riots as 'a most fortunate circumstance for ministers', he came close to accusing the government of fomenting the disorders.[84] The maxim that the convert is often more zealous than those brought up in a faith was exemplified by Fox's adoption of the radical canon. It seemed that Fox had, between 1774 and 1782, travelled the whole political spectrum. The American issue, the influence of Burke, and the new-found status in Westminster combined to effect a transformation scene worthy of a pantomime. Fox, the contemnor of reformers, had become Fox the Whig or even Fox the radical. It is a good and powerful case. There is another interpretation of these events, however, and one which might prove even more convincing. To that we now turn.

*

The first factor to cast doubt on the depths of Fox's professed convictions is his repeated claims that he had no real hopes of politics and much preferred the society of friends. Conventional nostrums of this kind take on more authority when expressed in letters to his closest friends, and are partly written in French, the language of ease:

J'aime tous les plaisirs de la vie, et avec des amis comme toi, des jolies femmes, de la bonne chose, on peut tres bien se passer d'etre ministre, surtout si on jouit d'une grande partie de l'éclat et de celebrité que formait le principal merite de cet etat. I am certainly ambitious by nature, but I really have or think I have subdued that passion. I have still as much vanity as ever which is a happier passion by far because great reputation I think I may acquire & keep, great situation I never can acquire nor if acquired keep without making sacrifices that I never will make.[85]

If Fox was sincere in his wish to resolve the American issue or promote reform, neither issue was allowed to interfere with the vividness of his social

round. Never abandoning his 'rakish life', Fox made speeches that were
unprepared by diligent research or sleep, for 'he was seldom in bed before
five in the morning, nor out of it before two at noon.'[86] Fox and his friends in
Brooks's still led in fashion as much as politics, though by 1777 they had
moved on from macaroni foppishness to calculated slovenliness, 'affecting a
style of neglect about their persons and manifesting a neglect of all usages
hitherto established'.[87] The reign of the *enfant terrible* in society was easier to
sustain than a comparable role in politics.

Freedom from office allowed him the luxury of a further visit to France
from November 1776 to January 1777, 'availing himself profitably of an
intimacy with the French nobility, in which his address always obtained him
a preference'.[88] A visit to Ireland was also possible. George III paid Fox the
indirect compliment of urging North to bring on as much business as possible while Fox was away, 'because real business is never so well considered
as when the attention of the House is not taken up with noisy declama-
tion'.[89] Watching Fox lose substantial sums at the gaming-tables in Paris,
Mme du Deffand for one refused to believe that any changes had been
wrought in Fox's character. Fox cared for nothing and believed in nothing:
'En effet, j'en pense à de certains égards, il n'a pas un mauvais cœur, mais il
n'a nul espèce de principes, et il regarde avec pitié tous qui en ont; je ne
comprends pas quels sont ses projets pour l'avenir, il ne s'embarasse du
lendemain. La plus extrême pauvreté, l'impossibilité de payer ses dettes,
tout cela ne lui fait rien . . . Il me semble qu'il est toujours dans une sorte
d'ivresse . . . Je lui aurai paru comme une platte moraliste, et lui il m'a paru
un sublime extravagant.'[90] In all of this, Fox seemed to regret his absence
from politics not a bit.

In England, throughout the period of the American War, Newmarket
and Brooks's were as much home to Fox as the House of Commons. It is the
period when his sexual and gambling excesses gave rise to the greatest
public concern. Even within a month of again taking office, there were few
concessions made to a wider opinion. George Selwyn found 'Charles at
Brooks with a mob of boys about him, talking treason and cutting out for
themselves the best employments of trust and profit . . . From a Pharo table
to the headship of the Exchequer is a transition which appears to me de tenir
trop au Roman.'[91] Throughout his career, Fox issued disclaimers to his
friends about his lack of ambition in politics, claiming that other values and
goals had priority. His behaviour demands that these protestations be taken
seriously.[92]

More tangibly, Fox was never pro-American in the sense that the resolution of the colonial problem was a priority, or in the sense that what was

offered to America could not be subject to delay or modification. He generally wished them well, but there were other considerations. Throughout the hostilities, Fox was much more anti-Bourbon than pro-American. Fox strongly shared the fear that France represented despotism in arms. French invasion scares were frequent. The attraction of American independence lay in the fact that it would detach the colonists from their French allies, thereby making a blow against France more feasible. It was not an absolute objective by itself. He told Fitzpatrick that

If the acknowledgement of Independence would not procure Peace, it is certainly useless. I own my present idea . . . is rather with Ld. Shelburne for being silent upon that subject, but acting as if it were acknowledged, withdrawing our troops from N. America & making the most vigorous attacks upon France or possibly Spain too. Whatever may be the conditions of Alliance between the United States & France I can not help thinking that they would act very lukewarmly against us when they found themselves wholly uninterested in the war & engaged merely by a point of honour.[93]

France, with the largest population in Europe, was a military threat to England for the whole of the eighteenth century. Fox was not alone or very original in seeing the American problem largely in European terms.

Most importantly, America was not, in Fox's view, an obstacle to the formation of new political alliances at home or to his own return to power. It was not a sticking point for him. In a most revealing letter to Lord North in 1780, Fox assured him that everything was negotiable:

In our conversation this morning I do not know whether I did not state one point in a harsher manner than was necessary, I mean in respect to the American War. The precise thing I should wish to say is this; that we are at present too little acquainted with the circumstances to come to any determination at all, & that whenever we shall know more of the situation of affairs we must act (as in all other wars) in the manner which that situation may direct.[94]

Such anodyne phrases meant precisely nothing and kept all Fox's options open. The brave words with which Fox championed the Americans in the House of Commons are not matched in his private writings. He was not intellectually opposed to the American cause, but nor was he emotionally engaged in its promotion. It could become a point of policy, but not at the expense of the more important conflict with France, or perhaps of his own return to office.

If America offered Fox no anchorage of principle before 1782, nor did his espousal of reform as a response to the despotic tendencies of George III. As has been noted earlier, his language in describing the King as a would-be tyrant could be colourful. But on other occasions he made speeches which were 'remarkably decent and respectful to the King'.[95] *Pari passu*, George would veer between denunciation of Fox and his lifestyle and 'commendations of him'.[96] There was enough family politics in Fox to prevent him becoming an out-and-out opponent of monarchy, and so much talent that it commanded George III's attention, if not respect. Ambiguity on this point punctuates Fox's behaviour in the 1770s. If, in 1780, he could be found speaking in favour of the economical reform of wasteful practices, he was, two years earlier, observed voting against a proposal to tax places and pensions as part of the war effort. In speeches to the House of Commons, Fox made little or no specific reference to George himself, and often argued that reform was necessary not to control the Crown, but to remove obstacles between king and subjects. A reduction in the power of the executive was as much for its own good as for that of the public generally. Supporting Burke's Economical Reform Bill, on 15 December 1779 he made this argument explicit:

I hope, therefore, for the sake of the public, for the sake of all public men, for the sake of the crown, and for the sake of the king upon the throne, that my honourable friend will add perseverance to the diligence he has already employed in his plan for lessening the public expences [*sic*] and reducing the ruinous influence of the crown.[97]

Such language could be taken as disingenuous, but this may be unjust. Between 1778 and 1780, there were many negotiations opened to explore the possibility of a coalition between North and some of the Whig factions. In these Fox consistently argued that the King was not to be coerced or pushed too far. Any kind of 'submission' on the King's part was not to be sought for or expected.[98] So temperate was Fox's approach to the subject of coalition that his uncle, the Duke of Richmond, was moved to stiffen his resolve: 'you will allow that we must expect more than the Removal of any of the Tide-waiters, or even one or Two obnoxious Men, when it is a whole system we complain of.'[99] The evidence does not make it clear that Fox did in fact object to a whole system. He may have disliked certain individuals like Sandwich and Germain, but that antipathy did not carry over to North and possibly the King. If George III, in return, harboured an implacable enmity to Fox, the latter was unaware of it before 1782. In the various coalition attempts that pepper the later years of the American War, Fox could not see any insurmountable obstacles in his views on the King's behaviour or in his drift towards the reformers. As with the American issue, he was uncommitted. The path leading back to an understanding with the men he had worked with between 1770 and 1774 seemed totally clear.

The strongest evidence that Lord North had not given up hope of reclaiming Fox, and that Fox had no objections to being reclaimed, comes from the repeated coalition attempts that were undertaken at the height of the American conflict. Quite how serious some of these negotiations were is not easy to determine. Some were clearly little more than conversations without full authorization from Lord North and the King. Others had more weight. All of them pointed to the gap between public and private statements by Fox on the subject of rejoining North. In the House of Commons, all was principle:

What! enter into an alliance with those very ministers who had betrayed their country; who had prostituted the public strength, who had prostituted the public wealth, who had prostituted what was still more valuable, the glory of the nation! The idea was too monstrous to be admitted for a moment. Gentlemen must have foregone their principles, and have given up their honour, before they could have approached the threshold of an alliance so abominable, so scandalous and so disgraceful.[100]

In private, Fox's views were very different. He was responsive to overtures from North, and not infrequently critical of the Rockingham Whigs for not sharing his enthusiasm for coalition. There was no hint in Fox's mind that any view he held or any action he had taken put a ban on his return to government.

The negotiations began in March 1778, when William Eden was asked by a ministry desperately in need of new strength to sound out Fox. Over dinner, Fox significantly 'stated himself to be unconnected and at liberty'. He also frankly admitted that all of North's Cabinet would be congenial colleagues except Lord George Germain. His only stipulations seem to have been that he should not be alone in rejoining the government, and that some employment should be found for Fitzpatrick and Upper Ossory. Eden concluded from the conversation that 'upon the whole it appeared sufficiently practicable to obtain his assistance, if he could be kept in countenance by others.'[101] Nothing was said about America or the other great issues of the day. In May of the same year, the dialogue was resumed, this time between Fox and Lord Weymouth.[102] When the negotiations failed, Fox could not make up his mind about who was to blame. In the same letter, he first suggested that the failure was 'entirely owing to themselves [Rockingham Whigs]', but then relapsed into the old expedient of blaming the King, being 'suspicious of the K's intentions, which nothing can ever remove, a desire of having it appear that *he* was yielding, to which it is impossible *he* can ever consent . . . There is no man who hates the power of the crown more, or who has a worse opinion of the Person to whom it belongs than I.'[103]

These disappointed words were written in January 1779. Negotiations with North were resumed in February. Fox was right to suspect the King's intentions,[104] but, by resuming talks, he could not have thought the situation impossible. In this he was right. Unbeknown to Fox, North was insisting to the King 'that without a coalition the present system must be overturn'd', and had shown him a list of office-holders in a new administration, in which Fox was marked down for a Treasurership of the Navy.[105] Once again Weymouth was the intermediary. Failure this time was attributed to a disagreement on the subject of who should head the new government.[106] Yet another round of talks in June 1779 foundered for a similar reason, namely that Fox allegedly was 'no way disposed to become a part of an administration in which Lord North is a principal'.[107] In fact, this was untrue. Fox had been enormously heartened by the coalition initiatives in the spring and summer of 1779. Whereas Rockingham was inclined to think that North and the King meant only to try to split the Opposition by endlessly dangling before them the prospect of office,[108] Fox was more optimistic. For him, there was no point of policy that was not negotiable, and only Germain and Sandwich were not to be tolerated as colleagues. As for George III, Fox was confident in the autumn of 1779 that Rockingham 'would receive a Message from the King who would deliver all things, without any reserve whatsoever, into your hands'.[109]

In December 1779, Fox's prophecy seemed almost on the point of coming true. The King, in commissioning Thurlow to talk to the Opposition, declared his readiness 'to blot from his remembrance any events that may have displeased him, and to admit into his confidence and service any man of public spirits and talents'. There were to be no vetoes on individuals and none had an assured future. Even Lord North's position was negotiable. Referring to Fox, George concluded that 'This ought to convince that person that I really mean a coalition of parties, and not to draw him in to support the present Ministry.'[110] Words such as these made it difficult for Fox to hold a consistent view about royal intentions. When coalition talks failed, he was inclined to blame George and fall back on the old nostrums about the dangers presented by despotic kings. More often in these years, he was privately prepared to believe that his relationship with George III was not so strained as to preclude his return to office.

The final round of talks were held in the summer of 1780. This time the negotiator was Frederick Montagu, a man well known in Foxite circles. He had a more restricted brief than that given to Thurlow six months earlier. George would not tolerate the Duke of Richmond in office, while Fox himself would have to settle for a place of profit rather than influence.[111]

Unflatteringly, the King thought that Fox might accept this proposal because he 'never had any principle, and can therefore act as his interest may guide him'.[112] Rumours circulating in London at the time suggested that Fox was so sunk in a financial mire that he had applied for posts in India.[113] So embarrassing was this negotiation that Fox could not bring himself to mention it to close friends like Fitzpatrick.[114] This time, the initiative came to nothing because the several groups in opposition, faced with the prospect of office, also faced the uncomfortable fact that they agreed on little except their opposition to Lord North: 'Lord Shelburne and Lord Rockingham are bitter enemies. Burke . . . is mad for toleration. The Duke of Richmond and Charles Fox agree with him, while the Duke is as violent for annual parliaments as the Rockinghams against them. Lord Shelburne, Lord Camden and the Duke of Grafton are as strongly anti-papistic.'[115]

Between March 1778 and July 1780, Fox had been involved in no fewer than six sets of conversations on the possibility of resuming his political connection with North. Some were more seriously intended than others. No doubt his friends were right to fear that George III's motives might be suspect, and that he was merely using the talks to highlight divisions among his opponents. In spite of these reservations, however, certain other points emerge that are of some significance. It is clear that Lord North had no objection to Fox as a colleague. It is also clear that Fox found few principles obstructing his possible return to power. In public, Fox systematically denounced North as incompetent and the King as malevolent. In private, in his view, nothing had been said or done that could involve a long-term breach with either man. Fox may have been naïve in thinking this. George III had very definite and very disparaging views about Fox by 1780. But, in terms of Fox's own political development, nothing seemed to have to become so fixed that it precluded a return to the family politics of enjoying office, not opposition. Not being born into the grand Whiggery, Fox was always more willing to enter into coalitions with those outside it.

*

Given these equivocations, the question of whether Fox had been given a new political orientation by the events of 1774 to 1782 admits of no simple answer. In retrospect, Fox's nephew thought that he had made a firm commitment to Rockingham Whiggery in the middle of the American War: 'Mr Fox had now resolved to connect himself avowedly with the Rockingham party. He told Lord John Townshend so at Chatsworth. Mr Burke in a letter directed to him in Ireland [in 1777], urges him to adopt that measure . . . he was already resolved to do so, though he did not in full form until 1778, or even 1779.'[116] The fact that, according to this account, Fox's conversion could not be more precisely dated is suspicious. Writing from memory, the nephew could only fix the moment somewhere within a three-year timespan. There was no clear and datable declaration of a change of loyalties. Ambiguities touched everything Fox said and did, and, with regard to reform issues for example, opened up a huge gap between public and private statements.

Such indefiniteness was an essential feature of the Fox character. Only two months before the collapse of the North government, Fox had no premonition that he was about to resume office: 'All that is to be clearly known is that this country is devoted, by the obstinacy of those who govern it (though God knows who they are) to certain and inevitable ruin.'[117] In the same letter, there is yet again an expression of the same distancing from public affairs that marks his whole career. Commitment was difficult because the labour of politics never totally captured his imagination: 'with respect to myself, I am very well in health and spirits; and having long since given up all hopes of things going right in this country, am very little personally affected with anything that happens in public.'[118] Fox had been pushed into politics by family pressures. To argue that he had, by 1782, abandoned North for Rockingham may be wrong in two senses. He had never been a Northite, in principled terms, and never became a Rockinghamite. Brave words about Americans and reformers had not materially dented his interest in a coalition with the opponents of those men. Rude words about North had not ruled out a renewal of their political association.

Interestingly, Fox chose, in those years, to define political loyalty not as coagulation around a set of principles, but as a function of friendship. Such an idea had a powerful and enduring influence on his response to events. In 1778, he told Fitzpatrick that

I shall be told by prudent friends that I am under no sort of engagement to any set of men, I certainly am not, but there are many cases where there is no engagement, and yet it is dishonourable not to act as if there was one. But even suppose it were quite honourable, is it possible to be acting with people of whom one has the worst opinion, & being on a cold footing . . . with all those whom one loves best & with whom one passes one's life?[119]

Defined in these terms, Fox's politics had no natural home. If he found himself at odds with North over America, he was equally at odds with Rockingham over reform and the possibility of a coalition. Subjugating all these to wider concerns about politics as friendship or association, either man would do as an associate. In a revealing letter to Rockingham in 1779, Fox, by taking the marquess to task on the coalition issue, demonstrated just how far he was from being of his coterie:

it has always been, and I believe always will be, my opinion that power (whether over a people or over a king) obtained by gentle means, by the goodwill of the person to be governed, and, above all, by degrees, rather than by a sudden exertion of strength, is in its nature more durable and firm, than any advantage that can be obtained by contrary means . . . In short, our difference of opinion is quite complete.[120]

If neither America nor reform could fix Fox as a Whig, there was one other development in these years that would go a long way to having that long-term effect. It is quite possible that George III, remembering Fox's resignations and hearing his abuse of the North government, had decided that he would never willingly admit him to office again. If the eighteenth-century commonplace that Kings were at liberty to choose their own ministers was honoured, Fox's ministerial career was at an end. The strongest hints of this decision had been given to royal negotiators in the coalition talks of 1778 to 1780. Fox himself, however, seemed to be oblivious of this fact. Having as yet no deep animus against the King, he could not believe that George entertained implacable hostility towards him. His interest in coalition had always been based on the assumption that he too would return to office. Senior figures in the Rockingham party, with a longer experience of the King's capacity to hate, found Fox's attitudes naïve. His uncle, the Duke of Richmond, lectured him firmly on the subject, arguing that this King always needed to be tied down to firm commitments: 'Not suspicion, but prudence requires us to be upon our guard.'[121] Proscription from office in the 1760s and 1770s allowed Edmund Burke, on behalf of the Rockinghams, to formulate the idea that George III was a would-be tyrant. Fox would come to the same idea by the same experience of proscription. The lesson would be learnt between 1782 and 1784.

3

Constitutional Crisis,
1782–1784

THE constitutional crisis of 1782–4 was the determining experience in Fox's political career. It had more impact than the French Revolution on his thinking. It would become the terms of reference against which future decisions were taken. Fox was personally shaken, and indeed hurt, by the events of these years. Throughout them, he had endlessly to respond to unforeseen events. In the confusion, old friendships were interrupted and new allies found. Four ministries in two years reminded many of the governmental anarchy of the 1760s. As in that decade, leading Whigs, with Fox to the fore, saw themselves as the victims of a chaos that had been deliberately engineered by George III, on the argument that it was the only circumstance that could allow the establishment of a royal despotism. According to Fox, nothing less was at stake in these years than whether English parliamentarianism was to survive. From that period he would later date what he would call the 'euthanasia' of the constitution.[1]

When North's government fell in March 1782, to be followed by a ministry composed of the two main Whig groups led by Shelburne and Rockingham, Fox's sky appeared to be cloudless. In public, Fox was boastful and unguarded: 'he talked of the King under the description of Satan, a comparison which he seems fond of, and has used to others; so he is *sans ménagement de paroles*. It is the *bon vainqueur et despotique*; he has adopted all the supremacy he pretended to dread in his Majesty.'[2] Loudly he proclaimed that North's majorities had only been sustained by 'means of corruption'.[3] Instead of accommodating royal feelings over the loss of a favourite servant, Fox insisted that North's removal had been due to a clear and open statement by the House of Commons: 'his majesty's late ministers were dismissed, because parliament disapproved of the system of their government, and . . . it was evident from parliament having gone so far to effect a removal of ministers, that it would be expected their successors should act upon different principles, and in a manner totally opposite.'[4] Fox was encouraged in his uncompromising stance by messages of support from reform organizations[5] and by an unopposed return for Westminster.[6] It was delightful for Fox now to be in a position to reward friends like Carlisle,[7] and to contemplate a Whig government so firmly established 'that no future faction shall be able to destroy them'.[8]

Within a month of the Rockingham–Shelburne administration taking office, the situation had changed with provocative suddenness. Fox could now 'hardly see one favourable circumstance in our situation'.[9] First, it had rapidly become apparent that the King had no intention of accepting the Whigs in office for one moment longer than was necessary. He described their arrival in power as 'the fatal day',[10] and assured Lord North of his continuing goodwill.[11] The King's disfavour was publicly expressed in a refusal to accede to any of the Rockinghams' requests for patronage. Such crumbs of comfort as there were went exclusively to the Shelburne Whigs, thereby creating jealousies between them and their Rockingham colleagues.[12] Little wonder that Fox was soon concerned that 'it should appear to the world that I have some weight in the disposition of employments.'[13] His concern would have been all the greater had he known that in March the King had had a private interview with Shelburne, during which, according to a memorandum in Shelburne's own hand, George expressed 'his bad opinion of Ld. Rockingham's understandg. & His horror of C. Fox. His preference for me compared to the rest of the opposition.'[14] From almost the Ministry's inception, George flattered Shelburne with the notion that, if he would only break with his Rockingham allies, he, with royal backing, should be sole minister. Shelburne, in effect, became a royal agent in the Cabinet.

The Fox and Shelburne families, though closely related,[15] were as hostile and suspicious of each other as only cousins can be. It seemed that Fox, as late as 1795, harboured 'an old prejudice' against Shelburne, which had been born in a 'transaction' between him and Henry Fox. Whatever the nature of this dispute, it soured family relationships for four decades.[16] Often outvoted in Cabinet, and unable to secure patronage for his friends, Fox quickly came to the conclusion that the Shelburne–Rockingham arrangement had been sabotaged by the King. Long before Rockingham's death on 1 July 1782, which was the occasion for the formal dissolution of the Ministry, Fox was clear that he had to bring this situation 'to the Crisis to which it must come & shall come'.[16] There was no strength in a government about the fall of which the press endlessly speculated, and whose imminent demise was whispered about at masquerades at the Pantheon.[17]

In Fox's opinion, evidence of a plot concocted by George III and Shelburne to destroy the Ministry was not hard to find. For example, on the question of economical reform, and on some aspects of parliamentary reform, Shelburnites and Rockinghamites had traditionally held similar views.[18] Suddenly, in Cabinet, Shelburne began to drag his heels on these issues. In April, Burke's Economical Reform Bill produced a 'very teizing and wrangling Cabinet', at which Shelburne appeared 'bothered' and spent some five hours 'throwing difficulties in the way'.[19] Disunity was made public in May, when the Lord Chancellor, Lord Thurlow, opposed a reform measure which had Cabinet approval, and, to add insult to injury, 'Ld. Sh. thought it right to compliment him upon it.'[20] It seemed clear to Fox, Burke, and many others that Shelburne was deliberately reneging on his commitment to reform, in order to split the Ministry. The reformers were to be the incidental victims of a royal plot to dislodge Fox and his friends.

So too were the Irish. Ever since 1779, the Volunteer Movement in Ireland had, in seeking some kind of legislative independence, found some sympathy in both Rockinghamite and Shelburnite circles. Fox was endlessly appealed to by Irish patriots like Charlemont and Grattan,[21] but, since Ireland was technically under Shelburne's jurisdiction, Fox prudently referred them to his colleague, in the confidence that they would receive a congenial response: 'it would be very imprudent in me (especially as it is not within my Department) to give any direct Opinion upon the various Points which make the Subject of your Letter.'[22] If a warrant were required for Shelburne's good behaviour, the Duke of Portland as Lord Lieutenant of Ireland, Fitzpatrick as his Chief Secretary, and Burgoyne as his army commander, collectively seemed to guarantee Foxite responses.[23] In spite of this, deviousness was early on display. Sheridan expressed his concern to Fitzpatrick about 'the style and tenour [*sic*], as they strike me at least, of THE *Secretary's* Despatches to the Duke of P. It is impossible not to see a reserve and a disingenuous management in them that cannot be very pleasing to you who are to act under them.' In all difficulties presented by Ireland in 1782, Shelburne's duplicity was 'the horrible part of the Business'.[24] Ireland was assisted in spite of Shelburne, not because of him.

Most dramatically, Fox, as Foreign Secretary, saw Shelburne compromising his schemes in European politics. Fox's plan was simple. France was and remained England's greatest enemy. The isolation of that country by diplomacy was his first priority. As he warned Frederick the Great, France aimed at the 'despotisme de l'Europe, avec de vues bien plus solides et mieux fondées que du tems de Louis quatorze.'[25] Such a threat could be countered, on the one hand, by putting together a triple alliance between England,

Russia, and Prussia, which 'seroit indubitablement celle qui conviendroit le mieux aux circonstances actuelles de l'Europe',[26] and on the other, by detaching the American rebels from their French allies. For this second purpose, Fox was reinforced in his view that American independence, freely granted, could only be to England's long-term advantage. In this, he once again encountered obstruction from Shelburne, under whose jurisdiction all colonies including America came. The press was very aware that the American issue was that on which the contest between Fox and Shelburne would be decided.[27] It was not a matter that could be resolved in isolation, but rather an essential feature of Fox's overall strategy in foreign politics.

Everything seemed programmed for a major confrontation. The peace negotiations were to be conducted in Paris. Fox, responsible for securing peace with France and Spain, had entrusted this task to Thomas Grenville. Shelburne, with responsibility for all colonial matters, dealt with the Americans through his envoy, Richard Oswald.[28] For three months, Grenville and Oswald received separate sets of instructions from London, and were predictably at loggerheads. Professional diplomats were appalled by this confusion in the expression of English policy. Kaunitz told one of them that 'there is again a flock of English at Paris. Is it possible that your ministry can hope to reap any advantage from such a mode of negotiating with the French Court.'[29] It was a chaotic arrangement calling for tight control from London. None was forthcoming. Instead, Shelburne exploited the situation to create difficulties.

The drama can be followed in Cabinet minutes. On 23 April, the Cabinet agreed to recommend independence for America, as long as all other territorial arrangements should be those of 1763, a policy reaffirmed on 18 May.[30] Five days later, a Cabinet attended by both Fox and Shelburne moved to agree the offer of independence without any conditions.[31] According to Fox, the Cabinet had been persuaded to take this step after receiving a letter from Grenville, which argued that only the offer of unconditional independence could detach America from her French allies.[32] Fox was so pleased with this development that he concluded that 'If any block to independence exists, it's at Versailles & not London.'[33] What he did not yet know was the extent to which Shelburne was playing a double game. In public, he supported the Cabinet's decision on independence for America.[34] In private letters to Oswald, however, he maintained the line that such independence was conditional upon other factors.[35] Charitably, Shelburne's motives might be attributed to a belief that Rodney's naval victory over the French, news of which reached home in May, gave England a stronger negotiating position in Paris. Without charity, Fox interpreted his action as part of a plot directed by the King to destroy the Ministry.

Predictably, Thomas Grenville soon began to complain to Fox that the negotiations had become 'a jumble'. Just when the Americans were on the point of settling, Oswald had arrived complaining volubly that 'the Rockingham party' were 'too ready to give up every thing'. Such was the mess that Grenville asked to be recalled. In his view, one English negotiator with full powers had to be appointed, 'or Ld. Shelburne must have his minister here, and Mr Fox his; by doing which, Mr Fox will be pretty near as much out of the secret, at least of what is essential, as if he had nobody here.'[36] Grenville had no doubt that Oswald and his master were deliberately upsetting the peace negotiations, and Sheridan agreed: 'If the business of an American treaty seemed likely to prosper in your hands, I should not think it improbable that Lord Shelburne would try to thwart it . . . I grow suspicious of him in every respect, the more I see of every transaction of his.' Significantly, Fox too was furious. He assured Grenville that Oswald's was 'a new intended commission of which the Cabinet here had never been apprized.' Calling for full details of 'this Duplicity of conduct', Fox tried to comfort Grenville: 'When the object is attained—that is, when the duplicity is proved—to what consequences we ought to drive; whether to an absolute rupture, or merely to the recal [sic] of Oswald and the simplification of this negotiation, is a point that may be afterwards considered. I own I incline to the more decisive measure, and so I think do those with whom I must act in concert.'[37]

With Rockingham seriously ill, Fox took the lead in forcing the pace. On 30 June, he proposed in Cabinet that independence should immediately be granted to America under the Great Seal. If America ceased to be a colony, then American affairs would be moved from Shelburne's jurisdiction to Fox's.[38] Shelburne disingenuously reported that this Cabinet meeting 'came to no final Resolution'.[39] In fact, Fox was outvoted, and his defeat on this issue crystallized a decision to resign. His experience of Shelburne's behaviour on Irish and reform issues, added to a deliberate sabotaging of the peace negotiations, convinced Fox that a plot to break the Ministry had been in place from its inception. The only way to make public the duplicity of George III and Shelburne was to resign. On 30 June, a resignation could only have been attributed to these concerns. Unfortunately, Fox did not resign until 4 July. In the interim, Rockingham died, and his death allowed other interpretations of Fox's resignation. Now, it could be argued that he went out because he and his friends were not sufficiently regarded in the redistribution of spoils and offices that followed the marquess's death. In fact, this is unfair. The intention to go out was firmly in place after the Cabinet of 30 June. The arrangement with Shelburne could not continue, if it gave George III the opportunity to neuter the Ministry's effectiveness.

On Rockingham's death, Fox put forward the Duke of Portland as his successor, to lead an administration in which Shelburne would play no part. Recent experience seemed to make such a proscription necessary, but adopting such a course was to play for very high stakes. The convention that the King should choose his own ministers had not been seriously challenged before. The Portland candidature, giving George III no options, was therefore deeply controversial. As Shelburne reported the matter: 'In truth, it is taking the Executive altogether out of the King's hands, & placing it in the hands of a Party, which, however respectable, must prove a compleat Tyranny to everybody else.'[40] Whether Fox and his allies had any right to insist that the new Prime Minister should be someone 'who lived & had habits with Ld. Rockingham's Friends'[41] became the central issue of politics. According to the King, predictably, Fox was attacking the just prerogatives of the Crown in a way that threatened the very balance of the constitution. In his view, though 'it may not be necessary to remove Him at once,'[42] Fox had rendered himself unfit for office.

The July resignation was one of the most decisive moments in Fox's career. In terms of losing both the argument and a great deal of parliamentary support, it was a disaster.[43] On the other hand, Fox's options were few. In his view, the Whigs had been caught up in a 'farce', whose title could either be 'Les Dupes' or 'Honesty the worst policy'.[44] George III had never intended the administration to survive, and Shelburne had been feeble enough to become his catspaw. For a king to undermine a ministry was an outrageous extension of prerogative powers and had to be resisted. As Fitzpatrick observed:

From the first moment I saw our *Beau-frère* [Shelburne], I was sure every thing had been settled in the *Closet*, & that he had the appointment of 1st Ld. of ye Treasury in his pocket. But if it is suffered there is certainly a total End of *Whig Principles*, & every thing more in the hands of Satan [George III] than ever. Charles is very decidedly of this opinion, & will move heaven & earth to resist the appointment; but the rest of the Cabinet are not equal to taking the decisive line of Conduct . . . If they let *him* have the treasury in his hands, it must inevitably be over with them as a party, & with Charles, & with the house of commons, & with every thing that is good.[45]

It was totally sinister that the King could not or would not work with the Whigs, who, as the men of great property in a political system predicated on property, were the acknowledged defenders of English liberties and parliamentarianism.[46] Conceivably, the King wished to be as despotic in England as in Hanover. As this nightmare of an idea gained currency, elderly Whigs remembered the destruction of an earlier administration in 1766.[47] The crisis was extreme.[48]

If Fox's resignation created a scandal by challenging the King's right of appointment, the decision to go out was not taken without advice. All his closest friends understood the point at issue and urged him on. Rockingham's long illness had prompted many of them to think over the question for some time before his death.[49] Portland, not the cleverest of men, had taken the point: 'Confidence I conceive to be wholly out of the Question. Power must be taken as its Substitute, & unless You can possess *that* & convince the Publick of your possessing it, Both Your Honour and Duty to the Country dictate your Retreat.'[50] Burke agreed, writing 'of the utter impossibility of your acting for any length of time as a Clerk in Lord Shelburne's administration'.[51] His only caveat was a prophetic word of caution about the necessity of carrying all the old Rockingham connection with him. Sheridan, the Prince of Wales, Burgoyne, and the Devonshires all agreed.[52] If one of Fox's major defects as a politician was a tendency to insulate himself against the cold of public opinion with the warmth of close friendships, that factor was never more in evidence than in July 1782. Fox thought that he would carry the day because his friends said so.[53]

After Rockingham's death, events moved quickly. On 3 July, each Cabinet Minister was told that Shelburne was to be the new Prime Minister by the King himself. Fox immediately replied that such a nomination was not tolerable. According to Shelburne, 'Mr Fox, spoke to the King in a strong way & seemed surprised to find that His M. dare have any opinion of his own.'[54] Next day, Fox went to Court, had 'an angry Conversation' with Shelburne, and, during an interview with the King of some five minutes duration, resigned the seals of office.[55] The experience left Fox's morale very much intact. That evening Horace Walpole noted that he dined with the Prince of Wales at Brooks's, stayed until four in the morning, and then went on to White's.[56] He shared with Sheridan the conviction that 'those who go are right; for there is really no other question but whether, having lost their power, they ought to stay and lose their characters.'[57] This was a fair point of view, but one that was not immediately obvious to those who were not at the centre of government, and therefore able to witness at first hand the tactics of Shelburne and the King. Before the resignation, little or no preparation had been made to convince the Rockingham party as a whole, let alone a wider political opinion, of the truth of Fox's case. Fox's departure from government would only be supported if statements about the King's despotic intentions were credible and provable.

It soon became clear that this case would be hard to make. By 8 July, Fox was admitting to the Duke of Leeds that only those with an intimate knowledge of politics could fully understand his position:

Upon the subject of his late resignation for which I told him I was sincerely sorry & feared the abrupt manner in which it had been done might prejudice him materially in the opinion of the world, he owned he thought it would, that it was impossible for any body to form a true opinion on the case who had not been in the Cabinet.[58]

Ominously, not even all former Cabinet colleagues took Fox's point. General Conway thought that Fox's resignation was nothing more than 'Caballing about Posts & Power',[59] while Thomas Townshend saw it as the product of irritation that Fox and his friends 'cannot fill up Offices to their wish'.[60] Most galling was the announcement by Fox's uncle, the Duke of Richmond, that he could 'see no reason at present for suspecting that the Measures on which we came in will not be pursued, and under this persuasion I think it would be very wrong not to support this Ministry merely because Lord Shelburne is at the Treasury'.[61] If it was not obvious to men such as these that Shelburne had been obstructing policy at the behest of George III, the scale of Fox's problem in convincing a wider world of the King's delinquency is revealed.

In the event, Fox's case was not accepted. Instead, contemporaries sought other explanations for his behaviour. For many, there was no need to look further than the general nature of Fox's character. He was a gambler in politics as well as in social life. Never having known restraint of any kind, he reacted instinctively when his wishes or ambitions were thwarted. The Duke of Grafton explained the resignation as simply a matter of 'Judgment and Temper'.[62] Even members of the Fox family had doubts. Lady Louisa Connolly approved of his politics generally, but thought that 'he was a little too hasty.'[63] Another cousin more brutally suggested that 'Charles is mad, & ruining himself.'[64] Within and without the ranks of the old Rockingham party, many people simply could not see the point of the resignation. For those not privy to Shelburne's performance in Cabinet or Oswald's behaviour in Paris, it was hard to take Fox's pronouncements seriously. His leaving government seemed to be dictated by nothing more than what Lord Temple called 'private grounds'.[65]

Alternatively, a contest between a king and the Whig aristocracy could always be characterized as an attempt at oligarchy on the part of a few great families. Horace Walpole saw the threat to the constitution not in terms of a royal despotism, but as Foxite exclusiveness: 'I hope we shall have a codicil to Magna Charta produced, for we are certainly to have a new War of the Barons, a struggle between the King and some great peers in which the people are to go for nothing.'[66] Referring to the pretensions of the Cavendish Dukes of Devonshire, Walpole insisted that his 'Whiggism is not confined to the Peak of Derbyshire'.[67] Gillray, in his cartoons on the crisis, showed Burke as a hypocritical Jesuit and Fox as 'Guy Fox', waiting for his opportunity to blow up the constitution.[68] Predictably, Shelburne was not slow to capitalize on these fears. The resignation and the ensuing crisis 'brings the point to issue, whether the executive is to be taken altogether out of the king's hands and lodged, as Mr Fox says, in the hands of a party, or, to speak more truly, in his own'.[69] Onlookers were asked to choose between the likelihood of George III's despotic intentions and Charles Fox's ambition.

For those at a distance from politics, there was simple confusion. Lord Pembroke, asking 'What did Charles Fox mean by throwing up', seemed to be under the mistaken impression that he had immediately asked to be reinstated.[70] The Bishop of Peterborough thought that Fox had 'hazarded all he had on one desperate throw against Poverty',[71] while Lord Sackville confessed to a friend that 'What still puzzles me is to account for the conduct of Mr Fox.'[72] From the vantage-point of Scotland, all was simply described as 'in confusion and the business of the public at a stand'.[73] Shelburne and Fox were thought to agree on so much that their argument was difficult to follow. Most people were not privy to Cabinet meetings or the King's backstairs influence. As a result, many were simply mystified, and it was this uncertainty that gave Fox a chance. In the first ten days of July 1782, he had to convince the political world at large that his resignation had been justified in terms of the constitutional dangers it signalled. In this he failed, with terrible long-term consequences.

There were two reasons for Fox's failure: he did not prepare the ground for his resignation and he chose the wrong issue to explain his behaviour. In his own circle, it was clear that Fox had resigned because Shelburne and the King were behaving in a dangerously unconstitutional manner. Yet, Fox told the world in general that he had resigned because he and Shelburne differed on the nature and timing of granting independence to America. This discrepancy was forced on Fox by the extreme difficulty of attacking a king openly. Eighteenth-century politics lacked a vocabulary that made this possible. Accusing a king of malpractice was hard to differentiate from treason. Fox therefore had to emphasize the American question and hope that the larger issue behind it would become obvious. As the Duke of Portland lamented: 'I really think that it is not less unfortunate for the public than for his own character that he cannot be at liberty to state every circumstance which induced him to take that upright and manly decision.'[74]

Further, at the end of a long and costly war, there was little popularity to be found in championing America. George III was clear that that alone would damn the resignation: 'I am glad Mr Fox is to try a question on unconditional American independence; I do not believe the Nation at large willing to come into it and great discredit will therefore attend the Party that proposes it.'[75] His advocacy of the American cause was 'far from being popular' and gave anyone with doubts about his general conduct 'a good plea for not following him'.[76] Nor was Fox's case helped by the fact that, just before resigning, on 2 July, in an attempt to commit Shelburne to the granting of independence, Fox had publicly and privately proclaimed the Cabinet's unity on this issue.[77] The public simply could not understand how, on 2 July, the Cabinet were united on the American issue, when Fox would resign on 4 July on the grounds that they were divided. The American issue had been the wrong one to take up, and it had not been argued consistently. Few could see that he had resigned on 'some great and essential ground of Politicks'.[78] The alternative explanations of frustrated ambition or oligarchical intent seemed much more plausible. As Fox felt the game slipping away from him, he admitted to Fitzpatrick that he 'did not think it had been in the power of Politics to make me so miserable as this cursed anxiety & suspense does'.[79]

If Fox chose the wrong issue on which to resign, his timing was also adrift. No attempt had been made to prepare the Rockingham party for what was to come. Not until 6 July did Fox address a party meeting at Lord Fitzwilliam's, in order to explain and persuade. The meeting lasted for nine hours, and Fox emerged victorious. Richmond was reduced to tears,[80] and 'the independent part of our late Party were perfectly satisfied with the account he gave of himself.'[81] But the damage had already been done. The Rockinghams did not resign *en bloc*, and Fox now led a diminished party. The only regret Thomas Grenville had about the whole business was 'the late hour in which it was done'.[82] Fox had at length carried most of the Rockinghams but, had he acted earlier, he might have carried more. Schoolfriends like Carlisle of course followed Fox, but, when asked to speculate about the future, Carlisle could go no further than 'God only knows.'[83] A huge crowd squeezed into the Visitors' Gallery of the Commons three days later to hear Fox's public apologia. Now the American issue was dropped. Still no mention was made of the King directly, and Fox confessed that 'for obvious reasons' he could not 'enter into a detail of the matters which had given rise to this difference'.[84] Consequently, fighting with one arm tied, he informed the Commons that he wished to ring 'the alarum bell'[85] and to warn them that 'such a system was to be begun, as he considered to be dangerous, if not fatal.'[86] For those who could read between the lines, 'the system' in question was the royal domination of politics.[87] It was a powerful performance that won him friends.[88]

No further attempts at self-justification were planned, but, at the last moment,[89] Fox took the opportunity of a Westminster reform meeting to offer his constituents an account of his actions. This time his words were more unguarded:

I own I had suspicions. I have long entertained suspicions, as to the general political principles of your present Minister [Shelburne]. When I became more immediately & thoroughly satisfied, that these suspicions were not badly founded, I esteemed it my duty to give a public indication of the state of my opinions, & to hold out the signal to the world, by retiring from his Majesty's service.[90]

Yet again, there was no direct reference to the King. His part in the skul-duggery had to be inferred from references to Shelburne's career and prospects. Significantly, not all the reformers in Westminster accepted his remarks. The powerful figure of John Jebb was unconvinced, as was Lord Mahon. A Firm and Free Club was started in the constituency with the aim of promoting radical purposes outside Foxite politics.[91] Fox was made bitterly aware of how costly his resignation had been, but was unrepentant. He told Portland that 'where there is not confidence there must be Power, and Power in this country must accompany the Treasury . . . we saw the thing in the true light.' The only remaining point of vexation was the con-viction that 'if we had resigned in a body, Shelburne must have yielded.'[92]

*

So traumatic had the July resignation been that some people thought that it marked the end of Fox's career. He was like 'Lucifer, past redemption'.[93] It was rumoured that he had given up politics for shooting,[94] and that he was intent on going to Gibraltar.[95] There was certainly a new mistress: 'I hear Charles saunters about the streets, & brags that he has not taken a pen in hand since he was out of Place . . . he lives with Mrs Robinson . . . I long to tell him that he does it to shew that he is superior to Alcibiades for *his* Countrymen forsook him when he was unfortunate, and Mrs Robinson takes *him* up.'[96] In fact, the disaster of July spurred Fox on to an unusual burst of activity. The battle with the King was very far from over.

Looking for new allies, Fox was aware that the House of Commons was divided into three factions: his own friends, the Shelburnites, and those who had remained loyal to Lord North. Any two of these could make a govern-ment. None alone could. With Shelburne beyond the pale, only North could be seen as a plausible colleague.[97] With him, Fox would command such a majority in the House of Commons that even George III would be cowed. If his recent and very public disagreements with North were an obstacle, they could be balanced by a family tradition that had made him a member of

North's government from 1770 to 1774. With quite astonishing speed and calculation, Fox visited North twice within a fortnight of his resignation.[98] Various politicians claimed the credit for promoting the idea of North and Fox resuming their association, notably Lord Loughborough and William Eden,[99] but for once Fox was very much prepared to take a lead. He had disagreed with North, but had always respected and liked him. He never liked or respected Shelburne, and recent experiences had done nothing to change his views. So enthusiastic was Fox that he made a formal offer of coalition in both July and August, claiming to North 'that it was by no means impracticable to reconcile their differences'.[100]

This was too sanguine. There were obstacles to resuming relations with North and they were real. Allegedly, some Foxites had not quite given up Shelburne, and continued to prefer him to North.[101] Certainly, the reforming speeches Fox made in Westminster unnerved Northites, whose hostility to most reform measures was notorious. Loughborough thought that 'Ch. Fox should keep out of West. Hall as a test that He wishes for a Coalition.'[102] Above all, the harsh words spoken by the two men since 1774, even if forgiven by the principals, were endlessly rehearsed in other quarters. The *Morning Herald* lamented the fact that Fox, the 'mock man of the people has crouched so low as to become a worshipper of Baal, whom he represented as some special messenger sent from the Luciferian regions, to scourge a devoted, because a guilty land'.[103] Predictably, for the whole period from July 1782 to February 1783, North was repeatedly reported to be uneasy about an association with Fox, and to be anxious not to close other options.[104] There were moments, too, when Fox felt qualms, always resolving, however, that 'it was best, though . . . it could not be lasting.'[105] He did not allow politics to interrupt his social life at Brooks's, and observers watching the would-be minister cutting and dealing found the whole scene ' "la plus parfaitement comique que l'on puisse imaginer", and to nobody does it seem more risible than to Charles himself'.[106]

In December 1782, any prospect of a Fox–North rapprochement was still so remote that Fox found himself voting in tiny minorities in the Commons, which merely emphasized his isolation and impotence as long as North held aloof.[107] Yet, embarrassing though it was, the courtship of North had to continue. From Fox's point of view, only the Northites could give him the numbers he needed to defeat George III and Shelburne. He bowed to this necessity. It was in terms of necessity that he later justified the association with North. Frankly he told the Commons that 'The motives which had induced him to agree to the coalition . . . were, that nothing but a coalition of party could remove the political obstruction given to the business of state.'[108] The coalition negotiations of 1778–80 appeared to be rehearsals for what was now unavoidable.

Two factors closed options and brought the Fox–North coalition into being: the necessity of both men to oppose the peace terms that Shelburne had secured with France and America, and the fear that some alternative, ministerial arrangement might leave one of them in the wilderness. Their joint concern about the peace terms was widely recognized. Fox, arguing that a disadvantageous peace was the inevitable result of not detaching America from France by a granting of independence, justified his role in the resignation crisis in July.[109] North was equally committed. The peace negotiations reflected inevitably on the conduct and success of a war for which he had been responsible. To argue that the peace terms were a just reflection of the military situation was to accuse himself of gross mismanagement. Instead, North had to argue that better terms could have been won, if the negotiating process had not been undermined by Shelburne's incompetence.[110] Predictably, therefore, Fox endlessly brought up the terrible nature of Shelburne's peace terms, in an attempt to force North to commit himself. Wriggle how he might, that was the hook on which he would be caught.[111]

Secondly, North was acutely aware that, although on paper his numbers were strong, most of his followers had been elected in 1780 as supporters of the King's government and administration. It would be unwise to keep them out of office too long. With Whig disdain, the Duchess of Portland called the Northites 'shabby people, who will be just as ready to leave him as to go with him',[112] while Burke observed that 'Lord North's (if it may be called *his*) party is within a trifle as numerous as ours on paper, but their weakness is that not one, literally not one, is attached either personally to him or to any principle whatsoever.'[113] Further, a rumour began to circulate early in 1783 that Fox, despairing of North, had decided to form an alliance with William Pitt, with whom he had hitherto been on friendly terms.[114] Whether such an arrangement with the son of his father's old enemy was a possibility would be a subject that would tantalize political observers until Pitt's death. Would the King allow it? Could the two most talented parliamentarians of their generation harmonize personalities that were as different as the North Pole from the South? North could not afford to speculate. Pitt detested him, and if he joined forces with Fox, North feared that he would be impeached on a charge of losing the American empire.[115]

These factors brought matters to a head between 12 and 15 February 1783. The peace proposals had been formally laid before the Commons on 27 January. Before they were debated on 17 February, North would have to break cover. On 11 February, Pitt and Fox had a widely publicized meeting.

In fact, both men quickly realized that an arrangement between them was not possible, but the very fact of their talking put North into a panic.[116] After passing another 48 hours in an agony of indecision, North met Fox at 2 p.m. on 14 February. According to the main account of that meeting, Fox promised North that no further attacks should be made on the influence of the Crown, and that he would not bring forward parliamentary reform. It seemed that Fox would offer anything to secure North.[117] On 16 February, a joint amendment to the peace proposals was agreed, and, a day later, the Fox–North Coalition came into public view in the debate on the peace. Shelburne's proposals constituted 'such a peace, that you shall sicken at its very name'.[118] Involving, as Fox claimed, the 'sacrifice of our chief possessions in America, Asia and Africa', it was not surprising that 'the situation of the country required a coalition of parties.'[119] What Fox would call the swingeing nature of the concessions made to France, Spain, and America was the consequence of Shelburne's delinquency in the previous summer. He had to be made to pay for his behaviour, and all political considerations were subordinated to that end.

*

The Fox–North Coalition was therefore conceived out of necessity rather than affection. It had been thrown together in haste, and the ambiguities that remained on almost every issue except opposition to Shelburne's peace were terrible. Fox had no time, and perhaps no inclination, to 'fully inform his own party of the true conditions entered into with Ld. North'.[120] Once again, as in July 1782, Fox's friends had to take much on trust. The reformers among them were guaranteed embarrassment by a union with North.[121] Those with sharp memories of the American War would have doubts. Any common ground had to be discovered after the Coalition was in place, not before its formation. Looking at his new situation in February 1783, Fox himself admitted that nothing but success was likely to justify it,[122] but for the moment that success was very visible. Shelburne was forced out of office and George III temporarily lost the direction of politics.

For the moment, it was 'King Fox compleatly'.[123] Fox and North together had a Commons majority in excess of a hundred, and not even George III could outface such odds. For over a month before accepting the Coalition as his ministers, George III tried unsuccessfully to find an alternative.[124] Temple, Gower, and Pitt all declined to lead an alternative ministry in the circumstances. Insisting that 'after the Manner I have been personally treated by both the D. of Portland and Ld. North it is impossible that I can ever admit either of them into my Service',[125] the King informed the Prince of

Wales that he was seriously thinking of abdicating and retiring to Hanover:
'The situation of the times are such that I must, if I attempt to carry on the
business of the nation, give up every political principle on which I have
acted.'[126] What made matters worse was that Fox and North presented him
with the *fait accompli* of complete Cabinet and governmental lists. For the
first time, an English monarch was not only to have no influence in the
nomination of a prime minister, but he was also to be excluded from
suggesting names for minor offices. The eclipse of the executive seemed
complete.[127] Almost plaintively, the King asked a friend to 'judge, therefore,
of the uneasiness of my mind, at having been thwarted in every attempt to
keep the administration of public affairs out of the hands of the most
unprincipled coalition the annals of this or any other nation can equal.'[128]

Fox was unimpressed by the King's tears and protestations. The harsh
experience of the previous year had taught him that George III set out to
destroy governments he disliked, whether they were generally supported by
the political nation or not. He could not be allowed to nominate to government, because his nominees would act as wreckers or spies, as Shelburne
and Thurlow had done the year before. Fox was aware that he was introducing new and controversial conventions into the practice of politics, but
he had no alternative. In an important speech of 6 March 1783, he set out
the new rules by which the power of the executive could be kept within proper
bounds:

It had been argued again and again, that the king had a right to chuse his own
ministers. In that particular, he rested on the spirit of the constitution, and not on
the letter of it; and grounding his opinion on the spirit of the constitution, he ever
had and ever would maintain, that his majesty, in his choice of ministers, ought not
to be influenced by his personal favour alone, but by the public voice, by the sense of
his parliament, and the sense of his people . . . It was no argument to say, 'I am a
minister, because his majesty has made me one.' The personal influence of the
crown was not the ground for a minister to stand upon.[129]

Fox, 'the acknowledged Minister',[130] was accepted ultimately by the King
'de la plus mauvaise grace possible'.[131] It was a public triumph, and Fox,
after what he took as the personal humiliations of 1772, 1774 and 1782, was
pitiless. He cheerfully observed to Grafton that '*he*, meaning the K. will dye
soon and that will be best of all.'[132]

In retrospect, the Fox–North Coalition, representing the junction of two
men who seemed to give up the pleasure of vilifying each other for the
greater entertainment of attacking the royal prerogative, was held up as an
example of infamous politics. Fox's obituary in the *Gentleman's Magazine*
referred to the Coalition as 'a stain in his life which all the ingenuity of his

political advocates could never wipe away'.[133] Indeed, at the moment of the Coalition's formation, some former admirers of Fox were unhappy,[134] but it is important not to predate its notoriety. In March 1783, the Coalition government was widely accepted. After all, most eighteenth-century ministries had been coalitions, often involving men who disliked each other intensely. As William Pitt drifted into association with the King, was that, Fox asked, not strange: 'If the coalition be disgraceful, what is the anti-coalition? When I see the right honourable gentleman [Pitt] surrounded by the early objects of his political, nay his hereditary hatred, and hear him revile the coalition, I am lost in astonishment how men can be so blind to their own situation, as to attempt to wound us in this particular point.'[135] It was the India Bill of November 1783 that gave the Coalition its malodorous quality. At the moment of its conception in March, it was perfectly acceptable. In April, all the Coalitionists were re-elected for their constituencies with a minimum of fuss, and this opportunity to give voice to a public outcry was not taken.[136] Foxites recognized that their wealth and talent would dominate the new arrangement, and that 'to *follow* or *lead* Lord North are two very different things.'[137] Northites consoled themselves with the thought that 'we had no Cause either to blame ourselves at this or to disclaim it; we had no Choice about it.'[138]

Inevitably, there was speculation about how long the Coalition government would last. Fox, with a strong majority in a House of Commons that in theory would run until 1787, was initially sanguine. It was that body which had the right 'to say who ought or who ought not to govern the country'.[139] On the other hand, the King's displeasure was public and unremitting. A reluctance to be co-operative in patronage matters was an early indication that he detested the Coalition and all its works.[140] After a month in office, Fox still thought politics were going 'very well', but added later in the same letter, 'cependant il faut voir.'[141] After two months in office bets were being taken at Brooks's that Pitt or Temple would be prime minister by Christmas, at odds of four to one against.[142]

Those odds would shorten dramatically in the course of the summer of 1783, as a series of crises underlined the extent of the King's hostility. In May, there was no royal backing in the affair of Powell and Bembridge, two officials restored to office by the Coalition even though they were being investigated for fraud.[143] In terms of the Coalition's foreign policy, Fox's direct responsibility, there was only obstruction and recrimination. As Fox struggled with the old policy of doing all in his power 'to ballance [*sic*] the enormous maritime force of the house of Bourbon',[144] George III brutally reminded him that the country's weakness was of his own making: 'Every difficulty in concluding Peace this Country has alone itself to blame; after the extraordinary and never to be forgot vote of February 1782 and the hurry for negotiation that then ensued it is no wonder that our Enemies seeing our spirit so fallen have taken advantage of it.'[145] All the King's communications with his foreign secretary are in the same cold, staccato style. Even more sinister, Fox's attempts to finalize peace terms with France and America were being frustrated. Little or no improvement on Shelburne's terms was forthcoming, and neither Vergennes for France nor Henry Laurens for America appeared to be in a hurry to secure peace. The reason, as Fox discovered, was that both men were being assured by friends of Shelburne that the King would shortly dismiss the Coalitionists, as soon as a suitable issue on which to act could be found. This all had a 'singular appearance'.[146]

In June 1783, it seemed that the King had found the issue he wanted. Only two years after coming of age, the Prince of Wales was forced to apply to the House of Commons to relieve him of enormous debts. He asked for £100,000 and was offered £60,000. Such a public admission of delinquency on the part of the Prince inevitably harmed the reputation of his friends in the Coalition. North and Portland had no sympathy with the young man's dissipation. In return, the Prince resented their moralizing and unwillingness to help.[147] For Fox, the affair was deeply embarrassing. Many people, including the King, regarded him as the Prince's tutor in debauchery. His own public indebtedness mirrored that of the heir apparent.[148] A Gillray cartoon showed him driving 'the white horse of Hanover from the Pinnacle of Glory to the Valley of Annihilation', crying 'Aut Cromwell aut nihil—so come up, old Turnips.'[149] Little wonder that, on 17 June, Fox believed that the Coalition government 'will not outlive tomorrow or at least that it will be at an end in a very few days'.[150] His fears were justified. The King took the opportunity to sound out alternatives, and only a total surrender by the Prince of Wales on the question of how much he was to receive defused a situation that could have developed into a major constitutional crisis.[151]

A month later, Fox had recovered his nerve. George III had drawn back from staging a coup, and the Coalition's strength in the Houses of Commons was a guarantee against the worst that the King could do:

Parliament is certainly our strong place, and if we can last during a recess I think People will have little doubt in our lasting during the Session. Perhaps I see this a little sanguinely, but I own when I look over our strength in the H. of Commons and see that all hopes of dissension between the two parts of the Coalition are given up by the Enemy . . . I can not help thinking of our being overturned in Parliament quite chimerical . . . If we last the Summer, the Public will think that the King has made up his mind to *bear* us, and this opinion alone will destroy the only real cause of weakness that belongs to us.[152]

Fox admitted that the 'next Session of Parliament will be a great Crisis',[153] but insisted that 'the Notions of a Change of Ministers' were 'entirely & necessarily groundless'.[154] In the summer of 1783, Fox was less concerned about politics than about the beginning of a two-year *affaire* with the Duchess of Devonshire.[155] In spite of endless speculation in the press[156] and in private letters,[157] the Coalition appeared safe though unloved. In this view, Fox fatally underestimated the sheer determination and bloody-mindedness of the King. For George III, Fox was such an anathema that 'every honest man and those the least interested in the support of this constitution must wish to do the upmost to keep him out of power.'[158] The King was doggedly resolved to destroy the Coalition at the earliest opportunity. Its very existence, in pitting Parliament against the King, legislature against executive, represented an ongoing constitutional crisis. It had to be resolved. The King had not won finally in July 1782 and nor had Fox in February 1783. A final encounter was yet to come.

*

Fox excitedly reported to a friend that the session of Parliament that began in November 1783 would be 'the most terrific . . . that ever was held.'[159] That its proceedings would be dominated by the affairs of India was agreed across the political spectrum. Disorder and suspected corruption on an epic scale made it imperative that the relationship between the government and the East India Company be put on a new basis. It was, however, a minefield of an issue, and Fox was under no illusions about the dangers:

I have but too much reason to think that upon our India Measure which will be our first, and upon which the fate of the Administration & of the country must depend, we shall meet with very great embarrassments and difficulties. The variety of private interests that will militate against us cannot fail of making it a most tempting opportunity to Opposition & therefore it is to be presumed they will lay hold of it.[160]

Great pains were taken to secure a full Whig attendance early in the Session.[161] Win or lose, there was no ducking the problem. As Portland observed, 'the evil . . . is grown so rank, all palliatives have been proved so ineffectual, the cure is of so much importance to the existence and character of the nation, that I pant for the experiment.'[162] The Foxite response to the problem of India had been entrusted earlier in the summer to Edmund Burke, who drafted the India Bill in consultation with Fox.[163]

At stake was the enormous patronage of India. Its potential was thought so great that it was feared that whoever controlled it could effectively buy up so much of the House of Commons as to threaten its independence. In whose hands therefore was the control of this patronage machine safe? The final, Foxite answer to this question was to invest control of Indian patronage in a Board of Commissioners, all of whom were close friends of Fox himself. It is some measure of Fox's appreciation of the difficulties in the situation, however, that before this wholly partisan solution was adopted he had tried to do a deal on the question with both the East India Company and with leading opponents like Pitt.[164] As Fox sent circular letters to all his known supporters begging them to attend Parliament,[165] he was aware that to allow a group of Foxites to control patronage networks in India would open the Coalition to the charge that they wished to use this new wealth and influence to confirm their oligarchical control of politics. Members of both Houses could be bribed. Rotten boroughs could be bought. As Sir Francis Baring informed Shelburne:

The Empire of Asia will remain compleately [*sic*] & absolutely in the hands of Fox . . . It is a system of influence & corruption as amazes me; it is however compleat, & if no other proof existed of the abilities & ambition of C. Fox, it will forever remain as a monument of the boldest & most artfull [*sic*] effort ever attempted by any subject since the restoration, for if he succeeds he will remain possessed of more real power & patronage than any future Minister can possibly enjoy supported by every thing which the Crown can give.[166]

Fox saw the plausibility of this point but, after the failure of his talks with the Company and with Pitt, he had few options. Clearly, the Crown could not be trusted with such an accession of influence. The only safe hands in which to lodge it were his own.

The Coalition's India Bill was debated in the House of Commons in late November 1783. According to Fox, 'the Question is really the most decisive one that ever came on.'[167] Its success or failure 'will be to a great degree decisive upon all Politicks'.[168] In major speeches on 18 and 27 November and 1 December, Fox set out his case. It was well known that the Company's government of India was nothing more than a system 'of anarchy and confusion'.[169] Its servants ignored its instructions and thought only of satisfying their own 'rapacity'. No confidence could be put in the Company's capacity to reform itself. Indeed, the government was called upon to save it from imminent bankruptcy. The Company's administration of India had been predicated on 'the miseries of mankind. This is the kind of government exercised under the East India Company upon the natives of Indostan; and the subversion of that infamous government is the main object of the bill in question.'[170] To transfer its authority to the Crown would be to exchange one potential tyranny for another. Fox proudly asserted that 'this bill as little augments the influence of the crown, as any measure which can be devised for the government of India.'[171] The only option was to call into being a board of parliamentarians, who, as commissioners and trustees for the patronage of India, would always be under scrutiny. The fact that the names put forward were all leading Foxites was justified by the claim that only such men were impervious to the blandishments of Court and Company.[172]

On 27 November, the Coalition's India Bill secured a second reading by the very comfortable margin of 229–120. Before the vote, Fox had thought that 'If we can beat them as I hope to do by a hundred or a hundred and fifty, it will give a most complete blow to the Enemy which they will find difficult to recover.'[173] After it, predictably, he could write that 'The more I reflect upon last night, the more I consider it as decisive in every respect.'[174] There was still the hurdle of the House of Lords to be overcome, but Fox was clear, on 2 December, that 'there is no cause to fear.'[175] He was oblivious to the campaign which George III had instigated to bully bishops and pressurize peers into defeating the Bill.[176] He simply could not believe that even this king would so publicly intervene in the deliberations of the legislature as to engineer the defeat of a measure which had been passed by the Commons by such a margin. On 6 December, Fox thought that the bill would pass the Lords by at least a majority of two to one.[177] Four days later, he told Mrs Armistead that he was still 'very sanguine, but the reflection of how much depends at this moment upon me is enough to make any Man who has any feeling serious'.[178] A slight doubt expressed to Portland on 13 December was soon dispelled,[179] and, on the day of the Lords' debate itself, Fox was still expecting a majority of twenty-five.[180]

On 15 December 1783, the India Bill was defeated in the Lords by eight votes. Fox was present to witness the full impact of the royal coup:

C. Fox was behind the throne during the whole time of the business yesterday, and seemed in great agitation . . . I am told, that his countenance, gesture and expressions upon the event were in the highest degree ludicrous from the extremity of distortion and rage, going off with an exclamation of despair, hugging G. North along with him and calling out for Sheridan—So Caliban, Stephano and Trinculo reeled off upon the disappointment of their similar project.[181]

George III heard of the Lords' decision at eleven at night. So anxious was he to be rid of the Coalition that he immediately sent officials to require the seals of office from North and Fox, without waiting for the light of morning. Allegedly, Fox, confronted with this demand, 'refused to credit it, for, he said, it was impossible to believe that the King in his actual circumstances would hazard such a step'.[182]

Paradoxically, the India Bill's defeat and the dismissal of the Coalition, instead of depressing Fox, left him in 'an extasy of spirits'.[183] For eighteen months or so, Fox had, by implication, been trying to convince the political world that George III was a malevolent king, whose determination to subordinate the legislature to the executive threatened the constitution. It had been a difficult case to argue because so much of the King's behaviour was only known to those who sat in Cabinets or were in Court secrets. Now, after his intervention in the Lords, to kill a measure which had overwhelming Commons support, he was exposed. It could now be loudly proclaimed that George III was a menace. Further, the Coalition seemed to enjoy a majority in three figures in the House of Commons, with no election due until 1787. Unless he took account of this fact, the King would provoke a constitutional crisis, which would widely be seen as of his own making. As Fox explained to Mrs Armistead: 'We are beat in the H. of Lords by such treachery on the part of the King . . . as one could not expect even from him . . . However we are so strong that nobody else can undertake without madness, and if they do I think that we shall destroy them almost as soon as they are formed.'[184]

Both sides were aware that the stakes in this crisis had been raised to an almost intolerable level. According to the King, what was at issue was 'no less than whether a desperate faction shall not reduce the Sovereign to a mere tool in its hands; though I have too much principle ever to infringe the rights of others, yet that must ever equally prevent my submitting to the Executive Power being in any other hands than where the Constitution has placed it'.[185] Alternatively, for Fox, the King's unconstitutional behaviour was 'so indecent and notorious'[186] that it threatened to establish 'a system of influence of the most dangerous of any yet attempted'.[187] Language now became totally uninhibited, and allusions to the Civil War and the return of a Stuart despotism were thought apposite.[188] Fox's denunciation of the King was now explicit. In a Commons debate on 17 December, Fox, calling on the English to decide whether they were to be 'freemen or slaves',[189] warned them that 'we shall certainly lose our liberty, when the deliberations of Parliament are decided—not by the legal and usual—but by the illegal and extraordinary exertions of prerogative.'[190] As the press pointed out, the argument was no longer about the India Bill. Rather, every voter must decide whether the balance of the constitution was now more threatened by Fox allegedly trying to take over the powers of the Crown, or by George III trying to undermine the liberties of Lords and Commons. No crisis had a sharper definition.[191]

In December 1783, Fox had no doubt that he would win. The Coalition's majority in the Commons was the ultimate guarantee. As the Duchess of

Devonshire brutally reported to her mother, 'we have the Majority still in the H. of C. which is suppos'd must rout them.'[192] When Temple, that 'd——d, dolterheaded Coward',[193] at the King's behest, tried and failed to form an alternative administration, Fox was not surprised, and amused himself with the observation that 'the Confusion of the Enemy is beyond all description, and the triumph of our friends proportionable.'[194] His cousin delightedly exclaimed that 'Never was there a more triumphant power than Charles', nor mortification to the folly of those who attempted such rash measures.'[195] No Foxite would have been surprised to know that George III was describing himself as 'on the Edge of a Precipice'.[196]

The hopelessness of the King's position seemed proved by the appointment of a 24-year-old as prime minister. He could find no one but William Pitt to outface the Coalition's majority in the Commons. Foxites, on hearing of the move, were almost incapacitated with laughter. Pitt's term of office was dubbed the Mince Pie administration because it would barely survive Christmas. Fox generously took bets that Pitt would be prime minister for at least a week.[197] Further evidence of Pitt's weakness was suggested by the fact that certainly once, and possibly twice, in the period between 22 December 1783 and 7 January 1784, he sought out Fox with offers of a coalition.[198] Fox's answer was a public rebuke in the House of Commons. He

talked of the weakness of young men in accepting offices under the present circumstances of affairs, and he mentioned their youth as the only possible excuse for their rashness . . . They did not seem to understand a pretty broad hint from that House, how improper it would be to come into power; it would, perhaps, require a broader one to convince them of the necessity of retiring.[199]

All in all, things looked 'well',[200] and, when Parliament reassembled on 12 January 1784, Fox was looking forward to 'the most decisive victory on our side that ever happened'.[201] According to the betting book at Brooks's, Fox was expecting a majority of three figures on the first question debated after the Christmas recess.[202]

Further, if Fox's position depended entirely on a Commons majority, it was a comforting fact that no election was due until 1787. In theory, George III could dissolve Parliament at will, and Fox was alive to this possibility,[203] but no monarch had exercised this prerogative in living memory. To do so would ignite controversial memories of Stuart kings, who endlessly dissolved Parliaments for no other reason than that their composition displeased them. Fox was pleased to discover that when he moved petitions, advising the King against 'a wanton or imprudent exercise of the prerogative' in the matter of a possible dissolution, he actually gained votes.[204] Dismissing

Parliament was so controversial a step that not even George III was thought capable of taking it.

Best of all, a wider political public seemed to have grasped the full significance of the crisis, and to have accepted Fox's interpretation of it. By the time of its defeat, the India Bill had only provoked two hostile petitions, one from London and one from Shelburne's borough of Chipping Wycombe.[205] True, some cartoons appeared showing Fox as Cromwell or Carlo Khan, riding down Leadenhall St. on the back of an Indian elephant, but others portrayed him as a new Demosthenes or as the 'Champion of the People'. Against anti-Coalition songs must be set images showing Pitt, riding the white horse of despotic Hanover, battling with Fox sitting astride the British lion.[206] The press was predictably divided on the issue, but a not insignificant number of newspapers found Fox's position neither hopeless nor unwarranted. The destruction of the India Bill had been so blatant that the political world at large had at least to draw breath before deciding between George III and Fox. The latter's achievement was that, at the worst, he had made the story of the King's delinquency plausible: at the best, he might, as he thought, succeed in establishing new ground rules for relations between Crown and Parliament. As the Commons reassembled, on 12 January 1784, Fox felt that he had an excellent chance of doing just that.

Fox's confidence proved sadly misplaced. Enjoying majorities of 39 and 54 in Commons' divisions on 12 January, he saw his majority dribble away over the next two months. By 8 March, it was down to a solitary vote.[207] Government effectively came to a standstill as Fox voted down whatever Pitt proposed. All MPs had to apportion blame for this alarming breakdown of government and act accordingly. Was Pitt culpable for standing in defiance of a Commons majority against him? Or was Fox guilty of using that majority against a man whom the King had chosen to be his minister? Faced with this decision, many Northites took fright. Elected as supporters of North and the King in 1780, they had now to choose between these two men. According to a list drawn up by Burke, fifty-one Northites, who had voted for the India Bill, now deserted to Pitt.[208] Lord North himself was reported to be so disturbed by the severity of Fox's language with regard to the King that he was on the point of abandoning politics altogether.[209] When Fox called a meeting to rally morale on 26 February, indicating that the game had gone too far to allow for retreat, some Northites showed 'a sort of boggle about the extreme'.[210] Fox was driving the Northites hard in directions that were new to them. That he lost many was predictable. What is surprising is that so many, including North himself and William Adam, stayed on.

If Northites had to choose between North and the King, reforming MPs had to follow either Fox or Pitt. Hitherto, these two young men had jointly been the hope of the reformers. Now, they were opponents and shackled by alliances to non-reformers. Which of them would prove to be the long-term friend of reform had to be debated at public meetings all over England, and the divisions set up at these assemblies fatally harmed the reform movement as a whole. Christopher Wyvill opted for Pitt, declaring that Fox wished to change 'our limited Monarchy into a mere Aristocratical Republic'.[211] William Mason thought that all politics would be corruption 'if Charles Fox had the Indies at his disposal'.[212] High-minded Yorkshire gentlemen, like William Wilberforce and R. S. Milnes, came to the conclusion that they had more to fear from 'the tyranny of Venice rather than that of France'.[213] Even in Westminster, things did not go smoothly. Fox carried a meeting of electors on 14 February, but not without overcoming considerable heckling, which included the throwing of a bag containing 'a noisome effluvia'.[214] It is in the course of such debates and meetings that the Coalition acquired its opprobrious flavour. Men remembered that North and Fox had not always been friends.[215] They knew that Fox was a declared bankrupt. For those in the reform movement, who could carry off the high moral tone of a tender conscience, it could indeed appear that the Coalition was attempting to seize the wealth of India for dishonourable purposes. Fox did not recover his standing among reformers until after the outbreak of the French Revolution, and reformers like Wyvill resumed contact only because Fox by then was one of the few people left in the reform field.

The third group to be under pressure were the country gentlemen, who, as MPs, prided themselves on their independence of thought and action. Normally reluctant to say anything disloyal about the King, many had been so alarmed by the progress of the American War that they had supported Dunning's resolution in 1780. Now, coming up to London after the Christmas recess, they found government at a standstill, a peace treaty still unsigned, and the symptoms of a national disintegration. Their first instinct was to effect a union of Fox and Pitt in an administration of national unity.[216] When that failed, they moved inexorably into support for Pitt. After all, Pitt's words were familiar and understandable. He argued that kings were allowed to choose their own ministers. It was an undisputed aspect of the prerogative. He was the Minister so chosen. Fox, in arguing that ministers depended, not on kings, but on Commons' majorities, offered something new, that failed to please traditionalist minds. Lord John Cavendish might dismiss these men as 'a very absurd Sett [*sic*] of people',[217] and it was true that they understood little of the Indian problem or knew much of Court intrigue. However, Foxites would have been wise to pay more attention to the worries and puzzlement of men, who, when in doubt, would bolt for the familiar rather than the innovative.

*

In March 1784, George III dissolved Parliament, even though it had three years of life left in it, and thereby plunged the country into the most acrimonious and bitterly contested election of the century. The constitutional crisis would now be settled by the political world at large. The King was fighting for a view of the executive that allowed it traditional powers in the formation of ministries and the influencing of policy. Fox, arguing on the evidence of twenty-four disastrous years from 1760 to 1784, set out to redefine the relationship between King and Parliament. The debate was awesome in terms of what was at stake. Both men were aware that this election was, in a sense, the critical point of their careers. If defeated, one threatened to abandon England for Hanover, and the other to throw up politics forever.

Fox lost decisively. MPs bought with royal money, reformers, and independents combined to destroy Coalitionists. As far as a public opinion can be identified in constituencies with a large number of voters, it operated overwhelmingly against Fox.[218] Long-established interests were overthrown by voters at all social levels. In Suffolk, a French visitor saw the Bunbury influence overthrown 'by farmers and freeholders who have only the bare qualifications of an elector'.[219] Lord John Cavendish was defeated at York, though he had thought himself 'as safe as at a Burgage Tenure borough'.[220] Most dramatically, Fox himself was challenged in Westminster. As the King informed Pitt, no tactics were to be ruled out: 'Though the advance made by Mr Fox this day can only have been made by bad Votes, yet similar measures must be adopted rather than let him get Returned for Westminster.'[221] In a poll drawn out over several weeks, duchesses famously exchanged kisses for votes and the level of vitriolic exchange was intense.[222] Fox was so unsure of his return that he actively sought alternatives in Bridgwater and Orkney.[223] The indignity of the Man of the People representing twelve voters from islands to the far north of Scotland was ultimately averted, but not before Fox had experienced the most profound pessimism[224] and the humiliation of a scrutiny.[225]

The election of 1784 was a total vindication of George III and his interpretation of the events of the preceding two years. Burke saw the Coalition's defeat as in some sense final, blaming Fox for relying too much on talented improvisation: 'As to any plan of Conduct in our Leaders there are not the faintest Traces of it—nor does [it] seem to occur to them that any such thing is necessary. Accordingly every thing is left to accidents; I thought Fox had great Faith in the Chapter of that Scripture.'[226] This is perhaps too severe. Throughout the crisis, Fox had indeed responded to events, but he had never enjoyed many options. The King, less public in his manoeuvres, with an assured power base within the constitution, could appeal to a whole range of traditional values, which made sentiment stronger than argument. Fox, by contrast, had to find theories to fit new situations as they unfolded. In the process, many sacred cows were slaughtered. A king could not choose his own ministers, if his nominees were simply to be used as spies and saboteurs. The old prerogative of dissolving Parliament had to be modified, if it was used capriciously by a king who found that the legislature thwarted his purposes. Above all, the peace and success of England since 1688 had depended on kings and queens, as managers of the executive, working harmoniously with the men of property, among whom Rocking-hams and Foxites figured prominently. If George III could not or would not maintain that harmony, rules had to be redrawn.

For Fox himself, the experiences of 1782–4 had a determining effect. For the whole of his subsequent career, they are the reference point for decisions. No other event, not even the French Revolution, had such an influence. The vindication of his actions becomes a recurring and obsessive theme. His loathing for the King and William Pitt was so profound as to be sometimes destructive of good judgement. In 1794, he accused them of establishing a 'system of vilifying parliament'.[227] In 1799, he was still insisting that 'the battle that We lost in 1784 . . . is the pivot upon which every thing turns.'[228] The hurt was deeply personal to Fox himself, and this had two consequences. On the one hand, he was now confirmed in his Whiggery. If he had needed a guiding principle or two in 1782, he had now been furnished with a hundred such. The vindication of his role in these years could call up astonishing bursts of energy and violence. On the other hand, his defeat had been public and complete, and this fact reinforced the desire, so often and sincerely expressed, to leave politics forever. Fox, the reluctant politician, found it easy to withdraw into the warmth of friendships and Foxite society. Writing to Mrs Armistead about the Westminster campaign, he assured her that 'I have serious thoughts if I am beat here, of not coming in to Parliament at all.'[229] Fox's career after 1784 see-sawed between an increasing desire to disengage from politics and spasms of intense effort to punish the men of 1784, who had inflicted such wounds on him and the constitution.

4

New Principles and Old Failings,
1784–1789

THE feverish politics of 1782–4 had ended, for Fox, in public and sensa-
tional defeat. Not surprisingly, their impact and influence cast long shadows,
and for Fox they were a formative experience. In 1784, all the factors which
were to govern his future responses in politics were in place. No subsequent
event, not even the French Revolution, was to change the agenda. Foxite
politics now had a clear definition and obvious priorities. Central to these
was the experience of George III's recent behaviour. It was evident that he
would never work willingly with Fox and his friends, a fact which was taken
as a deep personal insult. Exclusions of this sort, promulgated from palaces,
led on naturally to genuine concern about the extent and operation of executive power. This concern becomes the main theme of the Foxite litany. On
the other hand, defeat on the scale of 1784 had reinforced in Fox all those
inclinations to abandon politics that had always been part of his personality.
Too often thereafter the making of policy was left to others, like Burke and
Sheridan. At crucial moments, Fox, seemingly paralysed or indifferent, refused to exercise the influence that his name and talents secured him. He
was the undoubted leader and yet often refused to lead. He wanted to make
George III pay for the humiliation of 1784, but somehow lacked the will to
exploit opportunities to do so. As a result, divisions and animosities within
the Foxite group were allowed to develop long before 1789. It was the
French Revolution that would tear the party asunder, but Fox's refusal
either to lead or retire left the Foxites vulnerable and at risk.

*

The catastrophe of the 1784 election had been so complete that, not for the
first or last time, many contemporaries were tempted to conclude that Fox's
effective career in politics was at an end. Fox himself seemed to provide

ample evidence for this view. In spite of the fact that Pitt's administration was lacking in talent and open to attack on a number of issues, Fox, for the remainder of 1784 and the whole of 1785, was disinclined to exert himself. He refused to challenge Pitt on matters of finance, because he could 'not be enough Master of it'.[1] Sometime in the summer of 1784, he purchased a 'villa' at St Anne's Hill in Surrey,[2] which was to be his home for the rest of his life. Henceforth, party documents had to be ferried back and forth,[3] and no manager could ever be sure that Fox would appear for a particular debate or division.[4] When friends such as Portland urged him to attend for a particular vote, Fox agreed but felt obliged to add that 'I really do hate going to the H. of Cs. to such a degree that I wish not to be brought there for nothing.'[5] Even Pitt's India Bill, debated in June–July 1784, concerning the very issue on which the Coalition had fallen, could not excite Fox's interest: 'To be present at the daily or rather hourly equivocations of a *young hypocrite*, is at once so disgusting to observe and so infamous to tolerate, that the person who listens to them with forebearance [*sic*], becomes almost an accomplice in them.'[6] Even so, it was not surprising that, in the letters of Burke and others, there begins to appear the complaint that Fox still claimed the privileges of leading a party without really accepting its obligations.[7]

In response to his critics, Fox argued that Pitt would be more exposed as ambitious and incompetent by the absence of opposition:

It is impossible not to see that the majority is much more *against* us than for the Ministry, and their behaviour on the India Bill which had begun to excite much discontent till I opposed it is a very sufficient lesson to my mind . . . I know that, both on my own account and in consideration of the present state of the House, I can serve it better by lying by for a little while.[8]

Whatever force there was in this notion, many found it lame, as the public performance of the opposition appeared unmanaged and chaotic.[9] Little wonder that some individuals, like Lord Camden, decided to seek an accommodation with Pitt, claiming that the 'Coalition has destroyed the Whig party forever'.[10] As the Pitt administration was given time to establish itself, Fox seemed increasingly obsessed with his new mistress, Elizabeth Armistead, whom he seems to have filched from the Prince of Wales. In the summer and autumn of 1784, he appeared with her at leading social events, irritating his political ally, the heir apparent, and shocking reformers like Richard Price with this 'immoral and indecent conduct'.[11] As cartoonists depicted Fox as Satan, Guy Fawkes, Carlo Khan, Damien, Machiavelli, and, most often, Cromwell,[12] it became fashionable for literary men to write Fox's political epitaph.[13] For some, the only point at issue was whether Fox had abandoned politics or whether politics had abandoned him.

Epitaphs were not out of place in the sense that Fox never again gave such concentrated effort and attention to politics as he did between 1782 and 1784. Yet they described only one side of the tension in Fox's character. Much as he disliked day-to-day attendance at Westminster, the events of these years had given him a cause that kept him chained to the oar. When he did attend debates, it was to make the point endlessly that the power of the Crown had been enlarged to the point that it threatened English liberties. In 1784, he told the electors of Westminster: 'The true simple question of the present dispute is, whether the House of Lords and Court Influence shall predominate over the House of Commons, and annihilate its existence, or whether the House of Commons . . . shall have power to . . . regulate the prerogatives of the Crown, which was ever ready to seize upon the freedom of the Electors of this country.'[14] This was a stark message, but it was possible to follow the evolution of it in Fox's mind. The dismissal of the Coalition and the destruction of the Rockingham–Shelburne administration first led Fox to declare that he could not allow himself 'even to imagine that a monarch would appoint ministers whom he did not think possessed of the confidence of parliament'.[15] As he watched the workings of the 'dark and secret influence on the royal mind',[16] polite incredulity had to evolve into robust defiance. In specifically setting the Commons up against the Crown, Fox found the issue that would dominate the remainder of his career and that detained him at Westminster:

The House of Commons consequently were possessed of the power of putting a negative on the choice of ministers; they were stationed as sentinels by the people, to watch over whatever could more or less remotely or nearly affect their interest; so that whenever they discovered in those nominated by his majesty to the several great offices of state, want of ability, want of weight to render their situations respectable, or want of such principles as were necessary to give effect to the wishes of the House; in any or all of such cases they were entitled to advise his majesty against employing such persons as his faithful Commons could not trust.[17]

Fox's case was the more sharply defined because his opponents were equally anxious to make distinctions. George III went out of his way to congratulate Pitt on the speech he gave on 26 January 1784, in which he had insisted that neither the immediate appointment nor removal of a minister rested with the House of Commons.[18] The King insisted that 'if the two remaining Privileges of the Crown are infringed that of Negativing Bills that have passed both Houses of Parliament, or that of naming the Ministers to be employed I cannot but feel as far as regards my Person, that I can be no longer of utility to this Country, nor can with Honour continue in this Island.'[19] This implied threat to abandon England for Hanover underlined the depth of feeling between the two men. Their differing interpretations of constitutional propriety was clear. What was less immediately obvious but none the less influential was the deep personal animosity. George gave Pitt his promise that 'to oppose this faction', he would 'struggle to the last period of my life'.[20] Accusing Fox of political turpitude and of instructing the Prince of Wales in every vice,[21] the King declared war that would have no end. Fox reciprocated these feelings with interest. A position had been reached in which, as Dr Johnson described it, Fox had come to divide 'the Kingdom with Caesar; so that it was a doubt whether the nation should be ruled by the sceptre of George the Third or the tongue of Fox'.[22] As long as a desire for self-vindication remained, as long as injured pride stung, Fox could not cut himself free from politics.

One important outcome of this situation was that Fox conceived a deep loathing of William Pitt, whose very career was built upon his own humiliation.[23] In all the negotiations for an alliance between the two men, of which there were a surprising number between 1784 and 1806,[24] Fox's insistence that he could not serve under Pitt as prime minister was always one of the principal stumbling-blocks. He always insisted that Pitt should first resign by way of doing penance for his actions in 1784. Tragically therefore two men, who had so much in common on reform issues, were irrevocably prised apart. While admirers of Pitt saw him 'like Ajax, single and alone',[25] Fox always 'charged Mr Pitt with having come into office upon unconstitutional grounds, and upon such principles as were disgraceful to himself, disgusting to the country, and such as must necessarily deprive him and his coadjutors of the confidence of that House'.[26] The point at issue between the two men was clear:

I stand, said Mr. Fox, upon this great principle. I say that the people of England have a right to control the executive power, by the interference of their representatives in this House of parliament. The right honourable gentleman maintains the contrary. He is the cause of our political enmity.[27]

The very existence of Pitt as a leading politician was an affront. As a man of little property and no party, his career was so obviously based on nothing but royal influence. Allusions to backstairs influence in politics dovetailed nicely with endless innuendo that Foxites peddled about Pitt's suspected homosexuality.[28] He had to be destroyed for, as the Duchess of Devonshire put it, 'if Mr Pitt succeeds he will have brought about an event that he himself as well as ev'ry Englishman will repent ever after.'[29]

It must be emphasized, however, that, although Fox now had a clear line of policy and clear enemies, the fields on which he was personally prepared to fight were severely limited. He had, for example, no interest or part to play in the very dramatic developments in Whig party structure between

1784 and 1789. As Sheridan engineered the purchase of London news-papers and sponsored Foxite propagandists, and as William Adam began to put together a formidable infrastructure of funds, whips, and agents, there is no evidence that Fox took any interest in such matters.[30] The detail and organizational aspects of politics had always bored him. He was indeed prepared to dine with the radical Thomas Walker at a buff-and-blue dinner in Manchester, but only because it lay on his route between shooting parties at Delapré Abbey and Wentworth Woodhouse.[31] Fox seems to have had little or no appreciation of the long-term importance of such activity. For him, the battle against George III and Pitt should be undertaken in set-piece, but not always rehearsed, speeches on selected topics that would nar-rowly relate to the awfulness of 1784. He had a kind of tunnel-vision on this point, which, combined with an increasing disinclination to attend to politics on a regular basis, could make him a frustrating colleague. Two particular issues, the Regency Crisis and the impeachment of Warren Hastings, offered opportunities of the kind that Fox sought. Both could be related back to 1784, and this, for Fox, was their only point of interest.

*

The trial of Warren Hastings on charges of corruption and extortion as Governor of Bengal was one of the most spectacular events of the 1780s. Duchesses allegedly rose at unusually early hours to be sure of a seat in the public gallery. Fox himself could claim some interest in the government of India, but his appointment as one of the Managers of Hastings's impeach-ment was based on other qualifications. In 1773, according to Horace Walpole, Fox had joined in an attack on Robert Clive, denouncing him for corruption in India in a speech that was likened to that in which Cicero had harried Catiline.[32] When Clive escaped censure, Fox admitted that he 'really did not [think] it possible for me to be so much out of humour about any political event as I am about this'.[33] No further interest in Indian affairs is recorded in Fox's letters and speeches until May 1782, when he voted for the recalling of Hastings to England. Significantly in this debate there was no suggestion that an impeachment would follow, and, indeed, Fox went out of his way to refer to Hastings's 'unimpeached integrity'.[34] This was an unfortunate phrase, which was predictably flung back in his face on many occasions in the next ten years. Unlike Burke, Fox could not be seen to take up an Indian question because of long-standing interests and commitments. He, like most of the other Managers of the impeachment, all Foxite friends, had other motives for putting Hastings on trial before the whole of London society.

Quite simply, if delinquency could be demonstrated, in the person of Hastings, in the government of India, then the India Bill, on which the Coalition had been turned out, would be vindicated. George III, noting with astonishment the 'continual unsuccessful attempts to keep the remembrance of it in full force',[35] dramatically missed the point. India had been the issue on which the constitutional crisis had turned. India, therefore, had to be the issue on which the debate of 1784 would be continued. Fox had made this clear from the start. In February 1784, in supporting a move for more papers on India, he frankly informed the Commons that

it was for this reason that he wished an investigation into the whole affairs of the East India Company; that every proceeding of the court of directors might be examined into, and that every measure adopted by the new board of commissioners might be laid before the public, because he was convinced the more the real state of the Company's affairs became known, the less unpopular would be his Bill.[36]

Burke, to some extent, shared this view. Convinced that the involvement of Hastings in 'Tyranny, robbery and destruction of mankind' outdid any historical precedent, 'even in the worst times of the Roman Republick', he was equally clear that it was 'the Court and Ministry who evidently abet that iniquitous System'.[37] Fifteen of the eighteen Managers chosen to conduct the prosecution of Hastings were Foxites.[38] As Fox's cousin reported, 'The Trial, I understand, is likely to be a party business, and, of course, no justice done.'[39]

Party advantage could be secured on one of two fronts. First, the Hastings trial allowed Foxites to give voice to a conspiracy theory of some force. The Court and East India Company were accomplices. At moments of crisis, Indian money would be made available to fund George's schemes.[40] In return, government would generously remit Company debts. When Pitt, in August 1784, asked the Commons to forego £100,000 worth of debt, owed by the Company to the government, Fox thought this evidence overwhelming:

When we connect this present Act with the bill now pending in the Upper House for the regulation of that Company, may we not justly assert that, instead of establishing an English government over India, as the bill which I presented in the late Parliament professed and attempted to do, the inevitable tendency of the measures now in agitation is the establishment of an Indian government in England.[41]

The ill-gotten gains of tyranny in India, as represented by Hastings, would be used to finance the establishment of tyranny in England. To convict Hastings was therefore to convict George III and vindicate the martyrs of 1784.

Secondly, party advantage could be found in watching Pitt squirm. The Indian issue put the Prime Minister in a difficult situation. If he openly opposed Hastings, he would infuriate the King and the Company to such an extent that, as 'Fox himself had been wrecked by the East India Bill . . . Pitt might commit a similar error'.[42] If, on the other hand, he supported Hastings, he risked losing the support of country gentlemen and men of tender conscience like Wilberforce, who had been much disturbed by what they had heard about India.[43] In the event, he cleverly declined to dispute the Opposition's control of the impeachment, and, by so doing, was not associated with either its failure or its success. As the trial dragged on for several years, the Managers came to resemble 'scarecrows',[44] and Pitt's strategy was more than vindicated. However, in the earlier stages of the affair, the embarrassment had been severe enough. The connection between the issues discussed in the trial and the events of 1784 was so close that the kind of party vindication that Fox sought seemed only too likely to materialize.

During debates in the House of Commons on whether Hastings should, indeed, be impeached, and in set-piece speeches during the trial itself, it is to these points that Fox endlessly returned.[45] As a Manager, he was specifically commissioned to present the charge that related to the alleged brutality of Hastings towards Cheyt Singh, the ruler of Benares. In this role, he enjoyed enormous success. Queues formed at six in the morning to hear him speak, and such was the power of his arguments that even the Prince of Wales was seen to be taking notes.[46] But Bengal politics were never uppermost in Fox's mind. As he assured the Commons, when they were discussing the Rohilla War, the India Bill had been 'the most important measure of my life'.[47] He could not rest until it had been finally exonerated.

Once this retrospective point had been established, Fox had very little interest in either Hastings or his impeachment. The trial was to drag on from 1788 to 1794, but, as the minutes of Managers' meetings record, Fox was not assiduous in his duties. In 1787, he attended 2 meetings out of 10; in 1788, 6 out of 46; in 1789, 2 out of 26; in 1790, 3 out of 17; and in 1791, 8 out of 14.[48] It was thought by his family that, after dealing with the Benares charge, Fox was 'not likely to speak any more upon the Trial'.[49] Never ready to undertake the detail of politics, Fox was temperamentally incapable of a six- or seven-year involvement with the complexities of Indian government and finance. All of that devolved on Burke. As early as May 1788, Charles Grey was reported to be in favour of abandoning the impeachment,[50] and, a year later, a decision by the Managers to persevere was taken by Fox as a 'great slight of him'.[51] If the prosecution of Hastings had been initiated with the narrow objective of making a point about 1784, that point had been made very early in the trial. To continue year after year was a terrible drain on Foxite patience and resources.[52]

In taking this view, Fox was probably right. As the public at large gradually became bored with the trial, Pitt was able to throw more and more obstacles in the Managers' way with absolute impunity. As he was neither able to bring proceedings to an end nor secure convictions, Fox found himself endlessly seeking reassurance from the House of Commons that the Managers still had its backing, and repeatedly protesting against Pitt's constant attempts to make their task uncomfortable.[53] What had been partly initiated as a device to embarrass Pitt had become a tedious waste of Foxite talent. As Lord Bessborough laconically remarked, 'Hastings Trial I am afraid will not end this year. Pitt has a mind to keep it on to employ the Opposition.'[54] Fox's point had been effectively made in the first weeks of the trial. There was no reason to pursue the matter further, particularly if it distracted Whig efforts from other tasks. As the impeachment degenerated into farce, Fox was wise to distance himself more and more from it.

In so doing, Fox opened up an enormous breach between himself and Edmund Burke, who was, in Fox's words, the 'leader in this business'.[55] From the very start, Burke had been the man who carried the organizational burden of the impeachment. His knowledge of India was real and his capacity for detail exemplary.[56] Further, Burke was convinced that great evils had been perpetrated in India, and it was incumbent on him to pursue the men responsible for as long as was necessary. As early as 1785, he was acutely aware that he and Fox had very different motives for interesting themselves in India.[57] It was the short-term preoccupation with the symbolism of 1784 set against long-term concern to punish delinquency in India. Burke found it grinding, uphill work to keep Fox's interest at all. When Sheridan opened the Begums' charge against Hastings, one of the most important of all in the indictment, Fox was in Newmarket trying to win enough money to finance an excursion to Italy.[58] In December 1789, Burke reported to a sympathetic ear that, with regard to Fox and Sheridan, he continued to 'endeavour to awaken them to some sort of attention'.[59] Towards the end of the trial, it was not unusual to see Burke sitting alone, or nearly alone, in the Managers' box.[60] As Fox and his acolytes drifted away from the impeachment, it became a Burkean monopoly.

This experience had a devastating effect on the relationship between Fox and Burke. The latter felt himself abandoned by someone he had always regarded as a kind of protégé. It was hard to see Fox apparently preferring the company and advice of younger men like Sheridan, whom Burke detested, and Charles Grey, whom Burke did not know. Memories of the 1760s and 1770s allowed Burke to forgive Fox many things, but, long before the French Revolution gave him his opportunity, Burke was convinced that he would have to make a supreme effort to re-establish his intellectual authority within Foxite ranks. From Fox's point of view, therefore, the impeachment of Warren Hastings had gone disastrously wrong. What should have been the scoring of one or two quick points against Pitt and George III had become a protracted nightmare that he had neither the time nor the energy to terminate. Nor, if he was aware of Burke's feelings, was he willing to devote time to smoothing ruffled plumage. The impeachment weakened the Foxites significantly, and Fox himself must take some blame for this.

*

The Regency Crisis of 1788–9 presented an almost identical pattern of opportunities lost and party indecision. In late October 1788, George III had to be placed under restraint after the onset of what was widely believed to be insanity.[61] Such was the temper of politics that many people believed that he had been poisoned by Fox.[62] The King had suffered attacks of this kind before, but this time the madness appeared deep and permanent. Not only were oak trees addressed as the King of Prussia, but proof positive of an irreversible decline was that he was 'loud, turbulent, & threatening . . . He called Mr Pitt a rascal, & Mr Fox his Friend.'[63] A crucial factor in understanding the Foxite response to these events was their firm belief that the King would never recover. In Cheshire, the Crewe family made a special journey into Nantwich to buy mourning.[64] In late November, Fox himself told the Prince of Wales that, however much Pitt might prevaricate, medical realities made it certain 'your Royal Highness would be . . . sure of enjoying the situation that belongs to you in a few weeks.'[65] Even in late January 1789, when reports of a substantial improvement in the King's condition began to circulate, Fox and his friends continued to draw up lists of Cabinet members for their new administration, and to discuss the distribution of patronage.[66] The King had been dealt a mortal blow. Their friend and patron the Prince of Wales had to inherit power, either as Regent or as George IV. As they saw the situation, the strength of their hand lay in this inevitability.

The second crucial factor in the situation was that Fox was out of England as the crisis developed. It was fully three weeks old when he returned home on 25 November. For some weeks, he had been travelling in Italy and France, where English news was hard to come by, or, as some cynical observers remarked, easy to avoid:

it does still seem a sort of phenomenon to think of Fox lost for months to England in countries where the post goes twice a week, and England as totally lost to him; and that one on whom a nation seems at present altogether to depend should not know or inquire how the world wags from September to November, or with his own goodwill, to January.[67]

Throughout the crisis, Fox was to be accused of not offering effective or informed leadership, and such criticism started early. Fox seemed anxious to duck the challenge that the crisis presented, while, at the same time, being reluctant for others to take up the responsibility.

Sympathetic politicians like Lord Palmerston attributed this inertia to illness. Fox was 'much reduced and lowered by a Flux & other Complaints which he had before he set out & which he has not got rid of.'[68] According to Sir Gilbert Elliot, Fox was very ill for the whole period between 25 November 1788 and 20 December 1789.[69] Throughout the crisis, there was concern that 'the Poor Thing' might totally collapse under the weight of 'this unhappy Malady'.[70] On more than one occasion during these months, he was actually reported to be dead or dying.[71] At vital moments during the crisis, Fox had to miss meetings and debates, and it proved very difficult for him to keep up with fast-moving events. As explanations were sought to account for his miscalculations and misadventures, his incapacity was often referred to.[72] However, others made the obvious point that, in such circumstances, the leadership of the party should have been delegated, while the Archbishop of Canterbury uncharitably asserted that the illness was diplomatically assumed to cover political ineptitude.[73]

Having joined the crisis late, he abandoned it early. On 27 January, he left for Bath, and did not return to London until 21 February.[74] His absence threw 'a damp on the Party',[75] and even William Wilberforce had to admit that Commons debates without Fox were 'insipid and vapid'.[76] For nearly a month, Fox endeavoured to control his party's response to the issues raised in the Regency debates by exchanging letters with friends and party managers.[77] Inevitably, such a system was wholly ineffective, when reports of the King's likely recovery were first discounted, then doubted, then accepted. At each stage, political options changed, and decisions had to be taken quickly without reference to an invalid at Bath. This was particularly necessary because Fox was one of the last to believe that the King might indeed recover.[78] For much of the crisis, Fox was an absentee leader, but one who could not delegate his authority. A persistent theme in Foxite politics is thereby established. It could only be intensely galling to men like Sheridan and Burke, who saw their own ideas blocked and, as they saw it, opportunities lost.

Fox's views on the crisis were simple. If George III was mad, he was constitutionally dead, and events should take their course as though he were in fact deceased. As William Windham explained, 'It is, for the time at least just as if the King were dead. The same person must, upon all principles of reason, & all views of the Constitution, carry on the government, as if the King were actually dead.'[79] At death, property, under which description the Crown was included, passed naturally to heirs. For anyone or any institution, even the House of Commons, to set restrictions or limitations on that process was to raise grave questions about the security of property-holding in general. As French Laurence explained, Fox had to argue for the Prince's unrestricted right to the Regency, 'or he must have abandoned the *principle of succession* to the Trust of Executive Government . . . he sustained the character of a British Senator.'[80] Fox returned to the question many years later, in his *History of the Early Part of the Reign of James II*. Referring to the prerogatives of the Crown, he concluded that

> The Whigs, who consider them as a trust for the people, a doctrine which the Tories themselves, when pushed in argument, will sometimes admit, naturally think it their duty rather to change the manager of the trust, than to impair the subject of it . . . while, on the other hand, they who consider prerogative with reference only to royalty, will, with equal readiness, consent either to the extension or the suspension of its exercise, as the occasional interests of the prince may seem to require.[81]

Pitt countered this view with the argument that the Crown was not vacant, but only temporarily unoccupied. There was merely a hiatus in government, and the House of Commons had every right to determine who should fill the gap and on what terms. He and like-minded pamphleteers made great play of the fact that Fox, the champion of the House of Commons in 1784, was now anxious to deny that body any authority in deciding the terms of a Regency.[82] Foxites inevitably retaliated by pointing out that Pitt's new-found confidence in the House looked odd when memory recalled the way in which he had established himself as prime minister. Debating points aside, what was at stake at one level was a genuine doubt about whether a Regency would be required at all, and if so on what terms. At another level, the Foxites saw the path to office clear before them. The Prince of Wales was their man. He had stood by them in 1784. Then the question concerned the exact scope of the property known as the royal prerogative. Now the debate was to decide who should exercise it. There seemed to be every chance to destroy Pitt.

Fox's views were offered to the public in a famous speech delivered on 10 December. It was an open question whether his opinions were those of the party as a whole. Although they were based to some extent on a legal opinion drawn up by Loughborough, one of the most distinguished Foxite lawyers,[83] they did not seem to enjoy universal currency. A meeting at Burlington House on 4 December had not been able to come up with an agreed procedure for presenting the Prince's case.[84] Fox showed little interest in legal technicalities, historical precedents, or protracted party discussions.[85] The point at issue was too simple. He told the Commons that the situation they faced was 'as in the case of his majesty's having undergone a natural and perfect demise'.[86] That being so, 'There was then a person in the kingdom different from any other person that any existing precedents could refer to—an heir apparent of full age and capacity to exercise the royal power. It behoved them, therefore, to waste not a moment unnecessarily, but to proceed with all becoming speed and all becoming diligence to restore the sovereign power and the exercise of royal authority.'[87] With only a minimum of consultation, Fox committed his friends to the most uncompromising interpretation of the Prince's claims.

Fox's speech threw politics into turmoil. Some parliamentarians had never known 'more warmth upon any Subject'.[88] It appeared that Fox was arguing for the rights of prerogative and allowing the House of Commons no part in the crisis, a strange stance for 'the Man of the People'. As Palmerston observed, 'The declaration Fox made on Wednesday about the Prince's right seems to have been rather unfortunate, as it has been misunderstood by some of our friends not remarkable for clear comprehension and misrepresented by all the opposite party.'[89] If Foxites could be confused by claims made on behalf of princes, it was not surprising that the political world in general might accuse him of falling into inconsistency. Lord Spencer was not alone in wishing that the issue 'had never been stirred'.[90] Pitt, capitalizing on confusion, declared that he would unwhig the gentleman for life.[91] For Fox to deny the Lords and Commons even a consultative role in the setting up of the Regency was constitutionally doubtful,[92] but, more importantly, totally incongruous when set beside his claims for the Commons made since 1782.[93] What attracted Fox to this line of action was that it involved no negotiation or compromise with the men of 1784 or a Parliament that had been elected by fraud and whose very composition reflected his personal humiliation. When challenged with the idea that the 10 December speech had been a mistake, Fox was unrepentant: 'in mentioning the question of right, C Fox had let the cat out of the bag—he said so much the better for the rats are growing very troublesome.'[94] The Regency was to be a party measure serving narrow, party ends.

In subsequent speeches on 12, 16, 22 December, and 6 January, Fox elaborated and explained his position, but never really accepted the idea that the powers of a Regency exercised by the Prince of Wales should be set by a Pittite Parliament. 'The Constitution', he suggested, 'supposed each of its three branches to be independent of the other two, and actually hostile;

and if that principle was once given up, there was an end to our political freedom . . . The safety of the whole depended on the jealousy of each against the other.'[95] Claiming that his behaviour was consistent with the line taken in 1784, he went on: 'He had ever made it his pride to combat with the crown in the plenitude of its power and the fullness of its authority; he wished not to trample on its rights while it lay extended at their feet, deprived of its functions, and incapable of resistance.'[96] In other words, liberty survived because a resilient executive jealously surveyed the actions of a resilient legislature, and vice versa. The privileges of the Commons were at risk in 1784. The prerogatives of the Crown would be irrevocably damaged if the principle of natural succession were tampered with. This idea, together with that of the Crown as a property being passed on from father to son, gave Fox's views some coherence, but it was easily understandable that many contemporaries thought that Fox was simply dragging arguments out of the air. It seemed so odd that Charles Fox should be such a friend of monarchy.

The disorder brought about by the 10 December speech may have been unwise and unnecessary, but Fox was not unduly concerned that he had 'made some little confusion in the heads of a few old Parliamentaries, who did not understand him'.[97] Anything was to be preferred to dealing with Pitt. News that attempts at any such accommodation had had to be abandoned was always received 'to the great joy of Fox'.[98] What sustained him was the conviction that the King would never recover, and that sooner or later the Prince of Wales would have to be acknowledged:

We shall have several hard fights in the H. of Cs. this week and next, in some of which I fear we shall be beat, but whether we are or not I think it certain that in about a fortnight we shall come in; If we carry our questions we shall come in in a more creditable and triumphant way, but at any rate the Prince must be Regent and of consequence the Ministry must be changed . . . I am rather afraid they will get some cry against the Prince for grasping as they call it at too much power, but I am sure that I can not in conscience advise him to give up any thing that is really necessary to his Government, or indeed to claim any thing else as Regent, but the full power of a King, to which he is certainly entitled.[99]

Tactics were unimportant because overall victory was inevitable.

His confidence was not universally shared by his party. Lord George Cavendish reflected that 'On our side there was some misfortunes & perhaps some mismanagement. We despise Parliamentary Craft too much & are sadly deficient in it.'[100] Lord Palmerston agreed: 'I have often thought that we have more Wit and Ingenuity on our side than sound Judgment in managing Parliamentary matters.'[101] From within the ranks of his own supporters, there was grave dissatisfaction with Fox's performance. His

'refusal to consult was resented. Apparently anxious to avoid a detailed participation in the crisis, he refused to let others take a lead, and instead, by
sudden and unexpected pronouncements, committed the party to unforeseen positions. Sir Gilbert Elliot complained that 'Fox . . . has as great
difficulty or backwardness in *resolving* as if he had no interest or no judgment
in the affairs that are depending, and . . . he lets anybody else decide for him;
so measures are often the production of chance instead of wisdom.'[102] More
charitably, the classical scholar Porson diagnosed mere exuberance: 'Mr Pitt
conceives his sentences before he utters them. Mr Fox throws himself into
the middle of his, and leaves it to God Almighty to get him out again.'[103]
There was some truth in both remarks. Certainly great damage had been
done. Writing in 1802, the Duchess of Devonshire dated the divisions that
were to shatter the Whigs in the 1790s not from the French Revolution but
from the Regency Crisis: 'at the distance [of] 13 years I can trace the beginning of negligence and want of *ensemble* which together with the indulgence
of imprudent language has destroy'd the importance of the opposition.'[104]
Tensions produced by events in France operated on an already fissured party.
In particular, the Regency Crisis badly bruised Fox's relations with three men:
Edmund Burke, Richard Sheridan, and the Prince of Wales.

As has been noted above, the relationship between Fox and Burke was
under strain in 1788 over the Hastings affair. Now, their friendship was to
be further tested by the Regency Crisis. On the one hand, Burke was basic-
ally in sympathy with the Fox strategy of calling for the Prince to be allowed
an unrestricted regency, and of refusing all negotiations with Pittites. They
were 'men undoubtedly in legal Situations of Trust, to perform such functions as can be performed in Office, without resort to the Crown: But the
Kings [*sic*] confidential servants they certainly are not—and not only the
Rights of other Members are on a par with theirs, but all Idea of decorum
and preaudience on the Subject of the King, are out of the Question.'[105]
This being so, Burke agreed with Fox that 'now is the time to push.'[106] On
the other hand, he was appalled at the haphazard way in which the Foxite
response had been put together. In particular, he felt constrained to 'observe, that though there have been a very few consultations upon particular
measures, there have been none at all *de summa rerum*'.[107] There had been no
attempt to co-ordinate Whig activity at Westminster or to influence opinion
outside London.

Inevitably Burke, who took all politics in a deeply personal sense, felt
himself to be the principal victim of this chaos. In order to forward the
Prince's case, he had, unsolicited, devoted much time and energy to consulting historical precedents from the reigns of Edward VI and Henry VI. At

Burke's insistence, a special meeting of Whig leaders was convened to hear his findings, which took two hours to present. During this extended lecture, 'Fox kept digging his fingers into the corner of his eye, a trick he had when anything perplexed him.' Virtually no notice was taken of Burke's views, and what compounded the insult was Fox describing them to Sheridan as containing 'all Burke's bitterness'.[108] Burke detested Sheridan's lack of principle and feared his ambition. The Regency Crisis confirmed his suspicion that Fox would always take Sheridan's part against himself. The atmosphere in which the debate on the French Revolution would begin was therefore anything but calm.[109]

Matters were even more complicated than this, however, for Fox had also gravely offended Sheridan. From at least 1785, Sheridan had seen his career in politics as dependent on the reversionary interest of the Prince of Wales. For some years, he had been the errand boy for Carlton House, defending the Prince on all occasions and extricating him from personal and public indiscretion. It was often messy work, and men like Burke and Portland saw nothing in him but an unprincipled careerist. When the Regency Crisis started in Fox's absence, Sheridan set out to convince the Prince of Wales that the getting into office was everything. Large claims about rights were a diversion. If negotiations with the men of 1784 were required, that was a tolerable concession. If some of Pitt's administration should retain their offices, like Thurlow, to the disappointment of Foxites, that too could be accepted. Long before Fox returned to England, Sheridan was in negotiation with Thurlow to discover how best this plan might be effected.[110] This activity was deeply resented by senior figures in the party like Portland, who found that they could only contact the Prince through the intermediary of Sheridan.[111] It was such a public performance that many people recognized 'the steps which Sheridan has taken to secure his personal ground, and the jealousy which this has given to the rest of the party'.[112] Sheridan himself, by contrast, was cheekily delighted by the prospect of slipping quietly into office, with the benefits of a regular salary and an escape from the tedium of the Hastings trial. When challenged on the abandonment of a moral purpose, he simply replied that he wished 'Hastings would run away and Burke after him'.[113] The Prince of Wales was his patron, and this fact more than made up for the absence of wealth or title, the normal supports of a successful political career.

George Selwyn was right to speculate maliciously that Fox would not enjoy returning to England to find Sheridan calling the tune:

Charles you know is come; I have not heard anything more of him . . . I want to know, how he has relished Sheridan's beginning a negotiation without him. I have figured him, if it be true, saying to him, at his arrival, as Hecate does to the Witches in Macbeth, 'Saucy and bold, how did you dare to trade and traffic &c., and I, the mistress of your charms, the close contriver of all harms, was never called to bear my part,' &c. I will not [go] on . . . for fear of offending.[114]

When Fox found a negotiation in train with some of his opponents of 1784, he could 'not remember feeling so uneasy about any political thing I ever did in my life'.[115] When, as a consequence of these talks, he had to explain to old friends that their expectations of office might be frustrated, he confessed that he felt 'perfectly ashamed'.[116] Sheridan's behaviour clouded and compromised the stand taken in 1784. Consequently, the whole crisis was punctuated by bickering between the two men. Fox, like Portland, complained that Sheridan so monopolized the Prince of Wales that the formulation of party policy was severely compromised.[117] In return, Sheridan was sure that there was 'great treachery going on against him', and that he was the victim of 'abuse'.[118] To counterattack, he may well have used his contacts with the press to puff his own interpretation of events.[119] Certainly, the animosity between the two men was widely reported in newspapers, the Pittite press sarcastically congratulating Fox on a rumoured decision to exclude Sheridan from the Cabinet in any future Foxite government.[120]

For as long as Fox remained in contact with the crisis, there were altercations between him and Sheridan. On 20 December, for example, the Duchess of Devonshire reported that 'Fox was angry yesterday with Sheridan for letting some of our friends go out of town upon the idea of there being no debate afterwards; Charles made him excuses for having snubed [*sic*] him and Sheridan sd. quite as to a child—pooh pooh be as cross as you will.'[121] In early January, there was another major row, with Sheridan complaining that 'Charles Fox had been scolding him & that he had left him being in a great passion.'[122] Relations were restored two days later, but Sheridan had been so moved that 'if he had left the room in the anger he had been in, he never should have spoke to him [Fox] again.'[123] Many years later, Sir Philip Francis offered the view that Fox had only hated two men in his whole career, Horne Tooke and Sheridan.[124] This is too radical a judgement. Between 1789 and 1806, Fox, on a number of occasions, gave Sheridan the benefit of the doubt, or defended him against Burke and other detractors. Yet the two men were never close friends, intellectually or socially, and it is very clear that the Regency Crisis left permanent scars. Sheridan, in terms of birth, wealth, and talent could hope, like Burke, for office in a Foxite administration, but it would not necessarily be high office and there was certainly no question of his joining the party leadership.

Even before rumours began to spread, in February 1789, that the King would indeed recover, thereby pitching Fox and his friends once more into the political wilderness, it was clear that the Regency Crisis had revealed damaging shortcomings. It was felt that Fox had 'fail'd in judgement'.[125] Burke regretted that they had not made 'an honourable retreat . . . by an effectual defence of themselves'.[126] The leadership could not even agree whether to give a ball in celebration of the King's recovery.[127] They were reduced to writing self-justificatory memoranda explaining their conduct to the King[128] and teasing London mobs: 'The crowd was very great . . . They once stopp'd the P. & bid him cry God save the King, & he did, then Pitt for ever—wch he wd not do, but said Fox for ever—he then got in Brooks's open'd the windows and huzzad.'[129] Fox, Sheridan, Burke, and Portland had all suffered a grievous disappointment. The reign of George IV would be postponed for another thirty-one years. As mutual recrimination became the order of the day, Fox once again, and characteristically, began to have thoughts of retirement.[130] Yet to some extent, he had only himself to blame. He had come into the Regency Crisis at a tangent, and had attempted to lead when illness and unwillingness to consult made that task difficult. His justification must lie in the impossibility of delegating authority to Portland, who was not over-clever, to Sheridan, who was not over-scrupulous, or to Burke, who was not over-loved.

To compound these problems, the Regency Crisis exacerbated difficulties with the Prince of Wales. Ever since 1782, the Prince's loathing of his father had been one of the strongest cards in Foxite hands. The supposed mental and physical frailty of George III would, sooner or later, bring them into power as the servants of George IV. It was assumed that Fox would be the main beneficiary of this reversionary interest. Cartoons showed Fox as Falstaff and Prinny, improbably, as Prince Hal. It was well known that they were drinking companions and that women passed from one to the other as if by system. George III let it be widely broadcast that he held Fox principally responsible for the Prince's many failings, not least a tendency to vomit in public. Fox was indeed totally involved with Carlton House and its irregularities, but more often than not as someone trying to moderate Prinny's wilder activities. In March 1789, at the end of the Regency Crisis, there was 'a quarrel between the P of W & Charles Fox at Almack's', because a drunken brawl had led the Prince into the embarrassment of fighting a duel.[131] Fox intervened to stop the heir apparent borrowing money from the Duc d'Orléans.[132] With less success, he tried to shield the Prince from the murkier aspects of the racing world.[133] He did, however, stop a project that would have taken the Prince off to live in France.[134] All of this produced a close association between the two men in the minds of the public. One pamphleteer, addressing the Prince, found it impossible 'to distinguish between the Statesman whom you employ in the service of your country, and the buffoon whom you call to your midnight festivities.'[135]

In fact, this was to misrepresent the situation. Fox liked the Prince and was often consulted by Carlton House, but was always anxious to retain his freedom of action. Unlike Sheridan, whose whole career came increasingly to depend on Prinny, Fox preferred to describe himself 'as a party man' and although 'H.R.H. honor'd him with his friendship & good opinion which was very flattering to him . . . he did not live with them.'[136] Throughout the period 1782–9, there were moments of considerable tension between Fox and the Prince, which translated themselves into high politics. The most significant of these crises concerned the Fitzherbert marriage. In December 1785, the Prince determined to marry Mrs Fitzherbert, knowing full well that it could only be an illegal ceremony contravening both the Royal Marriages Act, which required the consent of the reigning monarch, and the long-standing prohibition on members of the royal family marrying Roman Catholics. On 10 December, Fox begged the Prince 'not to think of marriage till you can marry legally. A mock marriage, for it can be no other, is neither honourable for any of the parties, nor, with respect to your Royal Highness, even safe.' On 11 December, Prinny assured Fox that there was no cause for alarm and then promptly proceeded to 'marry' Mrs Fitzherbert four days later.[137]

The matter resurfaced eighteen months later, when the Prince once again had to apply to Parliament for relief from his debts. Fox, remembering the Prince's assurance, denied that any marriage had taken place, asserting that 'there was no part of his royal highness's conduct that he was either afraid or unwilling to have investigated in the most minute manner.'[138] Mrs Fitzherbert read Fox's words 'in the paper next morning', which 'deeply afflicted her, and made her furious against Fox'.[139] The Prince, failing to persuade Fox to retract, naturally turned to Sheridan to salvage whatever was possible in the House of Commons.[140] In retrospect, Prinny dismissed the episode as an attempt at 'gallantry to the lady',[141] but at the time the strain on Foxite friendship was intense. It was bad enough that the Prince of Wales should twice within five years approach the House of Commons as a debtor. Solid men like the Duke of Portland had not wished to be associated even with that: 'This measure being pushed on contrary to the Duke's advice, and carried through by Fox and the rest of the party, seems to be considered as a sort of separation and schism in the party, that may lead to discussion on other occasions, and perhaps to a total dissolution of what is called the Whig party.'[142] That the nonsense of the Fitzherbert marriage should be added to this unsavoury business was intolerable. Portland gave up speaking to the Prince, and, on the eve of the Regency Crisis, special meetings had to be convened to bring the two men together again.[143]

Fox too was outraged. Encouraged by the Prince, he had assured the House of Commons that truth was falsehood. Relations between the two men were never wholly repaired,[144] not least because the influence of Mrs Fitzherbert kept the dispute alive. In 1788, the Prince's secretary thought that

the Prince was afraid of Fox, & that his opinion of Mr Pitt was much altered since the negotiation on the subject of his debts . . . and that this coolness to Fox was much increased by Mrs Fit Herbert, who never would forgive his public declaration on her subject in the House of Commons, and had taken every opportunity of alienating the Prince's mind from him.[145]

Little wonder that backbench Foxites should conclude that 'we have great Plenty of Wit & Raillery & Eloquence on our side of the House but we have been accused of want of Judgment & we are going to prove the Accusation true.'[146] Difficulties with the Prince of Wales over debt and the Fitzherbert marriage inevitably meant that the Foxite response to the Regency Crisis would be incoherent. In the person of the future George IV, an association with the reversionary interest was a very mixed blessing for the party as a whole, and for Charles Fox in particular.

Importantly, for Burke, Fox, and Portland, the difficulty in handling the Prince of Wales was yet another indication of how far Sheridan's ambition could act as a wrecking factor within the party. Sheridan had become the general factotum of Carlton House, and it was widely known that 'The Prince of Wales' attachment to Sheridan gives umbrage to the Duke of Portland and Mr Fox.'[147] The Prince used Sheridan as his errand boy in moments of crisis, and seemed to prefer his advice to that of anyone else. In return, Sheridan appeared happy to abet the Prince in any scheme, however unprincipled.[148] No one was surprised that, when the Sheridans were evicted for non-payment of rent, in January 1789, Mrs Fitzherbert should offer them accommodation.[149] More seriously, Sheridan was accused of 'Great private treachery . . . courting the Prince and encouraging the Praise of him in the world and papers where Fox is abused'.[150] Sheridan's early prominence in the Regency Crisis was justified in his own mind by the favour he enjoyed with the Prince. According to Foxite grandees, Sheridan had become a harmful and irritating barrier between the heir apparent and responsible advisers. After 1787, relations between Fox and the Prince cooled dramatically. The two men met in secret to avoid the wrath of Mrs Fitzherbert,[151] and corresponded in terms of increasing formality.[152] Henceforth,

Carlton House stood at a tangent to Foxite politics, with Sheridan, not Fox, as the point of intersection.

*

On the eve of the French Revolution, Fox and his friends were ill-prepared to meet its challenges. True, in terms of party organization and funding, William Adam had worked miracles. True too, the Foxite creed, based on a fear of monarchical power and memories of 1784, had been to some extent vindicated in the impeachment of Warren Hastings, and had given coherence to Fox's response to the Regency Crisis. As the core of Foxite politics, concern about kings would remain plausible and relevant. All of this was positive and heartening. On the other hand, the period 1784–9 had emphasized the extent to which Burke, Fox, Sheridan, and the Prince of Wales had little in common except the martyrdom of 1784. These years vividly demonstrated William Eden's belief that 'we have all seen in Life that Differences of Opinion as to public Circumstances & Conduct generally affect personal Friendships & Partialities & sometimes in a great Degree.'[153] It was not, perhaps, surprising that within eighteen months of the fall of the Bastille, Burke, Fox, and Sheridan were each associated with a differing interpretation of events in France. The Foxites did not constitute a political grouping on which too much weight could be put, without running the risk of fracture.

To an extent, this was Fox's fault. He had not been able to control the Prince of Wales. He had not been able or willing to give much time to the Hastings impeachment. He had been often missing during the Regency Crisis. Throughout these years, there resurfaces that unwillingness to give time to politics that had always been part of his character, and which becomes more and more confirmed in his personality as he grew older. Never enthusiastic about the game of politics for itself and always happy to find other occupations, Fox established a style of leadership that alternated spasms of energetic activity with long periods of quiescence. It remained to be seen whether the French Revolution would so engage his interest as to break this pattern.

5

In Foxite Society

UP to the end of the 1780s, the prominence of Charles Fox in England owed as much to his position in society as to politics. He was a leading figure at Brooks's and Newmarket as well as Westminster. In all probability, Fox would not have been unhappy with such a mixed reputation. Fox enjoyed and encouraged friendships more than most men. Foxite politics was often an extension of friendship. Failure to impose his authority in politics frequently stemmed from an unwillingness to hurt a friend or trample on youthful ambition. Operating a moral code that was very much his own, Fox could be sometimes strangely insensitive to the interests of others, but such was his charm and magnetism that he was always forgiven. Breaking with Fox in politics was painful, and not least because it entailed the rupture of a valued friendship. Fox could be irritating and apparently self-centred, but he was always spontaneous, unaffected, and the enemy of anything that smacked of cant. He drank immoderately, was an excessive gambler, and saw no reason to make a secret of his many mistresses. In the 1770s, he had been an arbiter of fashion; in the 1780s, he became increasingly unkempt in appearance. On a day-to-day basis, social life was more exciting than politics, which too often became bogged down in details and amendments. Only the great parliamentary occasions roused Fox to give of his best. Quite often his best would be on show in other contexts.

Inevitably, Fox's reputation in the world at large was unenviable. The whole period is full of prints and verses that catalogue Fox's indulgence of vice. Brooks's was believed to be a place where anything could be the subject of a bet, from a game of faro to discovering the identity of the person who had defecated in Fox's trousers.[1] A Grub St writer, Charles Pigott, piously asked: 'Must it not become a national reproach to see the Minister of a great people constantly pass from the cabinet to the gaming table; from projects to advance the glory of the state, to schemes for the destruction of inconsiderate youth, or doting age.'[2] Very naturally, when another pamphleteer penned verses on the Devil's search for an heir, Charles Fox was an obvious candidate for the post.[3] Equally naturally, his changes of front in politics were attributed to a very distant relationship with anything that could be called principle:

> The Captain of the *Gang* is Fox, the old defaulter's son,
> By God, there's not a fault on earth—his *Honour* has not done.
> The tenets Catiline maintains, he values not a fig;
> For if a Tory he cou'd reign, he'd cease to be a *Whig*.[4]

It was distressing for many visitors to Brighton 'to see C. Fox walking on the Steyne on Thursday night with a vulgar looking *Putain*, a whore more mean looking than one of 2/6 on the strand [*sic*]'.[5]

Many people outside and on the fringes of Foxite society saw only self-gratification and irresponsibility, and the same kind of remarks are made about the politician that had been made about the adolescent. George Selwyn, from the perspective of an older generation, regretted that he could not 'trace in any one action of his life anything that had not for its object his own gratification',[6] and thought that Fox only complained about the King, 'because he cannot do more without a character than any other man ever did with one'.[7] To Selwyn, no stranger to vice himself, Fox had ruined himself in debauch:

Genius is an indefinite term. I never think a man really an able man, unless I see that he has attained the object of his pursuits, whatever they may be. I try Charles Fox by that test. He has had three favourite pursuits—gaming, politics, women. He addicted himself to play and thought himself a skilful player, but lost an immense fortune almost before he was of age. Power was his grand object, yet he has never been able to keep possession of it, scarcely for a twelvemonth. He was desirous of shining as a man of gallantry, and he married a whore.[8]

This is a severe judgement, but it was plausible and was shared by many, with incalculable repercussions for Fox's career and hopes in politics.

Further, Fox's reputation tarred those who chose to spend time with him. Sheridan became 'Sherry' in the cartoons, red-nosed and obviously the worse for drink. Productions like *The Jockey Club* and *The Female Jockey Club* pilloried his friends for the delectation of the public.[9] The Duke of Bedford lived with 'an antiquated demirep', and Fox with anyone, and 'his choice has not always been the most elegant or refined'. The Earl of Derby lived with an actress whom he subsequently married, and it was hard to know which was the greater crime. The Duchess of Devonshire turned Devonshire House into a gambling den, and endlessly deceived her husband, who

was a booby.[10] In 'Fox's Dinner' the themes of poverty, debauch, and
political irresponsibility are intertwined:

> At the Anchor and Crown
> Of noisy renown,
> A mob of the ragged and rough;
> All birds of a feather
> Assembled together,
> They call'd 'em the squad Blue and Buff.
>
> And sure such a clan
> In the mem'ry of man,
> As I am a song-singing sinner;
> So shirtless a rout,
> With their elbows all out,
> E'er met—so to torture a dinner.
>
> At the head of the gang
> Sat Charley the slang,
> His coat and he formed coalition,
> The very same day,
> As I have heard say,
> That North and he met in cohesion.[11]

It is hard to quantify the damage that this incessant propaganda did to Fox
and his friends. What is clear is that their social life was of intense public
interest, and that it was mostly written up in an adversarial manner. It raised
the question of whether the country's finances and prospects could be safely
entrusted to men whose own lives were so irregular.

What compounded Fox's offence in the eyes of many was his refusal to be
guided by outside opinion. Selwyn, irritatedly, referred to 'his infinite contempt of the *qu'en dira-t-on*, upon every point which governs the rest of
mankind'.[12] Fox lived in a hermetically sealed world of close friendships,[13]
which insulated him from a wider opinion. They operated values of their
own: 'Mr Fox's supporters seem to glory in the circumstance of that Statesman's having *sold* and *dissipated* the produce of two *Sinecure Places*. We should
think this almost as disgraceful as *living* by *Public Subscription*; and yet in the
catalogue of Opposition morals, neither it seems are considered as a disgrace.'[14] Fox was barely joking when, referring to Pitt's personal debts, he
offered the opinion that 'The only thing like good about him is his inatten-
tion to money.'[15] So incorrigible was Fox that so far from being ashamed of
the total shambles in his personal finances, he turned the circumstance into
an 'Invocation to Poverty':

> O POVERTY! of pale consumptive hue,
> If thou delight'st to haunt me still in view,

If still thy presence must my steps attend,
At least continue, as thou art, my friend.
When Scotch example bids me be unjust,
False to my word, unfaithful to my trust,
Bid me the baneful error quickly see,
And shun the world to find repose in thee.
When vice to wealth would turn my partial eye,
Or int'rest shutting ear to sorrow's cry,
Or courtiers' custom would my reason bind
My foe to flatter, or desert my friend,—
Oppose, kind Poverty, thy temper'd shield,
And bear me off unvanquish'd from the field.[16]

So unconcerned was Fox about the views of people outside his own circle that criticism was used to amuse his friends. Foreign visitors were astounded, when visiting Fox, to be invited 'to lounge over some caricatures . . . Mr Fox being the principal figure in each. Mme. Paliansky to this moment in a hopeless puzzle about it.'[17] It must have been maddening to the moralist that Fox was successfully impervious to his strictures. So careless was Fox in these matters that, as Macaulay later recorded, he could be generous to Pitt from a position of advantage:

Some paper was to be published by Mr Fox, in which mention was made of Mr Pitt having been employed at a club in a manner that would have created scandal. Mr Wilberforce went to Mr Fox, and asked him to omit the passage. 'Oh, to be sure', said Mr Fox; 'if there are any good people who would be scandalised, I will certainly put it out!' Mr Wilberforce then preparing to take his leave, he said: 'Now, Mr Wilberforce, if, instead of being about Mr Pitt, this had been an account of my being seen gaming at White's on a Sunday, would you have taken so much pains to prevent it being known?' 'I asked this', said Mr Fox, 'because I wanted to see what he would say, for I knew he would not tell a lie about it. He threw himself back, as his way was, and only answered: 'Oh, Mr Fox, you are always so pleasant!'[18]

Pitt's was a fragile public character that required the shield of discretion; Fox's was not.[19] With rare exceptions, Fox was unmoved by what the world in general thought of his behaviour. There would be a penalty in politics to pay for this, but it was also one of his greatest strengths.

Further, Fox insisted that there was a distinction between private and public life, which made it inappropriate to cite the shortcomings in one as a disqualification for the other. As one of his Scots supporters put it:

The friends of the present Ministers are fond of contrasting the virtues of Mr Pitt's private character with the excesses of Mr Fox. Mr Pitt is undoubtedly not accused of gaming, extravagance or any other particular vice. It is rather problematical whether a man will make the better Minister for having uniformly kept the ten commandments, and would not it be possible to find in history instances of those who, apparently correct in their private conduct, have atchiev'd the most capital publick mischiefs?[20]

When his gambling was cited in Parliament to suggest that he was unsuitable as a potential minister, Fox cheerfully admitted the offence, denied that there was any connection with public life, and concluded that 'it was a vice countenanced by the fashion of the times.'[21] None of this would reassure voters of a more conventional morality, but Fox's ambitions or interest in politics were not such that he was prepared to make concessions.

*

Late in life, an elderly Foxite, reminiscing about the last two decades of the eighteenth century, regretted the fact that public drunkenness was now liable to involve an individual with 'a little familiarity with a certain station-house and the police of the district. How differently people got "jolly" in my youthful days!'[22] Certainly, Fox in his youth drank immoderately. According to the autopsy performed on him in 1806, 'The whole substance of the liver was preternaturally hard, especially the right lobe, the interior structure of which was almost entirely scirrhous.'[23] The results were predictable. 'He . . . spews to an immoderate degree,'[24] noted Selwyn. Horace Walpole observed that Fox, Lord Derby 'and two or three more young men of quality' seemed to find entertainment, at the end of a drinking bout, in encouraging a mob to break all the windows in an opponent's house.[25] Neither hard drinking nor the violence that attended it was specifically Foxite. Nor was it usually worthy of note in the context of late eighteenth-century values. Even so, Foxite drunkenness was of such an order that it was remarked on in the press and in cartoons, and was made the more reprehensible when set alongside other misdemeanours.

One of the most notorious of these concerned Fox's relations with women. There was little or no religion in Fox's early life, and, without this or any other inhibition, sex was enjoyed to the full. Mistresses were shared between Foxites or passed on from one to another. When Richard Fitzpatrick's mistress, Lady Anne Foley, wrote to announce the birth of his son, she added as a postscript that 'This is not circular.'[26] Illegitimacy carried no stigma in Foxite circles, the bastard and the heir being brought up in the same nursery. At Brooks's, Fox's schoolfriends made sex the subject of crude bets: 'Ld. Cholmondeley has given two guineas to Ld. Derby, to receive 500 Gs. whenever his lordship fucks a woman in a Balloon one thousand yards from the Earth.'[27] It was a sport that Fox himself was happy to join in: 'I have received one Guinea from Mrs Benwell in consequence of which I promise to pay her five hundred pounds if ever Mrs Robinson lives with me or I with her.'[28] Little wonder that Fox became the recipient of confessions. Grave statesmen of the 1790s had in their youth complained of venereal disease and described their condition in great detail: 'I am now in a course of mercury, sick, miserable, & so sore that I cannot walk without difficulty; with a swelling in my thigh that promises in good time to be a bubo, and a soreness in my throat that indicates a disposition to ulcers. You cannot well conceive anybody more forlorn.'[29] Memories of his own youth would have made Fox a sympathetic listener.

Fox's more famous liaisons often punctuated political crises. Within a few days of resigning in July 1782, Fox, according to one of his closest friends, virtually gave up politics for Perdita Robinson, one of the leading actresses of the day:

Charles passes his whole day with Mrs Robinson, to the utter Exclusion and Indignation of the gallant Col. Tarleton, but not, I believe, of Capt. Craddock, for it is supposed that she has bad Taste enough to like fucking with him almost as well as with the late Secretary, whom I never see but at Mrs R's window, unless he comes to Brooks's after she is gone to bed, and gets drunk with Stanhope and Jack Townshend.[30]

As the Coalition administration prepared to fight for its very existence, Fox complicated matters by starting an *affaire* with Georgiana, Duchess of Devonshire, which to some extent irritated her husband.[31] It seems to have lasted nearly two years. When Fox found himself able to admire a beautiful woman platonically, this was so strange an event that it called forth verses:

> My heart is so fenced that for once I am wise
> And Gaze without Madness on Amorat's eyes
> That my wishes, which never were bounded before
> Are here bounded by friendship & ask for no more
> Is it Reason? No, that my whole life will belie
> For who so at variance as Reason & I
> Is't Ambition that fills up each chink of my heart
> Nor allow to one softer sensation a part?
> O! no for in this all the world must agree
> That one folly was never sufficient for me
>
> . . . .
>
> To Beauty our just admiration may claim
> But love and love only the heart can inflame.[32]

Artlessness and unselfconsciousness marked Fox the lover as much as Fox the politician. For the last twenty years of his life, Fox led a more settled existence with Elizabeth Armistead, but domesticity was a new experience for both of them, she having previously been the mistress of Lord George Cavendish and the Prince of Wales.

Once again, Fox was utterly indifferent to what a wider opinion made of his behaviour. In 1802, he revealed to his family and friends that he had been married to Mrs Armistead for eight years:

he was perfectly indifferent even then as to its being known or not, but as it was merely personal to him, it could not be very interesting to the public, and that she, satisfied with security without publicity, made it a point that it should be kept a secret . . . The odd thing is that people who were shock'd at the immorality of his having a mistress are still more so at that mistress having been his wife for so long.[33]

There was no connection in Fox's mind between private life and claims to office. If there were, it was debatable whether Pitt's sexual abstinence was more suspicious in a public man than Fox's indulgence. As a recent authority has noted, 'In 1784, when Fox was charged in a case of assault, he gave as his alibi that he had been in bed at the time with Mrs Armistead (she was willing to swear to it). He was much admired for his frankness.'[34] There was to be no subterfuge or concealment for the sake of winning office. Indeed, as Richard Fitzpatrick told his mistress, office was almost a distraction: 'we are all Ministers again, but the worst part of the Story is that I am once more a *Secretary* . . . But you must be very factious indeed if you are determined to devote yourself always to the *Arms of opposition*, and when your friends come into power you ought to have patriotism enough to sacrifice something as well as them for the *good of your country*.'[35]

Even more notorious was Fox's addiction to gambling. It was this more than anything else that confirmed the image in people's minds that Fox was a gamester in life and a gamester in politics. The hostile pen of Sir Philip Francis observed:

From his cradle to his coffin, he was a gamester, without positive avarice, except while he was engaged, from a pure unadulterated love of play. He was subject to other infirmities; but gaming was the master passion that ruled and ruined him. In that alone he was in earnest; and it followed him in many transactions which seemed to have no relation to play. Every object he contended for was a stake to be won, and made him, in the hazardous pursuit of it, just as prodigal of honour as of fortune, when he had nothing else to risk or to forfeit.[36]

A decision in politics was no different to the turning of a card or the throwing of dice. The betting covered all subjects. When involved in a fire in a country house, Fox and his friends 'got to a proper distance, and laid bets as to which beam would fall in first'.[37] For Fox the Turf was a positive passion. In the 1770s, he owned a string of horses in partnership with an old schoolfriend, the Duke of Buccleuch. In the 1790s, another Etonian, Lord Foley, shared the stable. Fox exhibited more enthusiasm than he often showed at Westminster:

when his horse ran, he was all eagerness and anxiety. He always placed himself where the animal was to make a push, or where the race was to be most strongly contested. From this spot, he eyed the horses advancing with the most immoveable look; he breathed quicker as they accelerated their pace; and when they came opposite to him, he rode in with them at full speed.[38]

Details of the performances of Fox's horses regularly appeared in the London papers, together with the sums wagered.[39] Fox's mastery of the complexities of horse-racing—weights, distances, past records—was taken by a French visitor to be proof positive of his 'genius'.[40]

Alongside horse-racing went card-playing on such a scale that moralists devoted whole pamphlets to a vice which they conceived to be, like the pox, an importation from France. As thousands of pounds changed hands, gambling was undertaken in high seriousness.

They began by pulling off their embroidered clothes and put on frieze great coats, or turned their coats inside outwards for luck. They put on pieces of leather (such as are worn by footmen when they clean the knives) to save their laced ruffles; and to guard their eyes from the light and to prevent tumbling their hair, wore high-crowned straw hats with broad brims and adorned with flowers and ribbons; masks to conceal their emotions when they played at quinze.[41]

Much of this activity was carried on in public. As passers-by looked through the windows of Brooks's, men with the highest pretensions in government could be seen winning and losing fortunes. Fox's good or ill fortune was widely known. The massive losses of 1774 were notorious. In 1781, just before the greatest political test of his life, Fox and Fitzpatrick opened a faro[42] bank at Brooks's, and allegedly won £30,000 in three months. New clothes were bought. Some creditors were even paid off. Selwyn had to admit that 'I never knew such a transition from distress to opulency, or from dirt to cleanliness.'[43] In December of the same year, Fox lost £10,000 at Newmarket.[44] As the world in general marvelled at these astonishing fluctuations in fortune, it was not surprising that, in April 1782, when Fox resumed office, cartoonists should portray him as the rogue in *Banco to the Knave*.[45] He was so completely the addict that he was almost equally indifferent to winning or losing: 'After losing large sums at hazard, Fox would go home,—not to destroy himself, as his friends sometimes feared, but—to sit down quietly, and read Greek.'[46]

Fox was involved in vice on a heroic scale. Those who condemned his morals often admired his stamina. Westminster, Brooks's, and Newmarket had an equal attraction, as Horace Walpole noted: 'Last week he passed twenty-four hours at all three, or on the road from one to the other, and ill the whole time, for he has a bad constitution, and treats it as if he had been dipped in the immortal river.'[47] So unselfconscious was Fox on these matters that friends like Fitzpatrick, who applauded his political triumphs, were free to write verses satirizing his obsession with gambling.[48] It was part of Fox's fascination that he never lived by rules that guided other men. He offered the electorate great talents as a public man, and saw little reason why his private life should come under public scrutiny. Dissimulation was foreign to his character. As long as he believed that his career in politics stood apart from his private life, he had no need of it.

*

Fox was indebted for virtually the whole of his life. Bankruptcies were not unknown and dunning tradesmen a commonplace. In these matters, as in others, Charles Fox never saw that any moral censure on his handling of money was in order, or that it was a problem which justified much attention. He never lived within his income, Micawberly believing that someone would provide. Strangely enough, they always did. It was part of the belief of Fox's friends that he was a man so set apart that they should finance his peccadilloes. Endless embarrassments over money, which would have crushed other men, were turned by Fox into jokes against himself. As ever, he refused to acknowledge that such matters were a genuine concern of the public, or that they reflected on his claims to hold high office.[49]

Initially, the obvious expedient to escape debt was to sell his inheritance. Between 1774 and 1777, Fox sold the annuity that had come to him in his mother's will, the Clerkship of the Pells, a profitable sinecure that had been secured by his father, and the family house at Kingsgate.[50] As Fox pleaded with intermediaries to help with particular sales, protestations of a willingness to lead a purer life were forthcoming, but were of little worth:

I must own fairly that in my present horrid situation it is impossible to employ my mind about any thing but the means of getting rid of the present Dun. If it be possible to relieve me I am sure I have smarted so much for my follies already that I may venture to say, that, so far from repeating *them*, there is no sort of life however laborious and unpleasant that I would not undertake with cheerfulness and joy . . . it is impossible to continue on the footing which I now am, without every day lowering myself in the opinion of Mankind by the shifts and excuses to which I am constantly driven.[51]

These words were written in 1774. Seven years later, one of the sights of London was the public bankruptcy of Fox. Londoners had 'the diversion of seeing Charles's dirty furniture in the street'.[52] As Fox's belongings were auctioned, he took refuge with a certain 'Mr Mann, an apothecary'. According to Selwyn, in the summer of 1781, in spite of events in India and

America, Fox's financial woes were 'now more the subject of conversation than any other topic'.[53] As contemporaries noted the similar problems of Fox's associates, like Sheridan, Fitzpatrick, and O'Bryen, they were not unnaturally tempted to ponder whether the Foxite desire for office was based on principle or the urgent necessity of a regular income.[54]

When everything was sold that could be sold, Fox had to fall back on the charity of his friends, and that appeared limitless. Selwyn was simply dumbfounded by the fact that Foxites 'have imbibed such a belief of the necessity of Charles's being the first man of this country . . . that they cannot conceive there should be the least impediment to it, arising either from his own conduct, or from that of others . . . The Messrs. Foxes must be indemnified, *coûte que coûte* . . . If Jews won't pay for them, the Gentiles must.'[55] Part of this willingness to subsidize must be put down to the fact that the careers and political aspirations of many of his friends would be realized if Fox triumphed, and would be ruined if he sank. Fox's career was, in a real sense, an investment. But it was also, in part, an acknowledgement that Charles operated under a special dispensation. He could not live by the general rule, and it was pointless to ask him to do so. If his personal finances were slightly less chaotic in his final years, this was not due to a new-found sense of the value of money, but to age and Mrs Armistead tempering his appetites.

Initially, it was the Fox family that bore the brunt of Charles's indebtedness. In February 1772, Henry Fox paid off his son's debts to the sum of £20,000.[56] Eighteen months later, a further £100,000 was lost for the same purpose.[57] What compounded difficulties was Holland's decision to employ a shady figure named John Powell[58] as his agent to negotiate with creditors. Rumours began to circulate that a bankruptcy was contrived to hide assets, and thereby swindle those to whom Fox owed money. 'If it is infamous to be a Bankrupt it is more so to pretend to be so when you are not, to save money which you are able to pay,' wrote George Selwyn. Recording the fact that Fox had just lost £900 at billiards in Bath, he went on, 'This £900 had it been pasd [*sic*] to the Annuitants to make up the deficiency which Powell stickles about, These annuities would at this day be in Ld. Hollds Hands.'[59] Fox himself thanked his father for having 'delivered me from certain & unexampled ruin . . . I am sure that is a satisfaction he may enjoy very completely',[60] but the scandal had been very public and very messy.

Horace Walpole was clear that Lord Holland's endless indulgence of his favourite son would serve no long-term purpose:

Why, Charles Fox's debts are like Caesar's. I really think that Lord Holland has done a bad deed in paying so much for him. The injustice to his family is great, and the example is pernicious, and neither in all probability will find any benefit by it. It

is a strange way to correct vice, that of furnishing fresh means to gratify it! The laws
of every country have provided a more efficacious one.[61]

Selwyn, too, confessed that 'Je me perds en ruminating on this matter.'[62] A
crisis which would have destroyed any other young man left Fox unmoved
and unscathed. London enjoyed the joke that the money that Henry Fox
was suspected of embezzling from public funds while Paymaster-General
during the Seven Years War should come back into circulation as payment
for his son's debts, but it was an awesome spectacle. Most astonishing was
Fox's insouciance. When his elder brother had a son, who would deprive
Fox of the title and income of a Lord Holland, thereby severely impairing
his creditworthiness, he wished the baby as well 'as if he had been a
daughter'.[63] When his father expressed surprise that Fox could sleep well
under such a burden of worry, the answer came back, 'Nay, Sir, do not
reprehend *me* on this subject, apply to my creditors;—rather wonder how
they can sleep!'[64] Throughout the whole business, Fox's attitude is not really
adequately described as immoral or amoral. He was simply untouched by it,
as though the debts had been accumulated by another person, perhaps the
'Carlino' invented to carry the burden of the indiscretions committed on the
Grand Tour.

   The same refusal to become involved with the consequences of his own
behaviour is demonstrated in his dealings with one of his greatest friends
from Eton, the Earl of Carlisle. It constitutes one of the bleakest episodes in
Fox's career. In 1773, Carlisle stood surety for £16,000 worth of Fox's
debts. He was then involved in paying interest of £2,000 a year, which was
one-sixth of his income. So great was this burden that Carlisle was forced to
mortgage his London house and adopt severe measures of retrenchment in
his own family.[65] At the same time, John Crewe stood surety for £8,000
worth of debt and Thomas Foley for £30,000. For these men, Fox's political
career was literally an investment. When Carlisle fully recognized the scale
of the commitment that he had taken on, he begged the Holland family to
release him from his obligations. He told Fox's mother that 'It was my
friendship & love for him that made me comply with his requests without
deliberation or considering the consequences.'[66] Such pleas fell on deaf ears,
Stephen Fox brazenly stating that he could not help Carlisle 'in justice to my
own Family'.[67]

   By 1775, Carlisle was talking of 'ruin'.[68] George Selwyn, Carlisle's trustee,
spent nearly ten years trying to extricate his ward from involvement in Fox's
debts. Cautioning Carlisle against doing anything 'which squints only towards setting Charles *free* and making him *easy*, as they call it,'[69] he recommended endless pursuit of Fox lest he 'may think that all the mire in which

he wallows, is as indifferent to you as to him'.[70] Carlisle was forbidden to discuss financial matters with Fox unless he were chaperoned by an adviser, and he was warned against Fox bursting into tears. In trying to account for the capacity of Fox to dun his friends, Selwyn was inclined to attribute it 'to a vanity that has, by the foolish admiration of his acquaintance, been worked up into a kind of phrensy'.[71] Fox's 'insensibility' to his friends' distress, for Selwyn, 'takes away from me every consideration whatever of the person'.[72] Even so, Carlisle continued to lend Fox small sums, and contributed significantly to the funds that were established to relieve Fox in old age.[73] Some of Carlisle's obligations were removed by Fox's gambling successes in 1781,[74] but the world had been struck by the way 'Charles bore both the sufferings and resentment of his friend with triumphant and impudent insensibility.'[75] Oddly, Fox's friends did not necessarily share this view. Carlisle himself was not untypical in asserting that Fox was not as other men, but rather lived under a special dispensation. Old men like Selwyn and Horace Walpole made stern remarks about Fox; his contemporaries forgave him. The man who determinedly lives life on his own terms is always compelling.

If the claims of friendship constituted one of Fox's major assets, so did his unmarried status and the possibility that, if politics took a particular turn, he might become the dispenser of great power and patronage. Some men saw these as a worthwhile investment. In July 1787, Thomas Coutts the banker wrote to Fox out of the blue offering him money:

Perhaps you will laugh at my letter, but I feel an impulse to write it, & to make you an offer, in case you have Annuities or Debts, to lend you money to pay Them provided you would like to be indebted *to me*—and that such a Sum as I can spare, would extricate you from hands that are less liberal than, I *Hope*, mine are . . . As to any Views to you—or any other, as a Public man—I am perfectly obscure & out of the Question—I have nothing to ask, & tho' You were now The Minister do I know of anything in Your Power that I would accept.[76]

The last sentence of this letter was transparently disingenuous. As Coutts more frankly admitted to another of his clients, the Duchess of Devonshire: 'If the King dies I lose a good friend; but I am in hopes I may still be employed by his successor. For I was his *first* banker, and he has always approved of my conduct . . . Mr Fox, I believe, your Grace will find much my friend.'[77] According to Coutts's records, £5,000 was lent to Fox in September 1787, and a similar sum in June 1788. Both loans 'were not to be pressed or any Interest even ask'd for'.[78]

Fox, predictably, was delighted by this unexpected offer. He expressed himself 'highly gratified to you for an offer of unexpected generosity . . . The reports of the world have not deceived you with respect to the embarrassed state of my circumstances.'[79] In August 1787, Fox gave Coutts an account of his indebtedness: £3,500 was owed in London, £1,500 in Paris, together with another £4,000 due to annuitants guaranteed by Fox in his own name or on behalf of Richard Fitzpatrick.[80] Ten months later, Fox had discovered that another £4,200 was owing.[81] Thereafter, Coutts became Fox's banker, and complete accounts of Fox's financial transactions are preserved in the ledgers of his bank. Predictably, the management of Fox's affairs was no sinecure. Quite often, Fox himself had only a vague idea of how weak or strong his personal finances were. Sometimes, Coutts had to tolerate bland assurances from Fox 'that it is at present wholly out of my power to settle our account'.[82] All of this was to be borne if it gave the bank social status and a hedge against an upset in politics.

There was another motive as well, however. Coutts had daughters of marriageable age. In his early correspondence with Fox, Coutts had ambiguously invited Fox to form 'a Connection' with him, insisting that, 'As to me my principal Ambition is to acquire the Friendship & acquaintance of men Eminent for Benevolent minds great Talents & respectable Characters . . . I am descended from respectable Familys [sic].'[83] As late as 1802, Coutts still entertained hopes: 'Our conjecture is that Coutts, whose folly and wrongheadedness about Fox is notorious, had taken steps to bring about a marriage between his daughter Fanny and Fox; that she had consented . . . but that Fox was conscious of the insuperable difficulty of being already married to Mrs Armistead.'[84] In the event, Coutts was to derive no benefit from Fox either as a statesman or as a son-in-law, but, in spite of these disappointments, he begged Fox to encourage his nephew, the third Lord Holland, to join his list of clients: 'I do not believe that the profit of an additional Customer can be an object to him but I know in many instances he is solicitous to be Banker to particular Persons, and with all his good qualities & good sense too he is a whimsical man in some things.'[85]

Coutts and Carlisle were the two men most prominently caught up in Fox's debts, but they were not alone. Foxite politics were, to some extent, an expression of tangled financial relationships. Fox lent and borrowed money with bewildering frequency, complicating political friendships. Lord Maitland pursued him for repayment of a loan that was over twenty years old.[86] When the Duke of Bedford left Fox £5,000 in 1802, part of that money was immediately diverted to rescue Dennis O'Bryen, his agent in Westminster.[87] At the very moment when Coutts was offering money to Fox in 1787, he himself was pressing Richard Fitzpatrick to repay a loan of £600.[88] Shortly before his death, Fox was begging Lord Lauderdale to 'deliver me from a considerable embarrassment'.[89] Many Foxite MPs were not unaware of debt and its problems, and inevitably bad blood was sometimes the result. The bickering and jealousy between Sheridan and Grey, which did so much to injure Foxite politics, was, according to Fox himself, 'upon private accounts relative to money matters'.[90] Another Foxite MP, J. B. Church, had particular reason to feel disgruntled. Within months of receiving Coutts's money, Fox persuaded Church to loan him £6,000 'to begin the New-market Campaign'.[91] In August 1791, he begged successfully for £2,500 more, in order to escape the 'most completely ruinous' situation.[92] Both debts were still outstanding at his death.[93] Over and over again, people gave Fox money with very little hope that it would ever be returned. They did so out of friendship or as an investment in a promising career. Their generosity fulfilled the prophecy that Fox would live under a divine dispensation from the rules that governed other men.

Fox's special status was spectacularly confirmed in 1793. On 4 June, a meeting was held at the Crown and Anchor Tavern in the Strand, presided over by Serjeant Adair. Philip Francis made the main speech, expressing the view 'that it deeply concerns and may effectually promote the service as well as the Honour of the Nation that the example of disinterestedness held out to the future by Mr F——'s publick conduct, should not descend to posterity unaccompanied by some evidence of the general impression it has made & the sense which His Country entertains of it'.[94] A Committee was organized to co-ordinate fund-raising on Fox's behalf, with T. Pelham, T. W. Coke, and G. Byng as Trustees.[95] Fox, as well he might, sent the meeting 'a very handsome letter'.[96] The collection of money started immediately, but the project was not universally popular. Mrs Crewe thought that her husband had been rushed into obligations against his wishes.[97] Giving money to Fox, at a time when his views on the French Revolution were beginning to alarm, was a political act. Scots subscribed anonymously or under the banner of 'the Independent Friends'.[98] Charles Dundas refused to help for fear that it would involve the loss of his parliamentary seat.[99] Foxites often found that the climate outside the cosiness of Whig Club dinners was chillier than they imagined.

Nevertheless, £41,000 was subscribed almost immediately; £55,000 had been raised by the end of 1793; and the final figure was £61,402. 6s. 0d.[100] Among the largest subscribers were the Dukes of Bedford, Norfolk, and Devonshire, his old schoolfriend Earl Fitzwilliam, T. W. Coke and W. H. Lambton. Over £21,000 was earmarked to pay off Fox's outstanding commitments, and the beneficiary proceeded to bombard William Adam with the details of remembered and half-remembered debts. Among them was the startling figure of £7,000 owed to Edmund Burke.[101] The remainder of the money was to be used to buy Fox an annuity of £2,000, to be managed by the Trustees. At Fox's request, arrangements were made for Mrs Armistead to be provided for, should he predecease her, particularly in respect of making St Anne's Hill 'quite free for her'.[102] It was a staggering amount of money to collect at a time when the Foxite connection was buckling under the pressure of the French Revolution. No doubt some of the subscribers contributed by way of paying a quit-rent, rather than as an earnest of continued friendship and association. Even so, many others offered him assistance out of real affection, and the conviction that Fox, as the principal opponent of the repressive governmental policies of the 1790s, had to be given a status in the world.

Such a public demonstration of esteem certainly irritated Fox's enemies. The refugee Archbishop of Aix, who called him a 'Demagogue and Rebel', noted that 'Fox seems to be in universal contempt both as a man & a politician all over the Continent, and his last mendicant pension has made his heart as contemptible as his mind.'[103] For a man of 44, after twenty-five years of parliamentary service, to be so openly dependent on charity was a chastening sight. Even those who felt 'a kind of satisfaction in his being relieved' were 'hurt by the kind of degradation which I think he suffers'.[104] Fox himself, as ever, felt none of these things. It was a matter of complete indifference what the world in general thought. He delighted in his friends and their kindness:

You will hear by others of what has been done & is doing for me. I may perhaps flatter myself but I think it is the most honourable thing that ever happened to any Man. The sum which *has* been raised is such as will pay all my debts that are in any degree burthensome and give me an income upon which I can live comfortably without contracting any more.[105]

At least now the option of retiring from politics could be properly funded, and it may not be coincidental that his marriage to Mrs Armistead took place in 1795, when he at last found himself to be in a position to provide for her long-term future. If in 1793, however, Fox promised to avoid debt in future, few of his friends believed that he would keep his word, and they were right. Fox died, as he had lived, in debt. In 1807, the Dukes of Bedford and Devonshire and Earl Fitzwilliam collected another £10,000 to pay off yet more clamouring creditors.[106]

*

An elector assessing Fox as a public figure in the 1770s and 1780s did not have an easy task. On the one hand, the talent and compelling personality were obvious. Brilliant speeches, often impromptu rather than prepared, made him a commanding figure in Parliament. His development of the great theme of the perils of an extended executive, personally played out in his own career, refashioned the agenda of politics. Cosmopolitan by nature and upbringing, he was accepted as an equal by the intellectual and social leaders of London and Paris. On the other hand, pleasure and the company of friends claimed as much of his time as politics. As cartoonists portrayed him as increasingly unkempt and debauched, electors had to assess the depth of scandal that surrounded him. When many feared that the swelling National Debt threatened state bankruptcy, was it reasonable to entrust government to the hands of a man whose personal finances were a shambles? Was Fox so acceptable in Paris that Francophilia might lead him to neglect British interests? Was it possible or desirable that men of tender conscience should make the distinction between private and public morality that would alone permit them to give Fox their votes?

Undoubtedly, Fox's political prospects were harmed by these considerations, although the exact extent of the damage is hard to quantify.[107] What is clear is that Fox himself never saw public opinion as of any consequence, and resolutely refused to make concessions to it. Foxite company was self-sufficient and self-congratulatory. The rules which governed their sexual and financial dealings were their own, and were quite separate from public life, where more general conventions obtained. Fox would very much have agreed with his friend Lady Bessborough, when she explained that

If I made use of the word *world*, it was as most people generally use it, I believe, as a short way of expressing that set of people they usually live with ... It is the people I live with constantly whose opinions I mind, either from fearing to give pain to those I love amongst them, or from hating the being teaz'd and plagued, which, however foolish it may seem, when it is repeated every day grows at length very unpleasant.[108]

The closeness of Foxite society was a strength in that warm friendships made political failures easier to bear. It was a weakness in that its values were not shared by wide sections of the electorate. Penalties had therefore to be paid, and the pressures of the French Revolution would bring this point home.

6

The French Revolution,
1789-1794

THE Foxites were badly prepared to meet the prolonged crisis provoked by the French Revolution. Their leaders were busy nursing the bruises that had been sustained in the Regency Crisis and in the ongoing impeachment proceedings against Hastings. Fox himself seemed ever more inclined to abandon politics altogether, or, at the very least, to subordinate them to the attractions of private life. Both factors encouraged men like Burke, Grey, and Sheridan to take initiatives, which all too often Fox would neither approve nor condemn. In the fast-moving and increasingly hysterical politics of these years, one of the oddest features of public life was Fox's refusal to take a line or to impose his authority on his friends and associates. At critical moments, he seemed almost paralysed. Spasms of activity alternated with weeks or months of dalliance. By 1794, the Foxite connection had almost disintegrated, leaving Fox with a rump of MPs and a handful of peers as supporters. This catastrophe was, more often than not, brought about by what Fox failed to do rather than anything more positive. The Foxite connection dribbled away because Fox could not or would not take steps to staunch the flow.[1]

In theory, the Foxite response to events in France should have been straightforward. She was 'the natural political enemy' of England.[2] With a population four times that of England, France represented an endless military threat that had expressed itself, throughout the eighteenth century, in repeated invasion attempts. Fox, in the brief interludes when he had charge of foreign affairs, was clear that his first duty was to contain 'the overweening pride and boundless ambition of France'.[3] He had opposed Pitt's commercial treaty with France in 1786 on the grounds that it was merely a French device to tie England down diplomatically, and to destroy long-standing alliances.[4] Fox was clear, in the late 1780s, that it was only France's indebtedness that prevented her from swallowing England whole. He told

Mrs Armistead that he profoundly hoped they 'would ruin their Credit', because that was 'the only means of saving the Country'.[5] Mercifully, the fiasco of an attempted French intervention in Holland, in 1787, proved to Fox that 'France was, in point of finance, in so imbecile a state, as well as in other particulars, that it was not in her power to break with us.'[6]

In rehearsing these well-worn Whig fears about France, however, Fox was objecting to a system rather than a people. In his speeches, the word 'France' becomes interchangeable with the phrase 'House of Bourbon'. From his travels and friendships, Fox had developed a great liking for everything French. What was objectionable was that the Bourbon monarchy was the supreme example in Europe of that monarchical despotism which Fox believed threatened England in the person of George III. What is more, he took the view that the political crisis developing in France could, quite possibly, end in yet further enhancing the power of kings. In January 1787, he told the Commons that 'Louis the sixteenth possessed abundantly more power than ever Louis the fourteenth could boast of, and that superiority, great as it was, would in all probability, be considerably heightened very shortly.'[7] Importantly, therefore, even before the Revolution began, there was a connection in Fox's mind between French and English politics. Louis XVI and George III were soul-mates in their desire to be despots. By reaction, Fox found his friends among those Frenchmen who opposed their king. Until the House of Bourbon's wilfulness was brought under parliamentary control, England could never be safe.

His many French friendships confirmed these opinions. According to Fox family tradition, France was 'the great hobby'.[8] On repeated visits, Fox had had as interpreters of French language and culture leading members of that liberal wing of the French aristocracy who were to play a prominent part in the first two or three years of the Revolution. He had been a gambling associate of Orléans and Lauzun. Talleyrand referred to the Fox family in politics, as 'vous qui êtes nos maîtres'.[9] There was between such men the feeling of sharing a common cause. Lafayette was fond of repeating something that Fox had told him to the effect that 'si nos deux pais peuvent avoir dans le même tems une administration libérale, la cause du genre humain est gagnée.'[10] Delighting in the title of 'French Whig', Lafayette was the obvious candidate for the job of showing Fox's nephew around Paris in 1791, thereby setting up an association that lasted for forty years.[11] As members of the same club with the same values, they applauded each other's successes. The Vicomte de Noailles wrote to congratulate Fitzpatrick on the formation of the Coalition ministry because England was now in 'les mains des personnes faites pour le gouverner'.[12]

Frequent cross-Channel visiting kept the contacts fresh. After the end of the American War in 1783, London was faced by an 'inundation' of French visitors.[13] After 1789, the tide flowed the other way, carrying innumerable Foxites to Paris to join in the excitement of the Revolution. Fox himself thought seriously of going over. While there, Fox's friends were chaperoned by Lafayette, Talleyrand, and Orléans,[14] and were not surprised to discover that 'almost all our men friends are great patriots'.[15] Capitalizing on these French contacts, Fox felt free to intervene personally in French politics. After the flight to Varennes, he wrote to Barnave urging moderation, for example, provoking questions in the National Assembly about the occult influence of Englishmen in France,[16] and doubts in England of the constitutional propriety of such behaviour. Lord Grenville angrily asked, 'Is not the idea of Ministers from Opposition to the different Courts of Europe a new one in this country? I never heard of it before, and should think that if it could be proved, I mean legally proved, it would go very near to an impeachable misdemeanour.'[17] In retrospect, Fox himself admitted that 'it was a foolish thing to do.'[18] However, being magnificently informed about French events, Fox could hardly avoid controversy. Frenchmen consulted him on constitution-making and Englishmen on the state of France.[19] On the basis of good reports, Fox could, for example, assure Thomas Coutts that his daughters 'are in as perfect safety in Paris as they would be in the Strand'.[20] Fox's intimate knowledge of France was no guarantee that he would interpret events in that country correctly. He might simply be wrong for very interesting reasons. But it certainly guaranteed a renewed prominence for him in England, where few men, certainly not Pitt, Burke, or Sheridan, had the same resources.

Much influenced by his French friends, Fox welcomed the end of the old absolutist order in France. One month after the fall of the Bastille, Fox wrote excitedly to Thomas Grenville: 'I say nothing of french News but if I were to begin I should never finish. It is I think by much the greatest Event that has ever happened in the world, and will in all human probability have the most extensive good consequences.'[21] What Fox thought he saw, in 1789, was a controlled attempt by people he called French Whigs to emulate the settlement of 1688 in England. Over the next two years, he applauded the putting together of a constitution that embodied the Whig values of a propertied franchise, religious toleration, and the ending of slavery. In a sense, this was to underestimate dramatically the dynamic of events in France, where a total remodelling of society was in prospect and not merely a readjustment among a political élite as in 1688. On the other hand, Fox was clear that this great experiment, if properly handled, offered dreamlike opportunities to replace absolutism with something better, and that the degeneration into violence after 1792 had not been inevitable. The mismanagement that led to violence should not obscure the glory of the original conception. Five days after the storming of Versailles, Fox was on his feet again: 'he is a wonderful Man, his toast of the Majesty of the People I suppose will make another Fuss, he loses himself very much in these sort of things, and yet how can one but bend to his amazing talents.'[22]

As France moved from absolutism to constitutionalism, so she ceased, in Fox's mind, to constitute the traditional threat to England. In July 1789, as Fitzpatrick set out for France, he was offered Fox's views:

It is not quite impossible but I may go too. How much the greatest Event it is that ever happened in the World! & how much the best! If you go without my seeing you pray say something civil for me to the D. of Orleans whose conduct seems to have been perfect; and tell him & Lauzun that all my prepossessions against french connections for this country will be at an end, & indeed most part of my European system of Politics will be altered if this Revolution has the consequences that I expect.[23]

Consequently, when the Army Estimates were debated in February 1790, Fox argued that military spending could be cut, because French threats had been removed by a Revolution in which he 'exulted'.[24] Again the analogy of 1688 was rehearsed, and when it was challenged by Burke on the grounds that the French were engaged in something altogether different in scope, Fox replied with some vigour that 'The reason why France had been so long settling her constitution, and why we had so soon adjusted ours in 1688, was owing to there being so much despotism to destroy in France, and so little which called for destruction when the revolution in our government took place.'[25] Fox's interpretation of events in France as a French 1688 managed by his friends Lafayette and Talleyrand was confirmed by visits to Paris by his English associates, and remained plausible until at least the flight to Varennes in June 1791.[26] In April of that year, Fox told the Commons that he 'admired the new constitution of France, considered altogether, as the most stupendous and glorious edifice of liberty'. France, he insisted, was now a country 'from which neither insult nor injustice was to be dreaded'.[27]

Anchoring French events in the tradition of 1688 also allowed Fox to contain the challenges of Sheridan and Burke, which had surfaced in the Army debates of February 1790. For reasons set out earlier,[28] both men were anxious to confirm their intellectual authority within Foxite politics. It was not surprising to many that both should have put up a startling interpretation of French events within six months of the taking of the Bastille. Burke talked of anarchy and Sheridan of democracy. Since Foxites overwhelmingly shared their leader's view that a French 1688 involved neither anarchy nor democracy, they watched the antics of the two outsiders with some amusement. Richard Fitzpatrick told his mistress that it had been 'a near race over the Curragh, for no two Irish heads ever displayed their absurdity'. As far as he was concerned, they might as well have been arguing about 'the Trojan War'.[29] James Hare also found the whole affair very funny:

I thought myself particularly fortunate in not being in the House of Commons on St. Patrick's day, for I should have died with the Reaction. Burke continues quite implacable, and his Son, Dr Lawrence, and every Irishman that has access to him, encourages him to persist in his Madness, I despair of a cure. He says, that is only the 'Dissolution of a Friendship, not the Creation of an Enmity', which, You know, is just what he would say, if he determined to poison Sheridan. Charles is perpetually talking it over, and is still full of astonishment at such a mixture of superior Sense and Absurdity.[30]

Fox later reflected that it was lucky that Burke had joined the ranks of those opposing the Revolution, because he 'would have got hanged on the other'.[31]

It was safe to laugh at Burke and Sheridan in 1790, but it may not have been politic. Their descriptions of France were indeed ridiculous. A revolution conducted by Lafayette, Talleyrand, and Mirabeau would never be democratic or anarchical. Therefore, most people within the ranks of the Foxites and many outside them concluded that Sheridan and Burke's views had less to do with France than England. They were, in fact, an extension of the enmities nurtured, in the Hastings Trial and the Regency Crisis, by an old man fearful for his authority and a young man on the make. The 1688 argument would easily defeat both. There was much truth in this analysis, but even so it was potentially perilous to leave two great talents in a state of disaffection. Fox made no move in 1790 either to restrain Burke and Sheridan or to coax them back into more orthodox views. Through indolence or disinclination, Fox took no action, and many Foxites, looking back on the whole period of the Revolution, regarded this as one of his major mistakes. In fact, it set a pattern. At critical moments Fox, almost psychologically distancing himself from politics, failed to act. Sheridan and Burke deserved attention, not for their views on France, but for the talent they showed, the services they had rendered, and the dangers they represented if they became focal points for disaffection.

In fact, Fox had always shown the greatest reluctance to discipline Sheridan, preferring to excuse and protect him. In spite of the embarrassments associated with the Fitzherbert marriage and Sheridan's meddling at Carlton House, Fox always entertained some sympathy for a man of enormous talent, who was endlessly frustrated by debt and who often found consolation in hard drinking,[32] circumstances not unknown to Fox himself. Unlike Fox, however, Sheridan lived under no special licence from friends who would always come to the rescue. Sheridan aspired to have a career like Fox's, without the latter's human and financial guarantees. Having so much in common established a certain rapport between the two men. Fox made no attempt to bridle Sheridan's trumpeting of radical ideas until July 1791, when he persuaded him not to attend a dinner celebrating the fall of the Bastille. After the flight to Varennes, caution was in order, as a constitutional outcome to the Revolution was for the first time in doubt. Even so, Fox was not sure that he done the right thing in putting pressure on Sheridan. He told his nephew that

I *rather* agree with you that it would be better that Sheridan should not attend the meeting of the 14th of July, if he can be absent without an appearance of being frightened out of the conduct he held last year, but I am far from thinking that it is *always* right to give way to unfounded prejudices.[33]

As Sheridan went on to develop an increasingly personal line on French and English politics, Fox refused to check him.

The problems of influencing Burke's actions were even greater. Fox always felt to some extent a pupil or dependant of Burke's, who had no right to give instructions to his master. He 'could not forget, that when a boy almost, he had been in the habit of receiving favours from his right honourable friend, [and] that their friendship had grown with the years'.[34] Before the House of Commons, Fox admitted that 'he was indebted to his right honourable friend for the greatest share of the political knowledge he possessed,—his political education had been formed under him,—his instructions had invariably governed his principles.'[35] At the same time, Fox was not alone in recognizing that Burke 'was a most impracticable person, a most unmanageable colleague . . . a damned wrong-headed fellow'.[36] When Burke published his *Reflections on the Revolution in France*, Fox considered it to be 'in very bad taste'[37] and as 'favouring Tory principles'.[38] In this, Fox was not out of line with most of the Foxite connection, but its publication established an alternative reading of the Revolution to that offered by Fox, which could become the basis of schism:

Burke tells me that Fox disapproves in the most unqualified manner his work on the French Revolution, both as to matter and composition . . . I regret the thing extremely also, because it threatens to embark Fox in a set of opinions, and in a course of politics, which will not do him credit, and in which it will be impossible for the truly respectable and weighty part of his support to follow him.[39]

The rejection of his book merely convinced Burke of a long-standing suspicion that Fox was lost to him. Through inertia and an unwillingness to lead, he was drifting inexorably into association with radicals. He complained to Fox's old schoolfriend Fitzwilliam that 'You know the facility of Fox. You know that he is surrounded and in many respects govern'd by those who have not 1/100th part of his parts, no share in his judgment; and principles absolutely bad. You know how they govern him; As people are always governed by impulse, by importunity and not by reason.'[40] The cavalier dismissal of his writings by someone whom he regarded as a pupil hurt Burke deeply. He was in every sense a difficult colleague, given to outbursts of temper and tears. His description of France seemed to be so wildly inaccurate that it could be ignored. Even so, in the crucial year of 1790, Fox made little or no attempt to comfort Burke or to keep open a dialogue. Suspicions were allowed to fester. As a result, Fox exposed his party to the danger that the slightest incident or remark could induce a crisis. That crisis came in the spring of 1791.

On 15 April, in the course of a debate on England's relations with Russia, Fox referred to France by saying

> that he could not help considering that revolution as a most stupendous work however it may appear to those who took a more superficial view of it. Burke at this time walking up the house attracted much attention; he rose to speak when Charles concluded but gave way to the impatient cry for the question with so much readiness that I took for granted that he felt no great anxiety to enter into any debate . . . Upon the whole I really do not apprehend that any further notice will be taken of this.[41]

In making this prophecy, Thomas Grenville could hardly have been more wrong. Even Fox recognized 'that perhaps I spoke with too much levity on the French Revolution'.[42] On 21 April, he sought Burke out to explain his position, using language that 'was really as conciliatory as it was possible to be',[43] and, in spite of asking Burke directly if he had been put up to anger by Pitt, in order to divert attention from a government struggling badly with a Russian crisis, worried Foxites were relieved to see the two men, after their meeting, walking down to the Commons arm in arm.[44] Further attempts to bring the two men together at this crucial point were frustrated by Fox setting off for a visit to Newcastle. Clearly, he realized that his relationship with Burke had been bruised, but not that it was mortally threatened. In April–May 1791, nothing new had happened in France to provoke a fresh debate. Fox had so far lost interest in the subject that he had not yet read Paine's *Rights of Man*.[45] His eyes were fixed on events in Russia. At this time, the French Revolution was merely one point of interest in a Europe that seemed to be diplomatically remoulding itself.[46]

When, therefore, on 6 May 1791 Burke, in the course of a debate on a constitution for Quebec, rose to damn Fox's stand on France and to announce a final rupture in their friendship and association, the effect, as Horace Walpole recorded, was stunning:

Prodigious clamour and interruption arose from Mr Fox's friends; but he, though still applauding the French, burst into tears, and lamentations on the loss of Burke's friendship, and endeavoured to make atonement; but in vain, though Burke wept too—in short, it was the most affecting scene possible, and undoubtedly *an unique* one, for both the commanders were in earnest and *sincere*.[47]

Burke complained of a 'systematik' campaign to discredit himself and his writings. He accused Fox of gratuitously undertaking 'an elaborate review' of Burke's career and ideas, and then of 'misrepresenting them, with little Logick and less candour'. He had concluded by accusing Burke of taking a bribe from Pitt to destroy the Foxites, 'an impudent calumny, which he well knew his friends the Presbyterians had been active in publickly propagating'.[48] Burke was so hurt that a recital of his woes at a dinner party took three hours.[49] He was in such pain that it engendered long memoranda of a self-justificatory nature,[50] another book, *An Appeal from the New to the Old Whigs*, and a focusing on Fox as the source of all evil. For his part, Fox hoped that Burke 'would forget what was past',[51] but could not be persuaded to take the first step towards reconciliation. A friendship that had run for nearly thirty years had fractured.

The break was very final. Thereafter, they met only very infrequently in the Managers' box at the Hastings trial or at forced social occasions. Burke, while admitting that 'it was with pain I broke with that great man for ever',[52] on his death-bed nevertheless refused to see Fox. Never the most forgiving of men, Burke carried his resentment to the grave. In Fox, the anguish was equally great, and his normally easygoing nature could not assimilate these experiences. In 1800, he guiltily refused Dr Parr's invitation to subscribe to a national memorial to Burke with plain words:

The truth is, that, though I do not feel any malice against Burke . . . I must own that there are parts of his conduct that I cannot forgive so entirely as perhaps I ought, and as I wish to do . . . To attempt to destroy me in the opinion of those whom I so much valued, and in particular that of Fitzwilliam . . . this was surely not only malice, but baseness in the extreme; and if I were to say that I have quite forgiven it, it would be boasting a magnanimity which I cannot feel.[53]

Significantly, what had hit Fox hardest was not Burke's attack on his politics, but his assault on his friendships. It was his point of maximum vulnerability.

For the moment, the loss of Burke to Foxite Whiggery carried few political penalties. Virtually everyone in the party thought that the fault lay with Burke in artificially creating a division that circumstances did not require, and comments were once again made about the possibly disturbed state of his mind. Romilly thought that 'Fox has gained much with the public by his conduct, and Burke has lost as much.'[54] Lady Elizabeth Foster simply recorded in her journal that 'C. Fox had done himself the greatest honor in every respect.'[55] An anonymous pamphleteer sternly informed Burke that 'Your name, Sir, has scarcely ever been mentioned during that period without a ridicule for which the intemperance of your conduct too often afforded plausible pretexts.'[56] The *Morning Chronicle*, the party's main newspaper, agreed.[57] For some months, as French Whigs indulged in the quiet task of constitution-making, Burke's views on that country had been construed by many as unbalanced. In 1791, Paris was still a place to visit rather than to fear. As a result, Burke's separation from Fox on the issue of France had an unreal, even a theatrical, quality that redounded to Burke's disadvantage.[58] He became an isolated figure, whose loneliness was not greatly eased even when so many of his prophecies came true.

In 1791, Fox could not be politically at risk from either Burke or Sheridan, because his thesis that the French were operating Whig values was still entirely plausible. According to this view, the politics of both England and France were based on the confrontation between those who favoured despotic monarchies and the friends of constitutionalism. To this extent, the debates of 1782–4 and the events of 1789, though different in form, were similar in content. Five days after the breach with Burke, Fox told the Commons that he was 'decidedly of opinion that the constitution of this country was more liable to be ruined by an increase of the power of the crown, than by an increase of the power of the people'.[59] The French Revolution had not actually changed Foxite priorities. It had merely given new life to the traumas of 1784, by working out the same debates in a French context. The only violence in England came, not from revolutionaries, but from the King and Church mobs attacking radicals and Dissenters.[60] In the long term, an analogy between English events in 1688 or 1784 and the French Revolution is a nonsense. It misses the special factors that operated in France, and perhaps the very dynamic of the Revolution itself. In the years between 1789 and 1791, however, the analogy had force. It was recognizable to Foxites generally and to men like Mirabeau, who hoped that the new French constitution would be framed on English models.

Predictably, Fox disliked the writings of both Burke and Paine on France, because both men took the debate to levels of discussion that had little to do specifically with the battles of 1784, where Fox insisted on making his stand. In the House of Commons, on 30 April 1792

Mr Fox said, he had read but one of Mr Paine's pamphlets, and that he did not approve it, and from what he had heard of the other, he was inclined to think, that he should not approve of that either; but he was not certain whether they had not done good, by leading men to consider of the constitution. In like manner the book of his right hon. friend [Burke] which he disliked as much as either of them, had, he believed, done some good, because, in his opinion, whatever led to a discussion of the subject was of service.[61]

Such statements comforted those who needed reassurance of Fox's basic suspicion of radicals,[62] and they were further soothed by his singling out Sir James Mackintosh's work as that which did most justice to events in France, notably the *Vindiciae Gallicae*.[63] Fox's views were thought to be so unexceptional that, in the spring of 1791, press reports suggested that some arrangement between him and Pitt might be in the offing.[64] Even Burke had to admit, poignantly, that Foxite views were harmless:

You know that the whole of those who think with the French Revolution (if in reality they think at all seriously with it) do not exceed a score in both Houses . . . It may be asked why I represent the whole party as tolerating & by a toleration countenancing, these proceedings. It is to get the better of their inactivity, & to stimulate them to a publick declaration of, what every one of their acquaintance privately knows, to be as much their Sentiments as they are yours & mine.[65]

In view of statements like this, Fox may have been justified, shortly after the Burke affair, in joining his cronies once more at Newmarket.[66]

What further guaranteed Fox's position was the fact that Burke had chosen the issue of France on which to distance himself from his former friends. That issue, of course, remained of great interest to Englishmen in 1790 and 1791, but, in those years, it was not the only point of interest in politics, and on these others Fox had scored a string of successes. In the second half of 1790, he had successfully forced Pitt to modify his policies in a dispute with Spain over a territorial claim at Nootka Sound in North America. In March–April 1791, he believed that the Foxites had prevented Pitt going to war with Russia over the latter's occupation of the fortress of Oczakov in the Crimea.[67] For this achievement, the Whig Club gave him a vote of thanks.[68] Good relations with Russia were confirmed by Fox sending a personal representative, Sir Robert Adair, to St Petersburg in July 1791, to open up a direct channel of communication between Catherine the Great and the Foxite opposition.[69] The Empress, in turn, wrote to her ambassador in London to desire he would send her the very best bust of Charles Fox, 'puisque c'était par ses talens et son éloquence qu'il avait épargné une guerre sanglante aux deux nations qui les aurait également ruinées, et qu'elle le placerait dans sa galerie entre Cicéron et Démosthène.' I suppose C. Fox is quite delighted.[70]

On top of being consulted by Frenchmen and flattered by empresses, Fox, in May 1791, sponsored the Libel Act and saw it successfully through Parliament. In giving juries, rather than judges, the responsibility of determining both the fact and the publication of libel, he believed that the power of the executive had been significantly reduced.[71] Another vote of thanks came from the Whig Club.[72]

Most significantly, Burke had made little or no impression on the grandees. Whiggery was predicated on the notion that property, broadly defined, was the basis of all rights in politics. It was property that interested a man in preserving liberty, and which gave him the leisure and education to perform this obligation. Those with great property inherited great influence. The titles alone gave them authority. The fact, therefore, that the Dukes of Portland, Bedford, Devonshire, and Norfolk, with the Earls of Carlisle and Fitzwilliam, remained with Fox stumped Burke. He might dispute the word 'Whig', by writing a pamphlet significantly entitled *An Appeal from the New to the Old Whigs*, but there was little serious doubt of where true Whiggery resided as long as Fox claimed the allegiance of men of great title. Fox's need of these men was of itself a guarantee of his good behaviour, because it was essential 'to their procuring to themselves that credit and confidence, which a great part of the nation have ever appeared unwilling to place in them'.[73] As the *Morning Chronicle* put it:

Can it be seriously imagined, that such persons—that the Duke of Portland, Lord Fitzwilliam, and Mr Fox (names never to be separated), and the great body of the landed interest of the country . . . would at the same time depart from those principles on which they had acted through life, and engage in wild and visionary schemes, in which they would have everything to lose.[74]

Portland was very upset by the tone of Burke's *Appeal*, admitting that 'I never read any work that ever gave me the pain which that has done, nor could it, had it come from any other hand.'[75] So far, Fox's standing among the grandees was unchallenged.

In the summer of 1791, therefore, Fox had good reason to feel pleased. The rupture with Burke had been personally distressing, but it had not involved political penalties. His anti-war stance over the Nootka Sound and Oczakov incidents gave him a certain popularity, which was confirmed by the passing of the Libel Act. Burke had tried to make the Whigs choose between Fox and himself before the flight to Varennes and the massacre on the Champ de Mars brought French events back to centre stage as matters for concern. His timing had not been of the best. As a result, Fox enjoyed his summer. He lost a lot of money at Ascot,[76] joined a shooting-party at Lord Fitzwilliam's house at Milton in Northamptonshire,[77] and then set off for a triumphal tour of the north. In Doncaster, which he entered to the ringing of bells, 'every Public house' had 'copious libations . . . and "FOX AND LIBERTY" the universal toast.'[78] In York, he was given the freedom of the city.[79] Back in London, Burke could only express dismay at what he called 'republican, frenchified Whiggism',[80] rightly seeing that 'This Russian business following the Spanish immediately has rendered them [the Ministry] unpopular; and Fox ascends in the other Scale.'[81] He not unreasonably saw his rejection as 'a slap'.[82] As long as French politics did not move outside the context of 1784 that Fox had given them, Burke's frustration could not be eased.

*

All this changed in 1792. In April, France and Austria went to war; in August, the monarchy was overthrown; and in September, the massacre of 2,000 people in Parisian prisons introduced a new period of violence. In addition, the French habit of issuing declarations of universal brotherhood suggested that the revolution would overflow the borders of France and take on a missionary aspect. In response to these events, many Englishmen had to revise their opinions. Liberties were now threatened from two directions: by the traditional enemy of despotic kings and, now, by democratic revolution. To determine policy, it was not enough to say that both were bad. A decision had to be taken as to which was worse. As Fox observed to Fitzwilliam,

You seem to dread the prevalence of Paine's opinions (which in most part I detest as much as you do) while *I* am much more afraid of the total annihilation of all principles of liberty and resistance, an event which I am sure you would be sorry to see as I. We both hate the two extremes equally, but we differ in our opinions with respect to the quarter from which the danger is most pressing.

As the kings and empresses of Europe lined up against France, Fox was clear about his own priorities: 'if the confusions there [France] should terminate in the re-establishment of the antient despotism I shall think it a decisive blow to all liberty in Europe, at least for centuries.'[83] All Foxites would have to make the choice between the dark events of 1784 or the pretensions of 1789 as the greater threat to Whig principle. For many, events in 1792 precipitated a decision.

The first of these was the formation, on 11 April, of the Association of the

Friends of the People, to press for parliamentary reform.[84] Among its members were Grey, Sheridan, and many young Foxites.[85] The idea of forming the Association seems to have appeared, in an impromptu manner, at a dinner party at Lord Porchester's.[86] Grey, in retrospect, argued that its object was to prevent 'mischief' by so reforming Parliament that neither George III nor Tom Paine could be thereafter a serious threat.[87] Other people denied it such high purpose. According to John Bland Burges, it was the brainchild of 'wild, unthinking young men', who, 'as the ostensible leaders of a democratical faction', held meetings 'attended by Presbyterian parsons and some desperate people'.[88] Significantly, Fox had not been consulted about the initiative, and had had no inkling that such a move was afoot. As Thomas Pelham reported,

he told me (what I knew to be the truth, notwithstanding what is *now* said) that he had never been consulted about it, & that on the contrary the Associators seemed determined *not to have any Advice* & particularly not *to have his*; this I know to be true for Lauderdale told me that they were determined not to consult Fox untill [*sic*] they saw the possibility of Success in order that he might not be involved if they failed.[89]

The appearance of the Association was a grave embarrassment for Fox. It was inept of his young friends to talk of abolishing boroughs and extending the franchise at a moment when French events were beginning to alarm significant numbers of people. At a Whig Club meeting on 7 June, Fox insisted that the timing of such a venture had been dreadful: 'However warmly he wished for a moderate Reform in the system of our Representation, he did NOT AGREE with a considerable number of his friends, who had revived the subject with such spirit and vigour, that the PRESENT was a PROPER season for AGITATING the QUESTION.'[90] Tom Pelham was relieved to discover that Fox shared his hope of soon being 'able to put an end to a scheme so very injurious to us as a Party and at this time so peculiarly improper for the Country'.[91] On the other hand, the simple fact that so many of his friends were involved compromised Fox in the eyes of the political world, and when the Associators brought forward a bill for parliamentary reform on 30 April, Fox, out of consistency to his past statements on the subject, was forced to vote with them, adding ambiguously that had Grey asked his advice, 'he should have hesitated before he recommended him to take the part he had taken.'[92] The ambiguity was lost on George III, who could not see 'any substantial difference in their being joined in debate by Mr Fox, and his not being a member of that Society'.[93] Votes of thanks to Fox by the Associators hardly helped to make convincing the distance he wished to preserve between himself and their initiative.[94] In fact, Fox had been angered by the Associators bringing forward parliamentary reform at a time when fear of all change was becoming more and more prevalent. His relations with Portland and the grandees were bound to be bruised. It was all very 'unpleasant'.[95]

The challenge of the Association was so damaging to Foxite unity that, in retrospect, Carlisle among others dated the disintegration of the party from the spring of 1792. What, therefore, needs explanation is Fox's failure to smother the idea at birth. That he could have done so is clear. While Grey, in his last illness, was being pushed in a wheelchair around Howick, 'he had stopped as usual before the bust of Mr Fox—amid his expression of affection and veneration for him he added 'Yet his influence over me was not always usefully exerted—He might have kept me out of all that mess about Reform; yet he never said a word.'[96] Fitzwilliam was equally sure that 'that abominable excrescence', the Association, 'would have signified but little, if one person (for ever to be lamented) had not given these Gentlemen protection and countenance'.[97] It seemed that Fox had been 'overborne by Grey'[98] or that 'upon this as upon most other occasions [he] will probably suffer himself to be led and perhaps act against his own judgment; this is his nature, and however one may lament it, there is no remedy.'[99] To some extent, Fox's paralysis or inability to act may be put down once again to illness. He was so unwell in the first week of May that his niece regretted that there was 'any Concern public or private to vex him'.[100] But this explanation alone will not serve. At critical moments, there was a pattern in Fox's career of an unwillingness to take a line and impose his authority. He could not discipline Grey in 1792, just as he had failed to handle Sheridan and Burke earlier. He hated bullying his friends, particularly if they amused and enlivened him. To use Grey's words, 'he did not like discouraging the young ones.'[101] Further, a disinclination to give too much time to politics, always present and now growing, made it too easy to allow others to set the pace.[102] The penalty to be paid was great. As the Foxite party was seen to be publicly divided on the issue of reform, the Association was named as 'one of those trials which are sure to separate the sheep from the goats'.[103]

Pitt was quick to note Foxite divisions and exploit them. He began to consult Portland privately about emergency measures that it might be necessary to enact to defeat foreign and domestic sedition. In particular, he invited the Duke to assist him in issuing a Proclamation against seditious practices in May 1792.[104] The spectacle of his friends being slowly drawn into association with Pitt was enough to prompt Fox to organize a half-hearted attempt at a common Foxite response. It was unsuccessful, not least because Fox was forced 'to trim, which is not natural to him, and he does not do it well'.[105] As a result, when the Proclamation was voted on, Foxites were to be found in both lobbies. Fox had no choice but to oppose the Proclamation sponsored by Pitt and Portland, because he held to the view that there was no sedition in England, and that the only threat to liberty came from ambitious kings and intolerant churchmen:

It was not, in his opinion, a republican spirit that we had to dread in this country; there was no tincture of republicanism in the country. If there was any prevailing tendency to riot, it was on the other side. It was a high church spirit, and an indisposition to all reform, which marked, more than anything else, the temper of the times.[106]

It was a point of view, but it was not shared by the Foxites as a whole.[107] Parliamentary divisions on reform and the Proclamation had clearly exposed the harsh fact that on these and allied issues connected with France, Foxites were in serious disagreement among themselves. Henceforth, Portland and Fox could only agree to differ, treating areas of contention as open questions.

It was too good an opportunity for Pitt to miss. Between May and October 1792, individual Foxites were tantalizingly told about jobs and offices, and the idea of a coalition between Pitt and Fox was explored through various channels. Loughborough, Dundas, Auckland, and a very naïve Duke of Leeds were employed as emissaries.[108] Fox had no choice but to let this hare run. To have blocked all coalition talks at the outset would have alienated Portland and Fitzwilliam, perhaps finally. As a result, Portland reported that 'Fox was a friend to coalition',[109] upon certain conditions. Those of a sanguine nature could reflect that, ironically, on issues like reform and religious toleration, Fox was closer to Pitt than to Portland, and that the two men had been friends and political allies between 1780 and 1783. Pitt himself assured Foxites that there was nothing 'which could induce him to wish, upon any *personal ground*, to exclude Fox from a share in the government'.[110]

In fact, there was never any possibility of these negotiations bearing fruit. Fox was convinced that Pitt only made offers to divide the Foxites further. To prove his suspicions, he set conditions which he believed Pitt could not meet. First, Pitt himself must resign the Treasury. Fox declared himself ready to act with Pitt but not under Pitt.[111] As Malmesbury recorded, 'Fox made Pitt's quitting the Treasury a sine qua non, and was so opinionative and fixed upon it, that it was impossible even to reason with him on the subject.'[112] Pitt's whole career, after all, had been built on the Foxite disaster of 1784. To leave him in place was, in a sense, to forgive him his political origins. For the two men to work together, the slate had to be wiped clean by Pitt exchanging the prime ministership for another post. Coalition therefore foundered 'from ye Impossibility that Mr Pitt & Mr Fox should both be the same thing'.[113] To use Lord Sheffield's words, the problem was 'How to arrange Pompey and Caesar, Pitt and Fox'.[114] In setting this condition, Fox could hope to demonstrate to Portland the depth of Pitt's insincerity. Portland shared all Fox's prejudices about Pitt's behaviour in 1784. He, too, must see that, if Pitt sincerely believed a coalition necessary to confront a national emergency, serving with Fox under some neutral leader was a price he should have been willing to pay.

Fox's second condition for an arrangement with Pitt was even more telling. He wanted an assurance that Pitt had kept George III fully informed of these initiatives, and that the King had no vetoes or objections to exercise. Portland, under Fox's supervision, made it 'a preliminary sine qua non that H.M.'s approbation should not only be understood, but that it should be un-questionably authenticated previous to any step being taken'.[115] Fox rightly guessed that Pitt had not raised the matter with the King. Since George's consent was absolutely required for any changes in the Ministry, Foxites could conclude that Pitt's coalition offers were nothing more than a joke or a diversion. Leeds talked of coalitions with George on 14 August, and Pitt did the same four days later. Both men predictably found the royal response chilly, with Leeds concluding that the King's 'dislike' of Fox remained 'in full force'.[116] Fox always suspected, and now no longer doubted, 'that Pitt has ever meaned any thing but to make a division among us'.[117] Even Port-land came to agree that Pitt and Dundas were taking 'a favourable oppor-tunity for breaking the opposition and dividing us and F.'[118] The Associators and the Proclamation of April–May 1792 had tested Whig nerves severely, and had uncovered terrible weaknesses, but Foxites were still so far distant from Pitt as to demand honourable terms for a coalition, and prominent among those was atonement for 1784.

*

At the same time that Fox was confronted by challenges at home, events in France were moving quickly towards the demolition of the thesis that the Revolution there was nothing but a re-enactment of 1688. On 10 August, the Tuileries Palace was stormed and the French monarchy brought to an end. Commenting on this incident, Fox sadly reflected that 'There is a want of dignity and propriety in every thing they do.'[119] 'It seems', he wrote to his nephew, 'as if the Jacobins had determined to do something as revolting to the feelings of mankind as the Duke of Brunswick's Proclamation.'[120] Then, in the first week of September, came the prison massacres in Paris:

I had just made up my mind to the events of the 10th of August when the horrid accounts of the 2nd of this month arrived, & I really consider the horrours [*sic*] of that day & night as the most heartbreaking event that ever happened to those who like me are fundamentally & unalterably attached to the true Cause. There is not in my opinion a shadow of an excuse for this horrid massacre, not even a possibility of extenuating it in the smallest degree.[121]

Fox was genuinely appalled by the course of events in France between June and September 1792. The violence had been bestial. His friends like Lafayette and Talleyrand were now exiles or prisoners. Henceforth, the Foxites would have no personal knowledge of the leading revolutionaries. All analogy with 1688 had apparently gone.

Once initial shock had been overcome, however, the question had to be faced as to why the Revolution had degenerated into violence. Fox had a very clear answer, but it was one that sounded increasingly idiosyncratic to the political world in general and to erstwhile friends in particular. Terror and destruction had come about because kings, emperors, and empresses had made it impossible for the Revolution to run straight. Would-be despots never accepted the constitutional values of the Revolution and set out to eradicate them by forming the First Coalition. France's generous ideals gave way to emergency measures, which included terror, because she was attacked, not because she was attacking. As Fox told the Commons,

What was the cause of the revolution of the 10th of August 1792? Be it remembered, that he was no advocate for the conduct of the jacobins; no liberal man would accuse him of it; though he knew he must put up with that ill-founded charge from others . . . In fact, his [Louis XVI's] fate was in a great degree owing to his avowed connection with the nobility of that country; a nobility whose views were hostile to the interests of the people . . . If this were admitted, he had a right to say, that the catastrophe was no more accelerated by the wickedness of those who were attacked, than by the baseness and folly of those who defended.[122]

The Coalition of Prussia and Austria was an 'unexampled and infamous conspiracy not against France but against Liberty in general'.[123] Its defeat at Valmy had to be welcomed: 'No, no public event not excepting Saratoga and York Town, ever happened that ever gave me so much delight. I would not allow myself to believe it for some days for fear of disappointment . . . The defeats of great armies of Invaders always gave one the greatest satisfaction.'[124] Brunswick's 'Proclamation' threatening Paris was morally more repulsive than the overthrow of the monarchy.[125] Louis XVI had never worked sincerely with the Revolution, but had rather sponsored the invasion of his country by his fellow despots, the 'Barbarians' in Fox's terminology. As a result, 'it was necessary at any rate to begin by getting rid of him and them.'[126]

After the summer of 1792, there was very little that Fox could positively favour in French politics for the rest of his life. Thereafter, he endlessly found himself choosing between evils. He was always clear, however, that, as usual, 'Whig' values in France had been undermined by kings. Louis XVI and his fellow monarchs had never given constitutionalism a chance. The Revolution had gone wrong, because it had never been allowed a natural, or unhindered, growth. On this idea, an analogy with England remained powerful. George III, according to Fox, was temperamentally at one with the French king and the Austrian emperor. Liberty was as much at risk in England as in Europe. This had been the whole pattern of George's reign, and the war in France merely brought matters to a head. Therefore, as Fox told Mrs Armistead: 'Any thing that proves that it is not in the power of Kings and Princes by their great armies to have every thing their own way is of such good example that without any good will to the French one can not help being delighted by it, and you know I have a natural partiality to what some people call rebels.'[127] Should the Coalition aristocrats be foolish enough to attack France again, he thought they would 'risque the existence of their monarchies, & so much the better'.[128] The Girondin administration deserved to be given a chance, because they, like Fox himself, had been the victims of despots.[129] Such a view linked French events with the preoccupations of Fox's past political life, but the idea that terror and violence had been the fault of kings rather than mobs was barely comprehensible to more conservative Foxites, who saw only an unparalleled assault on property and legitimacy.

By the autumn of 1792, this re-evaluation of European events as a despotic crusade attempting to stifle the experiment in liberty being tried in France was firmly fixed in Fox's mind. But it had only been worked out in letters to his niece, nephew, and mistress. The political world in general was not yet privy to Fox's thoughts. Instead, they saw only continued ambiguities. He had not joined the Associators, but he specifically told Carlisle that he did not consider them 'as separated from the Party, and . . . that it ought to be our object to prevent such a separation, if possible.'[130] In response to Pitt's offers of coalition, Fox had not vetoed discussions, but had been deeply sceptical of their authenticity. As a result of all this, the Associators were furious that Fox refused to commit himself entirely to their cause, and yet remained quite confident that he would ultimately do so.[131] On the other hand, Portland, Fitzwilliam, and the grandees were equally sure that Fox was no democrat and that nothing should be done to tip 'the Colossus' into 'the arms of the Tookes and Paines'.[132] In the autumn of 1792, Fox's leadership rested on the belief, held by both wings of the party, that he was theirs.

Complaints within the Foxite ranks about Fox were not that he had become either a democrat or an alarmist, but rather that he had relapsed into his old inertia. Lord John Cavendish, an old friend, wistfully reflected that

C. Fox has suffered himself to be led too far one way, by some hotheaded people whom I believe He thought He could lead, and has suffered himself to be led by them, and the greater part of our people more alarmed than I see any grounds for, so that I only say with Candide 'Il faut Cultiver votre Jardin.'[133]

No one quite knew what Fox thought. According to Lauderdale, he thought 'in such a half way', refusing either 'to retire to St Anne's Hill—or to join what he thinks the best of two *bad* parties'.[134] Carlisle thought 'he has an unlucky tumble' between two stools.[135] The problem was not helped by the extreme difficulty, in October–November 1792, of getting Fox to London at all. As a result, there was little or no party preparation for the new session of Parliament, and once again Fox had been startlingly absent from politics at a critical point. When begged to come to Town, Fox demurred, claiming to see

an end to all pleasant or comfortable prospects in Politics and even to much of the satisfactions of one's private life . . . I own myself disappointed that they [his friends] do not *feel* more as I think they ought to do with respect to Pitt, that they have not resentment enough against him for the year 84 at a moment when the consequences of that *revolution* as Burke used to call it begin to appear (for them at least) so formidable.[136]

The parliamentary year of 1792–3 would be one of the most critical in Fox's career. During it, his new views on France would become explicit, and options taken. Such views on France were controversial, but they were not hysterical or implausible. Unfortunately, he did little or nothing to prepare his friends for them. Little wonder that Lord Spencer should view the approach of the new parliamentary session with foreboding. He fully expected 'some mischief to be brewed there'.[137]

*

Between December 1792 and March 1793, a series of events dramatically changed the context in which European politics were to be discussed. French armies entered the Low Countries and threatened the Channel ports. A revolution that had been attacked was now attacking. In January 1793, Louis XVI was guillotined. On 1 February, France declared war on England. In response to these events, Pitt began to put together emergency measures that were designed to guard against the possibilities of foreign invasion and domestic insurrection. Fox, believing that war was unnecessary and domestic sedition non-existent, saw these same measures as merely the culmination of a design to abrogate civil liberty in England. The war gave the King an excuse to accomplish what had been his dearest wish for the whole of the reign. In sharp contrast to the summer and autumn of 1792, these months saw a spasm of activity from Fox that was unusually energetic. Significantly comparing Pitt to Bute, Fox insisted that the bills he now proposed would 'make the whole business of the country for years to come . . . This is a crisis indeed it is and we cannot prevent its being so by shutting our eyes.'[138]

Firing off letters in all directions in the first week of December, Fox determined to oppose, even if it involved a rupture with Portland and Fitzwilliam. As he reported to Thomas Grenville,

If you thought me feverish in London you will now perhaps think me delirious; but if what I just now hear is true, and the Ministers call Parlt. assigning as their reason the danger of Insurrection or Rebellion I *will* (though I know you dislike that tense and so do I) move the impeachment of them the very first day of the meeting support me who will. I am too agitated to write coolly or perhaps rationally but this appears such monstrous & unheard of wickedness that I lose all temper & patience. What can be their motive for wishing a civil war?[139]

When he came to write to Portland on the same day, he confessed himself to be 'much heated', and his favoured punishment for Pitt had escalated from impeachment to 'a french Lanterne'.[140] All ambiguity in Fox's pronouncements was to be abandoned, as George III was believed to be joining his fellow despots in an assault on constitutionalism not only in France but in England also.

For once, Fox set out to direct opinion rather than follow it. At a party meeting on 1 December, 'he had declared he would not accede to this temporary suspension of opposition; that he sees no danger; that the French revolution or the French principles cannot affect us.'[141] At the Whig Club, three days later, Fox, using highly coloured language for the time, declared himself to be 'an advocate for "The Rights of the People" ', invited his friends to defend those rights as Hampden and Sydney had done, and ended by giving the toast of 'EQUAL LIBERTY TO ALL MANKIND'.[142] So great was the controversy that this behaviour had engendered that ally and enemy alike spent the next ten days trying to discover what Fox had exactly said and what weight could be given to words like 'people', 'liberty', and 'revolution'.[143] In fact, Fox's case was quite simple. France, fighting all the major powers of Europe and struggling with civil wars in nearly half of its departments, offered no threat to England. Equally, that small number of Englishmen who advocated violence were so insignificant that to take Draconian measures was to flatter them. This being so, other motives had to be found for the steady erosion of civil liberties. In this search, Fox's attention was inevitably drawn to a king. In 1792-3, he thought, George III would complete the half-finished work of 1784.[144]

In the debate on the King's Speech, on 13 December, the attempt to put Pitt's emergency measures into the context of the whole reign became explicit. Fox invested this speech with high moral purpose, telling Mrs Armistead that nothing 'shall hinder me doing & saying what is *right*'.[145] He told the Commons that

It was not merely at the outset of their career, when they stood up against the declared voice of the House of Commons, that this spirit was manifested, but uniformly and progressively throughout their whole ministry the same disposition has been shewn . . . Is it not wonderful, Sir, that all the true constitutional watchfulness of England should be dead to the only real danger that the present day exhibits, and they should be alone roused by the idiotic clamour of republican phrenzy and of popular insurrection, which do not exist . . . We are come to the moment, when the question is, whether we shall give to the king, that is, to the executive government, complete power over our thoughts.[146]

In this debate, Fox was defeated by 290-50,[147] and further parliamentary initiatives in January and February to mitigate the severity of Pitt's emergency measures were no more successful.[148] The Foxites had been reduced to a rump, and, although a formal separation from Portland and Fitzwilliam was still eighteen months away, in essence it had already taken place.[149] Once the prospect of war became real, all the erstwhile Foxites had to choose between George III and Robespierre as the greater danger to Whig values. For Fox to continue to talk of 1784 seemed to many no longer relevant, when the political agenda seemed so substantially remodelled. Fox was bitterly disappointed by these results, admitting that 'the King is at this moment quite Master of the country', but this remark is followed by the reflection that 'it does not signify as long as one is satisfied that one is doing right, and I am quite so.'[150]

The clearest evidence of the new monarchical tyranny was offered by the trials for sedition which began in 1793. Radicals were harried, their writings prohibited, and their societies broken up. As some of them went on trial for their lives, Fox took the deepest possible interest in their cases, sadly reflecting, by 1794, that 'there is not a *pretence* left for calling Scotland a free country, and a very thin one for calling England so.'[151] Under Pitt's emergency laws, sedition had been defined so loosely that everyone seemed to be 'at the mercy of the government'.[152] In terms of contempt for justice, there was little to choose between the Committee of Public Safety and Pitt: 'I do not think any of the French soi-disant judicial proceedings surpass in injustice

& contempt for the law those in Scotland . . . You will easily believe that I shall not acquiesce in this tyranny without an effort but I am far from sanguine as to success.'[153] Showing unusual energy, Fox threw himself into helping with the defence of Muir and Palmer, raising their case repeatedly in Parliament, and ultimately, as a final gesture of loyalty, dining with them in the hulks before their transportation to Australia.[154] Palmer thanked him for his 'kindness to the sufferers for liberty',[155] calling himself 'an obscure individual crushed by the tyrannical hand of government'.[156] This case had for Fox been 'strikingly disgustful',[157] but it typified the new mood in politics that George III and Pitt had deliberately brought about. Determined to oppose this development, Fox left the cover of the ambiguities of 1792, cost what it might in terms of his own political future.

*

Pitt's central argument, in the spring of 1793, was that the French and their Revolution were so menacing that war was justified, and that that conflict made all his subsequent measures expedient. It was this claim that Fox had to meet, and he did it by arguing that the war was unnecessary,[158] being promoted in England by men whose motives were not made explicit. Technically, France declared war on England, but the French were only formalizing hostilities that had been generated in London. Pitt claimed that war was inevitable, because the French threatened the navigation of the Scheldt and the security of Holland. Fox admitted these fears to be reasonable, but insisted that they were negotiable. France, already struggling to hold off Austria and Prussia and to contain counter-revolutionary guerrilla wars, must, he insisted, be anxious to maintain peace with England. On 15 December 1792, he moved a motion that a minister should be sent to Paris to settle outstanding differences, declaring that his 'motive only was, that they might know what was the real cause of the war into which they were likely to be plunged'.[159] Pitt refused to take up this suggestion, and, what was more sinister, he and Grenville were known to be reluctant even to meet the French envoy Chauvelin, with whom Fox was in contact.[160] It seemed only too clear to Fox that a settlement by negotiation was being deliberately ruled out, and that the most charitable explanation for this was that 'Pitt in these businesses is a great Bungler.'[161]

Pitt's arguments about Holland and the Scheldt were simply not credible, and, if the motives for war were not therefore commercial or strategic, they had to be ideological. Austria and Prussia had been the initial aggressors,[162] and George III had now engineered a situation in which he could persuade the English to join them in a campaign to restore absolutism to France. Fox objected violently to 'our engaging to aid the restoration of despotism', by 'collusively' seeking 'pretexts in the Scheldt and the Netherlands'.[163] A refusal to negotiate with a particular government in France was of itself tantamount 'to saying, that we would dictate to them a form of government'.[164] The First Coalition of Austria, Prussia, and Russia, of which England was now the ally and paymaster, had, as Fox insisted in the Commons, firm objectives:

with all due reverence for crowned heads, was it impossible to conceive that kings might love, not limited, but unlimited monarchy; and that resistance to the limited monarchy attempted to be established in France, in the room of the unlimited monarchy, by which the country was formerly governed, might have been the true cause of the combination of some of the crowned heads of Europe?[165]

If further proof were needed, the partitioning of Poland in 1793 and 1795 between Austria, Russia, and Prussia, at which England barely murmured in protest, made the point. Fox deeply deplored the executions of Louis XVI and Marie Antoinette, but saw greater criminal intent in the elimination of a whole nation from the map of Europe.[166]

   Once George III had become the ally of his fellow monarchs, it was, furthermore, not only the liberties of France and Poland that were at risk. England too was threatened by what Fox insisted on calling 'the cause of Kings'.[167] The opportunity would be taken to undo all the constitutional gains of 1688. The abrogation of so many civil liberties in the spring of 1793 was simply the start of the process, and Muir and Palmer its first victims. As Fox lectured his nephew:

We live in times of violence and extremes, & all those who are for creating or even for retaining checks upon Power are considered as Enemies to Order . . . I feel it at the same time to be a most critical period, for if all these horrours [*sic*] abroad and at home can be endured with the bad success of the war, what will or rather what will not be the power of the Crown if Chance should ever make us prosperous?[168]

Pitt, though not a fool, had 'surrendered himself up entirely into the hands of the Court', not out of principle, but 'for the sake of office'.[169] For Fox, the issue of the war took on a black-and-white quality. What was at stake was not the navigation of a river in the Low Countries, but the real possibility that despotic monarchy could become the uniform pattern of government from London to Moscow. That in itself justified persistent calls for peace. Whiggery, historically defined as the containment of executive power, had never faced a greater crisis.

   This interpretation of events was not to be modified by new French atrocities. True, he admitted that 'the daily murders in France do really affect one's spirits.'[170] The execution of Louis XVI was an example of 'wild extravagance & unfeeling cruelty' that 'stained the noblest cause that ever was in the hands of Men'.[171] The death of 'the poor Queen' was 'attended with every circumstance that could contribute to make the act more disgusting & detestable than any other murder recorded in History'.[172] Crucially, however, such expressions are always balanced by reflections on the cruelties of despots, and their sins were the blacker if only because French atrocities were committed in the name of a threat that was real, whereas Pitt and his allies fabricated threats in order to persecute. As he put it, 'the danger which the Jacobins announced to their countrymen were [*sic*] not quite so ideal as our alarm.'[173] There was, therefore, 'some comfort in seeing that, while the French are doing all in their power to make the name of liberty odious to the world, the Despots are conducting themselves to shew that Tyranny is worse'.[174] Once war started, Foxites had no option they could positively favour. Jacobins were murderers of their friends. Despots were despots. There was no constitutional alternative. Forced to choose between two real evils, therefore, they had to opt for France, as having a revolution that was forced to go wrong but which yet might come right, against despotic certainties. 'Every thing in the world seems to be taking a wrong turn,' Fox gloomily recorded in the summer of 1793, 'and strange as it sounds, I think the success of the wretches who now govern Paris is like to be the least Evil of any that can happen.'[175]

So far had Fox broken cover with remarks such as these that many contemporaries simply came to the conclusion that he was 'leagued with the Jacobins'.[176] With French armies on the offensive, it was hard to believe that Fox genuinely feared George III more than the Committee of Public Safety. British spies in Paris reported to Grenville that Fox was being paid by the French.[177] He was accused of writing letters to Frenchmen 'of a dangerous tendency'.[178] Embarrassingly, Frenchmen wrote to him. Dumouriez, the leading French general in the early months of the war, asked Fox about the possibility of political asylum, expecting 'avec impatience une réponse de l'homme de l'Angleterre que j'estime le plus'.[179] It was compromising that Vergniaud, in releasing a former mistress of the Prince of Wales from a Parisian prison because she was a friend of Fox, should claim that 'Mr Fox is our friend; he is the friend of a free nation; he loves our Revolution.'[180] The caricature of Fox the *sans-culotte*, complete with *bonnet rouge* and dagger, becomes the stock-in-trade of cartoonists for the remainder of the decade. Close friends like Fitzwilliam found Fox's views on France puzzling.[181] Enemies thought them treasonable. Lady Stafford, for example, was clear that Fox 'does his utmost to bring this Country into the same miserable Situation in which France is'.[182] As rumours spread that the French were paying for pikes to be distributed in London, it was incredible that Fox should lean 'to opinions which, if not destroyed, must destroy all order and civilization in Europe'.[183] So controversial had Fox become that Mrs Crewe, in organizing a party, was not sure that he could be introduced to the 'corps diplomatique'.[184] Fox detested the Jacobins, but he was seen to prefer them to a cause for which England was fighting, and that alone was enough to convict him of the same opinions as Robespierre in the public mind.[185]

*

Fox's opposition to the war and the measures which it occasioned represented the major period of activity with regard to the Revolution. It was also the period when the Foxites ceased to be a viable party in opposition. At various dates in 1793, individuals like Loughborough, Windham, and Elliot formally severed connections with Fox. Others regularly voted against him while remaining in political association. In divisions, Fox could only muster fifty or so votes. The Foxites had become a rump or pressure group, with little or no prospect of seriously challenging Pitt. Portland and Fitzwilliam never broke with Fox until July 1794, but Malmesbury was not far off the mark in claiming, by May 1793, that the party was 'dispersed & broken'.[186] Breaking political friendships that had endured for many years was a painful business. Many men had simply delegated all political decisions to Fox. His politics became theirs. For Portland, for example, Fox was his 'vampire—he fascinates him, benumbs the operation of his reason & judgment & even of his conscience.'[187] Little wonder that, much to Burke's annoyance, it took them so long to throw Fox over. As for Fox himself, the splintering of old associations was acutely distressing in a man who rated friendship as more important than politics. He sadly reflected that he could 'not help loving the D. of P., and if with him the D. of D. & Ld. Fi. are to go I never can have any comfort in Politics again.'[188] Not surprisingly, according to his nephew, Fox once again began to think of leaving politics altogether and to take preliminary steps towards doing so.[189] Without undue theatricality, Fox longed 'for a lodge in some vast Wilderness',[190] and relapsed into inertia. No speeches are recorded between June 1793 and January 1794.

What delayed formal separation until July 1794 was a continuing reluctance on the part of Portland and Fitzwilliam to forgive Pitt for his behaviour in 1784. Fox was right to harp on this theme. Its power was astonishing. Even while grandees grew ever more fearful about France, that fear only slowly ousted the detestation of Pitt in their minds. As Portland explained,

It will not be denied to me that the characteristick feature of the present Reign has been its uniform & almost unremitting attention & study to debase & vilify the natural aristocracy of the Country, & under the popular pretence of abolishing all party distinctions, to annihilate, if possible, the Whig Party. For these express purposes the present Ministry was formed, & that they have most religiously adhered to & most exemplarily fulfilled the purposes of their creation every Year of their existence would furnish us with abundant instances.[191]

Lord John Cavendish put the matter even more simply: 'with the temper & disposition of Pitt & the Systems & Schemes of the K. & his friends, it is not possible for any man who has the feelings of a Gentleman to continue for any time to act with them.'[192] Deserting Fox on the French issue did not automatically involve association with Pitt. Using the memory of old battles, Fox could influence.[193] Foxites would join Pitt only when the irritation and fear of executive power, based on the experiences of 1784, gave way to apprehensions about France. What is surprising is not that that process eventually took place, but that it took so long to come about. When the thread finally snapped, in July 1794, Robespierre was effectively finished and the Terror was on the point of being dismantled. Fox's arguments against war, as involving new powers for the executive, had currency because, even to deeply conservative men like Portland, George III and Pitt were frightening, even if France ultimately became more so.

The parliamentary session of 1794 added little that was new to the debate. Fox continued to argue that Pitt 'had uniformly pursued the same plan of throwing all power into the hands of the crown, to be spreading a false alarm of danger from one quarter to cover a real danger from another'.[194] He continued to insist that the war had been started 'by artifice',[195] in order to reimpose the old order in France, and that such a policy was 'madness'.[196] With a handful of supporters, he opposed further war measures. The stationing of Hessian troops in England, allowing French émigrés to join the British army and, above all, the suspending of Habeas Corpus all represented direct threats to the survival of parliamentary forms of government. A royal plot was now visible for all to see. Fox told the Commons that 'We had no invasion to fear but an invasion of the constitution.'[197] With a hint of menace in his words, he proclaimed 'the complete extinction of liberty; and he dreaded to think what must be the shocking alternative which he, and others who loved the true principles of the constitution, must be reduced to in the impending struggle'.[198] Fox had so far abandoned all constraints on language, that, when old friends protested, they were simply told that they were 'very wrong'.[199] For Fox, the civil and parliamentary liberties secured since 1642 were at risk, and therefore the stakes of the game were too high for niceties.

Under the pressure of these events, the seepage of Foxite loyalties continued, though these political farewells took many forms. Thomas Grenville wrote to say that the war had to be supported, and that therefore Fox could no longer be, signing himself 'Ever, my dear Charles, very truly and affectionately yours'.[200] Portland separated from Fox after an interview that was 'without any acrimony or coolness'.[201] On the other hand, the Ponsonbys changed their political allegiances with less regret, accusing Fox of a 'passion of popularity', and adding that 'when vanity takes possession of a man there is no saying what it will make him do.'[202] Fox, in turn, sadly reflecting that 'Our old Whig friends are many of them worse Tories than even those whom they have joined',[203] felt, by March 1794, 'like Sisyphus, to roll up the stone again which long before it reaches the summit may probably roll down again'.[204] He was right to recognize the fact that the Foxite party of 1784 had disintegrated, and that a new grouping had to be formed, based on a rump of votes in the Commons and a handful in the Lords. Whether Fox had, or ever had had, enough interest in politics to accomplish such a mammoth task was to become a matter of much debate.

*

As party loyalties unravelled, Fox tried to mark the crucial moments in this process for the benefit of William Adam:

Regrets are vain, but one cannot help thinking, *if* Burke had died four years ago, *if* Lauderdale had not made his Association, for he was the sole cause of it; *if* our friends would have been right headed upon the subject of that association, or even after all *if* last winter they would have kept aloof upon the Question of War, & contented themselves with talking Nonsense about domestic alarms—I really believe any one of these *ifs* would have ruined Pitt.[205]

Missing from this otherwise comprehensive list is any sense of his own failures of judgement. He had not tried to mollify or coax Burke; he had not exerted his authority to stop the Association of the Friends of the People in its tracks; and he, of all men, had not kept 'aloof' from the war issue. Spasms of activity, like that between December 1792 and March 1793, so much alternated with periods of inertia that Fox as often followed events as led them. Such an approach was workable as long as Fox's French friends were in control in Paris, happily constitution-making on the 1688 model. When they were chased out of France, in the summer of 1792, Fox waited too long before coming up with a new interpretation of these developments. Then, as before, Fox's inertia allowed Burke, Sheridan, Grey, and others to take damaging initiatives.

To an extent, these failings were the consequences of Fox's great virtues. For him, friendship, particularly an old friendship, was more important than the most profound, political debate. He found the disciplining of friends an almost impossible task. Rather than have a confrontational interview or disagreement, he would prefer to do nothing, increasingly retiring to St Anne's Hill to avoid wrangling. Further, these years once again raised the very real question of just how far Fox cared for politics at all. He could appear strangely unmoved by either victories or defeats. In June 1794, at a moment of the greatest tension at home and abroad, Fox's niece took up her perceptive pen to tell her brother that it was still difficult to determine their uncle's politics: 'He affects to be as virulent as ever in politicks, but as he sometimes laughs at his want of candour, I think it is more a love of argument & dispute than any fixed principle to him.' He had described himself as 'being only furnished with the common cant of my party', and 'opposed by the common cant of the other'.[206] His family were not surprised that he should revive ideas of leaving politics altogether. In the great debate on the French Revolution, the losing of friends had probably been as grievous to Fox as losing the argument. It was not that he had no principle. Indeed, his fear of royal despotism was genuine, as was his sympathy for those whom he took to be its victims. It was rather that when politics failed him, or he failed in politics, he had the personal and intellectual resources to drift away without regret into other activities. The French Revolution had established and reconfirmed patterns in Fox's political thinking. It had also so marginalized him that, ever after, politics was little more than a hobby, to be indulged with increasing reluctance. For the last twelve years of his life, he more and more preferred other things.

7

Secession from Parliament,
1794–1801

WHEN Portland and Fitzwilliam formally joined the Pitt administration, in July 1794, obituaries of the old Rockingham party were speedily written. Robert Adair asked, 'who can contemplate without sorrow, or describe without shame, the spectacle of whim and degradation it now exhibits; dispersed and dishonoured,—its chiefs in hopeless bondage to the power they had combined to limit, and that haughty instrument of its will from whose hands they would have torn its symbols.'[1] Fox himself was profoundly hurt. Referring to Fitzwilliam's defection, he commented that 'nothing can ever make me forget a friendship as old as my life.'[2] It was hard for him to accept that they 'would disgrace themselves as I think they have done'.[3] In terms of voting strength, the Foxites were now a lobby group rather than a party. They were no longer a credible opposition, but rather a band who could only engage in guerrilla tactics on the edge of politics. Points and arguments could be made, but not carried. For much of the 1790s, Fox's correspondence is full of hopelessness. He told Gilbert Wakefield, for example, that he agreed 'in thinking that no nation ever was sunk in more deep ignorance than we seem to be at present; for we are not only in the dark, but have a kind of horror of the light'.[4] The challenging of Pitt and George III's system had become symbolic.

Even in the black depression of 1794 and subsequent years, a core of Foxite politics remained intact, to act as the basis of a revived party. James Perry ensured that the *Morning Chronicle* remained at Fox's service; William Adam somehow managed to keep a shadowy party organization in existence for the same cause; above all, the fifty or so MPs who stayed loyal to Fox represented some of the best talents in the old party.[5] In the Lords, the Foxite preferences of the Dukes of Devonshire and Bedford meant that the historic names of Cavendish and Russell gave the Foxite interpretation of

Whiggery a certain credibility. With these props, Fox could never be completely and finally marginalized. Indeed, his group was at least viable enough to afford refuge to men who found association with Pitt more than uncomfortable. By December 1794, for example, the Duke of Grafton was once more co-operating with Fox.[6] More significantly, Fitzwilliam, if not returning to a Foxite allegiance, was forced to abandon Pitt after a brief, but appalling, experience as Lord-Lieutenant of Ireland. In writing to Fox, asking for the renewal of their friendship, Fitzwilliam claimed that he had been a victim of Pitt's malice 'from the day we kiss'd hands'.[7] Only 'the old Obstacle Grey & Sheridan' checked Fitzwilliam in his wish to resume full Foxite politics.[8] Oddest of all, Lord Lansdowne, the Shelburne of 1782, was forced by his opposition to Pitt's war politics to vote with Foxites and renew Fox's acquaintance. Their family connection, as uncles of the third Lord Holland, did something to make this astonishing *rapprochement* easier, but old memories ensured that their union was plainly one of convenience rather than affection.[9] However depleted in numbers, Foxites provided a rallying point for all opponents of the war, and for such an alternative to be represented in politics was valuable. It meant that those who disagreed with Pitt would not feel obliged to seek solutions outside established politics.

Further, the grim experience of 1789–94 had only strengthened Foxites in their interpretation of the reign of George III. They had lost numbers but not conviction. One of Fox's favourite devices, in letters of the later 1790s was to talk of the 'euthanasia' of the constitution. By this he meant the smothering of evil liberty and parliamentarianism, for which the war was cited as excuse. This dreadful threat could only be countered by 'the union of great families, considering this as absolutely necessary to maintain the popular cause against the Court'.[10] Great families had great property, and it was the ownership of property that interested a man in resisting tyranny and which gave him the ability to do so. Parliament was the forum in which property defended liberty. 'A parliament', Fox once said, 'was so good a thing, however ill it might be constituted, that, if it were to consist of the first five hundred men who should be met passing in a certain street, at a certain hour, it would be better than to have none.'[11] In this Fox saw his basic disagreement with Pitt. He had told the Commons in 1786 that 'I stand upon this great principle. I say that the people of England have a right to control the executive power, by the interference of their representatives in this House of parliament. The right honourable gentleman maintains the contrary.'[12] In the 1790s, by calling up imaginary fears and unnecessary wars, George III had succeeded in reducing Parliament to subservience. In so doing, as Holland recorded in notes for a speech, he had recalled Whigs to their obligation of destroying the influence of the Crown, that pestilential disorder which pervading every aspect of our Constitution has rendered the most essential parts of our system the seat of debility and corruption. The duty therefore of a publick man is to direct all his endeavours to the purpose of diminishing this influence without actually altering the forms of the Constitution.[13]

What is remarkable about Foxite politics in the 1790s, therefore, is the degree to which their priorities in politics had been unaffected by the French Revolution. They continued to talk the language of 1784. The Revolution and George's war had simply sharpened old arguments. Most men adjusted their politics in this decade, in the belief that war abroad and sedition at home had set new agendas. Since Fox and his friends thought the war unnecessary and sedition non-existent, their priorities remained the same. Writing in 1800, he reflected that patience, not violence, 'is the character of the Common People'.[14] Only food shortages could stir them to protest, and even then it would take traditional forms.[15]

It was the conservatism of the poor, not their revolutionary potential, which should be wondered at. Equally, the so-called threat from France was a nonsense. In 1796, it was 'visionary'.[16] In 1798, 'there is very little chance of serious Invasion of this Country at least.'[17] When invasion fleets did indeed set sail, their failure caused Fox little surprise.

The unlikelihood of a French landing was a great blessing, because such an event, more than anything else, would underline how gruesome options were in the black-and-white politics of the 1790s. As long as Fox could concentrate on the defence of parliamentary values in a specifically English context, there was a role for him to play. If the French came, any parliamentary option disappeared, and it then became a choice of tyrannies.

From Events however which may possibly be good I except a French Invasion which can do nothing but mischief. It is bad enough to be obliged to be passively obedient to the present system, but when one has just made up one's mind to that, to feel oneself in a situation where one must make active exertions in support & for the Establishment of such a Tyranny is the very Devil. And yet I cannot help feeling that if the French come, this is what we must do.[18]

Having to 'prefer George III'[19] was a sad possibility, but it was inevitable if other options closed completely. Until then Foxites could express their 'readiness to fight with swords & guns against the french, and with anything short of swords and guns against the present Tyrany [*sic*] and for radical Reform'.[20] In rejecting the French Revolution and George III in the later 1790s, preferring to talk of English politics and 1784, Foxites occupied a narrow territory. In the fear-laden atmosphere of the 1790s, the relevance of their remarks seemed often obscure. Yet the Foxite option allowed a notion of politics to survive which was not predicated on emergency, that could offer a basis for debate when heads cleared and fears subsided. Even in the hopeless situation of October 1794, Fox severely reminded his nephew that 'party is by far the best system if not the only one for supporting the cause of liberty.'[21]

*

Between 1794 and 1797, Fox, even in his diminished position, believed that there was a serious contribution to be made in politics. First and foremost, as the leading politician arguing that the war was unnecessary, he quickly became recognized as the head of a peace party. Men like William Wilberforce, who had no sympathy for Whiggery or its preoccupations about 1784, found themselves sometimes voting or speaking with Fox against a war which they saw as ruinous. Fears for the National Debt, concern for bankruptcies, and the idea that hardship, rather than Tom Paine, could turn the English poor into revolutionaries, created a peace party that had to acknowledge Fox as an ally. His diatribes against continued hostilities increasingly won him friends. In an important speech of 10 May 1796, some four hours in length, Fox masterfully reviewed the whole course of the war, concluding that 'The great defect in the management of the war . . . has, in my opinion, been the want of a determinate object for which you have been contending.'[22] If a return to absolutism was not indeed in prospect, Pitt had gravely misled French émigré opinion in England and Europe.[23] If a constitutional future was hoped for, why was Lafayette still confined in an Austrian prison, and why had Alexandre Lameth been deported from England?[24] It was clear that Pitt's war aims had been confused at the outset, and had failed to become any clearer as the war went on. After two years of conflict, 26,000 men had been killed, £50 million in new taxes had fallen 'with terrible weight' on the shoulders of 'the middling ranks' of society, and all for objectives that Pitt could not define.[25] Many people who generally damned Fox's morals and principles could not help but give half an ear to words such as these the longer the war dragged on.

There was still work to be done, admittedly in a spasmodic and uncoordinated way, in symbolically opposing the government's further assaults on civil liberties. These could only be gadfly attacks, but they were useful in suggesting to dissidents that the political élite was not monolithically against them. Sympathy at least, and possibly change in the long term, was forthcoming without recourse to violence. Fox obviously relished denouncing the Loyalist Associations of John Reeves, as a system designed to run the country through 'the infamy of spies and intrigues'.[26] More ominously, an attack on the King's coach, as he drove to the opening of Parliament in November

1795, gave Pitt the excuse to introduce Sedition and Treason Bills, which Fox regarded as the most serious threat to English liberties yet. They were measures

whose direct tendency it is to prohibit all public discussion, whether in writing or in speaking, of political subjects . . . There appears to me to be no device at present but between an absolute surrender of the liberties of the People and a vigorous exertion attended I admit with considerable hazard at a time like the present. My view of things is I own very gloomy, and I am convinced that in a few years this Government will become completely absolute, or that confusion will arise of a nature almost as much to be deprecated as despotism itself . . . This is a great *Crisis*.[27]

Challenging the treason bills of 1795 represented Fox's only parliamentary campaign of any sustained character for nearly a decade. He spoke no fewer than ten times in debate, arguing that to check a free expression of opinion was to bottle up frustration to a point that it would become explosive. He warned the Commons that 'if you silence remonstrance and stifle complaint, you then leave no other alternative but force and violence.'[28] His anger was such that he agreed, though 'with a sort of reluctance', to a campaign to bring pressure to bear on Parliament from outside.[29] A petitioning movement subsequently enjoyed some success.[30] More spectacularly, on 16 November 1795, Fox addressed a public meeting on the subject of the two bills. His audience was variously estimated at between two and thirty thousand people.[31] It was a great Foxite success, as Wordsworth reported to Coleridge:

A little after 12 the Hustings being prepared, the Duke of Bradford &c. came upon it. Much hallooing & clapping on their appearance. The Duke was dressed in a Blue Coat & a Buff waistcoat with a round Hat. His hair cropped and without powder— Fox also cropped, and without powder,[32] His Hair grisly grey . . . After much acclamation Fox adressed [*sic*] the multitude stating the loss of liberties of the people, if the Bill passed, and calling upon them to come forward and support a Petition to the House of Commons against it.[33]

Fox hugely enjoyed the outing. It left him with the conviction that, although Pitt had reduced Parliament to subservience by corruption, Foxites had 'the popularity, and I suspect we shall have it universally among the lower classes'.[34] The élitist and closed world of Foxite Whiggery would always be suspicious of exciting mere enthusiasm, but, in the dire circumstances of 1795, other options were few.

Fox's sporadic sniping at the war and war measures between 1794 and 1797 did little to raise his reputation among those within the political pale generally, the peace party still being a small minority. In his anger, he often used words and phrases unguardedly, unaware or indifferent to the fact that, in revolutionary times, words change their meaning. In March 1795, he had advanced the startling view that the House of Commons was no longer 'the representive of the people'.[35] The success of the campaign against the sedition bills of 1795 convinced him that they were passed 'against the will of a great majority of the people of England', making 'obedience no longer a duty, but a question of prudence'.[36] The ambiguities raised by statements such as these alarmed contemporaries. By 'people', did Fox refer to the political nation or to the nation as a whole? Had he, in other words, abandoned the traditional Whig insistence on linking representation to property to become a Democrat? Even worse, if Parliament was no longer thought competent, was Fox recommending a defiance of its laws? Some of his speeches seemed to suggest this. In April 1796, he referred ominously to 'the right inherent in freemen to resist arbitrary power, whatever shape it may assume, whether it be exerted by an individual, by a senate, or by a king and parliament united. This I proclaim as my opinion. In the support of this principle I will live and die.'[37] Even if, as was no doubt the case, he was referring to the hallowed and respectable examples of resistance to arbitrary power offered by 1688 and 1642, these words sounded menacing in the charged atmosphere of 1795 and 1796. Foxites began to be described as 'factious traitors'.[38] According to Burke, Fox's politics 'are astray and absurd; and he cultivates and studies nothing at all at home but whatever is most wicked, unprincipled, dark, dangerous and traiterous [*sic*]'.[39]

The years 1794 to 1797 therefore set a new pattern of Foxite politics. They were no longer an opposition but a pressure group. The prospect of office receded: they could hope for a few old friends to rejoin them after experiencing the duplicity of Pitt; they could expect their peace initiatives to win votes in specific debates; above all, their existence offered a constitutional channel for dissidents to voice their opinions. No larger ambitions were realistic. Freed by this realization from the responsibility of potentially being members of a government, Foxites could indulge themselves in highly-coloured language. They had little to lose, except what little reputation they had. As the campaign against the sedition bills of 1795 indicated, they could irritate and alarm, but they could no longer materially affect the course of politics. The reduction of politics to a series of symbolic gestures greatly increased Fox's long-standing disenchantment with the whole business of public life. In 1797, he decided to secede from Parliament altogether.

*

Secession was determined on, at a dinner at Holland House in October 1797. It was not undertaken lightly. The main motive, as Lady Holland recorded, was that 'all their discussions end in the loss of time and temper, for Opposition are too unpopular to have anything left to hope for, and the system of party is obsolete.'[40] Implying as it did that the House of Commons was no longer an effective forum for the representation of the electorate, Fox's secession was a serious, some said treasonable, matter. As early as 1794, rumours circulated that Fox, like Burke, would shortly leave politics,[41] and, although these were unfounded, his family was fully aware that he 'seemed quite sick of politics', and that he looked forward 'to nothing with pleasure but the quiet of St. Anne's Hill, & how he bore the disappointment of being detained for the Habeas Corpus on Saturday I cannot tell'.[42] In April of that year, Fox began to describe the House of Commons as 'this cursed Place'.[43]

Never wholeheartedly a politician, he was convinced by the splitting up of his party in 1794 and the passing of the sedition bills of the next three years that the game had been lost. Admitting that Burke and Cicero might have been a little more robust in adversity, Fox nevertheless insisted that 'No good can ever be done now but by ways in which I will never take a share, and for which I am . . . unfit.'[44] Lords and Commons had been so infiltrated by the servants of the Crown that they had lost all capacity to challenge kings. Attending their debates merely gave them a spurious respectability. 'To this resolution', Lord Holland observed, 'his thorough conviction of the inefficacy of opposition his declaration last session & his opinion of the state of things altogether led him, & his idleness & joy at getting rid of Politics for the whole winter confirmed him.'[45] Foxites were divided by Fox's decision not to attend, but he had powerful allies. Grey, for example, agreed that there was no point in 'exertions wch. only subjected us to daily insult, witht. producing any benefit to the Country'.[46] Attendance would only 'encourage a delusion through the country, that measures were to be carried in that House by argument and the force of truth, when they certainly were not to be carried by such influence'.[47]

There was to be little change in Fox's thinking over the next four years. He believed that 'the Country is wholly without spirit'.[48] As the constitutional gains of 1642 and 1688 were reversed, the only surprising feature of politics was that no one protested. The King and Pitt had raised up so many spectres and terrors that they had become masters of everything. 'Neither of us I believe', Fox wrote to Lauderdale, 'expected that every vestige & shadow of what used to be called Liberty would be extinguished quite soon, and with such general good humour & acquiescence.'[49] He expected no change in the situation during his lifetime.[50] As a result, it was long an open question if he would again offer himself as candidate for Westminster in the general election expected in 1802. Equivocation marked his letters to his agent in the constituency: 'Events *may* happen as might make it right in me to attend, for which reason I do not go out of Parliament. On the other hand, I think any such Event so unlikely that it is not worth while to come into Parliament for the chance of it.'[51] In March 1798, Fox sold his London house.[52] For the rest of his life, he was physically and psychologically based at St Anne's Hill in Surrey. The miles between Chertsey and Westminster protected him from political importunity, except by the most determined. The break was very final. He told O'Bryen that 'I consider myself as having quitted London with little exception for *good and all* as the phrase is; I know there must be many who blame me, but I am convinced that in these times I can do no good, and therefore think I have a right to consult my ease.'[53]

Once the decision had been taken, Fox took his secession from Parliament very seriously. For nearly four years between 1797 and 1801, Fox effectively ceased to be a public figure. When this self-denying ordinance was broken, as in a single speech of March 1800, Fox insisted that he 'did it more in consequence of the opinion of others, than from my own; and when I came back, and read the lines 1451, 2, 3 of Lycophron

> Wretched me, why do I cry to stones which cannot hear,
> To the dumb wave, to horrid woods,
> Making vain noise with my mouth.

I thought them very apposite to what I had been about. In the last of the three, particularly, there is something of comic, that diverted me, at my own expense, very much.'[54] Outside Parliament, Fox occasionally attended annual dinners held at the Shakespeare Tavern in the Strand, on the anniversary of his return to Westminster.[55] As far as Fox had a platform in these years, however, he found it in meetings of the Whig Club. There, among friends, he could speak openly in a forum that did not carry the dangers of a public meeting.[56] Even these though he attended more out of duty than pleasure, and he never attended with that frequency that would satisfy his friends, arguing that 'nothing of what I think is fit to be said in public'.[57] He accepted that his presence was required from time to time to keep the Whig Club securely in Foxite hands, but even then expressed the wish that 'the Meetings could be less frequent'.[58] His retirement, according to his wishes, was not from Parliament alone, but from all platforms.

So complete was this withdrawal that he refused to make a parliamentary appearance on single issues, however startling or momentous their nature. The introduction of an income tax was immediately interpreted as an astonishing assault on the rights of property, but Fox was not moved even to read the Act.[59] For him, the passivity with which the proposal was received simply convinced him that 'Ergo tout est fini.'[60] Even more significant was Fox's refusal to implicate himself publicly in the ongoing crisis in Ireland, that began with the rebellion of 1798 and ended with the Act of Union in 1801. In theory, it should have excited his profound interest. His uncle the Duke of Leinster had been a leader of the Irish Volunteer Movement in the 1770s. His cousin Lord Edward Fitzgerald died in prison after leading the 1798 uprising. The Dublin Parliament, which the Act of Union destroyed, had been one of the few tangible achievements of the Rockingham–Shelburne administration of 1782. In one of his last speeches before seceding, Fox had gone out of his way to praise the establishment of a Dublin Parliament, arguing that, if its existence had not been able to pacify the country completely, the reason was to be found, as ever, in its benign influence being 'counteracted by the influence of the executive government and of the British cabinet'.[61]

All of this encouraged his friend Fitzpatrick to think that the Irish crisis might be sufficiently compelling 'to rouse him from his den, & to inveigle him from the Muses for one day'.[62] He was wrong. Fox was certainly much exercised by developments in Ireland, but with only limited results. He was happy to encourage patriots like Henry Grattan.[63] He spent much time lecturing his nephew on the value of the 1782 settlement, and in providing him with arguments that proved that the Dublin Parliament had no powers within that settlement to vote itself out of existence.[64] He detested the brutality with which the 1798 rebellion was put down, not least in regard to his own family,[65] accusing Castlereagh of 'profligacy & impudence' and the government of a wish to 'conceal & misrepresent all they can'.[66] Expressions of concern for 'poor Ireland' punctuate Fox's correspondence in these years.[67] Even so, its sufferings were not enough to bring him in from the wilderness. He encouraged others to attend and gave them points for their speeches, but that was as far as he could go.[68] As he explained to Grey, were he to make an exception of the Irish debates, such an 'exception will furnish an argument for attendance upon some other question, and thus the whole plan of my Secession completely destroyed'.[69] His withdrawal from public life was intended to be very final.

Naturally, Fox's seclusion prompted much debate. To many, he seemed to be showing a contempt for Parliament that, together with the other statements and actions, confirmed an impression of treasonable activity. If Fox refused to recognize Parliament as effective in its representative function, there was an implication that true political legitimacy might lie elsewhere. It was sinister that leading Radicals had already tried to call a rival

parliament, or convention. Denying Parliament's competence, or charac-
terizing it as so corrupted by royal influence as to be nothing more than a
club for the King's friends, carried large implications. Such suspicions were
completely unjustified, but they had a wide currency and materially black-
ened Fox's character yet further.

In fact, Fox's rejection of Parliament was passive. It involved no attempt
whatever to set up an alternative, or even to subject it to pressure from outside. As early as 1795, Fox had assured the Commons that 'he did not see
that his attendance at public meetings could be of any use to the public'.[70]
Fox left Parliament, not to find a new power base, but simply because there
was no fight left in him. George III had quite simply won. Meetings were
futile. As he confided in a friend:

I should agree . . . about trying for meetings if there appeared to be any disposition in
our friends to any activity, but I do not think there is, and it is sad work to be urging
People against the grain. I do heartily wish I could retire altogether from Politicks
with honour, for as to doing good I am convinced it is out of my power.[71]

Following a much-repeated pattern in his career, Fox refused to forbid
younger men from trying for petitions from the London area and Yorkshire
in January 1798, but had 'no hope of any good'.[72] When the attempt failed,
he was not surprised that the 'business will not do'.[73] He hated to discourage
those with energy or enthusiasm, but, throughout 1799 and 1800,[74] Fox's
inertia was a major factor in dampening petitioning movements and meetings of all kinds. Indirectly, he blocked them, as he confessed to Fitzpatrick:

The D. of B. must have misunderstood me if he thought I encouraged Meetings by
what I said at the Whig Club. And surely saying that Petitions could be of no use
unless they were very general, and unless too they condemned not only the war but
the whole system of Government, had a Tendency rather to discourage them.[75]

In taking this attitude, Fox gravely disappointed reformers. Men like
Christopher Wyvill had voted against him in 1784, but, as Pitt withdrew
more and more from reforming interests, they were forced once again to
seek his company and co-operation. Wyvill, writing to Fox in October 1799,
hoped 'to restore to the Public the powers of Animation which have been so
long suspended'.[76] His expectations were not fulfilled. Fox's secession from
Parliament in no sense implied that he would challenge its authority.
Indeed, he did much to persuade the others not to do so. Again and again,
Fox offers a diagnosis of a national mood that was so supine and acquiescing
that all political life seemed to be in suspension. There was no basis for resistance, let alone treason. It was a time to cultivate gardens. He was aware,
however, that there was a charge to answer: 'As to malicious interpretations, they of course will be given to one's conduct and will be more or less

believed, but nothing one can say can prevent that Evil. That Secession is a measure liable enough to misconstruction I admit.'[77] A refusal to flirt with movements outside Parliament was one answer to this accusation. He wanted peace, not activity in another sphere.

Another answer was to make secession personal to himself. It was Fox who left Parliament, not the Foxite group as a whole. Fox insisted to his nephew that 'there was not agreement of opinion enough on the subject to make it possible to take what one may call a *measure*.'[78] Sheridan and Tierney never seceded at all; Grey and Bedford did so intermittently. Crucially, Fox himself was very happy with this situation. He declared that he would 'not be at all sorry to find myself the sole Seceder', admitting that if he were 'younger', he 'should not like to give up the point'.[79] Even if one man had come to hold Parliament in such contempt that he felt obliged to absent himself from its proceedings, treason was hardly in question if he took no effective steps to find a remedy. He endlessly insisted to Grey and Holland that the old Foxite connection, as far as it remained a force in politics at all, could and should operate without him.[80] To close friends, he confessed a wish to

get quite rid of Politicks. As to the Publick Good I am sure it is no matter whether I do or not, as to Safety much the same, the only question is Reputation which I do not pretend to despise, but even as to that all one can hope for in these times is negative success in that respect, and, if hereafter it is said that I at least had no part in such & such things it is all I can look to.[81]

Foxite values were not to be unrepresented in Parliament because Fox had left it. The retirement of an individual is not treason.

Psychologically and spiritually, the secession of 1797 offered Fox enormous relief. Politics had never been the whole of his life. Perhaps public life had never been his major interest. To have done with it at last gave him great pleasure. He repeatedly told Denis O'Bryen that he was very unlikely to stand for Westminster in an election expected in 1802. Even when he did return to formal politics in 1801, the number of speeches that he made in Parliament was astonishingly small. The journey from St Anne's Hill to Westminster seemed harder and harder to undertake. In a profound sense, Fox never returned to politics after 1797. Even when he reappeared in the Commons, he behaved as a man performing a painful duty. All pleasure in politics had gone, even that of making Pitt's life as miserable as possible. Instead, contentment was to be found in his new family, old friends, and the pursuits of literature and history. Perhaps the demonstrable hopelessness of politics that prompted the secession finally allowed Fox to live the life that he had always wanted to live.

So personal was his retirement that he endlessly encouraged others to attend. As he explained to his nephew:

I own I remain very averse to the thoughts of more than one day in the *House* of *Commons* for *me*, but I do confine my opinion exactly to my expression, and I do not see why those who have any inclination or fancy there is any good opportunity should not attend. I am sure it would do no harm, and if it excites any sensation it would do good.[82]

Grey, always tendering for advice, was told the same thing.[83] Indeed, so anxious was Fox that his values should endure in parliamentary politics that, throughout the secession years, he was looking for someone to take over the leadership of his friends in a formal manner. Finally leaving politics would be easier if it were known that his battles would go on being fought by someone he could trust. He was sure that 'the more any new ones shew themselves the better'.[84] The obvious candidate was his nephew, Henry Fox, third Lord Holland. Family obligation had been one of the major factors taking Fox into politics and keeping him there. If that obligation could be handed over to a new generation, the abandonment of politics would be even sweeter. As one of the boy's guardians, Fox had taken enormous trouble to shape his personal and intellectual tastes. Exercising 'a sort of parental interest',[85] Fox gently told Holland what to think, what to read, and whom to like. In return, the boy idolized his uncle. He later recalled that 'I was, no doubt, swayed by my affection for him, as well as convinced by his arguments, to espouse the principles which have generally guided the popular party in this country called Whigs. He seemed to take pleasure in awakening my ambition, and directing it, both by conversation and by correspondence.'[86] In politics, he simply wished 'to be of service' to 'my U. Charles'.[87] Only in his marriage to the formidable Lady Webster did he act without his uncle's advice, and even then the new Lady Holland was wise enough not to confront or challenge her husband's established affections.

From 1797 onwards, Holland was pinched and prodded into taking a high profile in politics. Usually addressed as 'dear Young One', he was given advice on the procedures and tactics of opposition.[88] On Ireland, Fox provided arguments to be employed against the abolition of the Dublin Parliament, setting the historical and family context within which Holland was to speak.[89] Holland became in effect Fox's proxy in politics, with full licence to report and represent his uncle's views.[90] For two or three years, Holland was trained like a horse in a ring, and Fox clearly hoped that, sooner or later, he would so absorb family tricks that he would be able to perform unaided. Holland was more than happy to accept the challenge of those high expectations. He would be appalled, in due course, that his own son showed no interest in a political career, reminding him that

We Foxes owe as much to party as party can owe to us . . . I think you might have abstained from speaking in the way of disparagement of persons who have so often sacrificed their time, their money and their interests to opinions or if you will to illusions which they had in common with my Uncle & myself, or to their affection for him and his.[91]

Unfortunately, Holland simply lacked many of the credentials for the role that his uncle offered him. He was an amiable, easygoing man with many friends, but he was also a poor speaker, much embarrassed by a voice impediment; never commanded the intellectual authority of his uncle; and, importantly, suffered from a widespread belief among contemporaries that his political judgement was too often overborne by his wife. Holland was not equipped to lead the Foxites. The best he could do to serve his uncle was to turn Holland House into a shrine, where Fox's name and virtues would be venerated far into the nineteenth century.[92]

When Holland failed him, Fox turned to Charles Grey. This time, there was more formality about the handling of the mantle. Commenting on Grey's return to the Commons, Tierney made this plain:

This change has taken place in consequence of his having at last come to an Eclairessiment [*sic*] with Mr Fox the day before yesterday. Mr Grey is with his perfect, unqualified and distinct approbation to take the lead in the H. of Commons of which the friends of Mr F. are to be informed by himself, with a request that they will give their cordial support to this arrangement . . . I believe this to be a *real, bona fide*, transaction on the part of Mr Fox.[93]

There was no denying Grey's talent and promise, but he too could not quite fill the vacancy left by Fox's departure. For one thing, he was too much in awe of Fox, endlessly asking for advice and direction. For another, he was still only in his mid-thirties, with a parliamentary career that began as recently as 1786. As a result, it was not clear that he could impose his authority on Tierney, Sheridan, Fitzwilliam, and the Prince of Wales, with all of whom he had at one time seriously quarrelled. However strong the desire to leave politics altogether, Fox could not do so finally without accepting the risk that his values would not be safely transferred to a new party leader. The grooming of a successor had not been successful. It was a great disappointment.

Largely because no successor for leadership could be found, Fox's secession never developed into a final withdrawal from politics. He refused to attend Parliament, but retained his Westminster seat. To many people, within Foxite circles and without, this appeared to be nothing but an unsatisfactory half-decision. The logic of his arguments about the ineffectiveness of Parliament seemed to call for resignation. Denis O'Bryen, always against secession, reported that Fox's Westminster constituents were not too happy that they should be effectively unrepresented.[94] His appearances in the constituency were not undertaken willingly, lest, as his nephew explained, this grievance became too public and vociferous: 'however personally popular he may continue to be the measure of Secession is not one generally approved . . . Any desire expressed by his constituents or by any public meeting of his friends for his return to Parliament would be . . . distressing.'[95] Even Grey was convinced that Fox could not for too long claim the privileges and responsibilities of an MP without fulfilling the obligations. Rather 'he must determine either to return or relinquish our seats'.[96]

Westminster voters were not the only ones to express irritation. For men such as Richard Sheridan and Sir Philip Francis, a political career was not something that could be taken up or cast away at will. For them it was status and the prospect of salaries. Secession was a form of self-indulgence that Fox could literally afford, and they could not. Francis baldly told Fox that 'oblivion is Death'.[97] Much later, he wrote a character of Fox that is among the most hostile ever penned, including the phrase 'he *hated* very little, because in general he loved nobody'.[98] Fox's withdrawal was bound to compromise the careers of those who had remained loyal to him, and yet this fact seemed to concern him very little. Further frustration was involved for people like Sheridan and Tierney who saw themselves as potential leaders of a party. Fox's refusal either to lead or resign the leadership blocked them. In their view, it was very wrong for Fox to idle his days away at St Anne's Hill, while yet exercising *un pouvoir occulte* through Holland and Grey.

So impatient of Fox's behaviour did Sheridan become that, as early as 1797, he began to canvass the idea of an extended administration from which Fox would be excluded.[99] Maddeningly, Fox thought this idea very fair, only commenting on Sheridan's 'incurable itch . . . of distinguishing his conduct from that of those with whom he wishes to be supposed united'.[100] In a bizarre interview with George III, in May 1797, Fox himself gave his backing to the proposal, adding that 'he gave this advice with less scruple as he was himself determined not to accept office'.[101] He may well have been sincere in making these remarks, but they were unrealistic. Until he had finally departed from politics, his large shadow would fall across politics or politicians that were called Foxite. The political agenda for opposition had been defined by him. He had intellectually moulded many of the young men who had remained with him after 1794. For better or worse, the party was

Foxite. Until Fox cut the last thread attaching him to politics, all competitors were hamstrung. Had Holland or Grey been able to take on the burden, retirement would have held every attraction. As it was, only secession was possible. Ambiguities were inevitably set up in the public mind and among those with careers to worry about. The adulation of Grey and Holland was such that they were happy to live with these ambiguities. Sheridan, Tierney, Francis, and others were not. The complexities of politics between 1801 and 1806 have their origins in the jealousies engendered in the Secession years.

*

Fox's secession looked even more suspicious because contemporaries began to argue that he was so disgusted with Pittite repression and so sure that he was helpless to counteract it that, through levity or desperation, he became the creature of the Radicals. In truth, some evidence could be found for this notion. In the 1790s Fox noisily defended prominent radicals in court and out of it.[102] Further, with that carelessness with words that often enlivens a good dinner, on one or two notorious occasions he gave invaluable copy to his enemies. In February 1798, at a dinner in the Crown and Anchor, Fox, in company with Horne Tooke, toasted 'Our sovereign, the People'. That toast was followed by another, 'Three virtuous Men, Citizens, have stood up in defence of liberty— MAXIMILIAN ROBESPIERRE, COLLOT D'HERBOIS, and CHARLES JAMES FOX'.[103] For this *jeu d'esprit*, Fox was to suffer the indignity of seeing his name struck off the list of Privy Councillors. Nothing daunted, Fox allegedly rehearsed the toast at the Whig Club meeting in May, adding a cheeky analogy between the repression of Pittite government and that of the Terror.[104] According to one report, the February toast had been made by men wearing *bonnets rouges*, the uniform of the *sans-culottes*, who were in such an advanced state of drunkenness that they had to be turned out into the streets by the Crown and Anchor waiters.[105]

The spectacle of Fox dining with Horne Tooke was in itself startling. The two men had fought each other as candidates for Westminster as recently as 1796. That Fox should apparently have adopted Tooke's vocabulary seemed to indicate a strange conversion to radical thinking. Why, after all, should he shun respectable debate in the Commons in favour of raucous toasts in London taverns? Cartoons multiplied showing Fox as a French sympathizer and revolutionary. Pittite doggerel underlined the point:

> A whisper in your ear, JOHN HORNE,
> For *one great end* we both were born,
> Alike we roar, and rant, and bellow—
> Give us your hand, my honest fellow

Charles, for a shuffler long I've known thee:
But come—for once, I'll not disown thee;
And since with patriot zeal thou burnest
With thee I'll live—or hang *in earnest*.[106]

Fox's behaviour was likened to the tantrums a child might display if
thwarted in its demands: 'not possessing powers to comfort, in your proper
station, the justice and integrity of an enlightened administration, you have
descended to associate with the very dregs of the people, and at a tavern in
defiance of all law, precedent, or decency—have hiccoughed out insults on
your king, and blended constitutional sentiments with obscene toasts.'[107]
Pitt himself was so angry that he seriously suggested that Fox should be
commanded to appear before the Commons, in order to offer apologies for
his remarks impugning their authority, after which he should be sent 'to the
Tower for the rest of the Session'.[108]

There can be no doubt that Fox's behaviour on one or two occasions gave
credibility to the charge of radicalism, and cast the whole period of secession
in a darker light. In fact, however, Fox took no steps towards the Radicals at
all. He disliked their ideas and, although he might help them as individuals
suffering persecution, he never cared much for their company. He had never
liked Paine's writing, and subscribed so little to Godwin's views that he
returned the *Political Justice* to the bookseller unfinished.[109] Radical alliances
were never in question. Rather, it was the Radicals who sought him out,
and, when they did so, they were sent away with a brusque answer. They
were people to be kept at arm's length. This was notoriously so in the Westminster election of 1796. Horne Tooke was anxious to convince voters that
he and Fox stood on a joint platform. Fox vigorously denied this, telling the
electors that 'I ask your votes for me only.' As if to emphasize the political
distance between himself and Tooke, Fox insisted that 'it was the constitution of 1688 he loved.'[110] Quite specifically, Fox's supporters were forbidden
to canvass votes for Tooke.[111] All through the 1790s, Fox had debated
politics in an English context, centring on a fear of George III. Events in
France were read as a commentary on English politics. Not surprisingly
therefore, having declared a willingness to fight the French if they landed, he
distanced himself from Radicals with ideas that took them outside the
context of the English debate.

If Fox mixed with Radicals in the 1790s, it was for traditional Whig
reasons, and in no sense suggested that he had come to share their views. It
was always held by the Whig aristocracy that one of their historical functions
had been to lead and moderate cries for change. Radicals left to themselves
became desperate. In the seventeenth century, men called Russell and

Cavendish had resisted kings at the head of a coalition that included, and contained, men of radical temper. The Foxites of the 1790s, including Russells and Cavendishes, were doing nothing that their ancestors had not done before. Ancestor-worship was the only religion that many Foxites knew. As Fox himself clearly explained to his nephew:

At present I think that we ought to go further towards agreeing with the democratic or popular party than at any former period for the following reasons. *We* as a party I fear can do nothing and the contest must be between the Court and the Democrats. These last without our assistance will be either too weak to resist the Court and then comes Mr Hume's Euthanasia which you and I think the worst of all events; or if they are strong enough, being wholly unmixed with any Aristocratick Leven, and full of resentment against us for not joining them, they will go probably to greater excesses and bring on the only state of things which can make a man doubt whether the despotism of Monarchy is the worst of all Evils.[112]

To push Radicals outside the pale of reasonable debate or to harry them with the law was to court disaster. Whig contacts with Radicals were invaluable, in that they proved that the views of the latter could be taken seriously and given a hearing.

As for the two controversial speeches of 1798, Fox simply could not understand why the King, Pitt, and the political world in general had reacted so violently.[113] When Fox toasted the sovereignty of the people, he was, as he explained to the Duke of Norfolk, using that word in a traditional way to denominate those with the necessary property to make them political men:

The toast relating to the sovereignty of the People will be universally and I believe truly considered as the cause of your removal[114] and thus you will be looked up to as the marked champion of that sovereignty under which alone, King William and the Brunswick Kings have held their throne . . . this appears to me to be far the most violent and frantic measure of all that have yet taken place.[115]

Fox was toasting 'the people' defined by the propertied values of 1688, not 'the people' conceived by the egalitarian ideas of the democrats. Therefore, he thought his words unexceptional, 'for it is impossible to support the Revolution [of 1688] and the Brunswick Succession upon any other principle'.[116] What Fox failed to appreciate was that if, after 1789, words like 'the people' had begun to take on more than one meaning, the consequent ambiguity could be damaging. Fox was unquestionably sincere in his protestations, but with French fleets in the Channel, such words were better avoided. They do not, however, convict him of democratic leanings.

Not surprisingly, leading Radicals never really believed that they had captured Fox. Horne Tooke's advances had met with a very modest response. Thomas Spence was even more explicitly bitter:

> The Foxites next do meet to dine,
> And sing and toast o'er good port wine,
> Extol their chief up to the sky,
> Nay, they almost him deify;
> But nought afford to give relief
> To patr'ot woe, or patr'ot grief.[117]

If Fox occasionally drank with Radicals, many believed that this was a cynical exercise in electioneering. Francis Place, looking back on the 'poor lousey Whiggery' of the 1790s, concluded that 'It is now no use to talk of old Foxey, who was always insincere, always the friend of the people, when out of place, always willing to sacrifice them to get a place.'[118] On the crucial issue of parliamentary reform, Fox found it difficult to convince himself, let alone a wider audience, that it was absolutely required. Further his insistence on relating events in France to English politics did not recommend him to men who found in those same events something quite new and exciting. Foxite Whiggery and Radicalism remained two quite distinct political traditions, which eyed each other with justifiable suspicion.

*

If the Secession and drinking bouts with Radicals needed to be explained away, so too did Fox's very public involvement in the trials of certain men who had fallen foul of the repressive legislation of 1792–5. Holding Radical ideas only by the fingertips in no way precluded the offering of assistance to men in trouble, particularly, as was usually the case, when they were close personal friends or relations. Significantly though, these trials were not only regretted because convictions would trample civil liberties under foot, but also because acquittals would bring into contempt the government that had promoted the prosecutions. As he sadly reflected, in a letter to Thomas Coutts:

If they are acquitted, which I think the least Evil, it will bring not only Ministry but Government itself into a great deal of contempt; and if they are condemned it will be a beginning of bloodshed of which no man can foresee the consequence, and one hardly knows which most to deprecate of its probable effects either complete intimidation and destruction of all spirit of liberty in the country, or a real destruction of the Government productive possibly of plots & violence such as happened in Charles the second's time.[119]

Not the least result of the malevolence of George III and Pitt was the likelihood that they would provoke the revolution which they claimed to be defeating. They were mad to spread 'an alarm over this country, under the influence of which they made Englishmen forget and forego their natural feelings of justice and humanity'.[120]

Despite these real and identified risks, Fox found the trials of the greatest interest and importance. If juries recorded verdicts of not guilty in the cases of men charged with treason, then it would give the lie to Pitt's claim that treason existed. Once that point was established, all the emergency legislation that had been predicated on the threat of subversion would be undermined. Even Pitt's excuse for fighting an increasingly ruinous war might be brought into question. The acquittal of Thomas Hardy and other members of the Corresponding Society was therefore welcomed as a major political victory. It was quite simply 'a good thing that the criminal justice of the country is not quite in the hands of the Crown'.[121] Extending the argument, he told the Commons that:

For my own part, I hardly remember when I felt joy more nearly approaching exultation than on these acquittals. I rejoiced that the country was rescued from the foul stain attempted to be fixed on it. I rejoiced that we had escaped from the perils of constructive treason. I rejoiced that the people would see through the slanders by which they had been deluded into a ruinous war; and, as I believe they have done, more in consequence of those acquittals than of any other circumstance, recover from their delusion, and wish that war at an end.[122]

Fox's personal involvement in the trials of Radicals in no way indicated that he approved of their views. He helped them because he was genuinely concerned about their fate, and because their vindication was in a sense his. If they went free, Fox would claim that his description of the country, not Pitt's, carried the greater credibility.

In particular, Fox became involved in three trials in 1798, in a manner that attracted a great deal of adverse comment. Each of them, however, had special features that compelled his interest. The first of these was the trial of Arthur O'Connor at Maidstone. London juries were no longer trusted by the government, and consequently the proceedings had been moved to a provincial centre. This in itself excited Fox's indignation. He told Fitzpatrick that 'they want a Jury more likely to be influenced by the Court than they have found the juries of the Metropolis to be. It must be owned they are as unrelenting Hunters of lives as ever lived, and I suppose they will have as much pleasure the first time they kill after so many misses as ever had the most eager Shooter.'[123] The pursuit of O'Connor, 'a very good man',[124] was so inhuman that in thinking of Pitt, Fox now believed that 'Robespierre was not *much* worse.'[125] Fox, Sheridan and others travelled down to Maidstone to give O'Connor character references. Fox's evidence was explicit:

I have known Mr O'Connor very well these three or four years, and conversed with him frequently on political subjects; he lived chiefly with my friends, who are called the Opposition, and he also lived in esteem and confidence with me, and I believe with others. I can describe Mr O'Connor to be one of the openest characters I ever knew; he was perfectly open in his friendship.[126]

Using a favourite analogy, Fox saw O'Connor's acquittal as evidence that 'Robespierrism' could still be resisted in England.[127]

Giving evidence on behalf of a man charged with treasonous practices was to touch pitch. Guilt by association was all too likely a consequence of such behaviour in the neurotic climate of opinion in the late 1790s. Grey believed that they had acted correctly, but was worried about the forfeits to be paid: 'Nobody I hope who knows us, can suspect either Fox or myself, or any of those with whom we are most immediately connected on public principles, of any design hostile to the Country, but the generality will not distinguish.'[128] In fact, Fox's appearance on O'Connor's behalf is once again no evidence that he had moved significantly in a radical direction. His evidence had been given under subpoena, not freely offered.[129] His words were restricted to the character, not the politics, of the accused. Above all, although this assistance was readily offered, Fox was anxious to spend only one day in Maidstone. Unlike Burdett, Thanet, and others, he had no wish to sit through the whole trial. For once in his career, Fox seems to have exercised caution. When Thanet and Ferguson were convicted of disrupting the O'Connor trial, Fox took no action on their behalf.[130]

The second case was that of Gilbert Wakefield, a classical scholar of repute, who was imprisoned in 1798 for writing what was thought to be a seditious work.[131] His conviction Fox regarded as 'a death blow to the liberty to the Press'.[132] It was a further point of concern that Wakefield was an old friend of Fox. The two men enjoyed a protracted correspondence, mostly concerned with classical literature, that obviously gave enormous pleasure.[133] Wakefield was Fox's guide and tutor in the classical world, and for that reason alone was, as a scholar, held 'in esteem'.[134] That such a man should be imprisoned for two years for his writings was 'incredibly nonsensical'.[135] From the start, Fox offered all the help of which he was capable, telling Wakefield 'to make no scruple about applying to me'.[136] When his friend was committed to Dorchester Gaol, Fox continued to write, and to use his Ilchester relations in Dorset to ameliorate the conditions under which Wakefield lived.[137] For him, the incarceration of a classical scholar finally proved, if further proof was wanting, that civil liberties had been extinguished. To use words and analogies that Wakefield himself would have understood, Fox began to liken himself to Brutus, the last of the Romans, watching helplessly as the Roman republic gave way to the despotism of the Caesars.

The third and final case, that of Lord Edward Fitzgerald, was the one which touched Fox even more poignantly. Fitzgerald was his cousin,[138] and Fox held him in great affection. He was 'the warmest hearted and the honestest of Men',[139] and 'dear to me'.[140] A son of the Duke of Leinster, Fitzgerald had spent the early part of the Revolution in Paris, renouncing his title and marrying Pamela, the illegitimate daughter of the Duc d'Orléans. In 1798, he led an unsuccessful rebellion against English rule in Ireland, and was shot while resisting arrest, dying later in prison. Once again, in spite of the severity of Fitzgerald's crimes, Fox offered to help. He told Fitzgerald's brother that he was prepared to go over to Ireland if that were thought helpful, adding

If you see my dear dear Edward, I need not desire you to tell him that I love him with the warmest affection. When I hear of the fortitude with which he has borne his sufferings, I hear no more than what I expected from *him*, though from him only could I have looked for so much.[141]

Controversially, Fox wished that he 'should have escaped'.[142] What particularly rankled was the government's attempt to dispossess Fitzgerald's wife and children. A family petition was organized, protesting against 'the violation of property in taking that of innocent Persons in actual and legal possession'.[143] When this particular attempt was dropped, Fox was relieved, telling Adair that 'otherwise I think they would have surpassed not only Robespierre but themselves.'[144]

These public interventions on behalf of men being prosecuted for sedition gravely compromised Fox's character and reputation. Inevitably his association with such men branded him with their attitudes in the public mind, and gave credibility to cartoons that showed him as a Jacobin. In fact there was no truth in any of this. As many Radicals realized, Fox never came anywhere near their views or beliefs. He spoke on their behalf under subpoena, or by responding to the demands of friendship or kinship. If Fox were ever to slip inadvertently into treason, it would have been because, confronted with a choice between loyalty to friends and loyalty to country, he would have had clear priorities. In a period in which nationalism and national loyalties were less fierce and defined, Fox's position was not in theory so unreasonable. What made it so, in the minds of many, was the political context in which such views were held. Invasion threats, food riots, and naval mutinies suggested dangers that Fox took little or no account of. Fox was not a radical, but contemporaries had good grounds for suspecting that he was.

*

The years between 1794 and 1801 set a new pattern in Fox's life. His campaigns against the coercive legislation of 1795–6 were, in a sense, his valedictory performance as a politician. Defeat on these issues convinced him that Pitt had won. There was nothing more to be done. The destruction of constitutionalism would now proceed apace, and all Fox could do would be to comfort and support those who suffered persecution. The hopelessness that he felt after 1797 would be hard to exaggerate. In response to their situation, he was not, however, pushed into Radicalism. That in itself would have been a positive and energetic rejoinder. By contrast, Fox's politics become passive, even apathetic. Its energies were, instead, channelled increasingly into academic and domestic pursuits.[145] He married. He took up new languages and recovered his facility with old ones. He appeared in London only infrequently. He began to write history. Politics were something that he increasingly resented, as distracting him from interests that he really found absorbing. Even when the secession came to an end, it is to be debated whether, psychologically, Fox ever returned to full-time politics. In middle age, men contemplate power-holding, and either find it a worthwhile activity or a nonsense. Fox found it more and more a bore.

8

Fox, the Directory, and Bonaparte, 1794–1802

As far as Fox retained an interest in politics after 1794, it lay in a continuing concern for France and the possibilities of a peace. He never shifted from the view that the war had been unnecessary, or that a peace was always available. For much of the 1790s, the French were represented as defending themselves against coalitions of despots, while at the same time struggling with civil wars, bankruptcies, and famines. His logic demanded that they should be eager for an end to hostilities. As for the war itself, it was simply degrading to the high culture of the eighteenth century. 'There seems to me to be a spirit of violence & oppression all over the world in all political parties', he told his wife, 'that is quite disgraceful to an age so cultivated in all other respects as the present.'[1] His early friendships and travelling had convinced him that France lay at the centre of this 'cultivation'. He once confided to a friend that to 'abstain from saying something expressive of my admiration for them' would count as 'an act of great forbearance'.[2] As regime followed regime in France, Fox naturally approved of some and disapproved of others. What was constant was an underlying command of thought, style, and culture that England could only copy, but never match.

Old friendships survived the bright hopes that were lost in the violence of the Terror. Having once described the men of 1789 as the French descendants of the Whigs of 1688, Fox continued to find traces of Whiggery in the Directory, with the young Bonaparte being cast as the Duke of Marlborough.[3] As first Talleyrand and then Lafayette returned to active politics, so the Foxite connections in Paris once again blossomed. A reciprocity of political values was recognized by these men across the years. Lafayette defined the phenomenon as 'cette Sympathie de Liberté et de patriotisme qui Unira toujours, j'ose le dire, Certaines Ames'.[4] When Talleyrand arrived in London as a political refugee in the autumn of 1792, the Foxites had unhesitatingly compromised themselves by entertaining him. When Lafayette languished in an Austrian prison, Fox tried to offer assistance by repeatedly raising the matter in Parliament, and news of Fox's efforts reached the prisoner 'au fond de ma prison'.[5] Lafayette saluted the Foxites as 'les dépositaires des principes sacrés de Liberté et de justice dont les despotes et les Anarchistes tâcheraient d'effacer les traces'.[6] In return, Lafayette entertained Fox on his visit to France in 1802. When Fox died, in 1806, Lafayette was one of several Frenchmen to send letters of condolence.[7] The connection was maintained thereafter, as Fox's friendships became a legacy for his nephew.

As has been noted, this Francophilia was widely known and frequently resented. In cartoons and letters, he is transformed into 'Citizen Fox'.[8] The press delivered stern lectures: 'Your language, your sentiments, were felt as Gallican—If your harangues in the House of Commons, and at the Whig Club, were to be published under any one title, *Vindiciae Gallicae* is that which, to the feelings of a large majority of Englishmen, would best designate their general contents.'[9] He was accused of leading a 'Jacobine [*sic*] set',[10] whose objective was to 'truly frenchify us'.[11] Cartoonists joyfully worked this rich vein. In *Promised Horrors of the French Invasion* of 1796, Gillray showed a French army marching down St James's. A guillotine has been erected at Brooks's for the dispatching of the Cabinet, and Fox is exultantly flogging Pitt, who is tied to a post capped by a *bonnet rouge*. In *A French Telegraph Making Signals in the Dark* Fox was depicted in treasonable stance, as a lighthouse on the cliffs near Dover, from whose eyes beacons of light are directing a French invasion fleet towards the English coast. When the Fox family visited Paris in 1802, cartoons suggested that they were adoring pilgrims going to worship at the shrine of the new god. Such examples could be multiplied again and again. Fox's dandyism and vices had long ago marked him as a lover of France, and therefore as a figure of suspicion. In the context of the Revolution, suspicion could only be transformed into profound mistrust. The political world would have been much relieved and surprised had they known, in 1798, that Fox's name was on a list of those who were to be transported after a successful French conquest of England. According to the list's compiler, Fox was a 'Faux patriot; ayant souvent insulté la Nation Française dans ses discours, et particulièrement en 1786.'[12] Ironically, however, Fox would probably have been equally surprised to find his admiration for France questioned.

In fact, a confirmed Francophilia never led Fox to be uncritical about Frenchmen. As he carefully explained to the House of Commons in 1795, he had approved of the overthrow of the monarchy,

But at no one time had he given an unqualified opinion of the governments which succeeded that event; much less would he stand pledged to give the least countenance

to the scenes of blood and cruelty which had been the almost inseparable attend-
ants on the varied and successive governments that followed one another. He formed his
opinion of government by the test of practice, and not by theory and on paper.[13]

After 1792, no regime could be given Foxite approval. Robespierre was
simply 'that despicable miscreant' in Fox's words,[14] and 'the greatest Monster
in Modern History' in those of his nephew.[15] As for the Directory, it was
good in that it had put an end to the Terror, but, on the other hand, it was
corrupt, financially incompetent, and apparently incapable of doing what
was 'right', namely restoring confiscated property. Above all, Fox shared
Burke's criticism of the French that they had too much confidence in paper
constitutions and were too eager to change everything at a stroke. Counselling the Spanish in constitution-making in 1808, Holland recalled that

> My Uncle used to say that when a law could be made in *half an* hour there could be no
> liberty as it was his opinion that a want of respect for forms was one of the chief
> reasons of the violences & extravagances which the French assemblies & convention
> committed. Indeed the French have an inaptitude to forms.[16]

The acceptability of French regimes was to be measured by the same yardstick as that by which English governments were judged, namely the extent
to which they represented the political nation, however defined, within the
fixed rules of an accepted constitution. After 1792, all French governments
fell short of these requirements. Fox loved France, but criticized it in an informed manner, as only a friend could do.

It would have been easier to chastise the French if the Fox family had any
solution to offer for France's problems, but this was not the case. They were
clear that they were against certain options, and this allowed certain policies
to be formed. Beyond that, they were only too aware how bitterly French
society had been split open by the Revolution. That minimum of social and
political consensus, necessary to the operation of a quiet constitutionalism,
was missing. Therefore, Foxites contributed to the debate on France by
pointing out what would not do. First and foremost, they believed, by 1795,
that 'it is all over with the Monarchy there.'[17] After the resistance that Louis
XVI had offered to the institution of parliamentary proceedings, this could
hardly be a matter of regret. The return of his dynasty would be retrogres-
sive in the extreme. As he lectured his nephew, 'a greater evil than the restoration of the Bourbons to the world in general, and England in particular,
can hardly happen.'[18] Pitt was wrong to encourage exiled royalists and to
support counter-revolution within France itself. The death of the boy-king
Louis XVII was tragic, but, in making Louis XVIII the pretender, it at least
was likely 'to damp the spirit of royalism . . . as Monsieur is very generally

and justly [thought] odious and contemptible'.[19] Simply reading his pro-
clamations issued in exile was enough, according to Fox, to more than fulfil
'expectations of folly however high they may have been'.[20] The Bourbons
had learnt nothing. English governments would therefore be wrong to
pursue any policies, which in any way contributed to their restoration.

A second point of reference was an enduring belief that the war had been
started by the despots of Europe. France was the aggrieved party. In December 1794, Fox elaborated the argument for the benefit of the House of
Commons:

He would never forego inquiry into the causes of the war, and measures to prevent
similar calamities in future. This was due to the people, least [sic], in the enjoyment of
peace, they should forget their former sufferings from war, and again yield themselves up to delusion. Both the present and the American war were owing to a court
party in this country, that hated the very name of liberty; and to an indifference,
amounting to barbarity, in the minister, to the distresses of the people. It was some
consolation to him that he had done his utmost to prevent the war, and to know that
those who provoked it could not but feel, even while they were endeavouring to
persuade others of the contrary, that they must, in no very long space of time, adopt
the very course which he was recommending as fit to be adopted now.[21]

Fox took a consistently gloomy view of the war and its prospects. It was hard
to believe that France could actually be defeated, and, even if that happened, Pitt seemed totally unclear about what sort of settlement could then
be imposed. A war had been started in a panic. It had no clear aims and
therefore no obvious point of termination. Even in 1800, Fox's basic stance
was unchanged. He told the Commons that he would 'continue to think and
to say, plainly and explicitly, that this country was the aggressor in the
war'.[22] In wagers recorded in the Betting Book at Brooks's, Fox is uniformly
desponding: 'B. Tarleton bets Mr Fox 50 Gs that Mr Pitt ceases to be Minister on or before the 18 April 1796': 'Mr Fox betts [sic] Mr Stepney 5 Gs that
the French are at Brussels before the Allied Powers are at Paris, 30 April
1794': 'Ld J. Townshend 25 Guineas to 20 that peace is made between
England & France before the first of January 1796, 11 Oct. 1794'.[23]

If England was the aggressor, it followed that peace was possible as soon
as that country could be brought to give up hostile attitudes. Pitt, not the
hard-pressed government of the Directory, was the enemy of peace, because
only the hysteria surrounding a war enabled him to serve his master by elim-
inating English liberties. In August 1795, Fox assured his nephew that
'Peace is the wish of the French of Italy Spain Germany and all the world,
and Great Britain alone the cause of preventing its accomplishment, and
this not for any point of honour or even interest, but merely lest there should

be an example in the modern world of a great and powerful Republic.'[24] As Prussia and Spain began to make peace with France, Fox became even more convinced that such an option was open to all the powers in conflict with the French. Peace could be made 'by a negotiation of a few hours & by saying *done* and *done* like a bett at Newmarket'.[25] Taking Pitt at his word, that there was no wish to impose regimes on the French, Fox drained the conflict of all its ideological content. A negotiation with France would therefore turn on traditional points of difference concerning rivers and fortresses in the Low Countries and islands in the West Indies.

Fox's arguments became more insistent and convincing even to men like Wilberforce, as the cost of the war threatened England too with financial crisis.[26] From 1793 onwards, England became the paymaster of the crusade against France, doling out huge subsidies to continental allies, who then made their peace with France without consulting London. As early in the war as September 1795, Fox reported that 'there is a great scarcity of money in the Treasury.'[27] To the threat of a national bankruptcy was quickly added that of famine. The terrible winter of 1794–5, followed by a 'bad wet summer', sent bread prices rocketing. Fox could only marvel that 'the people of this country have the merit of Patience beyond all the world, when in the present state of things they can see quietly provisions and stores of all sort sent out of the country to fleets and armies for the purpose of restoring monarchy to France.'[28] Everyone knew that the government of the Directory and the people of France in general were equally hard-pressed. What was the purpose of a war, which Pitt himself insisted had no ideological intention? So commonsensical was this opinion that, even in the Pittite House of Commons of 1795, Fox believed that 'there are not twenty Members in the House who are not really with us in opinion.'[29] Only fear and corruption retained their loyalties. Once again therefore, a discussion which begins with an examination of French events comes back to the denunciation of the system of Pitt and George III. Whatever crimes had been committed by France, repudiated by the Fox family as 'Robespierrism', their diabolical nature was more than matched by a regime in London which had fostered a war that was clearly designed, despite Pitt's protestations, to restore the Bourbons and to confirm despotism in England.

It followed that the key to peace in Europe was a change of administration in England. In particular, Pitt had to be dislodged. He and his closest associates had been 'the aggressors'.[30] Theirs had been an ideological war 'to destroy the jacobin government'.[31] It became a standard theme in Foxite thinking that 'our Government is as determined as ever to make no peace without Monarchy in France which appears to me to be if possible more out of the chances than ever.'[32] He was not at all surprised by rumours that Pitt was on the point of recognizing the Comte de Provence as Regent.[33] So boxed in had Pitt become that he was literally incapable of making peace without an unacceptable loss of face. He would not be able to restore the Bourbons, and would therefore be left with a choice of a humiliating with-drawal or endless war. As Fox observed, 'it is impossible for a Ministry who have made war on the principles upon which these Ministers have made it, to make any peace except by unconditional submission on one side or the other . . . so that how long this War will continue God knows.'[34] The situation could only be unblocked by Pitt's departure from office.[35] Until the situation was resolved, Pitt avoided confronting the dilemma by telling the country over and over again that 'the French can not go on much longer' and that 'Royalty is sure to be re-established in France in a few weeks.'[36] Fox was prepared to concede that Pitt's capacity for self-deception had reached such heights that he might have begun to believe his own propaganda, but this only made his removal the more urgent. By 1796, Foxites were not even sure that a peace secured by Pitt, were that possible, would be something to applaud.

If it is once understood, that Ministers may safely make any war the most unjust or most impolitic, provided they can get out of it by a Peace *quelconque*, and that we are to acquiesce in their making such a Peace (nay to thank them for it), as can be justified only upon the consideration of the situation into which *They* have brought us, if This lesson I say is taught and subscribed to by opposition itself, what reason have we to hope that upon every passion of a King upon every party advantage that a Minister may fancy to himself from a war, we shall not be again involved in similar misfortunes to the present?[37]

While most contemporaries saw Pitt as a great war minister defending con-cepts of property against revolutionary aggression, Foxites cast him in the role of warmonger, whose whole political *raison d'être* came to depend on continued hostilities.

When, in 1796 and 1797, Pitt explored peace initiatives by sending Malmesbury and Hammond to Europe, Fox was not inclined to take them seriously. He recorded his 'doubts about their making or meaning to make the attempt in a proper manner, and still more about their success if they do'.[38] When the Malmesbury mission was announced, Fox sarcastically congratulated ministers on adopting a policy he had been advocating for the last three years.[39] When the enterprise failed, Fox registered little sense of shock. He told Grey that 'our way is so clear that we must be as ingenious as Malmesbury himself to go wrong. If it had been the object of Ministers to put themselves in the wrong I do not think they could have done more.'[40]

After all, Malmesbury had been sent out without clear instructions, and such clarity could not be forthcoming as long as Pitt's war aims remained fuzzy. The Prime Minister claimed that he was not necessarily committed to restoring the Bourbons. What then was he committed to? Until that question was answered, peace initiatives on the part of Pitt had to be denounced as a sham, designed to silence an increasingly vocal demand for the termination of war. 'Could there be', Fox asked, 'a more ridiculous farce?'[41]

In attacking the coherence and sincerity of Pitt's war aims, Fox consolidated, in some people's minds, the idea that he was a Jacobin sympathizer. In undermining the will to fight, Foxites were accused of behaving 'in a manner that must be very useful to France and makes them in fact very useful allies'.[42] As in the American War, Fox and his friends acquired the reputation of being leagued with foreigners, of being outside the nation. None of this, however, unduly concerned Fox, who was safe in the security of his own cosmopolitan values, and who was clearly so far from any possibility of holding power that he had no need to temporize or to moderate his views. Rather, since the war was the buttress of George III's system, an early peace was an absolute prerequisite for all future hopes in politics. Dismissing charges of being an ally of France, Fox instead identified an overblown National Debt as that which gave the French most hope.[43] Pitt was leading the country into a bankruptcy. In March 1797, Fox 'doubted whether the country could carry on a war for two or three years'.[44] England was less likely to be overwhelmed by the French than by the calamity of a breakdown in national finances. The fact that Pitt could neither identify the aims of war nor secure peace was therefore truly alarming.

Worse was to come. In Fox's opinion, the real reason for Pitt's reticence in public over war aims was not that they did not exist, but rather that they were contained in a private agenda to which he could not give voice. Insist how he might that he had no intention of imposing a regime on France, it was clear to Foxites that the ideological basis of the war had not changed with the fall of Robespierre. Pitt could not make peace with the Directory, because he wished only to restore the Bourbons. The evidence for this, in Foxite eyes, was overwhelming. In May 1795, Fox was still reiterating points that he had made for the first time in 1792–3. All the violence in France and the outbreak of European war was to be attributed solely to the fact that despots had refused to allow constitutionalism a natural growth in France. He told the Commons that 'The accursed confederacy of despots, for by no other name could it ever pass his lips, had given birth in the first instance to all the suspicion and consequent massacres which had taken place.'[45] It was sinister therefore that Britain had become the paymaster of the First and

Second Coalitions. These 'treacherous allies' took their subsidies and used them to wipe Poland off the map of Europe.[46]

Controversially, Fox expressed unqualified approval when French armies defeated Coalition armies. In particular, he had no sympathy for the courts of Austria and Naples, which he identified as the two powers most instrumental in attacking France.[47] As for Prussia and Spain, at least their venality overcame their commitment to a monarchical crusade. These powers simply took British money and then concluded a separate peace with France. It was amusing to hear Pitt loftily proclaim that no peace was possible without the concurrence of his allies, when it was clear that his allies were not so scrupulous. If Pitt believed his own words, he was foolish. If he did not, then his wish to consult allies was yet another tactic to avoid being forced into a peace which he did not want. Even more droll was the spectacle of George III making peace with France as Elector of Hanover and continuing the war as King of England. Again and again, Fox was at pains to establish why it was that Britain, with the exception of Austria, was the only belligerent power that could not find a path out of the war.[48] Burke angrily accused him of 'making every power in alliance with this Country odious',[49] and it was a charge that Fox would have cheerfully accepted. In the Foxite view, Pitt was the key to the question of war and peace. He sustained Austria's neurotic fears. He allied himself with despots, whose capacity for violence only gave way to their desire for money. He bullied powers like Denmark and America which wished to have no part of his war.[50] It was all part of the same pattern.

Until the very last year of his life, the war with France preoccupied Fox more than any other issue, and he persisted in thinking that Pitt was the prime mover in the whole business. Its ideological nature was apparent from the beginning. A Bourbon restoration in France was to be followed by the regularization of despotic practice in England. The emergency legislation enacted after 1792 would be systematized. France wanted peace, and was able to secure it with virtually every country in Europe except Pitt's England. To the degree that Pitt had staked his career on the war, his dismissal became a precondition of peace. Once a treaty was secured, it might even be just possible that the lost liberties of the 1790s might be salvaged. It was a distant and alluring prospect, but one strong enough to tempt Fox out of secession. Fox's views were unchanging over a long period, but then the interminable war set and preserved the agenda of politics.

*

These opinions were barely modified at all by the coming to power of Bonaparte. That a general should overwhelm a constitution was of course regrettable. The *coup d'état* of Brumaire was 'a very bad beginning . . . the manner of the thing quite odious'.[51] However, Bonaparte, in Fox's view, would be even more inclined to seek peace than earlier regimes, because his legitimacy was so much in doubt. Military men seeking power have to make themselves acceptable as well as feared. Guerrilla warfare was still endemic in much of western France. The new French government inherited a chronic financial situation. All of these factors pointed to a peace. There was nothing to be said for Bonaparte at the outset, except that he was a general who could not afford to fight. When the peace offer duly came, early in 1800, Fox was delighted but not surprised. The English Cabinet's refusal to treat proved that they 'must be quite mad'.[52] The terms that they offered to Bonaparte were so absurdly high, namely that he must 'restore Monarchy or shew us that you can behave peaceably for some time before we can treat, and this experience of peaceable demeanour is desired during the war'.[53] Without in any way admiring the form or the methods of the new government in France, Fox was less anxious to criticize it than to hound Pitt for missing a real opportunity for peace:

> That a great General like Bonaparte should be inclined to military means of effecting a military Government is less to be wondered at than lamented . . . by taking the common & beaten path of Ambition he has . . . done much against the liberty of mankind in every part of the world . . . The only good that could come from this Event, so pernicious to the cause of general Liberty, was Peace; and that you see our Ministers are determined to refuse.[54]

The Fox family was sure that Bonaparte was sincere in his offer, and that 'Peace & Peace upon good terms might be had nobody now doubts.'[55] So great was the opportunity that his nephew urged Fox to give up his non-attendance of Parliament. Politics now stood 'upon quite different grounds. A question for peace is so reasonable so unanswerable.'[56] Fox, sharing these views, was logically compelled to agree to attend at least one debate, though it was done 'against not only one's inclination, but one's judgment too'.[57] Consequently, Fox reappeared in the House of Commons on 3 February 1800, to make a speech that not only urged that Bonaparte's offer should be taken seriously, but also rehearsed arguments about the whole history of the war. His audience would have found them familiar. England had been the aggressor, even if the Declaration of Pillnitz had started the mischief. The rape of Poland exceeded in cruelty anything done by the French. Ministers who had allegedly tried to secure a peace with the Directory in 1796 and 1797 had no reason to snub Bonaparte, since all French regimes since 1789 had been born in violence. At least, 'this extraordinary man' might be able to stabilize France internally, which in itself would do much to suggest that any agreement undertaken by him could be made to stick. To miss this opportunity was to imply that the fighting would continue until there was a regime in France that Pitt was prepared to treat with, opening up the prospect of a war without end.[58]

This excursion back into politics was a dismal experience for Fox. The speech had been a powerful one and had been listened to with respect, but it had no effect whatever on events. A week before making it, Fox had diagnosed politics to be in such a dire state that it would never again be 'useful or fit for me to meddle in them'.[59] An appearance at Westminster had convinced him more than ever that Pitt would only accept a restored Bourbon monarchy, and that his peace initiatives of 1796 and 1797 had been solely motivated by a desire to mollify opinion. That opinion, by 1800, had dribbled away into apathy, and therefore Pitt was free of all pressures. Secession, consequently, remained the only sensible option. As Fox explained to Wyvill:

Mr Pitt's avowal of his former negotiations having been taken up in compliance with the wishes of the Publick appeared to me . . . the most important confession that could be made . . . To men capable of seeing it shews distinctly two things, first that to get even a negotiation set on foot, publick declarations of opinion are necessary, and secondly that negotiations managed by the present Men will always be a mere compliment to publick opinion, & a mean [*sic*] to get money.[60]

As ever, Pitt and George III were obstacles to peace.

In the course of 1800, Fox's opinion of Bonaparte rose dramatically. The securing of a European peace had become a yardstick by which all actions were to be judged, and by that measure Bonaparte was scoring well. Foxites seemed to be confronted by the novel spectacle of a peaceable general. In March, Fox assured his nephew that 'Bonaparte I think is going on better than I ever expected he would and seems still to be in hopes of peace with Austria.'[61] By July, the means by which he had achieved power were officially 'forgiven', as he had now 'surpassed . . . Alexander & Caesar, not to mention the great advantage he has over them in the Cause he fights in'.[62] He was to be honoured with a sonnet.[63] Both his interest and his inclination seemed to make him 'moderate and wise, and . . . pacifick',[64] even in the face of Pitt's insulting behaviour. As a usurper of power, Bonaparte badly needed to legitimize his authority in France, and an important aspect of that had to be a realization that 'the People of France are just now as I hear far more desirous of Peace of which they have been so long deprived, than of glory with which they have been glutted.'[65] Napoleon was shrewd enough to know that it was 'for the Interest both of his Glory and of his Power to continue in the system of Moderation'.[66]

By the beginning of 1802, Fox could only identify two faults in

Bonaparte's behaviour. The first of these was the Egyptian campaign of 1798, and, as he explained to his brother, there may even have been an honourable explanation:

Why Egypt should be of such importance either to the French or to Us I never could discover and I have always thought the Expedition there the foolishest part, perhaps the only foolish part of Bonaparte's Conduct, unless perhaps he had some views in it connected with the internal Politicks of France of which we are not informed, or (which I have always suspected) that he had a desire to be out of the way of either accepting or refusing the command of an army destined to invade England.[67]

His second failing was a function of 'his rage for Moderation'.[68] Quite simply, Napoleon trusted Austria too much, and was endlessly inclined to give that country the benefit of the doubt, when in fact the court of Vienna had shown itself to be Pitt's greatest ally in pursuing war. The Austrians were 'Villains'.[69] In defiance of English opinion, Fox delighted in Austrian defeats. Thus he told Fitzpatrick,

As to Bonaporte, you know what my apprehensions always were, and I can not help thinking they are in a great degree verified. For though he may, and I hope he will, trounce the Austrians . . . yet it is impossible to deny that he has lost, or at least risqued the losing of an opportunity. Every man has his weak side, and I have always thought Bonaparte's was the thinking Austria more inclined to peace and more to be depended upon than She is. I hope to God he will not suffer from his errour.[70]

Bonaparte's faults were a product of his pacific virtues.

So dominant was the peace issue in Fox's mind between 1799 and 1802 that it overwhelmed other considerations. As has been noted, he chose to forgive the violence of Bonaparte's coming to power. He also seemed determined to ignore or explain away many other aspects of Napoleon's regime that were neither liberal nor constitutional. French parliamentarians like Mme de Staël were dismayed that Fox, so admired in other contexts, should have misjudged the nature of Bonapartism so badly. It might be a fine thing to secure peace with a dictator after so much bloodshed, but the hard fact of dictatorship remained:

A cette époque, malheureusement pour l'esprit de liberté en Angleterre, et par conséquent sur le Continent, dont elle est le fanal, le parti de l'opposition, ayant à sa tête M. Fox, fit entièrement fausse route par rapport à Bonaparte; et dès lors ce parti, si honorable d'ailleurs, a perdu dans la nation l'ascendant qu'il eût été désirable à d'autres égards de lui voir conserver. C'étoit déjà beaucoup trop que d'avoir défendu la Révolution Françoise sous le Règne de la Terreur; mais quelle faute, s'il se peut, plus dangereuse encore, que de considérer Bonaparte comme tenant aux principes de cette Révolution dont il étoit le plus habile destructeur.[71]

This is a grave charge, and one to be given great weight, as coming from a witness who admired Fox and claimed to share his values. The only possible answer lies in Fox's ingrained belief that an end to the war, by whatever agency, was an indispensable precondition for the re-establishment of constitutional forms in England and France. If Bonaparte was apparently for peace, therefore, he wittingly or unwittingly placed himself on the side of the angels.

*

The flicker of a renewed interest in politics occasioned by the appearance of Bonaparte was confirmed by the fall of Pitt's administration in February 1801. Pitt had all along been identified as the prime mover of the ideological war against France. His efforts at peace-making had been a sham. By contrast, his successor, Henry Addington, was thought to be a joke, but at least a peaceable joke. An amateur medical man, Addington was regarded by Foxites as a man of very small brain. In letters, he was always contemptuously referred to as 'the Doctor'. However, if his survival as prime minister could guarantee the continued exclusion of Pitt and the war party, then he had to be supported. As Creevey noted, Fox 'will keep in the Doctor and preserve the peace. God continue Fox's prudence and Pitt's gout! . . . I see distinctly that Fox will at least have arrived at this situation that, tho' unable to be Minister himself, he may in fact prevent one from being turned out.'[72] Now, pacific overtures from Paris would be warmly received in London, and 'there is nothing easier to make Peace if the two sides wish it.'[73] Even the onset of another bout of mental incapacity from George III seemed divinely ordained to assist the peace process. Looking further ahead, Fox began to think that there was just a chance of rebuilding a Whig party on a peace vote. As he explained to Wyvill, it was a slim chance, but one that might make politics worth the game once more:

If there is a point that can be pushed successfully it must be the War, and then *perhaps* (but it is only *perhaps*) they who join the Whigs upon that point, may feel themselves obliged to acquiesce in others. At least it is worth trying.[74]

Incongruously, the very different characters of Bonaparte and Henry Addington might create conditions in which Foxite Whiggery could be reborn.

When peace in France came with the Treaty of Amiens in 1802, Fox was elated. It mattered little that France benefited considerably by the treaty. This fact merely proved that peace could have been had much earlier if either Pitt had not resisted it, or if the political nation had had the will to demand it. If these were the best terms available, Pitt would be hard put to it to explain why they had not been accepted earlier:

However it may have happened, it is an excellent thing, and I do not like it the worse for its being so very triumphant a peace for France . . . The sense of humiliation in the Government here will be certainly lost in the extreme popularity of the measure . . . this rascally people are quite overjoyed at receiving from Ministers what, if they had dared to ask it, could not have been refused them at almost any period of the war. Will the Ministers have the impudence to say that there was any time (much less that when Bonaparte's offer was refused) when we might not have had terms as good? Bonaparte's triumph is now complete indeed; and, since there is to be no political liberty in the world, I really believe he is the fittest person to be the master.[75]

Peace, concluded by anyone on any terms, was 'a great Blessing'.[76] It re-introduced a glimmer of hope into Foxite politics that had not been seen since 1794. Henry Addington would always be a figure of fun to the Foxites, but he was at least innocent of a desire to fight on to the point of threatening the country with total ruin. Simply to see Pitt out of government after seventeen years was to taste honey.

Fox's pleasure at these events was very publicly expressed at a large dinner held at the Shakespeare Tavern, on 10 October 1801, to celebrate the anniversary of his election for Westminster. His language was brusque and unrestrained. He admitted unqualified delight at the removal of Pitt, for 'We never could have had a Peace whilst the late Ministry continued in office.'[77] If the peace favoured France, that too was a matter for rejoicing:

It may be said that the peace we have made is glorious to the French Republic, and glorious to the First Consul. Ought it not to be so?—ought not glory to be the reward of such a glorious struggle? France stood against a confederacy composed of all the great kingdoms of Europe; she completely baffled the attempts of those who menaced her independence . . . Some complain that we have not gained the object of the war. The object of the war we have not gained most certainly, and I like the peace by so much the better.[78]

When even Grey was forced to protest about the freedom of this kind of language, Fox would not give ground. He merely restated the point that 'The triumph of the French Government over the English does, in fact, afford me a degree of *pleasure* which it is very difficult to disguise.'[79] Even though these words represented nothing new in Fox's thinking, it was not likely that they would win him many friends after a long, costly war, in which so many lives had been lost. According to French Laurence, it was 'a splenetick triumph in the present humiliation of the country'.[80] Even George Tierney found it a 'mortification'.[81]

There was no repentance in Fox, however. Everything that he fought for over the previous decade was vindicated in the fall of Pitt and the acceptance of peace terms such as these. As there was no hope of office, there was no point in bridling his tongue. As he told Grey, 'I do not know whether my Speech was or was not misrepresented, but I think it very likely that it really was liable to the interpretation you deprecate, & in that respect it was no doubt indiscreet, but you know that of late I have not considered much for myself what in a political view may or may not be judicious.'[82] The acceptance of Addington's peace wonderfully transformed Pitt into 'a figure at once both ridiculous & odious'.[83] Significantly, many of his letters to Grey during this crucial period still insist that he can only spare a day or two for politics, at the very most. Even the cracking of the ice in 1801 could not attract him back into politics on a full-time basis. He was free to speak his mind. Very different was the situation of men like Sheridan or Tierney, who still believed that there was a game to be played.

The best that Fox could promise, in response to the protests of his friends, was that, when the treaty came to be debated in the Commons, Grey and Sheridan should speak first, and he would try to match their words. By this device, he hoped that

he might not get into a scrape; for he says he never opens his lips now, let his intention be what it will, but he gets scolded and rated on all sides, offends every body, and has so many different meanings and words forc'd upon him that he hardly knows at last what was his own or what he meant either as to words or sense.[84]

When the debate came on, on 3 November 1801, he tried hard to keep to his undertaking. Although he reiterated his belief that the war had been fought to restore the Bourbons and that he was therefore happy that England's objectives had not been fulfilled,[85] he was 'on the whole moderate', and 'did not go into any violent invectives against Pitt or the late ministers'.[86] It was the best he could do. Quite simply, Fox felt himself to be vindicated by the events of 1801–2. They had not wafted him to office, but he had neither expected nor wanted that. It was enough that they should have proved the futility of Pitt's career since 1792. Aggression on the part of England had been thwarted by an unusual general, who used success in the field to compel his opponents to talk of peace.

*

All Fox's assumptions about France would be tested by the visit he made to that country in the autumn of 1802. For the first time in ten years, Paris was once again available to English visitors, and the Channel was choked by the curious, who wanted to view the effects of Revolution; by the artistic, who wanted to see the unparalleled collection of sculpture and painting now housed in the Louvre; and by those who wanted to see old friends. Foxites were anxious to do all of these things. Their Francophilia needed feeding, and there were many points of interest to investigate. Above all, Bonapartism comprehended men of the old order, like Talleyrand, and new faces which the Foxites were eager to see. The French élite had changed dramatically since 1792, and there was much to catch up on. None of this did anything to diminish Fox's reputation for holding a treasonous liking for foreigners, but, as ever, he discounted opinion outside his immediate connections. As Fox set out for Paris for the first time in fourteen years, the sense of excitement must have been extreme. So much of what he had been recently arguing would now be validated or proved to be nothing more than wishful thinking.

Details of the journey may be found in a journal kept by Fox to record his impressions. Fox was not a natural diarist, and the existence of a journal may of itself indicate the importance that Fox attached to this adventure. The party consisted of Fox himself, his secretary, John Trotter, St Andrew, St John, Robert Adair, and the newly acknowledged Mrs Fox. It set out on 19 July 1802, and was at Calais next day. All the people there were reported to be 'very civil', and Fox immediately became embroiled in controversy for choosing Arthur O'Connor as his dinner companion on his first evening on French soil.[87] According to Mrs Fox, few immediate changes could be seen in French life except that 'the people are not so smart in their persons but they certainly seem happier.'[88] At Lille a few days later, Fox was surprised to discover a florid invitation to a banquet in his honour. The mayor of the city proclaimed that 'Les grands hommes sont cosmopolites: ils appartiennent à tous les pays . . . Les autorités de Lille pénétrées d'admiration pour vos vertues . . . prennent la confiance de vous inviter à un banquet civique.'[89] The Fox party then went north, and in turn visited Ghent, Antwerp, Breda, Utrecht, Amsterdam, Haarlem, Leyden, Delft, and Brussels.

On 19 August, they reached Paris, where their company was augmented by the Hollands, Lord Robert Spencer, and Richard Fitzpatrick. A day later, James Hare, Thomas Erskine, and George Ponsonby arrived. It must have appeared as if the whole Foxite party had abandoned England for France, and possibly with a sense of relief. His money matters were, as usual, supervised by the banker Perrégaux, and his lodgings had been arranged by General de Grave,[90] who 'had got every thing very comfortable'.[91] They were in the Hotel Richelieu, rue St Augustin. Fox had desired that they 'be very near the great national library, in which case, said he, I shall be able to go there afoot, and I shall spend many half-hours, and perhaps hours, in the library, which I should not if I am obliged to go in a carriage'.[92] The ostensible reason for visiting Paris was to consult archives, in connection with the writing of his history of the reign of James II, and this project was taken seriously. Through the good offices of Talleyrand, he visited the appropriate librarian next day, and arranged to begin work. Thereafter, a daily pattern emerged of library work interspersed with visits to galleries and museums by day, and dinner-parties and theatre visits by night. Everything was of interest, but the Louvre collection was 'grand, sublime, every thing that can be imagined'.[93] It contained, among other things, his favourite painting, Domenichino's *St Jerome*, who was, perhaps significantly, a saint in the wilderness.

Very quickly, Fox became a curiosity, even a fashion. He was elected an Associé étranger of the Institut National des Sciences et des Arts.[94] Mme Récamier, noting that his 'picture was in every window', complained to him that 'before you came, I was the fashion.'[95] According to the not always reliable evidence of his secretary, Fox was even consulted about French governmental appointments.[96] Naturally, he was introduced to notable politicians, including many men and women who had played prominent roles in the Revolution: Barère, Santerre, Lally-Tollendal, Narbonne, Sieyès, Charles Lameth, Mme Cabarrus, Mme de Souza, Berthier, and Mme de Coigny. Above all, he re-established his old relationships with Talleyrand and Lafayette. From 24 to 29 September, he was Lafayette's guest at his country house, La Grange. There he planted an ivy which Lafayette showed to Coke of Norfolk in 1829, 'green and flourishing like his memory'.[97] Like Fox, many of these people had suffered ostracism or worse in the 1790s. They had common experiences to discuss and, in many cases, common values to explore. It must have been very reassuring to talk with people of like mind. Certainly memories of this visit could be traded on for favours for many decades to come.[98] There was a sense of relief that a terrible experience might have come to an end. Fox, looking around Paris, was elated, not only by the illuminations and fireworks, but by 'an appearance of enjoyment in every countenance beyond all description'.[99]

Fox's popularity and success in Paris was viewed with a jaundiced eye from the British Embassy. Officials found the court paid to Fox by Talleyrand and other foreign diplomats 'indecent' and 'offensive'.[100] In return, Fox seemed to flatter the French and belittle his own country:

The English Opposition Party here . . . seem to be exerting all their Industry to do their Country and its Government every possible Mischief, as it is natural to infer from their associating with several of the worst Class of His Majesty's Subjects who are here, such as the O'Connors, Corbett etc.[101]

In particular, Fox's repeated dining with Arthur O'Connor was thought to be suspect. O'Connor had been acquitted of treason, but to be seen in his company was still to touch pitch. When challenged on this point, Fox was predictably robust: 'It don't signify but by God I have not a heart to meet a man in distress whom I once knew when he was worthy of esteem & not take notice of him.'[102] As Adair reported home, fears about Fox agreeing with O'Connor simply because he sometimes shared his table were 'nonsense'.

Fox's 'Character is too big to mind these childish Criticisms'.[103] Even so, as Fox demonstrated a popularity and influence in Paris that he did not have in London, it is understandable that, when one embassy official heard that Fox was about to return home, his comment was 'Thank God!'[104]

Significantly, Fox showed no sense of urgency in the matter of coming face to face with Bonaparte. On 21 August, two days after their arrival in Paris, the Foxes were viewing pictures in the Louvre, when Napoleon drove by. As Amelia Opie recorded, Fox's reaction to this opportunity was not predictable:

all the company, myself excepted, crowded to the window; but our greatest man, I own, turned away, and resumed his station before the picture [Raphael's *Transfiguration*], while his wife observed to me that, considering Buonaparte was a republican, he seemed very fond of state and show. Again her distinguished husband went to the window, and again turned away. It was the first time he had ever seen ought appertaining to the consular government, and it was natural that his curiosity should be excited; but there was evidently a feeling uppermost in his mind, which struggled with his wish to indulge in it, and before the procession was out of sight, it had ceased to appear an object of interest to him.[105]

In his own journal, Fox simply noted that he 'saw from the window Bonaparte with his 8 horses, Mammelukes [*sic*.] etc.'[106] Fox was clearly hesitant to meet a man whom he had so praised as a bringer of peace to Europe. There was much to lose and everything to revalue, if the reality failed to match the image. In Fox's mind, as evidently in that of his wife, the ostentation surrounding Bonaparte was unpromising. Horses and mamelukes in large quantities had an imperial or monarchical quality that was unsettling.

The two men finally met on 2 September, when Fox was formally presented to the ruler of France. Napoleon clearly attached great importance to the occasion, and was anxious to impress. According to Fitzpatrick, he 'was very polite to all Englishmen presented to him, but most especially so to Mr Fox. The Consul addressed him in a speech evidently prepared, which he was sometime in delivering, & apparently anxious not to forget any part of it.'[107] Fox simply records a 'Long talk with Bony he talked almost all, was presented to Mme. liked her very much.'[108] In fact, as this laconic entry might indicate, the interview went very badly. Lady Bessborough, another witness of the encounter, thought that the two men had fallen out over the value or otherwise of a standing army:

Buonaparte also talk'd a good deal ... but in much too Princely a style, and seeming to dislike any difference of Opinion, he was startled and seem'd surpris'd and displeas'd at Mr Fox's answering rather abruptly to his lamentations on the necessity of keeping up a great Military establishment, un grand establissement [*sic*] Militaire est toujours odieux et doit l'être, car tout Gouvernement qui n'existe que par la force est *oppressif* et mauvais. (Mr F. told Ld. Robert he spoke bad French to soften it; that he meant *Tyranique*, but thought it was too harsh to say.)[109]

Fox was at last confronting what he had probably long suspected. His reluctance to meet Bonaparte related to an unwillingness to accept the fact that, although peace might be in Napoleon's interest, that alone did not give him Whig or parliamentarian credentials.

The two men tried once more to get on terms, over dinner the next day, but the outcome was hardly more satisfactory. Clearly irritated, Napoleon returned once again to a defence of a large standing army, and then went on to claim that the press in England had too much liberty, particularly with reference to commenting upon himself.[110] When Fox retorted that the freedom of the press 'was a necessary evil, and that in England people did not mind being abused in the News Papers, he [Napoleon] answer'd, "C'est tout autre chose ici." '[111] Later, Fox was to find himself defending Pitt against Bonaparte's accusations that the English prime minister was behind a plot to have him blown up with an 'Infernal Machine'.[112] In two encounters, Fox and Napoleon had found almost no common ground. At a final meeting on 7 October, not even the question of the slave trade could bring them wholeheartedly together. Both agreed that its abolition was desirable, but Napoleon then went on to dwell on all the 'difficulties' of putting such a policy into execution.[113]

Little wonder that Fox reported home ominously that he had found Bonapartist circles to be nothing more than 'a court'.[114] There was simply too much depressing evidence about Napoleon's desire to rule autocratically. The *ancien régime* was more in being in Paris than the Revolution. More surprisingly, Fox did not seem to share the common view that Bonaparte was a man of exceptional talent. On the contrary, 'He spoke very lightly of the abilities of Buonaparte. In conversation He found him very defficient [*sic*] upon every subject; no powers or extent of mind. He considers the predominance of Buonaparte as the greatest imposition, that was ever practised upon the world.'[115] It seemed that Fox's disgust at a military *coup d'état* in Brumaire 1799 more truly represented a correct response to the phenomenon of Napoleon than the accolades given in 1800 and 1801. Fox would certainly have been much amused that Bonaparte should have left Mrs Fox a lock of his hair in his will, as 'the relict [*sic*] of that great Man whose name I never heard him [Napoleon] pronounce unaccompanied by some expression of approbation, or of esteem'.[116] Fox would have been hard put to it to return the compliment. The visit to France had been hugely profitable in terms of the writing of his history and the renewal of friendships, but it had been a grave disappointment in necessitating a re-evaluation of Bonaparte himself and the regime he was constructing. On arriving back at St Anne's Hill on 17 November, he closed his journal with the words, 'dear, dear home . . . very very glad to be here & happy *so* happy that my Liz bore all the fatigues of the journey so well'.[117]

*

None of Fox's doubts about the Napoleonic regime seem to have been appreciated by a wider political public. Quite simply, the fact of the visit of itself compromised him. Fox was, perhaps, the most distinguished European politician to make the pilgrimage to Paris. By doing so, he gave respectability to a regime that was badly in need of it. Coleridge accused Fox of becoming 'the temporary courtier of Bonaparte', which was 'not delicate, not worthy of Mr Fox'.[118] Cobbett in the *Political Register* went further. According to him, Fox 'bows his grey head to the earth before him, and gathers up the crumbs that fall from his table', hoping to make himself 'Minister of this country by his [Bonaparte's] means'.[119] Contemporaries were hard put to it to explain why the journey had been necessary at all. It could only be sinister that Fox had been so flattered in Paris. At the least, it clouded the expression of English policy in Europe. At the worst, it smacked yet again of almost treasonous behaviour.[120] The Foxites began to be called 'the English Privy Council of the Consul' as a result of this 'flirtation'.[121] As ever, cartoonists quickly scented an opportunity and turned it into profit. Four prints appeared which depicted Fox's visit. The most vivid was Gillray's *Introduction of Citizen Volpone and his Suite, at Paris*. In subsequent cartoons, Fox is actually dressed as Bonaparte.[122] All of this was unfair and a savage misrepresentation of Fox's real views, but it had a real currency, and did nothing to enhance Fox's reputation at the very moment when he once again began to consider an active role in politics.

The visit to Paris had, indeed, greatly influenced Fox's thinking, but not in the way that many of his contemporaries feared. First, his hopeful assessment of Bonaparte in the years 1799–1802 had been totally undermined. It is quite possible that he feared it always would be once he came face to face with the man. Certainly, the interview was strangely delayed. Fox seemed anxious to see everyone in Paris except Napoleon. When the two finally met, Fox had to face the cruel fact that Bonaparte was no Whig. In spite of this, Fox continued to believe that the Consul was for peace, not unfortunately because he was a peaceable man, but because he needed it. His control of France was uncertain. Assassination attempts punctuated an enduring civil war in the west of France. Having come to power by *coup d'état*, he had only the legitimacy of armed force. All these factors convinced

Fox that Bonaparte could not afford another major war, which would yet further destabilize France. On the day after his return to England, Fox told Lauderdale,

As to War I can only say that my opinion is clearly that it will *not* be. I can tell you my reasons for this opinion in two sentences. 1st. I am sure that Bonaparte will do everything that he can to avoid it. 2nd. that, low as my opinion is of our Ministry, I cannot believe them quite so foolish as to force him to it, without one motive either of ambition or interest to incite them.[123]

So clear was Fox that the peace could be maintained that, although every inclination still suggested a withdrawal from politics, he felt obliged to resume parliamentary duties to promote this narrow objective. Writing from Paris to the Duchess of Devonshire, Fox signalled his limited return to public life:

Do not be angry with me for saying *d'avance* that I strongly suspect I shall not think your reasons good, and that I am more and more for complete retirement. I heartily wish I had not been overpersuaded to come into Parliament, but as I am there, and notwithstanding my system of withdrawing, I must take some opportunity of declaring my wish in favour of peace, and pray tell this to everyone whom you can suppose at all desirous of knowing my opinion. I think the folly of the last two wars, wisdom, in comparison of the scheme of undertaking one now.[124]

Within four days of arriving home, he notified Holland that he planned to attend the opening debates in the new Parliament, even though 'I am told I shall be as much abused for pacifick language.'[125] Peace was the hope that dragged Fox partially out of retirement. Peace was the measure by which he judged the characters and actions of other politicians. It regenerated a spark of interest in politics. If peace could be secured, so much of the horror of that terrible decade 1792–1801 could be undone. Repressive legislation would have to be repealed. The persecution of Radicals would have to stop. Best of all, as the Pittite system, predicated on war, unravelled, the sufferings of 'Fox's martyrs' might win some belated vindication. Here was a theme which, though not strong enough to tease Fox back into full-time politics, was tempting enough to suggest a magnificent, valedictory resolution of his career.

9

Books and Domesticity,
1794–1802

THE years 1794–1802 saw Fox develop and consolidate a lifestyle that had little or nothing to do with politics. Secession from Parliament was the easier because there was an alternative way of living, with which, as he grew older, he became increasingly comfortable. Foxites had always guaranteed politics some of the day, but not the whole of it. Pittites generally were more single-minded. The authentic Whig assessment of public life is captured in a comment made by Fox's niece in August 1794, shortly after one of the greatest crises in her uncle's political career:

My Uncle Charles who is confessedly the most indulgent of Politicians is likewise the one, who has the greatest variety of occupations and amusements that bear no relation to these subjects—*Fireside Enjoyments*. He & Mr Windham *did* last year in the midst of parliamentary opposition to each other, sit up at the literary club, tête à tête, till two o'clock in the morning, the word politics or any thing relating to them, not being mentioned by either of them.[1]

Increasingly, Fox was not to be found in London at all, but at his country house, St Anne's Hill. Its purchase gave him access to 'Nightingales, Flowers, Litterature [*sic*], History etc all which however I conceive to be good and substantial reasons for staying here.'[2] More and more these are the subjects which fill his correspondence. London kept in touch by trekking down to Surrey, but such was the honour contained in an invitation that a new verb was coined to describe it, 'to Charley it'.

As Fox, in the decade of his forties, began to accommodate himself to a new lifestyle, its centre was Elizabeth Armistead. Ever since 1781, Fox had mournfully expressed a half-wish that he could lead a more regular life. It was Mrs Armistead who guided him to it:

Charles has been very free from that dreadful disorder in his bowels this winter: his chief complaint is, that he grows old, but the effects of age he laments most are not those which are commonly thought the worst. His complaint is that he cannot be as foolish as he was formerly about women, and that though he takes great pains to fall in love, he cannot bring it about; this I wonder at, as he has always begun by taking the thing into his head, which is not the usual process. Whenever he has a fancy for any woman it makes him so unhappy and so ridiculous that I most sincerely hope his complaint may continue.[3]

Long before their marriage, Mrs Fox, as Elizabeth Armistead became in 1795, had begun to effect changes. In manners as well as morals, discernible improvements were noted in Fox. His dress was less slovenly, his hours were more regular, and his drinking was more tempered. He even abandoned the practice of spitting on carpets, a practice which had gravely 'hurt Lord Shelburne, who is a man of great neatness'.[4]

There can be no doubt that the Foxes were enormously fond of each other. Fox called his wife 'The Lady of the Hill'.[5] For her, Fox was 'my old one' or 'the full of days'.[6] The earliest surviving letter from Fox to his future wife is dated 7 May 1784, and its content and tone set a mood that lasted until his death:

It may sound ridiculous, but it is true that I feel every day how much more I love you than even I know. You are *all* to me. You can always make me happy in circumstances unpleasant and miserable [and] in the most prosperous. Indeed, my dearest Angel the whole happiness of my life depends upon you. Pray pray do not abuse your power.[7]

She became a point of consolation and sympathy when political life went badly, and increasingly a substitute for it. In 1787, he warned her that 'the remaining half of my life whether it is to be happy or otherwise depends entirely upon you, indeed it does. I never can be happy now I have known you but with you.' She was 'a full compensation for every disappointment'.[8] Unlike Fox's nieces, Lady Holland and Caroline Fox, unlike his former mistress the Duchess of Devonshire, Mrs Fox showed no interest in influencing politics, and little attention to the subject at all. In her company, Fox's mind would be directed to other things. For this reason alone, she was not much liked by Fox's political nieces.

In a quiet and unostentatious way, Elizabeth Fox used her power over her husband to domesticate him, and even to teach him economy. Towards the end of his life, the two of them could be seen shopping in Chertsey for 'china—cheap china I mean; for they seem great economists'.[9] As Fox explained to a friend, by 1797 his wife's approbation was the yardstick by which he measured nearly everything:

My Liz says she wishes she could shoot too, and so do I with all my heart, and when I have made a good shot I often think how I should like to turn round and see my dear Liz's lovely face smiling and encouraging me, and even when I do it, I should like to hear her find fault with me and see her look contemptuously as she does when I am awkward at carving.[10]

This influence was apparent very early in their relationship for, when she suggested that their relationship should end because her debts were even more compromising than his, Fox merely assured her that he could change his 'name and live with you in the remotest part of Europe in poverty & obscurity. I could bear that very well, but to be parted I can not bear.'[11] On his fiftieth birthday, in the dark political days of January 1799, Fox presented his wife with a poem, which in its simplicity and sincerity is far removed from the Latin verses addressed by a precocious Etonian to pretty cousins:

> Of years I have now half a century past,
> And none of the fifty so blest as the last.
> How it happens my troubles thus daily should cease,
> And my happiness still with my years should increase,
> This defiance of Nature's more general laws
> You alone can explain, who alone are the cause.[12]

For eleven years, from 1784 to 1795, Fox and Mrs Armistead lived together without marrying. Even for a man of his temperament, Fox had to make some allowance for the fact that his mistress came from the *demi-monde*, and that he was not the first, nor even the second, man to act as her protector. Living with such a person was permitted in Whig circles. Marrying them, and thereby complicating dynastic and inheritance claims, was more controversial. Fox formalized the relationship in September 1795, because Mrs Armistead would be 'more comfortable' as Mrs Fox. 'So', he told her, 'on Monday Morning you must say Love & obey . . . I have no coat but a blue one.' After the ceremony, he promised that they would 'go year after year for the flitch at Dunmow'.[13] Although Fox claimed that he was not much exercised by the matter,[14] the marriage was not made public until 1802, even to his immediate family. His excuse for doing so then was that he was anxious to take Mrs Armistead to Paris as his acknowledged wife.

When Fox told his niece the news by letter from Paris, he insisted that he was 'quite happy that a Secret which never need have been one, is now divulged'.[15] That Fox should show some uncharacteristic sensitivity to what other people might think was justified by the minor sensation his announcement occasioned. As Lady Bessborough noted: 'The odd thing is that people who were shocked at the immorality of his having a mistress are still more so at that mistress having been his wife for so long.'[16] Mrs Fox might be received at Napoleon's court, but she could never hope to expect the same favour at the court of George III. Fox's nephew loyally backed his uncle up, proclaiming that 'an unequal marriage [was] more respectable in the eyes of the world than living openly with a mistress.'[17] But his sister Caroline never really accepted the new Mrs Fox and nor did his wife. The latter had herself been a divorcee when she had married Lord Holland, and her view of Fox was much coloured by the cold reception he had given her. According to Lady Holland, Fox seemed to be operating a double standard. According to Fox, Lady Holland had scooped up his beloved nephew and ward, without giving him time for reflection, and traded on the Fox name ever after, whereas he was conferring status on a woman for showing unstinted affection for nearly twenty years.

If members of his own family found Fox's marriage difficult to accept, the social world in general predictably enjoyed imposing penalties. When Mrs Fox gave a ball, it was described in a *bon mot* that circulated around London to the effect that 'there was all the world, but little of his wife'. When Fox himself was asked to describe the occasion, he referred his questioner to the twenty-second chapter of the first Book of Samuel, verse two: 'And everyone that was in distress . . . and everyone that was discontented, gathered themselves unto him, and he became a Captain over them.'[18] St Anne's Hill was not only now politically suspect for its denial of Parliament and for its Francophilia, but it was also socially out of bounds to all but the hardiest. Its *habitués*, like Fitzpatrick and Lord Robert Spencer, were men of a type whose private lives gave them little to lose. None of this could have helped to revise the opinion of the world in general about Fox's suitability for high office. For this, however, Fox continued to care little. Visitors recorded that dining 'with Charles en famille . . . is really an edifying and pleasant sight'.[19] After his death, Mrs Fox turned the house into a shrine.[20]

The comforts of St Anne's Hill were reinforced by other residents. There was an illegitimate daughter of Fox's called Harriet Willoughby, born in August 1781 and therefore almost certainly not the child of Mrs Armistead.[21] She was 'cross-eyed, otherwise pretty'.[22] There was also an illegitimate son called Henry, the dates of whose birth and death are disputed. Samuel Rogers noted that he died 'a few years' after Fox at the age of 15, while Farington believed that he had been born in 1774 and had died in February 1804. Both sources agree that the boy was deaf and dumb, and that Fox talked to him 'by his fingers'.[23] The boy's disability was a source of great sorrow, not only in personal terms, but also because it precluded him from taking on the responsibilities of a Fox in politics. As a result, as Fox told his nephew, that burden fell fairly and squarely on him: 'Poor Harry tho' an excellent Boy from his misfortune is not what can look forward to with much satisfaction so when I have a mind to build castles and to look forward to distant times with pride & pleasure I must think of you & only you.'[24] The boy was boarded out to a schoolmaster in Kent, deliberately protected from any pressure his parentage might have brought upon him. As he is not mentioned in Fox's will, it is likely that Farington is right in placing his death in 1804. In that document, another boy named 'Robert Stephen' is mentioned, who may have been yet another illegitimate son or some kind of ward. Little is known of this person except that he was reported to be living in America with Fox's schoolfriend Lord Bolingbroke.[25] The household also included a factotum called Basilico, who was sometimes used as a messenger to friends in Europe.[26]

Fox, not unreasonably, was anxious that his own lack of concern about money would not prejudice the well-being of his dependents. Thomas Coutts became Mrs Armistead's banker in 1789, and through him Fox began to make his mistress/wife semi-regular payments.[27] Fox was delighted that his great friend Francis Duke of Bedford, on his death in 1802, should have left Harriet Willoughby an annuity of £100 per annum, and Mrs Fox an annuity of £250 per annum. His wife was also receiving £200 a year from another of his closest political allies, the Earl of Derby.[28] Most worrying was making provision for 'poor Harry', who clearly needed a great deal of care and attention. The bill for supporting him in 1797, for example, was so high that Fox was afraid that effects would have to be sold to pay for it.[29] The last years of Fox's life were clouded by the realization that he was in no position to guarantee his wife and children an assured financial future. It is quite likely that this consideration alone would have been enough to keep him chained to politics, in the hope that office-holding might relieve his burden.

Money worries aside, life at St Anne's Hill was a bustling, even noisy, affair. Lord Albemarle, remembering a visit there as a small boy in the last year of Fox's life, recalled that Fox spent every morning in the library, but that

At one o'clock was the children's dinner. We used to assemble in the dining room; Fox was wheeled in at the same moment for his daily basin of soup. That meal despatched, he was for the rest of the day the exclusive property of us children, and we all adjourned to the garden for our game of trap-ball. All was now noise and merriment. Our host, the youngest amongst us, laughed, chaffed, and chatted the whole time. As he could not walk, he of course had the innings, we the bowling and fagging out; with what glee would he send the ball into the bushes in order to add to his score, and how shamelessly would he wrangle with us whenever we fairly bowled him out.[30]

Fox had played cricket in his younger days, though a combination of overweight and a lack of caution often led him to be, symbolically, run out.

In the last decade of his life, the Fox family drew closer. Fox's younger brother Henry and his wife were usually abroad, but the correspondence with St Anne's Hill is warm and full. The Hollands too were often travelling in Europe, but their political loyalty could always be counted on. The formidable Lady Holland was always 'extremely afraid of my Uncle Charles', but was sensible enough never to challenge his authority in any way.[31] Around the family group was a penumbra of old friends, for whom weekends at St Anne's Hill were always pleasurable: Lauderdale, Fitzpatrick, the Bedford family, Lord Robert Spencer, and occasionally Grey. Little wonder that Fox should conclude that 'I am here well and happy, and shall be truly sorry if any thing should make it necessary for me to enter again into publick Business.'[32] There was 'no place that I mind bad weather so much as this'.[33] Very quickly, the Surrey countryside and a domestic circle offered consolations of an irresistible kind to a man who had failed in politics, but who had never given politics his whole life. Fox took to domesticity with suspicious ease. Gone were the days when, having admitted to his father that he had been visited by the clap, he would be amused by the old man replying that he only wished he had energy enough to suffer the same misfortune.[34]

*

Increasingly, politics had to compete with the diversions that life in the Surrey countryside could provide. Fox was no farmer, but in his later correspondence there are references to agricultural prices, turnips, and the rebuilding of barns and outhouses. A few months before visiting France, worries about Napoleon coexisted with the question of 'Barn or no Barn'.[35] Throughout his life, too, Fox was keen on shooting. Unlike his nephew, who only killed one pheasant in his whole life, a circumstance that brought on considerable bouts of remorse, Fox was 'a very keen sportsman'. He was so keen in fact that 'he would not unfrequently [*sic*] put the shot into the gun before the powder.'[36] However, his pleasure was not to be bought at the expense of others, and he denounced the Game Laws as 'unfit to exist as laws in a free state'.[37] The retreat from politics seemed to have a positively rejuvenating effect. Grey, after reporting house parties at Woburn Abbey, where Fox swam and played tennis into his fifties, mused that it was 'fine to grow young at 50'.[38] On another occasion, he noted that

Fox is in the highest spirits. Every thing seems to be a source of enjoyment to him & I hardly know which to envy most, his admirable disposition or his unrivalled Talents. When I descend from admiring him, to think of myself, how I sicken at the contrast.[39]

When illness began to curtail his range of activities, Fox became 'chess mad'. On being interrupted by public business in the middle of an intriguing game, 'he wish'd all the Politicks of Europe at the bottom of the sea and the Politicians with them.'[40] It goes almost without saying that at the charades, verse-making, and epigrammatic puzzles that filled the after-dinner hours in Whig houses, he was an adept.[41]

The real opportunity in country living, however, was the possibility of pursuing intellectual interests more systematically than a life of politics allowed. In these matters Fox had clear preferences. He had no interest in theological speculation or political science. His reading and research lies almost exclusively in English and European literature and in history. Although it is difficult to pronounce with any confidence on the quality of Fox's personal religion, church-going is never mentioned by him or his friends, nor are religious questions mentioned in their correspondence. His private life had not obviously been based on the Ten Commandments. When, as he lay dying, he ruminated on the question of Christianity, he did not appear able to go beyond a very standard deism, and even for this the only real evidence comes from John Trotter.[42] Fox's nephew, Holland, disliked many aspects of Trotter's book, accusing him of attributing to his uncle many views that he never held. Foremost among these was a sense of obligation towards religion. In his own account, Holland insisted that if, in his last months, Fox allowed himself to approach religion, it was purely and simply to give comfort to his wife.[43] If this was the closest Fox came to religious feelings, even on his death-bed, it may be fair to assume that theological puzzles did not greatly interest him.

Indeed, he was generally suspicious of all things speculative. He had not hurried to read Burke or Paine, and had preferred Mackintosh to both. He had found Godwin unreadable, and his letters are free of quotations from the high priests of the French Enlightenment. He had tried to read *Le Contrat Social*, but had had to give it up as too 'extravagant'.[44] Indeed, he thought that 'Rousseau's absurd to the last degree. I have read but little of Rousseau . . . (for I have not his works) but I suspect his general character to be somewhat like that of his namesake . . . nowhere any *good sense*.'[45] Even the chic new theories in the study of political economy left him cold. Fiscal debate had never been a Foxite speciality. Its general propositions failed to interest him and its detail bored him to death. As he observed to Grey, 'You know, Grey, you and I don't mind these things.'[46] With some justice, throughout his career, Fox was accused of a wilful ignorance of the handling of money: 'when he became Chancellor of the Exchequer . . . Charles Fox, if the story be true . . . never could understand what Consols were—he knew they were things that went up and down in the City, and he was always pleased when they went down, because it so annoyed Pitt.'[47] Certainly, he would have been incapable of initiating the Pittite reform programme in financial and economic life that was enacted in the 1780s. Political economy was 'that most nonsensical of all Sciences'.[48] Its practitioners were bores. When Holland showed an interest in the agricultural reforms proposed by the Spanish reformer Jovellanos, Fox, almost yawning on paper, simply commented, 'As to your Jovellanos, if that is his name, the subjects he treats of are, I believe, very fit to be studied but not by me. The truth is I can not endure them.'[49] For Turgot he had nothing but 'contempt'. As for Adam Smith himself, Fox found him 'tedious'. One half of *The Wealth of Nations* could be 'omitted with much benefit to the subject'.[50] All these theorists could not command his attention or respect, because 'their reasons were so plausible but so inconclusive'.[51] Edinburgh thinking and political economy would enter the clear stream of Foxite politics in the next generation, through the medium of Holland House. Fox himself stood outside all such considerations.

In fact, Fox had other priorities. Literature was, for him, 'in every point of view a preferable occupation to politics'. In particular, poetry was the means by which men 'first discovered themselves to be rational beings'. It was 'the great refreshment of the human mind' or, more finally, 'the only thing after all'.[52] After 1794, his correspondence, particularly that with his nephew, takes on more and more of a literary tone. As Holland corrected Fox's attempt to write Italian, so Fox, in return, corrected his nephew's Latin. A long poem in Latin of 1793 brought forth such stringent comments as 'obscure and bad', 'very awkward this', 'not Latin', 'nonsense or so'.[53] So, too, in conversation, friends noticed with surprise and some alarm that Fox increasingly preferred literary to political subjects.[54] The only remaining question for them to answer, after this discovery, was whether the end of politics allowed Fox to develop new interests, or whether his release from public life had allowed him finally to lead the life that he always would have preferred. The ease with which he slipped away from Westminster, without regret or a backward look, suggests that the second of these options might be the more plausible.

Just as literature was accorded a primacy over other pursuits of the mind, so within literature there were hierarchies of value. In every respect, ancient authors were to be preferred to the moderns. Fox had never lost his Etonian control of Latin. From 1796 onwards, he made a determined effort to recover his Greek. According to his wife, 'he does nothing now but read Greek all day and I suppose he will know it better than Dr Parr.'[55] The classics had always been important to Fox, and now offered endless consolation. He had discussed Roman history with Gibbon in Lausanne;[56] a new secretary was primarily engaged because he could converse sensibly on the subject of the *Iliad*, accepting Fox's view that 'Hesiod, Pindar, Eschylus [*sic*], Sophocles, Euripides, Appolonius Rhodius [*sic*] & Theocritus, are the most worth reading.'[57] Fox had long enjoyed the friendship of the savant and classical scholar Dr Parr, and from 1796 that association was complemented by his taking up of Gilbert Wakefield. Their relationship began with Wakefield dedicating a book to Fox, and it blossomed into an uninterrupted correspondence that was only cut short by Wakefield's death in 1801.[58] It is a remarkable correspondence, in which the appreciation of Greek writers is interspersed with scholarly asides about Greek accents and the editing of texts. Without doubt, Wakefield greatly assisted Fox in his classical studies, and helped him to leave a permanent mark by materially contributing to the dating of the Greek poet Lycophron.[59]

So all-pervasive did classical preoccupations become that they began to colour the context of politics. Fox was fond of comparing the 1790s with the first century BC. He liked to think of himself as Brutus, vainly trying to save representative institutions. Pitt is sometimes called Octavius or Augustus. Another character from antiquity with whom he closely associated himself was Dion, who, having saved the people of Syracuse from the tyrant Dionysius, was then torn to pieces by a mob. As he explained to Denis O'Bryen, 'Pray read Plutarch's life of Dion the character of all antiquity the most to my fancy and the turn of my vanity would make me like more to have his fate than any other.'[60] If Fox believed himself to be of a generation that would witness the end of parliamentary government and the imposition of a new despotism, the classical world offered many examples and precedents that could frighten and console. His sense of helplessness and hopelessness made parallels with the plight of Dion and Brutus easy to draw. No contemporary writer could offer serious competition. As Fox assured Fitzpatrick: 'If the ancients did all these things better than the Moderns I can not help that, and their example, because it is better, not because it is old, ought to be followed as far as it can without flying in the face of fashion too much.'[61]

As far as any 'modern' poetry was worthy of praise, it was rarely to be found in England. Fox's sharp preference for European writers was another aspect of the un-English quality of his character that so many of his contemporaries suspected. He knew Spanish well enough to have read *Don Quixote* in the original, and he used this language exclusively in his letters to his nephew.[62] In Italian and French, he was of course even more proficient.[63]

Significantly, and unusually in his generation, however, Italian literature was to be preferred to that of France. In his lectures to his nephew, he asserted that 'Italy is of all Europe the most worth seeing and if you do not see it now you probably never will, and . . . if you do not go to Italy you never will learn thoroughly the Italian Language & for want of it be deprived of some of the greatest pleasure that you who love poetry can enjoy.'[64] On another occasion, Holland was firmly counselled that 'If I were to know but one language besides my own it should be Italian.'[65] Dante, Ariosto, Boccaccio, and Metastasio were, in his view, the supreme masters. Their works are discussed at length in a long correspondence that Fox undertook in retirement with the Italian writer Serafino Buonaiuti, whose *Tancia* he thought 'the best specimen in any language of what Pastoral ought to be'.[66] Italian literature also figures in letters to M. G. Lewis, for whom Fox seems to have been employed as a translator, and R. P. Knight.[67]

With rare exceptions, English literature was a poor, grey thing, when compared to that of Europe. One exception was Dryden, with Fox maintaining that 'no expression could be correctly used in English composition which was not found in Dryden.'[68] Pope had written some useful lines, and, among his contemporaries, Burns and Campbell were worthy of some consideration.[69] Even so, the list is a short one. Significantly, Fox saw no value whatever in the Lake School of poetry, and seemed indeed to be actively hostile to it. On Coleridge's suggestion, Wordsworth had sent Fox a presentation copy of *The Lyrical Ballads*, accompanied by a personal letter expressing the hope that Fox would enjoy them. He was to be disappointed.[70] Through the good offices of Samuel Rogers, the two men were brought face to face, but the encounter was frosty:

I introduced Wordsworth to Fox, having taken him with me to a ball given by Mrs Fox. 'I am very glad to see you, Mr Wordsworth, though I am not of your faction', was all that Fox said to him,—meaning that he enjoyed a school of poetry different from that to which Wordsworth belonged.[71]

Almost immediately after this entry, Rogers recorded Fox's preference for Ariosto and Metastasio, and that he was in the habit of reading Homer through annually.[72]

In rejecting the Lake Poets, Fox set a pattern that was to be followed in subsequent generations. Coleridge and Wordsworth never figured among the company at Holland House. Foxite objections to their work were twofold. First, as literature, it gave primacy to what Fox took to be a formless and undisciplined outpouring of emotion. They seemed to subjugate reason to feeling. Rhapsodies on clouds and daffodils had little argument in them, and were displeasing to a metropolitan aristocracy. Worse, their lines carried real political menace. If individual feelings were to be given precedence over social norms and constraints, the consequences could only be alarming in the period of the French Revolution. If blacksmiths and shepherds were to be endowed with philosophy, why should they not vote? Politics, even if controlled by Pittites, was a matter for dialogue and debate among educated men. As Francis Jeffrey insisted:

Now the different classes of society have each of them a distinct character, as well as a separate idiom; and the names of the various passions to which they are subject respectively, have a signification that varies essentially, according to the condition of the persons to whom they are applied . . . The question, therefore, comes simply to be—which of them is the most proper object for poetical imitation? It is needless for us to answer a question, which the practice of all the world has decided long ago irrevocably. The poor and vulgar may interest us, in poetry, by their situation; but never . . . by any sentiments that are peculiar to their condition, and still less by any language that is characteristic of it.[73]

Poetry, in the 1790s, by its subject-matter and structure, could not avoid also being politics. Fox's rejection of Wordsworth and his friends was more than an aesthetic judgement. Foxite Whiggery felt altogether more at home in the classical world. Reading two ancient and three modern languages, Fox was not short of reading-matter that offered more pleasure and less risk than the foggy productions of the Lake District.

*

For a Whig in retirement, literature was a resource and a consolation, but it was not the principal area for study and research. In these matters history reigned unchallenged. Whigs had always had an acute awareness of the past. Their creed, defined as that which defied despots and defended constitutionalism, was at least 2,000 years old. The first Whig martyr was Socrates. Their opponents willingly accredited Whiggery with this lineage, but argued that its first practitioner had been the Devil, who had quite rightly been expelled from Heaven for resisting legitimate authority. When in personal and political adversity, Whigs tended to fall back on past victories for support and vindication. This was made the easier because Russell Dukes of Bedford and Cavendish Dukes of Devonshire carried names that were prominent in the seventeenth-century litany of parliamentary struggle. It was no accident that Fox, in turning to the writing of history, should choose to describe the reign of James II. The wickedness and despotic tendencies of this man could be made into a telling analogy with those of George III. Cavendishes and Russells, in remaining true to Fox, were doing nothing more than re-enacting the brave deeds of their ancestors.

What was odd, and faintly amusing, was that in berating James II Fox was in fact destroying the reputation of his great-great-great uncle.

As a parable, the history of James II's reign was avowedly didactic. Unfinished at his death, it was prepared for publication by Holland, who was clear what sort of duty lay before him.

Next summer I hope to be able to get out my poor Uncle's history, an imperfect work but one which will if possible add to his reputation & I sometimes flatter myself infuse into posterity some little portion of that spirit of liberty which he & he alone preserved in this country for years.[74]

In its political purpose, the book became a model for subsequent Whig historians, of whom there were many. In opposition for so much of the period 1760–1830, they had a lot of free time in which to ransack the past for a defence of their present difficulties. According to Lord John Russell, one of the most prolific writers of history in the next generation, the book was 'a work which contains more sound constitutional opinions than any other history with which I am acquainted'.[75] For Francis Jeffrey and the young writers of the *Edinburgh Review*, it contained 'the only appeal to the old principles of English constitutional freedom, and the only expression of those firm and temperate sentiments of independence, which are the peculiar produce, and natural protection of our mixed government, which we recollect to have met with for very many years'.[76]

It was unquestioned in Whig circles that James II was the Demon King of English history. Fox was all the more appalled to discover, therefore, that the history of his reign had been written by men like Hume and Rapin, who had not been friendly to Whigs.[77] David Hume had been 'an excellent man and of great powers of mind, but his Partiality to Kings and Princes is intolerable'.[78] Their factual errors were numerous, as Fox knew from family anecdote trickling down from his Stuart ancestors.[79] He was in the privileged position of being able to challenge Hume with what the Duchess of Portsmouth had told his grandfather, the Duke of Richmond. Quite apart from the making of a major historical analogy, there was much work to be done in simply setting history straight.

The project seems to have been put in operation towards the end of 1799. On 22 January 1800, Fox could write to O'Bryen to say that 'Whoever has informed you that I am going to publish any thing soon, has wholly misinformed you; it is true that I have thoughts of writing something upon English History, and that I have begun doing some little but very little indeed towards it, but I do not want any Copyist at present.'[80] By the late spring of that year, the tempo of the work quickened. Sitting in St Anne's Hill, Fox began to recruit by letter the services of a wide range of people.

Historians like William Belsham, Sir John Dalrymple, and Andrew Stuart were consulted on points of special interest.[81] Talleyrand and Lafayette were to help with the French archives. Using Lauderdale as his principal amanuensis, Fox invited the Richmonds, Devonshires, and Russells to go through their family holdings for anything that might prove helpful.[82] Charles Butler gave assistance on the workings of the anti-Catholic laws, and Senator Barthelemy on the whereabouts of James II's papers in Paris.[83] Holland was ordered to fetch and carry books from Lansdowne House.[84] Without ever leaving Surrey, Fox could write seventeenth-century history by mobilizing the archival holdings and energies of his friends and relations. His attitude to Stuart history was, in this sense, proprietorial.

Predictably, the prospect of a book by Fox on such a subject excited considerable interest. Holland, who was Fox's business manager in the project, was offered the huge sum of 4,525 guineas for the manuscript by William Miller. Longmans were also reported to be interested.[85] Its translation rights were ultimately to become a matter of negotiation and competition as well.[86] By 1802, Fox was so taken with his historical endeavours that his visit to Paris was as much an opportunity to consult archives as to see Bonaparte. The first of these activities certainly gave him more pleasure than the second.

In outline, Fox hoped to begin his history in 1685 and to carry it forward into the reign of William III, thereby putting James II's years in context. This scheme never came to fruition. Fox started with the section on James II, and died before the period after 1688 could be covered. He was 'determined not to look into King William's reign till I have finished K. James's'.[87] Oddly for a man of undoubted verbal fluency, writing did not come easily to Fox. In 1802, he complained to O'Bryen that 'The History after all goes on very slowly, and I assure [you] I have nearly as much difficulty in arranging Prose sentences to my mind, as even Verses. Surely Thucydides could not be 68 when he began his History.'[88] According to Lady Elizabeth Foster, the *History* became such a preoccupation that Fox began to worry that it was eating into the time that should be spent in the reading of novels, and 'found that if he wrote his *History* at night it agitated him, and when he went to bed he thought over what he had written, and thought one word wanted changing, and another would be better elsewhere, and it kept him awake'.[89] All through the tangled politics of the years 1802 to 1806, Fox's mind was half-engaged on the problems of the seventeenth century, rather than on those of the early nineteenth. In its unfinished state, it was eventually published in 1808, with its 277 pages covering up to 1685 only.

The thesis of the book was very much in accord with standard Whig interpretations of English history since 1066. Century after century, a battle had been joined between those with despotic ambitions and those who saw their mission as that of defending parliamentary life. Foxites saw themselves as lineal descendants of the righteous in these contests. At Holkham in Norfolk, T. W. Coke decorated the hall with bas-reliefs showing moments in history when liberty reasserted itself. In the depiction of the scene at Runnymede, the faces of the barons forcing King John to concede Magna Carta are those of members of the Cabinet that passed the first Reform Bill. History was personal to the Whigs. In an introductory chapter, therefore, Fox sketches the awfulness of the Conquest and the magnificence of Magna Carta. All then proceeds smoothly until the arrival of the Tudors. The reign of Henry VIII, in particular, saw the build-up of despotic ambitions in the monarchy, and, by reaction, the first stirrings of a renewed feeling for liberty:

It is now the generally received opinion, and I think a probable opinion, that, to the provisions of that reign, we are to refer the origin, both of the unlimited power of the Tudors, and of the liberties wrested by our ancestors from the Stuarts; that tyrany [*sic*] was their immediate, and liberty their remote, consequence.[90]

Little more is said about the Tudors, and Elizabeth is passed over in silence, for the very good reason that, although Russells and Cavendishes later proved themselves very good patriots, their families had been built on Tudor patronage. For Fox, detailing a Manichaean struggle between liberty and despotism, the sixteenth century was an embarrassment to be dealt with as quickly as possible.

He was on stronger ground on reaching the Stuarts. It was under James I and Charles I that English parliamentarianism was seriously threatened. The men in opposition to those kings were martyrs and heroes in the Whig pantheon:

Their first object was to obtain redress of past grievances with a proper regard to the individuals who had suffered; the next, to prevent the recurrence of such grievances, by the abolition of tyrranical [*sic*] tribunals, acting upon arbitrary maxims in criminal proceedings, and most improperly denominated courts of justice. They then proceeded to establish that fundamental principle of all free government, the preserving of the purse to the people.[91]

Looking at the dark politics of the 1790s, Fox saw terrible parallels. Suffering individuals, arbitrary jurisdictions, and an inert House of Commons all demonstrated that the work of the seventeenth-century patriots needed to be done all over again. Cromwell offered no relief. His regime was 'in substance monarchical and absolute, as a government established by a military force will almost invariably be'.[92] The power of this remark could not be lost on a generation which stared at the phenomenon of Bonaparte across the Channel. As for Charles II, Fox's great-great-grandfather, he allowed certain extensions of liberty, such as Habeas Corpus, but was essentially too idle and easygoing to do more, and in particular to check the evil designs of his younger brother.[93]

Having set a historical stage, Fox came at last to the unqualifiedly evil figure of James II. He, inheriting a family predilection, set out to rule without Parliament, and to remodel the basic structures of English government, in emulation of those in France. It was this ambition, rather than James's Catholicism, that Fox sought to attack. By studying his reign, according to Fox,

> We are taught, generally, the dangers Englishmen will always be liable to, if, from favour to a Prince upon the throne, or from a confidence, however grounded, that his views are agreeable to our own notions of the constitution, we, in any considerable degree, abate of that vigilant, and unremitting jealousy of the power of the crown, which can alone secure to us the effect of those wise laws that have been provided for the benefit of the subject.[94]

It was a simple fact of life that men like the exercise of power, and preferably without restriction. This rule applied to amusing, good-natured men like Charles II and to wicked men like his brother. Power always had to be under restriction and supervision therefore. The disasters of 1685–8 were simply a direct result of Parliament men putting too much trust in the promises of the two Stuart brothers. In fearing a return of Cromwellian politics, they put their faith in princes and were predictably confounded.

The book therefore had a profoundly didactic purpose. History in Whig hands was a weapon in contemporary battles. Holland was clear that Fox was taking the 'opportunity in instructing his countrymen in the real nature of their Constitution', and expressing 'the hope of impressing on mankind those lessons applicable to all times, which are to be drawn from that memorable occurrence [1688]'.[95] Arguing that James II's reign presented parallels with those of Tiberius and Domitian,[96] Fox knew very well that similar comparisons between the 1680s and 1790s would easily enter the minds of his readers. For Judge Jeffreys, read the Scots judges who sentenced Muir and Palmer. For the persecution of Richard Baxter, read of the sufferings of Joseph Priestley. If Gilbert Wakefield was a scholar persecuted under George III, John Locke had suffered under James II, for 'Tyrrany [*sic*] when glutted with the blood of the great, and the plunder of the rich, will condescend to hunt humbler game.'[97] Fox made a hero out of Argyll and nearly succeeded in giving the same title to Monmouth. Inevitably, there must have been a clear association in his mind between their misfortunes and his own.[98] Quite simply, their historical responsibilities were the same. Succeed or fail, they had to try to contain the power of the executive. Increasingly, Fox seemed to be seeking to justify his career, not in parliamentary debate, but in the parable and the parallels offered by the study of history.

*

In the years of the secession, literature, history and an intense family life filled whatever vacuum politics had left. Fox so revelled in these rediscovered interests that it is possible to argue that they reveal the real man. In theory, Fox returned to some sort of attendance in Parliament in 1801, largely to make and sustain a peace with France, but, psychologically and temperamentally, he never returned to politics. The dismal encounter with Napoleon had convinced him that there was nothing to hope for from European politics in his lifetime. English politics were even more depressing. In reaction to these thoughts, Fox, as ever following sound classical precedents, retired to cultivate more personal and, perhaps, more satisfying interests. If he had not been pushed into politics by an ambitious father, if he had had an elder brother or a nephew who could have vindicated the family name in politics, public life might have been bypassed altogether. After 1797, it effectively was. In the last five years of Fox's life, almost everything in politics carried a feeling of anticlimax. As Christopher Wyvill recorded, as late as 1804 Fox

assured me, that He was growing old & indolent; & Power was now no material Object to Him. That when young, he owned, he might look with some degree of Ambition to share with others in Governing the Country. But that was over with Him. He was fond of his place in the Country, fond of reading & loved to be quiet & was happier there, than in the bustle of London. Of the present struggle he seemed to be weary, & to wish himself at St. Anne's Hill.[99]

IO

Political Life Resumed,
1801–1806

FOX resumed political life in 1801, but on terms. His interest in politics was at best part-time. Between 1801 and 1806, only twenty-two performances are recorded in the collected edition of his speeches. Letters to friends continue to address themselves to literary and agricultural topics as well as the continuing iniquities of Pitt. The wish to retire finally is frequently rehearsed, and with an increasing sense of urgency, as, from 1802 onwards, he became the victim of recurrent fevers and other types of illness.[1] As has been noted in an earlier chapter, with the single exception of the war issue, he had become intellectually disengaged from politics, finding compensation in historical and literary pursuits. Throughout these years, messages had to pass back and forth between St Anne's Hill and Westminster to keep Fox abreast of events. His attendance in Parliament could never be guaranteed. He had little expectation of office, and less ambition of holding it. He could not quite let politics go, but he always held it at arm's length.

Quite apart from personal predilections, there were more practical reasons dictating his actions. First, he remained convinced that the House of Commons, and the political world generally, were more anti-Fox than pro-Pitt. To appear and speak at all regularly was therefore to force men to support Pitt, who, in Fox's absence, might have been the target for much criticism. As he bluntly told Grey, 'the House tho' not favorable to him, were still willing to support him against *me*, & that, therefore, it would be best that I should stay away.'[2] Secondly, on the central issue of containing Crown influence, Fox believed that that battle was over. George III had won it so decisively that injured patriots could do no more. In 1804, in talking of monarchical authority in England, he assured Holland that 'There is not a power in Europe, no not even Bonaparte's that is so unlimited.'[3] As a corollary, the House of Commons had so declined in

stature and influence that it was no longer a body that was worth the effort
of trekking to Westminster:

according to my notion the Constitution of the Country is declining so rapidly that
the House of Commons has in great Measure ceased and will shortly entirely cease to
be a place of much importance. The whole if not gone is going, and this Consideration ought to make us less concerned about the particular Situation (in regard to the
Publick) in which we may be placed.[4]

In the Parliament elected in 1802, Fox thought that 'there are Pittites 58,
Grenvillites 36, Foxites 69, and all rest Ministerial.'[5] Against odds of this
magnitude, there was nothing that could be done. In retreat in Surrey, Fox
could only reflect, with a mixture of sadness and apprehension, 'What is, or
rather is not the power of the Crown?'[6]

These arguments led Fox to rehearse the theme of a final retirement
again and again. In May 1802, he told Grey that 'Perhaps it was rather
shabby in me to be absent, but I do not care, and the smallness of the Minority makes it of less consequence . . . All opposition seems to be out of the
question, perhaps for ever; and we may boast, I suspect, that we were the
last of the Romans.'[7] In November of the same year, he declared that he had
'done with Politicks'.[8] In December 1803, only a month before alliance with
the Grenville party brought a new edge to political debate, Fox was determined 'to attend very little'.[9] When a general election became due in the
autumn of 1802, he expressed his wish to retire from Parliament altogether,[10] going so far as to say that if Sheridan were to succeed him as MP
for Westminster, that would be 'what I should on every account like best'.[11]
He was dissuaded from this plan by Denis O'Bryen, his agent in the
constituency, but, not surprisingly, many Westminster electors were unhappy about being represented by a man who hated to attend Parliament.

No doubt there was something of the theatrical in these oft-repeated
statements that never led to action, but they were regularly enunciated until
the end of 1803. Opposition continued to be seen as symbolic rather than
useful. Fox occasionally dipped into politics, but never gave them his full
attention. Such ambivalence was maddening to some of his constituents,
and profoundly irritating to ambitious young men like Tierney or those, like
Sheridan, who thought that continued opposition was viable. The former
first complained of 'soreness'[12] about Fox's conduct, and then went on to denounce him as 'my worst Enemy'.[13] The blind faith that Foxites continued
to hold in the actions of their leader was beyond Tierney's comprehension:

I understand he goes into retirement again this day, to be heard no more till some
other unlooked for chance sends him to Parlt. to favour us with another speech . . . As
the last display was on this side Royalty, the next I presume will be in concord with

Horne Tooke, and thus this exalted Patriot will enable himself to be useful, as he calls it, if occasion should serve, either against the Crown in this reign, or for it in that which is to come. His Friends however give out that he has no meaning whatever in what he does, and seem to think this a very Satisfactory explanation of the Proceedings of their great Statesman . . . Mr Fox may finish his History, and his friends may go to the Devil.[14]

Reflecting that Fox's presence in London might be explained by an interest in politics, but could just as easily be accounted for by Mrs Fox's need of salt baths, Tierney broke with Fox, describing himself as 'an outcast. I have presumed, without consulting Mr Fox, to think for myself, and therefore must be a damn'd Rogue. Q.E.D.'[15]

What divided Fox from men like Tierney was a basic difference of opinion about the public mood of politics. Sheridan, Tierney, and their associates saw the resignation of Pitt and the coming of peace in 1801–2 as the opening up of a whole range of new possibilities. Fox could not agree. The preposterous figure of Addington as Prime Minister, always contemptuously referred to as 'the Doctor', proved to him that royal nomination was the only real force in politics. The return of Pitt to office in 1804 gave further proof of this, if further proof was wanted. All these events were symptomatic of an underlying malaise, unless, as Fox put it, 'death is a fitter description than sleep for the general state of all political feeling and sentiment . . . The insipidity of the H. of Commons is beyond conception.'[16] There was no energy to be found anywhere in Parliament, or in the political world at large.[17] Fox had always been fond of describing the triumph of executive power as the 'euthanasia' of the constitution. That condition now seemed to have set in with a vengeance. As a result, it was 'of little importance' to be 'wholly out of every intrigue, and every connection, except with the remnant of our old friends'.[18]

*

Fox's return to politics in February 1801 was therefore in response to specific circumstances, and had particular objectives. It was, in fact, narrowly associated with Pitt's resignation in that month, after his failure to carry Catholic Emancipation against the wishes of George III. At last, the ice on the frozen surface of politics had cracked. At first, Fox simply could not believe the rumour of Pitt's resignation.[19] When he did, it was thought such a good thing in itself, whatever else might follow, that he rejoiced without qualification:

If Pitt be out, whatever may be the grounds he goes out upon, and however speedy and certain his reinstatement may be, it must be productive of some good; since whatever the result may be, such divisions among them as those must have been which have produced such an event, must weaken them. Besides no inconsiderable part of Pitt's strength consists in his long and *uninterrupted* enjoyment of power.[20]

It was, mildly embarrassing that the issue on which Pitt left government should have been Catholic Emancipation, since Foxites were largely in agreement with him on this point, but at least their motives were different. Fox and his friends patronized religious dissent because it was right to do so; Pittites only considered such actions as matters of expediency.[21] Even so, Pitt's departure from government changed the nature of the game. When his nephew suggested that 'something can be done now',[22] Fox was inclined to agree. As an earnest of his new intentions, he took a lease on Sir James Sinclair's house in Hertford St.

When Addington succeeded Pitt, Fox was unusually rendered almost speechless: 'Addington Chancellor of the Exchequer as against Pitt! If I do believe it, it must be quite incomprehensible.'[23] At first, he was inclined to think that Addington really had had a quarrel with Pitt, and that it was not 'all a mere juggle',[24] but on the other hand it was hard to think 'that Pitt goes out *merely* because he can not carry an honest and wise measure'.[25] There simply had to be 'some *dessous de cartes*'.[26] How could a man whom Foxites thought dangerously stupid succeed a man of great, if malign, abilities? Was it really possible, after a seventeen-year association, that Pitt and George III had finally quarrelled? These questions were answered for Fox, when the details of the new ministry were published. 'Juggle or no juggle', there was no fundamental change in the nature of the government at all. It remained simply monarchical government by royal agents. Addington was even more the King's poodle than Pitt had been:

This Ministry cannot last, say our friends; so say not I . . . The King's power is, as we know, great; and when exerted in conjunction with his Ally, the Church, and therefore in the way and upon the points he likes best, and into which he will enter with the greatest spirit, will not be easily foiled; and you may be sure this Ministry is one quite to his heart's content.[27]

The personnel of politics had simply been rearranged. The fundamental nature of the power that passed from Pitt to Addington was unchanged. Both men existed only by royal sanction.

This being so, Fox's excitement quickly subsided. It was clear that George III was still the master of politics. It was likely, if only because he refused openly to oppose Addington, that Pitt remained hopeful of returning to royal favour very soon. Foxite prospects were not much affected. The only thing to be done was to reiterate traditional arguments:

The line of Conduct to be taken seems quite clear . . . Removal & Censure of Pitt and his Associates, Religious Liberty to its utmost Extent, Reform in Parliament, Liberty in the Press, in which I include pardon in all instances, & Indemnity in others, to Libellers, etc,—not only Peace but a good Understanding if it can be had with Bonaparte, and every thing that is mild and conciliating to Denmark, Sweden etc.[28]

There might be fun to be had in pressing Catholic Emancipation measures, in the hope that the difference of opinion between Pitt and Addington was genuine.[29] More mischief might be had by probing the depth of Addington's professed love of peace. But this was all peripheral to the hard fact of politics, which was that nothing had really changed. Fox summed up his assessment of the situation for Grey by writing that 'as to the new Ministry I am so doubtful whether it is best they or the old one should be appointed that I hardly know, if I had the chance, which way it would be.'[30] Even if the ice of politics showed hair-line cracks, it was still firm enough to assure George III a safe footing.

Between February and December 1801, this thesis was proved to Fox's satisfaction. He told the Commons, on 25 March, that the Addington ministry 'are come in distinctly and expressly to support the system of the former'.[31] They enacted the same penal legislation, using the same excuse of an imminent French invasion. Their attitude to the suspension of Habeas Corpus was so similar to Pitt's that there was no reason to bother to oppose them, because the situation was still hopeless.[32] So little had changed that Fox thought 'this Enlightened Age as it is called is as much given to persecution as the most barbarous.'[33] As with Pitt's recent administration, the stifling of liberty was justified by the spreading of hysterical rumours, and this 'false Alarm had caused these various measures against liberty and that general submission to the Crown, which have produced not a state of turbulence, which was the species of Evil likely to be produced by them, but a state of Slavery and Insensitivity to the blessings of the old Constitution.'[34] As in the 1790s, the glaring inadequacies of the Addingtonians were tolerated with 'Indifference'[35] by the vast majority of the political nation, so that 'it must be almost a miracle to bring back any love of liberty among us.'[36]

The secession from Parliament had been abandoned, but it now became clear that Pitt's disgrace was not in itself enough to tempt Fox back to a regular attendance at Westminster. He was entirely happy to encourage Holland in his efforts to build up opposition numbers, as in the 1790s.[37] As usual too, he was eager for Grey to take initiatives in leadership, including conversations with Addington in the spring of 1802 about a possible coalition of forces to secure a peace, but he was not surprised when these negotiations proved fruitless, and was even mildly relieved.[38] He was certainly not prepared to take undue trouble himself. Addington was a very much stupider version of Pitt, but he would stand because the all-conquering power of the Crown backed him. Formal opposition was pointless. Fox's attendance was sporadic, and limited to certain debates in which he felt particularly interested. The most notable of these concerned the question of war and peace. Pitt and Addington could not really differ on Catholic Emancipation because George's opposition to the proposal could break either of them. On the question of continuing the war against Bonaparte, however, Fox thought there might be a difference worth exploiting. Ever since 1793, Pitt had become so personally identified with the war that he could never make peace but on terms that would exonerate him. Addington, by contrast, and no doubt for reasons that were very un-Foxite, seemed to be more accommodating. Here was a chance. After 1801, Fox, still based in the sanctuary of St Anne's Hill, operated single-issue politics, and the most important of these was the winning and maintaining of peace.

*

The peace question dominates Fox's correspondence in the years 1801–3. It was the point on which he was prepared to support Addington as long as the Doctor remained pacific. It was virtually the only issue on which he showed spasms of energy. In the debates on the peace preliminaries, Fox not only attended Parliament, but did so with just a hint of warmth.[39] He was unconcerned about the detail of the Treaty of Amiens. Indeed, as he told a friend, if the terms were favourable to the French rather than the English, that in itself would be no bad thing, because it would emphasize the futility of trying to impose governments on other countries. The values of 1793 would therefore be discredited:

The war has ended as you say without any proper disgrace to the Men concerned in it, but I can not think as you do that the principles of it have not been in a considerable degree disgraced, so much so, that I should hope the grand principle of it, I mean that of dictating to foreign Countries a Government such as we approve, is as completely destroyed as a principle can be destroyed.[40]

A bad peace, from England's point of view, would vindicate Fox's whole stance on the war, namely that it had been undertaken for ideological objectives that could never be realized. The discomfiture of Pitt by the same reasoning made it even more attractive.

Thereafter, the Treaty of Amiens was, in Fox's opinion, to be maintained at all costs. There was 'nothing that . . . can lead him to disapprove of it'.[41] So important was it that, for the first time in four or five years, Fox began to think that meetings and petitioning could be once again actively encouraged, although he still doubted their ultimate efficacy.[42] As long as peace held, Addington had to be supported, in that his administration's success guaranteed the exclusion from power of Pitt's bellicosity. If this policy involved the putting on ice of issues like Catholic Emancipation and the abolition of the slave trade, because Addington was no friend to either cause, that was a price that had to be paid. The maintenance of peace was a priority, because ten years of war had been the basis on which George III and Pitt had tried to build a despotism. Fox still doubted that the friends of liberty would recover their nerve, but there was no chance of their doing so as long as the war continued.

As has been noted in an earlier chapter, this belief in peace had not been shaken by his visit to Paris in 1802. Napoleon himself had been found to be unattractive, but Fox returned home with the firm idea that he needed peace desperately to secure his regime:

My notion of B's Politicks is this, that when I first went to Paris he was foolishly sure about our Newspapers but ill disposed to the Country and still less to the Ministers . . . Afterwards when he suspected (whether truly or falsely) that we should interfere, he began to be terribly afraid of a War which might in France be imputed to his Rashness . . . France must in some degree recover her commerce, and the more she does, the more she will be afraid of a War with England—But what signifies France? Bonaparte can do what pleases *him* without consulting the nation . . . and I feel morally certain that Bonaparte and all his friends are of opinion that War with Engd. is the only Event that can put his Power in peril. An Army is a most powerful instrument of Government, but that it is not in all cases one upon which Dependence can be had, is proved by the history of every country where very enormous Armies are maintained . . . Whatever ridicule may be attempted to be thrown on the title of Pacificator you may be sure that whatever hold he has (perhaps no great matter neither) upon the *People* of France arises from the opinion that he alone could make Peace, and that he will be best able to maintain it.[43]

Fox at no time seems to have considered the alternative thesis that Napoleon's success within France lay in constructing a war machine and an empire, in which crucial sectors of French society had vested interests, with the result that it was war, not peace, that sustained him. Almost certainly, Fox, on his visit to France, had listened with too much credulity to the over-optimistic opinions of men like Lafayette.[44] Fox's description of Napoleonic France as a regime that could only stand if peace were maintained was further evidence, in the minds of his critics, of a dangerously blinkered Francophilia.

In England too, Fox believed, 'the wish for Peace is warm & general.'[45] In spite of Pittite attempts to saddle him with the title of 'Agent of the 1st Consul', the anti-war mood was such that Fox felt that he now had the backing of the House of Commons for the first time since his triumphs in foreign policy in 1790 and 1791.[46] As he explained to Grey in a long and important letter, there were overwhelming pressures pushing the English towards peace:

Besides the mischiefs of War in a constitutional view of which we have had such Ample experience, the certain misery it must occasion by the repetition of Income Taxes etc etc and the imminent danger of Bankruptcy, a most material consideration in this case, is the moral certainty of failing in our object, & of aggrandising France still more than we have done. I therefore lay as a foundation, that the main object at present is to preserve peace.[47]

The case for peace was so powerful that even the Addingtonians could see it, in spite of being '*dreadfully* foolish; I say dreadfully, for they are so much so as quite to frighten one with the thoughts of having any thing to do with them'.[48] Pittites and Grenvillites continued to oppose peace, not because it was rational to do so, but because their whole political careers had been so compromised by the years of war that they could not honourably disentangle themselves, since their war aims had been unrealistic from the start.

Quite simply therefore, in the months between his return to England in November 1802 and the resumption of war in May 1803, Fox's whole politics were, as he explained to Grey, 'not a support of Addington's Ministry (which must depend on future circumstances) but a support of Addington's *accommodation* with France'.[49] He was 'obstinate' in the opinion that 'Bonaparte's wish is Peace, nay that he is afraid of war to the last degree.'[50] None of the many disagreements between England and France in this period seemed in themselves or cumulatively a *casus belli*. Napoleon's belligerence towards Piedmont, Malta, or Switzerland was regrettable, but they were details that needed to be tidied up rather than fought over.[51] If the French government's behaviour often gave rise to irritation,[52] there was nothing more at stake than the exchange of 'reciprocal Billingsgate'.[53] Talk of rearmament in England was 'mere folly' because it was bound to alarm France.[54] If some people found passages in Napoleonic speeches 'grating', this was 'a symptom that the nonsense talked here has produced a strong effect upon his mind'.[55] Everything could be settled, and 'a few civil words would have done all.'[56] Never considering the argument that a man like Bonaparte who achieves power by military force might only retain power by exercising it, Fox persisted in seeing England as the only potential aggressor,

I will endeavour to be as prudent as I can, but if I am to shew a feeling for the wounded honour of the country you or somebody must shew me the wound, for the life of me I cannot find a single instance since the definitive treaty where the Govt. of France has behaved ill to *us*, many, God knows, to their own people and to the Swiss. It is not affectation indeed when I say that among all I have heard and read upon the subject I cannot find one fair ground of complaint on our side.[57]

It was a stance he was to uphold until he himself became Foreign Secretary in 1806.

When the peace collapsed, therefore, Fox was inclined to blame the English government alone. Addington, an uncosmopolitan figure, had always dealt with the French 'very awkwardly'.[58] Holding 'vapouring language',[59] he was constrained by George III's suspicions about France, and by the wish to re-establish political links with Pitt, who, in refusing to oppose the King's ministers, was clearly holding himself in readiness for a return to royal favour. The shadows of Pitt and the King fell across Addington and terrified him once again into thinking of war.[60] The Doctor was simply too maladroit in his handling of France, and lacked the stature to stand up to Pitt and the King. As a result, he had not 'left B. any alternative but War or the most abject humiliation'.[61] If war returned, therefore, 'it is entirely the fault of our Ministers and not of Bonaparte.'[62] Fox's worst fears were realized in May 1803, but the case England made for resuming hostilities was, he thought, 'weaker than it was possible for the most prejudiced Man to suppose'.[63] In fact, in retrospect, Fox believed that the war of 1803 had been the work of the same men who had provoked the conflict in 1793, and that their motives were the same. England went to war in 1803 ostensibly to defend Malta and the Swiss, just as the Low Countries had been cited in 1793, but the real purpose of the hostilities lay elsewhere. In both cases, war was the result of George III's determination to destroy a French government of which he disapproved, and to continue to rule without any effective parliamentary restraint on his actions, on the model of the 1790s. Looking back on the outbreak of war, Fox assured Lauderdale that he was 'mistaken when you say that I thought the new men drove the Doctor into the War. I always thought it was the K. & the K. alone, & think so still.'[64]

*

Once war had been rekindled, the usefulness of Addington evaporated. The Doctor was known to be in favour of slavery, and against Catholic Emancipation and the reform of Parliament. A more un-Whiggish figure could hardly be imagined. The peace had been his only link with the Foxites, and that had now been severed. Alternative partners in coalition could only be the followers of Grenville or Pitt. The latter option was not absolutely ruled out, with Fox suggesting to O'Bryen that, if such a move was suggested, he would need 'to ballance [*sic*] the different arguments that may be brought *pro* or *con*'.[65] Memories of 1784, however, made it unlikely. Fox would say 'nothing dispraising of P. except doubting his sincerity and decision',[66] and, as in previous negotiations, he would have to insist that Pitt resign all claim to the leadership of the new coalition. Fox could not serve under his rival. Further, a junction with Pitt would be 'such a disgusting measure'[67] in the eyes of Sheridan, Erskine, and others, that it was far from clear that Fox would retain their loyalties. Pitt's concern for slaves and Catholics, though suspected as motivated by pragmatism rather than principle, went some way to interest Foxites, but nowhere near far enough to divest him of the character of being soiled goods.

This reasoning left Grenville and his friends as the only group with whom there was a realistic hope of acting in concert. True, Foxites had been for peace and Grenvillites for war, but with the rupturing of the Treaty of Amiens, that point was now academic. From March 1803 onwards, specu-lations about Grenville's personality and politics began to infiltrate Fox's correspondence. It was clear, after the crowded politics of 1801–3, that new patterns were in formation, and that 'jumbles . . . would ensue'.[68] Fox and his friends were forced to re-evaluate: 'As to men, the folly and hollowness of Addington is, you know, my aversion . . . I have no liking for the Grenvilles or the Cannings: but both of them have, I believe, notions of acting in a party not dissimilar to my own.'[69] Unlike Pitt and Addington, whose whole careers had been built on the status of being royal puppets, because they lacked the personal fortune that would have allowed them to be anything else, Grenville's wealth and intelligence, in Fox's opinion, gave him the freedom to challenge the Crown, if the need arose, and to do so through the agency of party. Grey agreed. As he informed Fox, it was this ability to act on party terms that singled out the Grenvilles as preferred partners: 'I am, as you are, nearly indifferent as to the different Parties, except that I think there is vigour & ability on the side of the Grenvilles, & a principle which while you are acting with them would make them more to be depended on, which appears to me to be wanting in all the others.'[70]

In the summer of 1803, Fox's interest in the Grenvilles was visibly growing. He listened without demur to a lecture from the Prince of Wales on the necessity of a Fox–Grenville coalition.[71] Significantly too, he thought he could detect a softening in the traditional, Grenvillite hostility to France:

In a letter which was shewn to the P. I stated that whatever mutual concessions might be made on smaller matters, I never could be of a party with any men who did not hold that Peace upon certain terms with the Govt. of France, whatever that Govt. might be, was desirable. Indeed I think Ld. Grenville's speeches, as I have read them, are not against peace in general and the very words of their Resolutions that by *remonstrances etc Peace might have been preserved*, are inconsistent with the notion of the sort of war which is now talked of by some.[72]

As far as Fox was concerned, Grenville had become 'unexceptionable'.[73] Most significantly, he was aware that men like Sheridan and Norfolk, bracketing Grenville with Pitt in the criminality of 1784, would be appalled by the idea of coalition, but he was not prepared to accommodate their concern, even at the price of schism.[74] No one was keener than Fox on keeping the memory of 1784 green, but he focused it on the person of Pitt. Others preferred a more general anathema, and this provoked Fox almost to petulance:

The only argument was the one you urged of its being disagreeable to my friends . . . but what do these friends mean? Are they absurd enough to think that we ought to avoid rather than seek the support and agreement in opinion of other parts of Opposition? in other words that we must never gain any accession of strength? This can not be any rational man's view.[75]

The wickedness of 1784 had been the establishment of Crown government. To fight that hydra, it was illogical to seek alliances with Pitt or Addington. Neither of them could or would oppose George III. That option only came with the private means and broad acres owned by the friends of Fox and Grenville.

Although a full understanding was not to be reached until the spring of 1804, at least six months earlier Fox was energetically trying to moderate attacks on Grenville in Foxite publications, and to undo Sheridan's mischievous machinations to discredit the Grenvillites.[76] The more that Grenville showed his willingness to oppose Addington, Pitt, and their royal master, the more he expiated any residual guilt for his role in the outrage of 1784. To attack him, therefore, was folly. In a long letter to O'Bryen, written in June 1803, Fox formally states the case for a coalition with Grenville. He argued, significantly, from hard pragmatism rather than affection:

I still think as I did about the attack upon the Grenvilles and especially upon Ld. Gle. To prove how impolitick it is, it is only necessary to observe that we are exactly doing the work of the Court. Are not they abusing the Grenvilles every day? have they not had even the impudence to call them Bloodhounds? . . . Even the milk & water Adn. gets to something like Invective when he speaks of them. And why are *we* to attack them? as Warriors? are not they the true Warriors who make a wicked war, rather than those who talk absurdly against peace? . . . You will suspect me of denying that we have sufficient cause of complaint agst. the Gs, but, alas, against whom have we not? and is this the moment, when the Court is in direct & bitter hostility to them, and, when moreover Pitt & They seem to be every day getting further distant from each other, is *this* the moment for us to attack them? . . . I can not help thinking that among the different Corps of the Enemy, these Gs are those that have preserved most of something like a trifle of reputation.[77]

Grenvilles had been good Whigs earlier, in the eighteenth century. On the evidence of their willingness to oppose King's ministers after 1801, they seemed to be recovering their family form.

If a willingness to attack George III was the first factor drawing Foxite and Grenvillite together, the second was the situation in Ireland. Both groups believed that Ireland could only be pacified finally by the granting of Catholic Emancipation, which Fox himself regarded as a matter of principle as well as expediency. When war was renewed, in May 1803, English politics was dominated by the fear of a French invasion, with the firm conviction in many minds that that invasion force would first land in Ireland. As Fox realized, this situation created a national mood that was unfavourable to all notions of change. He believed that 'a picture of a People so terrified as we have been was never before exhibited';[78] but, not for the first time, he took a line that marked him out as singular. In his view, the invasion would not be attempted and, if attempted, would fail. Quite simply, 'the chances are so many against success that the Enemy will not try it.'[79] Although he formally offered his services as a JP and, more incongruously, 'as a Soldier'[80] to defend London, he never gave up the conviction that the French would not come.[81] His letters to close friends in the summer and autumn of 1803 are a mixture of scepticism about a French invasion and enquiries about turnips, ploughs, and rye grass. He appeared most preoccupied with the fact that, although he had 'no pretension to farming knowledge', he had '*une grande ambition* to acquire it'.[82] Even at this date and in these circumstances, St Anne's Hill is still his preferred base.

The invasion scare alarmed Fox in one sense only, namely that it increased the likelihood of major disturbances in Ireland. Ever since the great rebellion in 1798, in which his Leinster relations had been so closely involved, Fox was clear that Irish grievances should be met with concession rather than repression. The threat from France simply made this more urgent. While most politicians argued that a national emergency was not the time to consider reform, Fox insisted that the emergency made the reform all the more imperative. As he informed Grey: 'That there should be a part of the U. Kingdom to which our laws nominally at least extend, and which is nevertheless in such a state as to call for Martial Law etc so repeatedly, is of itself ground for reconsidering at least the System by which it is governed.'[83] It was absurd for ministerialists to argue that the bringing of Ireland back under Westminster control in 1801 had settled the problem.[84] True, for the moment, it was comforting to see 'Irish & English Jacobinism quite separate',[85] but a conjunction between the two, possibly in association with the French, could not be ruled out in future. As a result, the immobility of

Pitt and Addington on the subject was comic, but dangerously comic: 'there must be a fundamental change in the system of governing Ireland, to give even a chance of future quiet there. Oh! if you had heard the Doctor in answer to me on that subject! it was quite below himself. *What can I say more?*'[86]

The first element in a proper response to the Irish situation was the formation of a party in England which would be seen as clearly pro-Irish by Irishmen. As he explained to Grey, in October 1803:

it does, I confess, seem to me that the appearance of any thing like a strong party in favor [*sic*] of the Irish might be very useful in regaining the affections of some, and retaining those of others to this country. Besides, I have, I own, a little desire to rescue ourselves from the infamy of acquiescing in the baseness of conceding the most important of all national points to the private opinion of the King.[87]

It was George III's veto which blocked Catholic Emancipation. A king was, as usual, to blame. The problem of finding a coalition that would appease Ireland therefore dovetailed with the problem of finding a coalition that would stand up to the King. Fox was clear that the Prince of Wales could and should be a leading member of such a coalition, because 'the Irish, having hopes from a new reign, would be less inclined to France, and less willing to join in any rash attempts at risings etc.'[88] The age and repeated illnesses of George III suggested that his malign influence would soon be removed from office, allowing his son to bring in an administration friendly to Catholic aspirations.

The creation of a party friendly to Ireland led directly to Grenville. It was true that 'that Rascal Pitt'[89] claimed to be pro-Catholic, but his whole career suggested that he would never stand up to George III on this or any other issue. Grenville might, being pro-Catholic and independent of royal patronage. To force the issue, Fox from the autumn of 1803 onwards began to urge that petitions from Irish and English Catholics should be encouraged, to expose the hollowness of Pitt's pretensions, and to acclimatize Grenvillites to the company of Foxites in the same lobby. If Irishmen like Grattan and Ponsonby were taken aback by Fox's enthusiasm, and if they asked for a delay in bringing forward petitions until they could properly muster their forces, Fox could only acquiesce, but in doing so he was at pains to point out that he 'deferred to the judgment of others',[90] rather than followed his own. He was also anxious to assure his nephew that the delays were in no sense the fault of the Grenvillites:

It is not the fault of the Grenvilles that the Irish question is not brought on; when one knows one's letters may be opened one can not write comfortably especially about

Individuals, but that it is not brought on is a sad thing indeed. I repeat the Gs are not in fault, and *they* will, if there is an occasion, behave well about it.[91]

By the end of 1803, a Fox–Grenville understanding was effectively in place. From Fox's point of view, Grenville was pro-Catholic and prepared to defy kings. What is more, there was even some hint that, on the war issue, Grenville was coming to the view that peace had been lost through Addington's incompetence, and that it might be regained. Parliamentary reform would continue to divide them, but that had never been a matter to engage Fox's full sympathy. Everything else pointed to a match.

*

By December 1803, in the seventh month of the renewed war, the incompetence of Addington was, according to Fox, so glaring that his removal from office was a national duty and probably a kindness to the man himself. He told Lauderdale that,

as I have been persuaded to come into and attend Parlt., it must be understood unequivocally that I am in opposition, and, tho' less actively perhaps, yet just as substantially as to the Doctor as to Ld. North or Pitt. Indeed the fellow's bringing on the War in the way he did makes me feel more outrageous against him than against any one. It is no excuse that he is a fool.[92]

To let him continue in office would be to invite the suspicion that 'a Minister without abilities is best for the Country.'[93] Significantly, Grenville had come to the same conclusion. For him, Addington's government was 'manifestly incapable'.[94] The dreaded word 'coalition' began to be bandied about again, and found its defenders. Old friends like William Windham, who had abandoned Fox between 1792 and 1794, re-established contact with him to defeat Addington.[95] Windham hoped that, after 'an interval of twelve years or more',[96] formal meetings would give way to the reinvocation of old friendships. Letters such as these must have been particularly agreeable for Fox to receive. George III's support for Addington, with disastrous consequences for the search for peace and the prosecution of the war, resurrected arguments about the dangers of executive power that sounded sweet and familiar to the ears of men who remembered 1784. These, together with the necessity of doing something about Ireland, all pushed politics in one direction, dovetailing the worries of 1804 with those of twenty years earlier. Foxite politics suddenly had a renewed currency.

One of the leading authorities on the Grenville party has credited Fox with the sole responsibility for the coming into existence of a Fox–Grenville coalition.[97] It would be truer to say that both sides moved to an understanding at roughly the same time, prompted by roughly the same motives.

On 26 January 1804, Grenville's brother Thomas invited his old friend Fox for a ride. As recorded by Fox, Grenville baldly stated his family's 'wish to co-operate with me (and friends of course) in a systematik opposition for the purpose of destroying the Doctor's Administration', and went on to suggest possible lines of attack. Fox replied that he 'thought with them upon all the subjects discussed and that I felt no repugnance to agree to the Proposal'.[98] To Grey, Fox insisted that this overture had been 'wholly unsought', but that it had been made with 'an openness and appearance of cordiality . . . that pleases me'.[99] In order to carry his friends with him into yet another coalition with men Foxites had recently vilified, it was important for Fox to argue that the arrangement had not been his initiative, but it had rather been a natural confluence of two complementary political traditions.

Only one further obstacle remained. The Grenvillites insisted openly that Pitt should be given the chance of acceding to the coalition that would oust Addington.[100] Fox was happy that the invitation be issued, in the knowledge and expectation that Pitt would refuse to attack a minister appointed by the Crown. Foxites called this reluctance 'lingering after Addington'.[101] In the event, Fox and his friends were proved right. In the crucial months of January to March 1804, George III was calling Fox 'his personal enemy' and 'the cause of all our Miseries'.[102] As Fox suspected, Pitt would never challenge the King, particularly after the onset of another bout of what was thought to be madness in George in February 1804.[103] Pitt's whole career had been built on being a royal stooge. It was too late for him to learn new tricks. The Grenvillites were brought to the same conclusion, when a rumour began to circulate that Pitt, in 1801, having encountered unexpected royal opposition to his proposals on Catholic Emancipation, offered to abandon them as the price of staying in government, without consulting or informing any of his Cabinet colleagues, notoriously Grenville himself. When Fox heard this story, without doubting it in detail or substance,[104] he simply exclaimed 'quel homme!'[105] As he rightly surmised, Grenville was now so angry with Pitt that he hastily dropped any attempt to include him in a new arrangement.

In February–March 1804, the Fox–Grenville coalition became an acknowledged force in politics, but it was an understanding that operated only within certain parameters. Grenvillites were acutely aware of the fact that they were numerically inferior to the Foxites, and that much of their talent was confined to the House of Lords. *Pari passu*, Fox was clear that the purity of the new arrangement was guaranteed, because 'we have so decisively the lead in the H. of Cns.'.[106] Grenville would, furthermore, hardly relish Pitt openly stating it as his opinion around Westminster that clearly Fox 'had gained most by the Coallition [*sic*]'.[107] On top of this, memories of years of antagonism could not be easily overcome. For these reasons, the coalition had the limited objectives of removing Addington, and of co-operating on issues where their opinions were in harmony. The terms of the contract were explicitly set out by Fox in a letter to William Smith:

A proposition of the most frank & handsome nature came from the Grenvilles . . . proposing a junction for the purpose of putting an end to this Ministry & substituting one on the broadest basis in the room of it. To this proposal my answer was that having consulted various persons, I thought it better that there should be no formal junction or arrangement of any sort, but that upon such measures as the two parties concurred in approving we might have that degree of concert which was necessary for giving efficiency to our opinions. How far such concurrence in Parliament might or might not lead to more intimate political connection future circumstances must determine. I will not conceal from you that if I had followed my own opinion entirely, I should have gone farther, but not to go this far was surely impossible. The measures to which particular reference was had, were, the imperfect defence of the Country & the affairs of Ireland, upon which our opinions were the same.[108]

More succinctly, Carlisle, from a Grenvillite perspective, simply described the coalition as a device 'to get rid of the present evil'.[109]

So loose was the arrangement that when, in May 1804, Addington resigned to be replaced by Pitt once more, Fox assured Thomas Grenville that his family was free to consider their options: 'I wish you & them to understand most distinctly, that I have not the smallest notion of any engagement, either express or implied, or any thing like an engagement with me that ought to influence them.'[110] Grenville, by return of post, thanked Fox for his generosity of sentiment, and agreed that everyone was 'unfettered by engagement'.[111] It was hardly surprising that the new coalition should be so tentatively put together. With the exception of Thomas Grenville, that family had been politically opposed to Fox for twenty years. Closely allied to Pitt by kinship, the Grenvilles were not the natural allies of Foxites. In the event, their determination to fight the war determinedly, in pursuit of a peace with defined objectives, together with an ongoing concern for Ireland, drew them closer and closer to Fox. Grenvillite and Foxite edged slowly towards each other, snuffling the air and looking for pitfalls. As in the case of Lord North in 1783, so now with Grenville, Fox would have to convince his friends that an alliance could now be formed with a man whom they had for years described in terms that would have made the waiters at Brooks's blush.

*

Fox was right to expect trouble, and he set out to convince old friends that the coalition was well founded, but that it was one of the most unstructured variety. Lauderdale was asked, 'Can there be less of connection between persons who agree on particular questions, and in their hostility to Ministry, than that which consists only in such concert as is necessary to give their debates and divisions what strength they can?'[112] When Lauderdale remained unconvinced, Fox appealed to history: 'I do not deny the truth of the objection you state to this junction, but it applies to all junctions of the kind, and would, if attended to, make all resistance to the Crown more impossible even than it is.'[113] George Tierney was confirmed in his apostasy from the Foxites by the news of the arrangement, and set out more energetically than ever to undermine Fox's authority.[114] Erskine and the Duke of Norfolk were so upset that they could now be found voting against Fox in certain divisions.[115] At a stormy party meeting held on 21 March, Fox was much criticized for flirting with the Grenvilles. John Curwen, a respected back-bencher, argued for many in saying that the difficulties England faced were not principally the result of policies adopted by Addington, but by the whole drift of politics since 1784. Grenville was therefore as much responsible for everything that Foxites found disgraceful as Pitt.[116] On a similar theme, Coleridge, in an open letter to Fox, reminded him that he had refused to coalesce with Grenville between 1792 and 1794 on '*principle*', going on to ask, 'what is it that *so suddenly* altered the complexion of this party? What is it that has miraculously cleansed away their Ethiopian hue?'[117]

Predictably perhaps, and not for the first time, Sheridan emerged as the leading dissident. Avoiding 'Sheridan's contrivances'[118] was an irritating necessity for Fox throughout the negotiations with Grenville. Sheridan detested Grenville to such a degree that, when they both inadvertently visited Fox at the same time, they had to be shown into different rooms.[119] In his view, an alliance with Grenville would leave the King only one option, that of recalling Pitt, an outcome which Sheridan insisted was the worst of all possibilities. Ever since 1797, he had been annoyed by Fox's seceding from Parliament, yet clinging on grimly to the party leadership. That Sheridan saw himself as a possible successor to Fox, even if very few other people did, was unashamedly admitted, and most recently proved by the anxiety he showed to follow Fox as Member for Westminster. Fox had hitherto always protected Sheridan, and had gone out of his way to explain his skittish behaviour. In the Regency Crisis and in the early years of the French Revolution, Fox had positively refused to discipline someone for whom he felt some affection and sympathy. Sheridan's meddling in the negotiations with Grenville, however, may have been the last straw. Fox began to speak of Sheridan's 'folly', and Sheridan returned the compliment by describing Fox as 'a thorn in his breast'.[120]

In the spring of 1804, Sheridan opened a campaign to turn the Prince of Wales against the idea of a Fox–Grenville coalition. With George III once more incapacitated, the views of the heir apparent were of critical importance. It is, perhaps, no coincidence that Fox's correspondence with the Prince resumes in 1803, with a degree of warmth that had not been exhibited since the French Revolution and Mrs Fitzherbert's loathing of Fox had soured their friendship. In the summer of 1803, the Prince had found the notion of a Fox–Grenville alliance exciting. Six months later, and possibly because of Sheridan's activities, he was wobbling on the issue.[121] Thanks to the intervention of the Duchess of Devonshire, Sheridan's poison was counteracted, but it was clearly uphill work.[122] It was with an obvious sense of relief that Fox was able to assure Lauderdale that 'The best thing is that the P. is much more right than from Sheridan's tricks one would suppose, and I have reason to think that Sheridan sees this himself.'[123]

As with the more famous Coalition with North in 1783, Fox's association with Grenville was secured at a price. Even if most of his friends ultimately bowed to the inevitable, with the possible exceptions of Sheridan and Tierney, the political world at large was once more tempted to think that a man who could associate with former opponents must be a man of little principle. Little wonder that this new coalition should have been undertaken on the loosest of terms, and with no guarantee of surviving very long. Anything more structured would have put an insupportable strain on party loyalties. This consideration affected Fox's subsequent behaviour in opposition, and was the motive for some of his most controversial decisions when the coalition came into office. If he could find the time and energy to accomplish the task, there was much work for Fox to do in convincing friends and the public alike that 1783 and 1804 were of a pattern. The politics of both years were dictated by a determination to check the King's domination of events. Pitt symbolically represented the validity of that concern in both periods. The only new feature in 1804 was that the triumph of George III and Pitt put off peace indefinitely, and committed the country to a catastrophic war. Grenville, like North before him and unlike Pitt, was at least prepared to face up to kings without blinking.

*

When Pitt took over from Addington, in the spring of 1804, he was aware that, in point of talent and, if Addington joined Fox and Grenville, in point of numbers, his ministry was weak and likely to remain so. His first step, therefore, was to try to broaden the basis of government, even allegedly offering 'to include Fox in the arrangement short of making it a sine qua non'.[124] The very fact that Pitt was constrained to make such an offer was welcome to the Foxites for, as Thomas Creevey noted, it demonstrated how desperate a situation he was in. Nothing but necessity could have prompted him to act in this way:

> The King has communicated to him that he will see him tomorrow or Saturday, *which communication Pitt immediately forwarded to Fox*. There is, I hope, much value in these facts: they show, I hope, that the Monarch *is done*, and can no longer make Ministers; they show too, I hope, that Pitt thinks so . . . We are all in better spirits—by 'all', I mean the admirers of Fox and haters of Pitt.[125]

Even so, the omens were unpropitious. When George heard of what Pitt had to propose, he simply remarked that 'with respect to Mr Fox, after he had been dismissed from the Treasury before he was of age, and after his speeches and conduct at the Whig Club, for which he had been struck out of the Privy Council, he wondered Mr Pitt should think of presenting such a name to his Majesty.'[126] When the two men met, on 3 May 1804, George told Pitt that he could only regard the idea as a 'personal insult'.[127]

Next day, Fox called a meeting of his friends, and declared that, since the King's veto applied only to himself, the Grenvillites and Foxites generally should feel free to accept office if they wished.[128] In the event, Pitt's initiative failed either to divide Foxite from Grenvillite, if that had been his intention, or to bolster his weak administration. Foxites like Creevey had no intention of abandoning their leader, and were simply 'struck dumb and lifeless by the elevation of that wretch Pitt to his former fatal eminence'.[129] More significantly, the Grenvillites refused to re-enter government, restating their belief that it was a time for a union of 'men of all descriptions, and without any exceptions'.[130] In fact, the experience of April–May fused Foxite and Grenvillite more closely than Fox himself could have anticipated. What had been the loosest of associations took on the character of something firmer. As for Fox himself, his exclusion from power was almost a matter for rejoicing, in that it gave him a new excuse to prefer St Anne's Hill to Westminster. As his niece reported:

> My Uncle Charles [is] much merrier & more careless than before his exclusion from Ministry was decided, he said he should go down to St. Anne's the next day & stay at least one night. I said that you owe that liberty to Pitt, you are so far indebted to him—'That I am, indeed', he answered most heartily.[131]

Long memories influenced the performance of all the actors in this particular playlet. From Fox's point of view, it was almost more gratifying to watch Pitt struggling to exert the authority of a ministry that was always vulnerable than to be Pitt's colleague in an arrangement that had some strength.

Fox always doubted Pitt's sincerity, and the experience of April–May 1804 had done nothing to alter this view. Pitt was 'a mean low minded Dog'.[132] He was 'not a man capable of acting fairly & on a footing of equality with his Equals'.[133] According to Carlisle, who knew Pitt and Fox well, the two men could never be brought to work together, because Pitt would always be faced with the insuperable problem that 'in that orchestra Fox will in the public view be considered to lead the band'.[134] If both men were able, Fox's personality was so large and compelling that it would always cast a shadow over his rival. More seriously, as his equivocations on Catholic Emancipation, slavery, and the pursuit of peace suggested, Pitt had so completely based his career on the patronage of the Crown that he had, in a sense, become psychologically dependent on the executive. Accordingly, as Fox explained to Grey, nothing of substance could be expected of him:

You know this sort of hydrophobia upon the Catholick question . . . [His] views are so narrow and his fear of committing himself against the Court & its corrupt interests meets him so at every turn that he cannot act like a Man . . . the Court! the Court! he cannot bear to give up his hopes there, and upon this principle wishes to narrow every question of opposition so as to be pledged to nothing.[135]

Quite simply, Pitt represented in his own person the betrayal of 1784 and the Foxite suffering of the 1790s. Even Fox found it hard to forgive.

Not surprisingly therefore, a second Pittite offer of accommodation, between June and October 1805, also came to nothing. From the beginning, Fox would have preferred that the project had not been raised at all.[136] It was a kind of 'impudence'.[137] Although it was mildly diverting to make contingency plans and to sketch out the details of a Foxite Cabinet,[138] he was all along certain that it was 'sure to end in nothing' and that there would be 'no overture'.[139] Even when Pitt made a special journey to see the King at Weymouth, allegedly to persuade him to drop his veto on Fox, there was a firm belief and hope in the Foxite camp that this was nothing but more posturing. Fox's own comment was forthright enough: 'I still hope there will be nothing . . . At any rate I have strong confidence in the insolence of his character making him offer such a Basis, as every Body will see the propriety of immediately rejecting.'[140] In fact, there is some evidence to suggest that, on this occasion, Pitt had been entirely sincere.[141] He was only too aware that, in a period of major warfare, an opposition of Fox, Grenville, and Addington would always threaten, and might ultimately overwhelm him. Trying to convince Fox of his sincerity, however, would be even more difficult than trying to persuade the King to re-employ a man he detested.

Even if Pitt could be believed, and even if George III could be brought to reinvest Fox with his livery, the negotiations of April–May 1804 and

July–October 1805 barely touched on two other obstacles upon which Fox set great weight. It was vital for him that he should not do anything to suggest that he was joining the system established in 1784. Symbolically, but crucially, he must not be asked to accede to Pitt's administration. Rather that administration had to be dissolved, allowing Pitt and Fox jointly to construct another. As he explained to Robert Adair,

The great distinction however between acceding to a Ministry and co-operating in the forming of a new one, is what is principally to be insisted on, and this distinction (clear & intelligible, as I think, to every man) is I *know* particularly felt & understood by Pitt; as, when there was a possibility of our situations being reversed, I mean in the then expected event of a Regency or a new reign, Ld. Gr. Levison [*sic*] particularly stated how different Pitt would feel in the different cases, supposing the proposition to come from us.[142]

On the same point, he was adamant that 'nothing ought to be consented to unless he [Pitt] will consider the present Ministry as annihilated in all its parts and consult about forming a new one. He will never I think bring his mind to this.'[143] Further, to emphasize the fact that any arrangement meant a complete break with the past rather than a continuation of the system founded in 1784, Pitt himself could not be allowed to remain as prime minister. He and Fox would both have to serve under a third person. Foxites would have to 'insist that, after what has passed, Pitt should not be the ostensible Head of any Ministry in which we are to bear a part'.[144] The more that Fox became convinced that Pitt could not possibly accept either of these conditions, the more he claimed to expose Pitt's duplicity. As a corollary, the more the Grenvillites rebutted Pitt's offers to receive them back into government, the sweeter their company became.

*

Throughout the period of the Addington and Pitt governments from 1801 to 1806, Fox responded to events in a way that his critics within the party called listless. Initiatives were not to be expected of him. These came from Sheridan, Tierney, Windham, and others. Fox's role was to set the parameters of debate when chances occurred or negotiations were offered. For him, it was not this or that ministry that was at fault, but the whole system of Crown-dominated politics. According to Foxites, 'the general era of decline may be said . . . to have commenced in the year 1784.'[145] Putting the whole of George III's reign into perspective, Fox posed the crucial question to Windham, in November 1804.

Is it too much to charge upon the system of this Reign, that the errours [*sic*] of it, to use a mild term (the corrupt Servility of it, as I should term it,) have lost first America, then Europe, and that, if persevered in, Ireland must be the next Sacrifice? How soon England itself will follow is a matter of Speculation on which there may be different opinions.[146]

It was not surprising to Fox that Pitt should have refused to oppose Addington between 1801 and 1803, or that Addington should have been prepared to serve under Pitt from 1804 to July 1805. Both men knew that their only possibility of a career in politics lay in the character of royal puppets. Fox's contempt for them and their master lay at the heart of his politics: 'C'est de la pure & vraie canaille que tous ces gens là.'[147] He was delighted that the fragility of their administrations should be exposed because, as royal nominees, their discomfiture 'saw the cause of Royalism (in the bad sense of the word) lowered too'.[148] Addington was a stupid and incompetent man, who was the sycophant of kings. Pitt had great abilities, but he had chosen to prostitute them in the same cause. When news reached him that Pitt might well be suffering from a terminal illness, Fox uncharitably commented that he 'should be very sorry to have Pitt escape in such a manner from the complete disgrace that must at last befall him'.[149] In other words, the period 1801–6 saw the introduction of new issues into politics, notably the question of war and peace, but had not fundamentally changed the basic nature of the debate. Fox accordingly found it hard to rekindle genuine enthusiasm for renewed exertion. His whole career had been moulded in reaction to 'the dreadful Power of the Crown'.[150] The war had so increased the powers of the executive that by 1805, as Brougham put it, 'the country can never have a chance with the Crown.'[151] In his rare appearances in the House of Commons, Fox used words and arguments that had barely changed focus in the last twenty years:

To return, however, to the prerogative of the Crown. If it be, which I do not deny, the prerogative of the king to choose his own ministers, it is equally the right and the duty of the House of Commons to judge of the capacity and the intentions of those ministers; and if they should be found deficient in the confidence of the House of Commons and in the confidence of the country, such disapprobation is a strong and fair ground for the king to dismiss them.[152]

George III had made and unmade administrations at will, and Pitt and Addington had acquiesced. Writing to Thomas Coutts, Fox insisted that Pitt had 'for the sake of office surrendered himself up entirely into the hands of the Court'.[153] He was 'a sad stick',[154] who had given the game to George III.

In considering coalitions and new arrangements, it was not enough to indulge in 'mere trading'.[155] As Fox explained in a long and important letter to Windham, any new administration of which he was to be a part had to signal a complete change in governmental values:

Speaking of the new system of Government, I should perhaps say these last *forty*, instead of twenty, years; but the general effect on the manners and character of the

Nation, being of course produced gradually, is, of course, of a later date, and I may allow the Child to be twenty years younger than the parent. I am as thoroughly convinced as you or Cobbett can be that, till there is a revolution (do not take fright at the word) in the system and principles of the Government, and till such a change shall have produced its correspondent effect on the genius of the People, we can never hope to be what we were, or by any means to be *upon the whole* equal to the French, and, therefore, whatever change of Ministry has been, is now, or may hereafter be, projected, my preliminary question is this,—Is it of a Nature to be in fact, and to be generally understood to be, really and *bona fide* a Change? a Change not of names only but of Character?[156]

This was so dramatic a condition to set that it seemed to some that Fox had lost all sense of political realities, but he was clear that, until it could be realized, the pleasures of St Anne's Hill were not to be exchanged for wearisome involvement in a system that he regarded as corrupt. Only Grenville, as experience gradually suggested, had any inkling of what Fox felt and thought. He at least would oppose kings.

*

The understanding between Fox and Grenville was struck in February 1804, and confirmed by the failure of Pitt's offers in 1804 and 1805. Socially and temperamentally, the two groups had little in common but a concern for Irish Catholics and a belief that, if the war were fought effectively, peace might be negotiated. These ideas brought them together and kept them united. As Fox put it, 'it was agreed with the mutual consent of both parties, that we should make no engagement of any sort, but simply cooperate upon such measures as were agreed upon.'[157] As the months passed, the more Fox came to know Grenville and his friends, the more he found them 'steady and honorable'.[158] In April 1804, he declared that he was 'well satisfied with the conduct of the Grenvilles'.[159] By December of the same year, he was inclined to dignify his coalition with the Grenvilles with the title of 'newly coalesced Opposition'.[160] Grenvillites may have lacked the social agility to cope with a dinner at Holland House or a weekend at St Anne's Hill, but they demonstrated again and again that, having taken a party line, they could defend it. As Fox knew, it was essential to confirm their union by endlessly rehearsing those issues on which they stood on common ground.

For much of 1804 and 1805, therefore, Fox tirelessly promoted the Irish and Catholic questions. As he explained to Windham, he would 'not have come into this Parliament (which it is not affectation to say that I did very reluctantly), if it had not been in consideration of the Catholick Question'.[161] Fox and Grenville believed Catholic Emancipation to be 'absolutely necessary'.[162] In November–December 1804, he was anxious to bring forward a bill for the relief of Catholics, but agreed to defer it when Irish Whigs pleaded for more time to mobilize opinion.[163] In April 1805, when 'almost all our friends' were still unsure about the timing of such a measure, Fox thought it would be 'shameful' to put it off any longer.[164] Significantly, Grenville's enthusiasm to do something for the Catholics matched Fox's. When a bill was introduced into the Commons, in May 1805, Fox's nephew was told to 'thank God and Ld. G's and my stoutness'.[165] The initiative earned him a round of applause from the Catholic hierarchy in Ireland, who assured him that he had 'established another Epoch in the history of your public life'.[166] Catholic Emancipation became the talisman of the Fox–Grenville alliance, and its reiteration made firm friendships that had been tentative. When the issue failed to find a place in the early programme of the Talents Ministry after January 1806, in which Fox and Grenville were the leading figures, both men would have to struggle to find explanations. For the moment, while in opposition, the Catholic question was a powerful weapon. Its endless airing would confirm the Fox–Grenville understanding and embarrass Pitt in his dealings with the King.

Complementing the problems of Ireland and its Catholics was the more general question of the war with France, which had been resumed in May 1803. From the outset, Fox believed that it was unnecessary, being fought allegedly for objectives that had very little to do with England's real interests. Undertaken for 'Malta, plain Malta', it was not 'wise or justifiable'.[167] It was 'the foolishest of all Wars!'[168] Conflict was promoted by crude government propagandists like Cobbett, whose paragraphs simply 'disgust'.[169] As a result, as Lord Minto noted after an interview with Fox, 'Peace seems the grand ruling principle of his politics and all his party's.'[170] He was only too aware that the peace might not be advantageous in its terms, but that, with little likelihood of the war going well, it was simply realistic to accept what was available. He thought that 'the days of Chivalry are past, and that one must aim more at what is achievable with a hope of durability than what one might wish to achieve or really succeed in doing.'[171] He was anxious to fight the war effectively as long as hostilities could not be avoided, but was equally keen that peace initiatives should be in evidence. He gave thanks for the 'Herring Pond and Wooden Walls',[172] and was cheered by Nelson's success at Trafalgar, but only because it was more likely to force Bonaparte, too, into seeking a peace.[173]

Publicly and privately, throughout 1804 and 1805, Fox repeatedly claimed that a peace of some kind could be secured. Only the incompetence of Addington and the malevolence of Pitt prevented its realization. England's indebtedness and trading problems created a peace party of growing strength and vociferousness. In France, equally, Bonaparte was thought to be 'uneasy about the war',[174] and 'would like Peace if we would give way in any thing'.[175] These Foxite assessments were reinforced by their correspondence with foreigners, which the onset of hostilities seems barely to have interrupted. Their cosmopolitan quality had always given them a distinctive voice in politics, and, although contacts in Europe misled as often as they informed, Foxites cherished them and were inclined, perhaps over-inclined, to give them credence. While the war was in progress, Talleyrand continued to perform small favours for Fox.[176] Generously, Foxites passed on information to the more insularly-minded Pitt. When the American ambassador in Paris, while on a visit to London in June 1804, met Fox to express 'very strongly his opinion of the pacific disposition of the French Govt.', Fox requested an interview with Pitt to relay the information.[177] Russian friends like Czartoryski and Novosiltsov were encouraged to think of an alliance with England, but not before St Petersburg too had explored the possibility of a peace with Paris.[178] Friendships in Europe had always led Foxites, controversially, to launch diplomatic offensives that frequently confused the expression of British foreign policy. Talking and writing to foreigners did nothing to reassure men of Fox's patriotism, and some thought he was 'actually in the pay of France'.[179] What justified such activities, in Fox's mind, was that a peace might be had if Pittite obstructionism could be somehow circumvented.

In stark contrast to these policies, Pitt seemed determined to continue to offer huge subsidies to European states in an attempt to keep the war effort against France alive. One after another, they were prepared as sacrificial victims to be gobbled up by Bonaparte. In September 1805, Pitt remorselessly urged Austria into a war that could only lead to her destruction,[180] and, when that destruction came on the battlefields of Ulm and Austerlitz, Fox's resigned comment was, 'These are wonders indeed but they are not *much* more than I expected.'[181] When Prussia refused Pitt's blandishments, going so far as to think of becoming an ally of France, Fox was delighted:

I heartily hope the K. of P. will not join, for while he keeps aloof there is always something to look to, and some new war to *threaten* France with, but if he engages . . . the illusion will be all over, and Bonaparte will *appear* to be what he is, complete master of the Continent.[182]

Pitt's ill co-ordinated and ruinously expensive alliances in Europe had, by the end of 1805, simply had the result of 'making Bonaparte as much in effect monarch of Germany as he is of France'.[183] Peace might still be had, in Fox's view, for reasons that had been set out repeatedly since 1801. Bonaparte wanted and needed a peace, as long as the established and legitimate powers of Europe would accept him. With every defeat, however, the position of a future English negotiator worsened. Pitt appeared to be caught in a vicious cycle. He could hardly continue fighting without a credible European ally, but on the other hand he personally could not afford to conclude a peace on the sort of terms that were available in 1804 or 1805, as military reversal followed military reversal. By contrast, Fox was in a position to make a bad peace, being so totally uninvolved with the war that had made such a peace necessary.

Questions of war and peace were potentially difficult for a Fox–Grenville coalition to answer with a united voice. The Grenvillites had been uniformly hostile to France. They had opposed the Peace of Amiens, while Fox had supported it. As the situation unfolded, however, Fox hoped that he and Grenville could find common ground on two points. First, if there had to be war, then it should be waged competently. The inadequacy of Addington had brought Fox and Grenville together; the failures of Pitt might seal their understanding. Secondly, because he believed that Grenville was a pragmatist rather than an idealist, Fox hoped that, when it became clear that there was no possibility of opposing Bonaparte in Europe, his ally would accept the inevitability of peace. As he explained to Grey: 'if events should occur (and most probably they will), which will extinguish all hope of Austria continuing the contest, then I think our friends will come nearly right.'[184] The great French victory at Austerlitz was therefore to be welcomed, in a sense, because it proved to all rational men that war could not go on.

*

At the end of 1805 therefore, only a month or so before the formation of the Talents Ministry brought Fox and Grenville into government, their alliance had a very clear public face. They were seen to be committed to the relief of Roman Catholics and, more particularly, to the searching out of a peace with France. Few administrations had taken office with such a defined programme. For Fox, returning to government after twenty-two years in opposition, it was the opportunity to vindicate those years in the wilderness by bringing those policies to a triumphant conclusion. In the event, he was only allowed nine months as a minister, and the onset of a terrible illness impaired his effectiveness for virtually the whole of this time. It was Fox's triumph that, at the end of 1805, he had moulded a situation in which he could return to power against the wishes of George III. It was his tragedy that his brief experience of government should cruelly expose the limitations that royal authority and misguided Francophilia could still impose on his hopes and aspirations.

The Talents Ministry,
1806

THE failure of the coalition negotiations of 1805 highlighted the essential weakness of Pitt's government, and then, in the early days of 1806, it became clear that Pitt himself was mortally ill. At first, Fox refused to believe it. Uncharitably, he told his nephew that 'I must know Pitt's Resignation for certain before I believe it, even if he is dying the ruling Passion will prevail, and in these moments as in all the past O! let me keep my place shall be his last.'[1] Within days of his great rival's death, Fox was reported to be talking of him 'like a b———g———d. His party had much ado to conceal their joy and hopes at the prospect . . . of the termination of Pitt's career.'[2] When news of death finally came, there was a spasm of charity, but it was short-lived. Lady Bessborough reported Fox as turning 'pale as ashes', and as muttering in a low voice, 'I am very sorry, very, very sorry', and then 'one feels as if there was something missing in the world—a chasm, a blank that cannot be supplied.'[3] For much of his career, Pitt had given point to Foxite politics by personalizing everything they detested. His removal from the scene in no way invalidated their concerns, but they now had to be differently focused. A determined enemy gives as much definition to life as a valued friend. The loss of both is keenly felt.

Fox regretted the function that Pitt had fulfilled in his life and not the man himself. He was deeply embarrassed by proposals that Pitt's debts should be paid by a grateful nation, and that he should be accorded a state funeral in Westminster Abbey. Grenville pressed Fox to agree to both ideas. In the event, Fox conceded the point about the debts, but felt obliged to oppose the Abbey proposal. The first would merely render assistance to an individual, while the second would seemingly condone policies and a public life that Fox thought damnable. Never addressing the Commons 'with more pain', he explained this distinction clearly:

I must say, that the country at present is reduced to the most dangerous and alarming situation—a situation which might call for any thing rather than honours to be conferred, upon him, who had the direction of the measures which brought it to this state . . . I esteem him the more culpable, as without that splendour of mental endowment, which enabled him to throw a veil over the hideous deformity of the system alluded to, I am fully persuaded, that it could not have resisted the attacks made upon it, and consequently could not have existed, and spread its baneful influence half so long.[4]

The 'system' referred to was the infiltration of executive power into all branches of the constitution. Even though Grenville begged Fox to remain silent as a personal favour, Fox voted against the idea of a state funeral.[5]

For over twenty years, Fox had found it impossible to like Pitt or to credit him with one sentiment that was sincere. Potentially so alike in their views on reform and, from 1780 to 1783, great friends, Fox and Pitt had been so repelled, one from another, that their attitudes were barely rational. Pitt loathed Fox's irresponsibility, while Fox had nothing but contempt for an introverted bachelor who could move neither duchesses nor mobs. Above all, Pitt's ambition and indigence had led him to sell himself to the 'system' of royal influence. The most important point about his death was that that 'system' could now be challenged from inside for the first time since 1784. As Fox insisted to Denis O'Bryen, 'The System must be completely destroyed *now* or *never*, in this K's reign at least.'[6] All experience proved that ruthlessness had to be employed, and 'the taking of anything short of complete Power would be worse than anything that has yet happened'.[7] Fox was not hypocrite enough to pretend that, having detested Pitt living, he grieved for him dead; nor, in this instance, did he have charity enough to dissolve the torments of a long rivalry in reflections on common mortality.

Even so, the clear possibility that Pitt's death would bring Foxites back into government was not unreservedly welcomed. The wish for retirement and seclusion was still strong. As Fox explained to his favourite cousin, he took office in the Talents Ministry because he had to, not because he wanted to:

You are quite right in surmising that my new situation will not add to my happiness, except in the case (which I fear is far from a probable one) of my being able to do some great good. What I owe to the Publick and to a set of Political Friends whose attachment to me has been exemplary left me no choice about taking an opportunity which has been so long waited for.[8]

Another cousin was sure that Charles was 'without the least shadow of interested motives'.[9] From the start, he was not over-sanguine that the coalition that sustained the Talents would be any more cohesive than other coalitions of which he had had experience. The only argument he accepted for coping with the terrible difficulties with which the new administration was beset was that if they failed, the country would be sacrificed to 'the miserable administration which alone could succeed us'.[10] In the event, Fox was proved right. Being a member of the Talents government was to prove endlessly frustrating. It was almost merciful that, by May 1806, the onset of the illness which was to kill him reduced Fox to being a spectator of politics rather than an active participant. Pitt had indeed gone, but the 'system' endured. From the start, it imposed constraints on what the 'Talents' could do, and effectively neutered their aspirations in government.

*

It was clear from the beginning that the Talents Ministry was yet another coalition, which inevitably subsumed within itself many old tensions and points of conflict. Grenville and Addington had been Fox's political opponents for over twenty years. Grenville and Fox favoured Catholic Emancipation, while Addington opposed it. Addington and Fox still believed that Napoleon could be brought to peaceable ways, whereas Grenville doubted it. One of the few areas of common ground had been an inability to work with Pitt, and this was no longer pertinent. Compromise was inevitable, and, as principle was watered down to accommodate new friends, so charges of inconsistency were bound to arise. All the arguments of 1784 could be rehearsed. Gillray nicely caught the mood in a cartoon, *Making Decent—i.e. Broad Bottoms Getting into Grand Costume*. In a theatre dressing-room, the Talents are shown preparing for office. Fox is actually being given a shave, as he hastily hides buff-and-blue clothes and a *bonnet rouge* behind a chair. Addington is lost in a puff of powder. Lord Henry Petty, the new Chancellor of the Exchequer, is struggling into robes that are far too big for him. Grey is shown cleaning his teeth, to enable him to eat his own words, and Grenville anatomically is allowed the broadest bottom of all.[11] Necessity rather than affection had led Fox to co-operate with Grenville and Addington, but it was harsh necessity and that alone might bind him to his new allies.

Predictably, the infant administration was not thought to be long for this world by many critics, some of whom blamed the Foxites for trying to dominate the development of policy and the distribution of places. They were accused of showing too great a 'Spirit of Party', too much violence of language, too unforgiving an attitude to former opponents.[12] Even if Foxite lions could now lie down with Addingtonian lambs, the opportunity may have come too late for any real good to be done. As the Duchess of Devonshire observed: 'At any other time I should rejoice and exult in the assemblage of talent and integrity which we now can boast of, but, alas! in these times what is to be done? It is uphill labour, and it must be to the regret of everyone that the proposed junction was not suffered to take place when it might have saved Europe.'[13] Fox was in no way as pessimistic, but it can hardly have been encouraging that some of his oldest friends saw the Talents Ministry as conceived in despair and born in dejection.

On the other hand, some Foxites argued that, by January 1806, Fox and Grenville had been co-operating in politics at some level for almost two years, and that in that time they had come to respect each other, as loyalties were tested and found to be firm. Creevey, in retrospect, found the Talents one of the most plausible of all the coalitions of George III's reign: 'Fox and Grenville had been acting together openly in opposition. When Pitt got the Govt. in 1804, he could not induce Grenville to accept office and leave Fox. When Pitt died, and old Nobbs [George III] sent for Grenville to make the Govt., the latter would not listen to any prejudice against Fox, but made the Crown divide the Govt. between them.'[14] They seemed to have developed 'a perfect confidence in each other'.[15] Obituaries of the Talents noted how well and how quickly the disparate parts of the new government came to work together.[16] Underlying the whole experiment was the knowledge that, if they could not work together, they would all become victims of a renewed Pittite system, under the direction of Hawkesbury and Castlereagh. Indeed, it was rumoured that the King was actively canvassing this possibility.[17] Fox and Grenville had to find each other's company congenial. The only alternatives were a return to the wilderness or a share in a Pittite government on Pittite terms.

To avoid this nightmare, Foxite and Grenvillite had not only to love each other, but had also to simulate affection for Addingtonians. As long as they too were associated with the Talents, Hawkesbury and the heirs of Pitt had little chance. Courting 'the Doctor' was hardly a task that Fox would relish, but, keenly aware of political realities, he had begun to make official overtures as early as 15 January.[18] Inevitably, this development sparked off yet more controversy. Fox and Grenville were in favour of trapping Addington to prevent the revival of a Pittite system. Others, like Windham, argued that if Grenvillite and Addingtonian returned to government, the Pittite system had effectively been revived. Fox and his friends were simply 'at their mercy'.[19] Attractive and sinister though this point was, it was swept aside, in the hope that the common experience of office would banish old hostilities and set new agendas. A formal offer of co-operation was sent to Addington from Fox and Grenville on 29 January, and accepted after days of hard bargaining.[20] In Fox's view, the King's control over politics had been so overwhelmingly established in the 1780s and 1790s that it could only be toppled by treating with some of George's former servants. It was not an ideal situation, but it met the realities of the hour. Foxite expectations were not high, and therefore great disappointments were unlikely.

Problems immediately presented themselves, not least the question of how offices and patronage should be distributed. It was not simply the difficulty of ensuring that all three parts of the coalition should feel equally accommodated. Rather, it was the sheer number of claimants. Foxites who had suffered twenty years of opposition were looking to their reward. Grenvillites and Addingtonians had, since 1784, had many years of associating office with profit. For Fox himself, there were family pressures and the demands of those like Thomas Coutts who had lent him money against the security of his political prospects. He tried very hard to meet his nephew's preferences,[21] and gave his younger brother Henry a military command, which he thought himself 'not competent to fulfill [*sic*]'.[22] Such was the pressure, however, that cousins were disappointed, one of them complaining that Fox had been bamboozled 'into giving away everything till they have nothing left for those they *love best*'.[23] Rough letters had to be written to claimants for peerages. One such was brusquely informed that there were 'at least twenty Claimants for Peerage whom I should prefer'.[24] As in 1783, coalitionists discovered that the spoils of office could not satisfy everyone with a claim. Disappointed applicants were only then too likely to damn the union.

Most worrying was the possibility of damage done to the Fox–Grenville understanding by arguments about patronage. Fox was determined that Ireland, and by extension control of the Catholic issue, should be in the hands of his friends. He fought hard to have the Duke of Bedford appointed as Lord-Lieutenant, and to implant as many Foxites as possible in the Irish bureaucracy. Even so, it was uphill work. He told Bedford that, as far as patronage was concerned, 'I cannot help retaining my old prejudices on matters of this sort, & am already most exceeding sorry that I have been persuaded to acquiesce so much as I have done in what is called a conciliatory system here.'[25] The Treasury had been conceded to the Grenvillites, but even so Fox felt justified in complaining to Thomas Grenville that 'I recommend a Man because he is a Grenvillite, you seem to accept a Man *though* he is a Foxite.'[26] Later the same day, Fox sent another note, exploding with indignation: 'Indeed, my dear Grenville, I cannot bear it, I can not.'[27] Worst of all, Grenville insisted on retaining his sinecure as Auditor of the Exchequer on becoming First Lord of the Treasury, thereby theoretically putting himself in a position to audit his own accounts.[28] Inevitably, the purity of his and, by extension, Fox's intentions was widely called into question. The squabbling about places and offices was ugly and very public. It was harmful to the reputation of a man like Fox, who for years had been railing against corruption in government.

Equally clear was the fact that a number of issues could only be accommodated if they remained open questions. Foremost among these, as Grenville explained to Grey, was any reference to the first Pitt government of 1783–1801: 'When it was first considered between Mr Fox and myself whether the public circumstances of the country and the state of our opinions as to future measures, would admit of our cooperation, the most distinct reserve was expressed on both sides as to former opinions to which we still adhered respecting past transactions.' Grenville himself was still sure of 'the necessity and wisdom of the measures of 1792 and 3'.[29] Fox could not in fact attack Pitt's record without impugning Grenville's. He was rather brutally told by Grenville that in no way could they 'improve either the situation of the public or our own by accusations against our predecessors'.[30] Fox had little choice but to accept this uncomfortable advice, but he insisted that Pitt's second ministry, from 1804 to 1806, should be fair game for the critical artillery of his friends. Not to attack on this front would be as 'impolitic for ourselves as unfair to the Publick'.[31]

Accepting that a veil had to be discreetly drawn over the events of 1783–1801 was an enormous concession on Fox's part. In the wilds of opposition, his ragged army had always rallied to a recitation of the evils of those years. The catechism involving royal wickedness and Pittite flirtations with despotism had comforted and confirmed. This whole vocabulary was now undermined. Fox was uncomfortably reminded that his partners in coalition had been leading actors in events he had made a profession of condemning. Worse still, they seemed to be thoroughly unrepentant. In a very real sense, therefore, the Fox–Grenville understanding was to be dated from 1804. It had nothing to say about earlier events and personalities. It had no history. This fact alone came close to convincing many contemporaries that it also had very little future.

On top of all this there remained the problem of George III. Bouts of illness, each more alarming than the last, in no way diminished his determination in politics in general, or his loathing of Fox in particular. His personal veto had blocked Fox's re-entry into government after 1801, and, as late as 27 January 1806, he was still clear that he would not 'suffer [Fox] to sit in any cabinet that is to advise him'.[32] On 6 February 1806, Queen Charlotte spoke to Fox for the first time since 1788.[33] Both blamed him squarely for debauching the Prince of Wales and for turning him against his parents. Fox himself was keenly aware of the charge, and vigorously denied it, arguing with some justice that Prinny was quite able to find his own way down the primrose path without assistance.[34] In due course, the King forbade the Prince to attend Fox's funeral.[35] Before he could resume office, Fox had to go through the macabre ceremony of being readmitted to the Privy Council, from which he had been expelled by George in 1798.[36] No one could be under any doubt that the royal curse on Fox's career was still very much in place.

In particular, the King's continuing opposition to Catholic Emancipation made an Irish settlement almost impossible to bring off. Emancipation had been one of the firmest points of common ground between Grenvillite and Foxite, and now the King was undermining it. Fox and Grenville had described it as 'the great publick question on which the component parts of Opposition could consistently and cordially concur'.[37] In retrospect, they would both be criticized for squeezing no firm promises out of the King when the Ministry was formed,[38] but in all probability they had very little chance of doing so. A new status for Roman Catholics would require a new king. If the Talents ministry was to do good in other areas, the Emancipation issue could not be given any kind of priority. Addington was amazed that Fox was found to be 'always peculiarly respectful and conciliatory in his manner towards the King'.[39] This was not affection, however, but rather a bowing to the inevitable. Nothing could be done for Catholics but, if the King were kept sweet-tempered, something might be done for slaves, and a peace for Europe might be established. It was messy but unavoidable. It opened up Fox yet again to charges of inconsistency, but the only alternative was a return to the wilderness.

Grimly, Fox set about the task of positively dissuading Catholics from offering petitions or holding meetings. They were told that such activity would 'rather hurt than benefit their cause'.[40] According to Joseph Farington, he 'rested this recommendation chiefly upon the public prejudices which prevailed in England, and which have been of late widely and actively diffused'.[41] This was hardly a convincing argument, in that public attitudes in 1806 could have changed little from those of 1804 or 1805, years in which Fox had positively encouraged Catholics to act. The real, but unspoken, motive lay in his acquiescence that the whole matter should be shelved 'till after the death of the King'.[42] When Catholics understandably complained that they had been abandoned, Fox bluntly 'answered, that it depended entirely on the Roman Catholicks themselves, to decide between a friendly ministry without immediate discussion of their claims, or the immediate discussion of their claims with a hostile ministry'.[43] There was logic in this response, but neither option offered Catholics any real hope. As a result, Fox's reputation as a committed reformer suffered badly. Even his nephew, rarely inclined to take an independent line against his uncle, was moved to tell him that the abandonment of the Catholics 'was a *stain*' on the whole Talents enterprise.[44]

All in all, Fox's return to government involved a terrible cost. An unseemly squabble for jobs had been accompanied by a general amnesty for the criminals of 1783–1801 and the desertion of his Catholic friends. Further, it was clear that concessions of this magnitude in no way softened the King's view of Foxites. Contemporaries legitimately asked the question whether the Talents experiment had therefore been a mistake. In reply, Holland offered the only possible response. His uncle 'would not have submitted but for the hopes of *peace* & the acquiescence of the Catholics'.[45] It all came down to a matter of priorities. Was it better to remain virginally pure in opposition, or was it better to be able to exercise power at a price? Was it more sensible to do some good or no good at all? Catholic suffering could not be alleviated as long as George III lived. That of the slaves might be. Above all, Fox believed that he, as Foreign Secretary, might be able to secure a permanent peace with France. Since the exercise of despotic power by the executive was in large measure predicated on war, the attainment of such a peace would bring George III's domination of politics to an end, with very great consequences. A peace was the precondition for much else, and should therefore have priority. From a Foxite perspective, the experiment of the Talents should be tested in this area, and this area alone.

*

Ever since Bonaparte's accession to power, Fox had never modified his view that France was in search of an enduring peace. As Francis Horner recorded in January 1806:

Mr Fox was of opinion before the commencement of the present war, that the real intentions and wishes of Bonaparte, however hostile he was to this country, were to make his subjects a commercial people; to keep his own power, of course, as absolute as possible; but to reduce the military spirit and system to which he originally owed it. It is needless to say what ought to have been the policy of this country, upon such a supposition.[46]

Fox was 'sure that two civil sentences from the Ministers would ensure Peace, but they have not the spirit to pronounce them'.[47] In the event, as Fox painfully discovered as Foreign Secretary in 1806, this was to be a tragic misreading of the French situation. Napoleon saw the security of his regime not in pacific policies but in the transformation of France into a war machine that would subsume existing vested interests and create others. If Fox was wrong, however, he shared his misconceptions with French liberals like Lafayette, who subscribed both to Fox's distaste for Bonaparte as a person and to his belief that the general had to opt for peace. As an old friend, Lafayette took pleasure in seconding Fox's ideas: 'Graces soient rendues, mon cher Fox, à vos nobles efforts pour conserver la paix entre nos deux nations. Je pense bien comme vous sur les maux de tous genres que la guerre entraînerait sans qu'on peut en espérer aucun resultat consolant ni pour nos deux peuples, ni pour la cause générale de l'humanité.'[48] He too gave credence to the view that 'Bonaparte souhaite la paix.'[49] In retrospect, such notions were hopelessly adrift. What must be remembered is the fact that they were plausible immediately following the resumption of war in 1803. Napoleon seemed so threatened in France itself that common sense dictated that he should be pacific.

Further, Fox had long held the view that he himself was uniquely qualified to negotiate a treaty. His long experience of France and his many friendships in that country were qualities which, as he told Coutts the banker, could now be put to real use:

There have been moments in these last eight months when I should have wished to have some power, because I own that I *think* I could not only have saved the country from the nuisance of the present War, but have made such arrangements as to give us a rational prospect of durable peace, and that I should from particular circumstances have had advantages for such an object which others have not.[50]

These qualifications were acknowledged by contemporaries, who were, as a consequence, forced to take Fox's claims to office seriously once more. It really did appear that 'the character and direct influence of Mr Fox, with the French Rulers, might procure the best possible terms.'[51] Fox's long-established Francophilia still drew charges of Jacobinism,[52] but, after 1803, it was seen by more and more people as something that could be turned to national advantage. Further, 1806 was the year when peace prospects were brightest. After Napoleon's victory at Austerlitz, not even the Grenvilles, the most bellicose of the Talents,[53] were 'mad enough to wish for another campaign in Germany'.[54] As Fox assured his nephew, Pittite policies involving foreign alliances were exploded, and 'future exertions on the Continent . . . are out of the question.'[55] Circumstances seemed to conspire to make propitious the moment when Fox would chat to his old friend Talleyrand, now French Foreign Minister, to bring peace to Europe.

Contemporaries were fully aware that Fox was 'ambitious of entering with Talleyrand into the lists of negotiation, and of building his reputation upon an advantageous Treaty',[56] and were not therefore surprised at the speed with which talks were set on foot. Compliments flew in profusion across the Channel. Talleyrand, recalling his years in exile, remembered that 'Tous les amis de M. Fox avec lequel, à plusieurs époques, j'avais eu des relations intimes, cherchèrent à me rendre le séjour de Londres agréable.'[57] He assured his English friends that Napoleon's intentions were 'toujours pacifiques', and that the Emperor fully recognized 'les principes d'honneur et de vertu qui ont toujours animé Monsieur Fox'.[58] France had absolutely no claims to make against British territory, and therefore, in Talleyrand's view, 'La paix avec la France est possible et peut être perpétuelle.'[59] It seemed conceivable that the old rivalry between England and France, based on a scramble for territory and trade, could give way to a new understanding, founded on the fact that Foxite and Bonapartist had at least in common a wish to undermine the Europe of despotic monarchs and intolerant churchmen. Talleyrand and Fox both saw themselves as victims of such people in the 1790s.

In return, Fox poured out honeyed words. Talleyrand was 'l'homme de l'Europe avec qui personnellement j'aurois le plus de plaisir à coopérer'.[60] According to Talleyrand's *Mémoires*, the two men had met before 1789, and their friendship had been confirmed in their joint proscription in the 1790s. There was no difficulty about Fox asking Talleyrand for favours, such as the release of prominent Englishmen trapped in France by the resumption of war in 1803.[61] In return, Fox reported to France that a certain royalist émigré in London had embarrassingly requested an interview to give details of a plot to murder Napoleon. Fox admitted that 'ma confusion étoit extreme de me trouver dans le cas de converser avec un Assassin déclaré.'[62] His tact and sensibility were warmly appreciated in Paris, and taken as 'le présage de ce qu'on peut attendre d'un cabinet dont je me plais à apprécier les principes, d'après ceux de M. Fox, un des hommes les plus faits pour sentir en toutes choses ce qui est beau, ce qui est vraiment grand'.[63] This exchange of soft words and small favours seemed to rekindle hopes that the men of tolerant and constitutional values might be able, as in the 1770s and 1780s, to undertake a great work for 'la tranquillité de l'Europe et la félicité du genre humain'.[64]

Only a few months later, the mood had completely changed. By July 1806, Fox had few illusions left about the likelihood of peace, and cartoonists reverted to accusations that he had been simply dazzling the public with tricks and potions. In Gillray's *Experiments at Dover, or Master Charley's Magic Lantern*, a wary John Bull, looking at the beguiling pictures that Fox's magic lantern was throwing on to cliffs on the French coast, is made to say, 'I will tell thee what, Charley, since thee hast become a great man, I think in my heart thee beest always conjuring.'[65] Equally, public statements in Paris had become more menacing. The *Moniteur*, on 8 June, sharply informed its readers that

Si les affaires du Continent prennent ici une direction convenable, ce n'est pas la faute de l'Angleterre, qui a fait tout ce qu'elle a pu pour les brouiller de nouveau. Qui ne voit, en effet, à découvert, la politique des Anglais? Semer la trouble et la discorde parmi les puissances du Continent, et tyranniser les mers pour faire à leur gré le monopole du commerce.[66]

Compliments had given way to insults. As Fox was to discover to his cost, a Franco-British understanding could not be established in isolation. After fourteen years of European conflict, other powers had to be considered, thereby presenting problems all over the Continent. Worse, as he listened to Bonaparte's ideas about how the new European order might be structured, Fox could not avoid the conclusion that the new France was uncomfortably like the old France, keen to dominate Europe territorially, and no friend of constitutions and free peoples. The peace on which the Talents had staked so much was not available. Even Talleyrand was a Frenchman first and a Foxite second, and this realization clouded the last few months of Fox's life.

*

A series of specific problems underlined the point that the differences between England and France were of an order that could not be overcome by the invocation of nostalgia for times past. The first of these concerned the occupation of Hanover. Prussia had been no part of the coalition against France since 1795, and it was clear that its invasion of George III's German electorate had been undertaken with the blessing of Paris. Worse still, the annexation had occurred without any formal declaration of hostilities between Prussia and England. As Fox complained to Talleyrand, it was an outrage perpetrated 'en pleine Paix! après les declarations les plus solennelles! En verite cela fait mal au cœur'.[67] George III was predictably furious at the action of France's protégé, and made it clear that there could be no question of swapping Hanover for some other territory, as part of a general peace, and that, in his view, an immediate embargo should be placed on Prussian goods.[68] For once, Fox agreed with his king. It was pathetic for Prussia to claim that Hanover had to be taken, because Anspach and Bayreuth had been lost to France.[69] Prussia's opportunism had to be resisted with all possible energy. As Fox assured Grenville, he was 'on the most mature reflection, of opinion that too much cannot be said or done against Prussia, and that the taking from her of Poland or any other part of her Dominions would . . . tend more to stop the career of the Enemy than almost any other Event'.[70] Referring to the Prussian problem, Fox gloomily told Bedford that 'our bed of Roses is not very comfortable'.[71]

In these circumstances, it was not helpful of Talleyrand to insist that Prussia should be invited to discuss the terms of the projected peace. Some contemporaries regarded this notion as so provocative as to be proof positive that

France had no serious intention of ending hostilities. Fox himself could only be disturbed by reports reaching him through diplomatic channels that, when confronted with the question of Hanover, Talleyrand was merely dismissive of the whole affair. Allegedly, he told a friend that Hanover was no longer of importance because 'Pitt est mort . . . dans ces changemens futurs l'opinion va plus vite que la politique.'[72] It was simply not credible that a man of Talleyrand's experience could seriously believe that England's concern with Hanover had died with Pitt. Therefore, some other motive had to be found for the French patronage of Prussia, and that which most immediately came to mind was that it was the weapon which Paris would use to thwart all negotiations for a peace. Fox himself could find few answers to suspicions of this kind.

Complementing the problem of Hanover was deep concern about the future of Sicily. In 1806, French troops controlled much of the Kingdom of Naples, and now threatened Sicily. Fox was clear that, should the French succeed in winning control of that island, England's naval superiority in the Mediterranean would be seriously at risk. Such an outcome could not be allowed, even if the French were acting with the real or forced consent of the King of the Two Sicilies.[73] In this crisis, Fox's family involvement was strong. His younger brother, Henry, was not only given a military command in Sicily, but was also endowed with 'a Diplomatick Character'. His instructions were precise: 'To the Court you will of course be as civil as possible, but do not let them have their way in any thing that is wrong . . . you must judge also what pecuniary succour and to what amount can be afforded to the King of Naples with some security for its being well employed.'[74] Henry Fox's dispatches made gloomy reading. The Neapolitan court was 'strange' and 'uncertain', and could not 'be depended upon for two days together'.[75] It was dominated by a queen whose ideas were 'absurd wicked and indeed *impracticable*'.[76] Worse, she was 'prepossessed against me and our Name'.[77] In spite of this, the British ambassador to the Court of Naples was instructed to tell the King that no French troops should be allowed into Sicily,[78] and the Neapolitans were assured of 'all the assistance and support' that the British government could give.[79] Talleyrand's refusal specifically to abandon claims relating to Sicily and Malta offered yet more proof that his master was not seriously interested in peace.

The final point in dispute concerned Russia. England was an ally of Tsar Alexander I, and Fox was clear that his participation in the negotiations for a peace was essential. He instructed the British envoy in St Petersburg to assure the Russians of his loyalty 'in the most distinct manner possible'.[80] This generosity was prompted not only by a feeling of obligation to an old

friend, but also by the practical recognition that geography dictated that
Russian pressure would materially assist the removing of Prussia from
Hanover.[81] All issues were open for discussion between the allies, except
those relating to Malta[82] and Hanover. Russian diplomats were equally accommodating. Prince Czartoryski assured Fox that he was anxious 'de conserver vos sentiments personels', and that he wished to work with him to
secure the happiness and tranquillity of Europe, 'à y rétablir les principes
qui en feront les bases'.[83] It seemed that, even after the disaster of Austerlitz,
the Russians were still to be depended upon to oppose France. The Comte
d'Antraigues was sent to England as Czartoryski's special ambassador, and
confirmed to Foxites that his master had 'a determined disposition to resist
the encroachments of the *tyrant*, as he calls him'.[84] The Russian alliance, one
of Fox's favourite gambits throughout his career, had never seemed more
valuable.

Unfortunately, Talleyrand vetoed all Russian participation from the
start. On 1 April 1806, he bluntly informed Fox of the fact:

Je dois vous dire qu'ici nous jugerons que vous ne voulez pas la pais, si vous
compliquez la question et si au lieu d'une Négotiation, vous voulez un Congrès.
Nous sommes en guerre; nous voulons faire la paix. Si vous faites intervenir la Russie,
il faudra aussi que nous fassions intervenir la Prusse. Il n'y aura pas raison, pour
qu'une troisième, une quatrième Puissance ne soit pas admise ou appellée, et voila les
élémens tout préparés d'une 4ᶜ Coalition.[85]

To George III, untroubled throughout his reign by any prejudices in favour
of France, Talleyrand's ploy was transparently to separate the interests of
England from those of Russia. For once, Fox was forced to agree that the King's
suspicions seemed 'but too well founded'.[86] Under considerable pressure from
the Court and his Grenvillite colleagues in the Cabinet, Fox had no choice
but to be equally sharp with Talleyrand. He was told that 'il nous paraît être
impossible, vu l'étroite alliance qui subsiste entre les deux gouvernemens que
celui de l'Angleterre puisse commencer une négociation, sinon provisoire, sans
la concurrence ou tout au moins le consentement préalable de son allié.'[87]

As Fox's tone became firmer on the Russian issue, Talleyrand's mingled
obstinacy with sarcasm. He reiterated the French view that 'lorsque entre deux
puissances égales, une d'elles réclame l'intervention d'un tiers, il est evident
qu'elle tend à rompre cet equilibre si favorable à la juste et libre discussion
de leurs intérêts.' He went on cheekily to add that the Anglo-Russian alliance was so strong that the Russians were in fact negotiating separately with
the French without Fox's knowledge, and condescendingly concluded with
the words, 'Croyez moi d'ailleurs; nous connoissons mieux ici les opinions
du Continent qu'on ne les connoit à Londres.'[88] Each dispatch from Paris

concluded with a personal paragraph in which Talleyrand asked to be affectionately remembered to Fox's family and friends, but the situation was clear. French interests could only suffer if she were forced to negotiate with England and Russia at the same time. By contrast, unilateral talks with each country in turn would bring considerable benefits. Fox was only too well aware that to follow French prescriptions was impossible, if English interests were to be protected. It mattered little whether Talleyrand was playing the Russian card out of a genuine concern or simply as a way of thwarting the setting up of negotiating procedures. The result would be the same. Peace was impossible. As Fox informed him, 'puisque vous ne voulez pas chez vous que nous traitions conjointement avec la Russie, il faut donc que cette guerre continue, mais je me flatte que nous la ferons desormais en gens qui s'estiment.'[89] Remembering that in 1782-3 England had agreed to negotiate with France and her allies separately, Fox could legitimately ask why France could not be obliging in 1806.[90] Talleyrand's querulousness could only be attributed to the darkest of motives.

In April 1806 therefore, three months into the Talents administration, negotiations for peace looked doomed almost before they had begun. It was comforting that the collapse of his talks with Talleyrand had 'occasioned no difference or even shade of difference in the cabinet',[91] but there was very little else about which to be optimistic. To Grenville, Fox confessed that he 'was exceedingly vexed, tho' not surprised, at the going off of the negotiation'.[92] Indeed, the experience must have appeared calamitous. Ever since Napoleon's coming to power, Fox had argued that France was essentially pacific. His visit to Paris in 1802 had confirmed him in this view. Association with Grenville and Addington in the experiment of the Talents had, to a large extent, been predicated on the possibility of securing a peace. Now, the exchange of a few letters with Talleyrand proved that an end to the hostilities was only the remotest of possibilities. Foxite credibility was so exposed that Fox himself was reduced to the expedient of begging Grenville to release him from the agreement not to attack Pittite policies since 1792 as the real reason for the hopelessness of British diplomacy in 1806:

I feel this so much that I hope you will reconsider the propriety of your desire that we should abstain from accusing our Predecessors. We are not nor can be safe in *character*, perhaps not even in other respects if we do not shew that the present state of affairs is in a great measure owing to the absurd and, in the event, ruinous line of conduct, pursued by the late Administration.[93]

Grenville declined this request, on the grounds that to attack Pitt would be to divide the Cabinet, and, as a result, Fox was left in a position of extreme discomfort.[94]

Grimly, he had to accept the fact that he would have to try again. In June, the Cabinet was persuaded to send Lord Yarmouth to Paris, on a special mission to make soundings about the resumption of peace negotiations. Desperately, Fox wanted Yarmouth to have full powers to negotiate.[95] The Cabinet, more cautiously, gave him a very clear brief: the problems of Sicily, Malta, and Naples were to be settled on the basis of *uti possedetis*; and Russia had to be fully involved in all conversations.[96] In other words, the Cabinet could not be convinced in any way to modify the terms that had proved unattractive to France in April. Yarmouth arrived in Paris on 16 June, and saw Talleyrand almost immediately. Predictably perhaps, there was little progress. He was told that England should be content with the return of Malta, Hanover, and the Cape of Good Hope; that to return Sicily to the authority of the King of Naples would be nothing more than 'a hollow truce'; and, most wounding of all, that it was ridiculous for the British to refuse to negotiate without the Russians, when the latter were quite happy to abandon allies.

Fox received this report 'with much suffering'. He was profoundly aware of how far his own career was caught up in the negotiations. Much of what he had argued in the 1790s was now being tested and, in France's 'Tergiversation' and 'Cavil',[97] was being found wanting. Fox frankly admitted to Yarmouth that 'I feel my own Glory highly interested in such an event, but to make peace by acceding to worse terms than those first suggested to you by M. Talleyrand wd. be as repugnant to my own feelings as it wd. be to the Duty I owe to the K & Country. We sacrificed much in giving up the joint negotiation (I mean joint in form) on which we first insisted, in return for such a sacrifice to hear further of increasing demands, I cannot very well bear.'[98] Worse was to come. On 26 June, Fox had assured Yarmouth that the Russians would keep faith with England.[99] On 20 July, Yarmouth had sadly to confirm that the Russians were indeed treating separately with the French.[100] He concluded that 'We are now alone.' Fox was appalled at this 'extraordinary step'.[101] If Talleyrand really had succeeded in dividing England from Russia, Fox's bargaining position had been immeasurably weakened. Perhaps Paris really did understand Continental politics better than London after all.

Yet so great was Fox's need for a peace that each new humiliation offered by Talleyrand had to be accepted. The Talents ministry had secured the odd success, notably on the slave trade,[102] but it was clear from its inception that its extraordinary composition would only be free from ridicule if it could indeed end the war. Conversations with Talleyrand in March and April and the Yarmouth mission in June now suggested that the prospects for peace were as remote as ever. For Fox, this was a stunning experience.

He had insisted that the French were inclined to be pacific. He had insisted that the war had been the responsibility of George III and his brother monarchs. He had described its purpose in ideological, not territorial, terms. All of this was being proved false. He was completely trapped by his former opinions and, when Yarmouth reported each new French demand, Fox could only repeat that the British government 'continues ardently to wish for the Conclusion of Peace'.[103] In August, Lauderdale was sent to join Yarmouth in Paris, as an envoy with full negotiating powers. He could only report home about 'the complete system of Terror which prevails here'.[104] There was so little prospect of peace that French friends of the Foxites were too frightened even to call at Lauderdale's hotel. Disillusionment was total.

Contemporaries were only too aware of the grisly nature of Fox's predicament. The young Palmerston feared that a desire to salvage his political career would lead Fox to conclude a peace that could not be in England's long-term interests:

A peace negotiated by Fox, and concluded by Ld. Lauderdale cannot fail of being a *chef d'œuvre*. I am most heartily sorry for it, it is a wretched thing and I cannot help thinking the majority of the sensible part at least of the Country will be of the same opinion . . . I cannot see how at present peace can bring us any thing but dishonour and defeat.[105]

Observers of politics noted that 'Charley Fox eats his former opinions daily and even ostentatiously, showing himself the worse man, but the better minister of a corrupt government.'[106] According to these accounts, if the Talents could not bring the French to an honourable peace, what possible reason was there for Fox, Grenville, and Addington to call each other friend and colleague? Enemies for most of their political lives, their new-found co-operation was based on the hope of peace or on nothing. It was a tragic conclusion to Fox's career. The French were not pacific, but bellicose. Old friends like Talleyrand were not Foxite enthusiasts interested in the dissemination of constitutionalism, but the willing servants of autocrats interested in territorial expansion. Just conceivably, Pitt and George III had been right after all. Perhaps the claims of Roman Catholics and Irish Patriots had been put aside for no purpose. These were chilling thoughts for the last few weeks of Fox's life. A contemporary uncharitably observed: 'I did not expect what I may venture to call an ostentatious dereliction of all the principles produced in his long political life by C. Fox . . . He should have died, for his fame, a little sooner; before Pitt.'[107]

*

That the experiment of the Talents ministry was, from Fox's point of view, a catastrophe is undeniable. It is, however, some measure of mitigation that he was seriously ill for almost the whole time. Fox's lifestyle had not been that which would have suggested much concern with general health or longevity. From 1802 onwards, he had been plagued with intermittent illness. According to his secretary, the disease which was to kill him struck with some force for the first time in December 1805, just before the Talents project was set on foot. No doctor was consulted until March 1806, because Fox had a horror of the profession.[108] The symptoms were varied and seemed to indicate that more than one vital organ was affected. By late May, his condition was already bad enough to give rise to serious concern. His cousin noted, on the twenty-first of that month:

I saw C. Fox for *one hour* that he came of a Sunday to see me, & happy was I to *see* that his dropsy & water in the chest and the Lord knows what of his liver, &c., &c. is all fabricated. *He is very very anxious* & very much worried, but he sleeps well if he *can* get to bed by 12; if not, he lies awake & *thinks*, & owns that it *wears* him. He is also billious [*sic*] with heat & worry, & he chose to *frisk* to B. House in silk stockings out of *respect*, & so got a pain in his bowells [*sic*].[109]

It is doubtful, while the negotiations with Talleyrand were in train, that Fox was in any position to give them his full attention. Intimations of mortality were probably as much a matter for reflection as the fate of Sicily or Hanover.

At the beginning of July, the illness was making such strides that any attention to politics was becoming difficult. Robert Adair was told that Fox himself was too ill to write: 'What the nature of his complaint is cannot be ascertained. It began with violent pains in the thighs accompanied with loss of Appetite & great debility. He is however better in every respect excepting the pains which still continue with great violence though less constantly.'[110] On 17 July, the illness was diagnosed as 'bile' and not life-threatening. Even so, his cousin was clear that a complete withdrawal from politics was essential: 'those who love him may be well off if by the sacrifice of public business he prolongs his life. But do not say this, for there is a degree of *malign* joy at the hopes of his death among the Opposition that is savage, & one hates to indulge such sort of people with *such* pleasures.'[111] By the end of July, a more sombre tone had set in among Fox's friends and relations. His illness was now described as 'a dropsical complaint',[112] of the kind that often proved fatal. Old friends hastened to repair whatever damage time and the vagaries of life had done to affectionate relationships, but they found him 'despairing of Peace', and so ill that, according to his old schoolfriend Carlisle, 'all my vision of repairing a large division in our early friendship & affection vanishes for ever.' There was clearly too little time left to make all smooth once again.[113]

On 7 August, Fox underwent the excruciating operation of tapping, which was described by his secretary: 'about five gallons were taken from him. The water followed the stab with great violence; it was very fetid and discoloured, and as it were, a mass of blood which, on being exposed to the air, coagulated within half an hour.'[114] Some relief was experienced for a while, but a week later the dropsy once again began to assert itself. On 31 August, the tapping operation had to be repeated.[115] It was all too familiar a pattern. Legs and abdomen would become distended with water, which could only be removed by the crudest of incisions. Those who had given Fox up as an active politician in early July now had to accept the fact that he was unlikely to recover. His nephew's account of the illness, the fullest and most substantial, makes it clear that, throughout the Talents ministry, Fox was never remotely well, and that from March or April 1806 onwards, his actions were those of a terminally sick man who suspected the gravity of his situation.[116]

Mrs Fox kept a journal of the last few weeks of her husband's life. She attended the whole time because 'We had agreed some years ago that whichever was likely to die first, the other should stay by all the time, and to try to look gay and cheerful; but, my God, who could do it?'[117] In his last days, Addington was relieved to hear that *The Book of Common Prayer* was read aloud, and that Fox 'frequently clasped his hands together, and shewed strong signs of devotion'.[118] He would have been less happy to hear that the reading of scripture alternated with the reading of Virgil, and that Fox's nephew was clear that his uncle allowed a certain amount of religion to infiltrate his last days only out of consideration for Mrs Fox. Fox himself had never been a church-goer, nor had he ever allowed revealed religion to influence his thought and actions. His whole life had been lived within the context of enlightened rationality. If Charles Fox ever approached religion, it was only in the very last days. It is hard to imagine whether he would have found heaven or hell the more amusing.

As death drew nearer, 'He suffered little, but was occasionally dejected: in general, however, he preserved his complacency, and smiled when any friend approached him.'[119] He died at 5.45 p.m. on 13 September, in the Duke of Devonshire's house at Chiswick, where he had spent his last weeks, in the presence of Mrs Fox, Holland, Harriet Willoughby, John Trotter, Richard Fitzpatrick, Lord John Townshend, and Lord Robert Spencer. These witnesses were understandably unsure about the last words that Fox uttered. According to Trotter, he turned to his wife and said, 'I die happy. I pity you.' According to Mrs Fox herself, the words were 'It don't signify, my dearest, dearest Liz.' In their philosophy and warmth, these sentiments more plausibly represent the man. It was a good death in the company of family and friends, but it left enduring memories. Mrs Fox closed her journal with the words, 'Merciful Father, let me adore Thy great goodness to me. Oh! make me worthy of it, and of my dear departed angel's affection for me.'[120]

*

A post-mortem revealed that, although heart and lungs were 'perfectly sound', other organs had succumbed to the strain imposed upon them by Fox's early life: 'The cavity of the abdomen contained about seven pints of transparent fluid. The whole substance of the liver was preternaturally hard, especially the right lobe, the interior structure of which was almost entirely scirrhous. The gall bladder was small, and its membranous coat thickened: it contained a small quantity of viscid [sic] liquid, and thirty five gall stones, each about the size of a large pea, and of a dark green colour.'[121] To die at 56 was to have lived a full life, given eighteenth-century expectations, but the sense of loss was profound. Grenville regretted a man 'with whom every day was uniting me more closely'.[122] Lauderdale had lost the friend he had 'loved most on earth'.[123] Lafayette, in a letter to Mrs Fox, was sure that the death of her husband 'ajoute . . . au deuil général de l'Humanité.'[124] Even the Prince of Wales was deeply moved:

without Him, I can neither be of use to the Country, my Friends, nor to myself. He has not only been the Friend of my heart, but with his all powerful mind he has instructed me, & with his hand from the earliest days of my Youth, has led me along the path of True Patriotism, what am I then to do without my Friend, my Supporter, & such a Friend, & such a Supporter too, 'tis too much, too much.[125]

Such was the number of tributes that they were collected together, and published, under the title *Characters of the late Charles James Fox*.[126] It was an extraordinary recognition of qualities that had rarely been allowed to be expressed in office or official positions, but which were all too obvious in spite of that.

Fox's will was a simple document: £250 was given to Lord Holland and to 'Robert Stephen a Youth now living with Lord Viscount Bolingbroke in America'; an annuity was secured for Harriet Willoughby. Everything else was left to Mrs Fox, who was requested to give presents to Holland, General Fox, Fitzpatrick, Lord Robert Spencer, Fitzwilliam, James Hare, the Bishop of Down, Lord John Townshend, Miss Fox, and Mr Bouverie, because, although 'there are many others whom I love and value to the greatest Degree . . . these are my Oldest Connections'.[127] Since he is not mentioned in this document, it is fair to assume that Fox's son, Henry, had died before 1806.[128] For a man who had lived his whole life with a total disregard for financial propriety, Fox's executors were left with a surprisingly simple task.

The funeral took place on 10 October. Two days earlier advertisements in the main London newspapers warned those intending to come that so great were the numbers expected that names should be sent in advance to the undertakers. Gentlemen were requested 'to come provided with black silk scarves, properly fastened on their right shoulders, and black silk hat-bands and gloves, and dressed in plain mourning, with or without powder'.[129] It was a point of pride, repeatedly referred to in the Foxite press, that, although Fox's funeral unlike Pitt's was a private affair and not ordered by the state or the nation, the numbers attending were as great as those who had turned out for Pitt a few months earlier, and were better behaved:

The solemn dignity of the obsequies derived its most affecting interest from the circumstances of the whole being the spontaneous effusion of popular feeling. There was no national or public arrangement. This was not a ceremony ordered by the State, and conducted according to the etiquette of the Herald's College; but it was the voluntary and heartfelt tribute of a sensible people to the memory of a Statesman who had devoted his life to their service . . . No funeral ordered by the State could have been so truly honourable to the deceased.[130]

The procession from St James's to Westminster Abbey set off at two in the afternoon. The entire Cabinet attended, and over a hundred MPs followed the coffin on foot. The pall-bearers were drawn from the heart of grand Whiggery: Devonshire, Norfolk, Carlisle, Albemarle, Fitzwilliam, Holland, Thanet, and the Lord Chancellor. By the Prince's order, his Volunteer regiment marshalled the crowds. Along the route several bands of musicians played the Dead March from *Saul*. The service was read by the Dean of Westminster, and Fox was laid to rest in a grave, eight feet deep and 'bricked and paved'. Throughout, the depth of grief expressed had given the whole day a dignity that was often missing from such occasions: 'what particularly contributed to the effect was, the orderly demeanour, silence and sorrow of the immense multitudes which were assembled in the streets. They required neither the civil nor military authorities to keep the lines and preserve order.'[131]

Management of the funeral arrangements had fallen to the lot of a committee chaired by Samuel Rogers. The total cost came to a staggering £2,840. 7s. 21/2d.[132] Nothing daunted, the Duke of Bedford called a meeting three years later to raise funds for a statue to Fox in the Abbey, for which the sculptor Westmacott gave an estimate of £6,000.[133] The task of collecting the money was entrusted to William Adam, who was to be preoccupied with this responsibility for the next seven years.[134] No doubt, part of the reason why this sum was so difficult to find was that Fox's friends were also being dunned to pay off debts outstanding at his death.[135] In the event, funds were found, and Fox's grave is now marked by a magnificent memorial, showing the dying statesman lying on a couch and dressed in a toga, attended by two women also dressed in classical draperies. At the foot of the couch kneels the figure of a weeping Negro.

*

1806 was a terrible year in British politics. It not only saw the deaths of two men, who had dominated politics for over twenty years, but it also saw the public exposure of their policies. Pitt could not win his war. Fox could not secure his peace. Napoleon's victory at Austerlitz clouded Pitt's last days, suggesting that his grand strategy of a European coalition to contain France, pursued since 1793, was in ruins. Equally, Fox's humiliating failure to bring Talleyrand to a serious discussion of peace was a terrible indictment of much of what he had been arguing for nearly two decades. Catholics and other reformers had been told to stay their demands until peace had been secured, and now they could reasonably accuse Fox of betrayal. The great achievement of ending the slave trade[136] could be set against this record of failure, but it hardly moved the overall balance. Both Pitt and Fox died in disillusionment. Little wonder then that, when Foxite and Pittite cults sprang up in the years following their deaths, worshippers glossed over the traumas of 1806. Rather, the reputation of the two men was predictably to be established by reflection on their careers as a whole, and by discussing the general ideas and principles they were thought to hold. This must be the task of the final chapter.

12

Reform and Liberalism

Fox very quickly became the subject of hagiography. From the Foxite cults of the early nineteenth century to the biographies written by twentieth-century Liberals in search of ancestors,[1] the line of argument was clear. Fox was to be hailed as a keen reformer in religious and political life, and his arguments on these issues contributed mightily to the formation of the liberal creed of subsequent centuries. In fact, although there are strong liberal themes in much of what Fox said and wrote, he was never the reformer that later generations would have wished him to be. His advocacy of change was restricted to certain issues, and was motivated by specific experiences. He never developed an overall philosophy of life that could guide in matters moral, political, and religious all at the same time. Certain arguments engaged his sympathy and attention. Others did not. He would probably have been flattered, but almost certainly he would have been more amused, to discover that he had been credited with forming the ideas that guided the sober men in frock-coats who led Victorian Liberalism.

Fox's reputation in this area must rest on the fact that he was almost entirely free of the influence of organized religion. There is no record of church-going at any stage of life. The sermons and homilies that made up so great a part of eighteenth-century reading found no place in his library. This being so, Fox was able to argue that the whole field of moral choice should be open to the individual, without any constraints imposed by political or religious establishments. His own life had been very much lived on these assumptions, often to the scandal of contemporaries, and Fox wanted them extended to others. Some of his earliest parliamentary performances were given in favour of what might be called humanitarian issues, often involving a softening of clerical control. He voted, for example, for a diminution in the number of offences that carried the penalty of capital punishment. In April 1771, he spoke against a bill that sought to prevent divorced women from marrying the co-respondents in their cases. As a junior minister, he gave great offence to the Prime Minister, Lord North, by supporting and acting as a Teller for a bill to relieve Dissenters of the necessity of taking a religious test as a condition of entry to Oxford and Cambridge.[2] Dissenters and Roman Catholics often looked askance at Fox's private life, but they learnt early in his career that he was a friend. Having little religion himself, Fox could hardly object to anyone else's.

What is not nearly so clear is whether Fox approached the institutional life of England with the same open-handed willingness to advocate change. Unlike nineteenth-century Liberals, Fox was always very circumspect about attacking long-standing constitutional arrangements. His political vocabulary never moved away from the conventional worship of the Glorious Revolution, and the reiteration of the standard view that English liberties were guaranteed by the metaphor of the balance, whereby the privileges of the Lords and Commons complemented the prerogatives of the Crown. It was all well-worn stuff, and reaffirms the extent to which Fox remained his father's son. As a result, whenever parliamentary reform was in question, or whenever there was a suggestion that the constitutional relationship between England and Ireland might be amended, Fox's response was so hedged about with equivocation that contemporary reformers were inclined to give him up. Men as disparate as Wyvill, Place, Jebb, and Flood, at various points in their campaigns for constitutional change, despaired of him. Fox's liberalism therefore comes down to the simple proposition that he claimed for others the freedom that he so expansively exercised in his own life, in terms of behaviour, thought, and belief. This objective in no way implied constitutional change. Fox was so committed to a pride in the values of eighteenth-century parliamentarianism that he endlessly advised Frenchmen to copy them. Changes of the sort he desired could be secured without significant alterations in political thought or practice.

*

After his death, there was a lively debate on the question of where Fox had exactly stood on the issue of religion. In retrospect, some writers tried hard to claim him for Christianity, or at least for a milk-and-water deism.[3] In fact, Fox had very little contact with the Church. Few clergymen were numbered among his friends. Those that were were sociable vicars like Henry Bate, who could turn an epigram as expertly and drink as hard as any man in London. A rare exception was William Dickson, Bishop of Down, for whom Fox wrote an epitaph. Significantly, it dwells on the bishop's public virtues, rather than his piety or theology:

Of his publick Character the love of Liberty, and especially of Religious Liberty, was the prominent feature, sincere in his own Faith he abhorred the thought of holding out temptations to Prevarication or Insincerity in others, and was a decided Enemy, both as a Bishop and a Legislator, to laws whose tendency is to seduce or deter Men from the open and undisguised profession of their Religious Opinions by Reward & Punishment, by political Advantages, and political Disabilities.[4]

In fact, Fox was clear that genuine toleration was usually only to be found in those who stood at a tangent to organized religion. Samuel Rogers recorded him as saying, in 1805, that 'The only foundation for toleration is a degree of Scepticism and without it there can be none, for if a man believes in the saving of souls, he must soon think about the means; and if, by cutting off one generation, he can save many future ones from Hell-fire, it is his duty to do it.'[5] Certainly, cartoonists and religious pamphleteers never gave Fox the benefit of the religious doubt. Gillray's *Repeal of the Test Act* of February 1790, for example, embraced motifs that enjoyed a wide currency. Fox, standing on a balcony, supervises, with the aid of a speaking trumpet, a riot in which bishops are being clubbed and in which the Dissenter Joseph Priestley expertly oversees the demolition of churches. When Fox's secretary attempted one of the earliest biographies of his employer, he consulted members of the family, after which he assured them that he had 'wholly expunged the Passage in which I had spoken of Mr Fox as a Believer in a future State'.[6] He was probably right to do so.

Free of a determining, personal belief, Fox could take aim at those laws, notably the Test Acts, which sought to impose penalties on non-Anglicans. Against them he brought two arguments, one historical and the other philosophical. Fox the historian was only too well aware that Anglicanism had been defended in law in the sixteenth and seventeenth centuries, because it was believed with some justice that it was the form of religion which alone felt sympathy for a system of government under which property-owners and the values of property were pre-eminent. Catholicism was too closely associated with monarchical despotisms in France and Spain, and Dissent with the levelling reputation of the Cromwellian period. By the end of the eighteenth century, however, Fox was sure that the old link between dissident religion and political threat had been broken. Most of the states in continental Europe now employed ministers and soldiers of all religions. Adopting a favourite tactic of invoking the new enlightenment of his generation, Fox argued for an end to old slogans:

For base and insidious purposes, a clamour has been excited that *the Church is in Danger* . . . In these enlightened days, however, it has lost much of its influence and efficacy, and if there are those who really conceive the Church to be in danger because the State is no longer disposed to be unjust; I will only say that they must be very timid indeed.[7]

All experience seemed to prove his point. During scares over Jacobite invasion and French fleets, English Catholics had, by and large, demonstrated nothing but loyalty to the Hanoverians. The day was long past when a Pope could exercise real, political power. To argue otherwise was to set off an 'alarm which can be accounted for on no rational principle'.[8] As for the Dissenters, they had resisted the blandishments of James II, and had, for more than a century, done nothing worse than indulge in undue sobriety. The fact that the Church of England continued to persecute them made that Church the enemy of rational Whiggery. Fox was adamant that 'a point of Toleration is the last thing upon which the Church ought to be consulted, and we are the last persons who ought to consult her upon anything, for if the Church Party is not the most determined enemy of the Whigs there is no trusting experience in any thing.'[9] Foxites should rejoice that the set of historical experiences that had given the Test Acts whatever historical validity they had possessed were now gone forever. On no account should they be shy in challenging the Anglican monopoly. Rather, their well-developed historical consciousness counselled boldness.

If history proved that the Test Acts were no longer useful, the new philosophical insights of the eighteenth century proved that they were unjust. Claiming free judgement in religious matters as a right shared by all men, Fox came close to using that Painite vocabulary which he always disavowed in politics. Contemporaries, listening to his speeches in favour of toleration, could be forgiven for thinking him a full subscriber to natural rights philosophy. In March 1791, he assured the House of Commons that 'Toleration in religion was one of the great rights of man, and a man ought never to be deprived of what was his natural right.'[10] A year later, as events in France gave many words a new edge, Fox's remained unrestrained:

Toleration was not to be regarded as a thing convenient and useful to a state, but a thing in itself essentially right and just. He, therefore, laid it down as his principle, that those who lived in a state where there was an establishment of religion, could fairly be bound only by that part of the establishment which was consistent with the pure principles of toleration. What were those principles? On what were they founded? On the fundamental, unalienable [*sic*] rights of man.[11]

Almost certainly, Fox's use of phrases about natural rights owed more to Locke than to Paine,[12] but his belief that demands for toleration could be firmly based on principle rather than utility was firm and unshakeable.

Warming to his theme, he increasingly argued that the state had no right to regulate or influence matters of private judgement, as long as opinion never translated into action injurious to the commonweal. A firm distinction ought to be drawn between Church and State,[13] based on the assumption that 'No human government had a right to enquire into private opinions.'[14] He and his friends had always followed private judgement in matters of religion, if only by largely ignoring it, so why should the same facility not be extended to others? A sense of urgency entered the argument as the religious revivalism of the late eighteenth century underpinned many of the moralistic crusades of which the Foxites were often perceived enemies. Therefore, when Irish Catholics were prepared to campaign for relief on the practical grounds that they were no longer dangerous, Fox insisted that 'it was necessary to go one step higher, and maintain that no man should be punished for opinions or for the publication of opinions.'[15]

Keeping the debate reverberating at the level of how natural rights theories should modify Church–State relations carried one further advantage. It sharply distinguished Foxite participation in the campaign for religious toleration from the Pittite. The issue was in a sense always bipartisan. Pitt himself and many of his friends supported Catholic and Dissenter petitions. According to Foxites, however, their interest was fraudulent. Fox endlessly argued that Pittites only took up toleration when circumstances left them no other choice. Theirs was a severely utilitarian approach to the problem. If Pitt supported an extension of the franchise to Irish Catholics in 1793 or full emancipation in 1801, it was only because a chaotic and threatening situation in Ireland forced him to concede. By contrast, as Fox lectured the Commons in the emancipation debate of 1801, his friends had other, loftier motives: 'As a right, the right honourable gentleman [Pitt] denies the claim of the catholics. He would give them nothing as a right— but he thinks the concession expedient. This, Sir, is not my sense of the catholic claim. I would grant it, not merely because it is expedient, but because it is just . . . the rights of man in the strictest sense of the word.'[16] On these views, Fox never saw toleration as a bipartisan issue but rather as a Foxite monopoly in which Pitt occasionally bought a few shares when the terms of the market were right.

Armed with these arguments, Fox's voting record on the toleration issue was impeccable. As early as February 1773, when Dissenters petitioned for the abolition of the requirement for all those entering Oxford and Cambridge universities to subscribe to the Thirty-Nine Articles, Fox supported them with the full armoury of irony and sarcasm. Recalling his own recent undergraduate days, he mockingly confessed to the House that he had been too young to 'swallow down the sublimer mysteries of religion'. It was ridiculous for young men to be 'trained solemnly to attest and subscribe to the truth of a string of propositions, all of which they are as entirely ignorant of as they are of the face of the country said to be in the moon'.[17] Once established, his support for toleration was never conditional. In September 1780, for example, when anti-Catholic feeling in the wake of the Gordon Riots led him to place an advertisement in the London papers, reassuring his constituents that he would never prejudice the Protestant religion by doing anything 'to establish Popery in this kingdom',[18] a severe attack of conscience forced him to confess to Edmund Burke that 'if any one were to think that I had given up in the smallest degree the great cause of Toleration for the sake of a point of my own I should be the most miserable man in the world.'[19] Although his support for religious toleration caused embarrassments with Portland in the 1780s and 1790s, as it had with North in the 1770s, Fox allowed himself no flexibility on the issue.

Normally, leading Foxites were happy to allow respected back-benchers like Henry Beaufoy to take the lead in co-ordinating petitions and presenting bills. From the late 1780s, however, there is evidence that Fox was interested in taking a more prominent role. Dinners of London Dissenters began to be chaired by leading Foxites, who gave toasts that mingled sympathy with promises of help. Most noticeably, the campaign for relief from the Test Acts that was organized by Dissenters in 1789–90 was very much directed in a manner that made it easy for Fox to lead it at Westminster. As addresses poured in, thanking him for his help and concern, Fox was well pleased.[20] It was a matter of some satisfaction to be told that Dissenters had given Pitt up as a false friend and that it was 'only under the protection of Mr Fox and his Friends that we are to hope for relief'.[21] As fear of France and all its works spread through England after 1789, fewer and fewer people could contemplate change with equanimity. As a result, patronizing Dissenters and Catholics became more and more Foxite.

Not all of Fox's friends were entirely pleased with this development. Dissenters had voted overwhelmingly for Pitt in the determining election of 1784, and Lord John Townshend for one was clear that the party should never forget 'their shameful conduct in the year eighty-four'.[22] Dr Parr was 'concerned to see Fox a dupe to their cunning'.[23] Dissenters had repeatedly shown themselves to be unworthy political allies, and therefore being too closely associated with them would only 'alarm the country, and not fix the Presbyterians'.[24] None of these thoughts gave Fox reason to hesitate. In a long letter to Fitzwilliam, he set out his motives for taking such a prominent part in the campaign of 1789–90. He was aware that Dissenting votes, which had been lost in 1784, might be recovered, but this point is something of an afterthought:

I feel myself so much inclined to the *cause* of the Dissenters that without any further consideration I should be very glad to take any part they desire of me and not at all sorry that they should apply to me; but I am sure you think with me that I ought not to move any thing in my present situation which I do not mean to support *in earnest* if ever I am in power . . . My opinion is not only that it is right to support them on account of their cause but that there is a *chance* of getting very important support in return at the General Election.[25]

As far as Fox was concerned to attend Parliament and take politics seriously, his vote for religious toleration was assured.

   In view of this record, his decision to postpone the forwarding of Catholic claims on his return to office in 1806 was all the more startling.[26] Criticism came not only from political opponents but also from within his own family. His defence must lie in the onset of the debilitating illness that would eventually kill him; in the impossibility of securing the agreement of George III; in a reluctance to sacrifice the opportunity to abolish the slave trade, by returning to the opposition benches; and in the determination to make the securing of a peace with France his first priority. Significantly, the hesitation of 1806 had no long-term impact on Fox's reputation as a champion of toleration. His name would be intoned in the cause of Catholics and Dissenters for the next thirty years. In 1829, when Catholic Emancipation finally reached the statute book, Lady Holland proudly reported to her own son that 'The world are very just, & ascribe the merit entirely to Fox & Grattan and those worthies who first agitated the matter. Those at the eleventh hour, & Canning even, have not the glory. The old Whigs have acted admirably, & are much respected for their high, disinterested & zealous conduct.'[27] The Fox family had a habit of adopting whole groups of people as their protégés, and their correspondence very much suggests that they saw Catholics and Dissenters in this light.

*

The other issue which Fox narrowly argued in terms of individual liberty was that of slavery and the slave trade. It was a matter on which he felt deeply. As he himself expressed it to Mrs Fox, it was 'a cause in which one ought to be an Enthusiast and in which one can not help being pleased with oneself for having done right'.[28] It was not an issue on which compromise or half-measures could be contemplated. Quite simply, 'the slave trade ought not to be regulated, but destroyed',[29] because 'There was no medium; the legislature must either abolish the trade, or avow their own criminality.'[30] William Wilberforce, who rarely admired Fox's politics and often blenched at his morals, willingly testified to his unswerving assistance on the slave question. Writing to Holland in 1832, he was happy to 'assure your Lordship

that I am scarcely more convinced that I am myself an honest Abolitionist
than that you are and ever have been such . . . your strong likeness to your
warm-hearted Uncle and his inextinguishable zeal in that good Cause
would alone maintain that impression in my mind.'[31]

If Fox could be criticized by some contemporaries for equivocation in the
matter of religious toleration, no such opportunity was offered them on the
slave question. All political embarrassments had to be endured rather than
surrender it. In 1792, for example, when his relationship with Portland and
Fitzwilliam had never been more strained, Fox frankly informed the latter
that the slave question was not a matter for negotiation:

The second [point] is the Slave Trade which I was very sorry to hear you mention in
the way you did yesterday as having any connection with those foolish and wicked
opinions your Sheffield Neighbours wish to propagate. Upon the point I must fairly
own I think so seriously and so warmly that I should prefer the abolition of it to any
political good that can be gained or even wished, for the Party or the country. I am
very sorry the D. of P. and you are not of the same opinion with me, but when I have
said that I can say no more, because I can not ask for concessions from my friends
upon a subject in which I am determined to make none myself.[32]

This view set a pattern for his whole career.

Such firmness carried the additional benefit of giving Fox another reason
to explain his detestation of Pitt. According to Foxite lore, the Prime Minster
was only prepared to support the slaves as a private Member of Parliament.
He never agreed to make it a government-sponsored issue, or a condition of
his staying in power. As a result, he effectively ruined all chance of reform.
As Fox reported to his nephew in 1796:

I was yesterday in an expected majority upon the Slave Trade 93 to 67 for bringing
in the Bill, but I fear we shall do no good for tho' Pitt spoke very well I can not think
him in earnest, as Dundas took so eager a part on the other side. What a rogue Pitt is!
it is quite unpleasant to think that a Man with such parts should be so totally devoid
as he seems to me of all right feeling.[33]

In this matter, as in all others, Pitt was accused of ensuring that George III's
prejudices would prevail. The King supported slavery, and Pitt guaranteed
that no changes would be enacted as long as he did no more than support
them with his single vote. As Fox bluntly informed Wilberforce, the slaves
had become victims of the system of executive-dominated government set
up in 1784: 'the Cause is, as long as the present ministry lasts, a desperate
one, and that during the prevalence of the present System there is no chance
for any Proposition founded upon the principle of Humanity, Liberty or
Justice.'[34] Either Pitt was not sincere at all on this matter or, if he was, 'how
determined and irresistibly powerful must that Government be, which has

been uniformly both willing and able to defeat us, though supported by the sincere cooperation of the most efficient member of its Administration.'[35] The slave issue could be neatly accommodated within the Foxite nightmare concerning Pitt and the politics of 1784.

In debate, Fox once again indulged in the language of natural rights. Asserting that 'in the sight of Heaven all mankind are equal', he went on to claim that 'Personal freedom must be the first object of every human being; and it was a right, of which he who deprives a fellow creature is absolutely criminal in so depriving him.'[36] Slaves were denied this freedom solely on the wicked assumption that black men were somehow inferior to white men:

There was an argument which had not been used at all, but which was the foundation of the whole business; he meant the difference in colour ... Such a custom could not now be tolerated; and as to the pretext, that what would be great cruelty to us, who profess strong feelings and cultivated minds, would be not injurious to those who were ignorant and uncivilized, it was the height of arrogance, and the foundation of endless tyranny.[37]

Until assumptions based on differences of colour were discarded, the European mission to civilize Africa could not begin. In the broad canon of Foxite Whiggery, a race was to be judged by the extent that it approached civilized values, not by accidents of colour. After all, Frenchmen and Spaniards were as much in need of Foxite lectures on parliamentary government as the inhabitants of Africa.

In 1806, just before his death, Fox had the great satisfaction of seeing the slave trade abolished. Its disappearance was incorporated into his *nunc dimittis* in one of his last speeches in the House of Commons:

So fully am I impressed with the vast importance and necessity of attaining what will be the object of my motion this night, that *if, during the almost forty years that I have had the honour of a seat in parliament, I had been so fortunate as to accomplish that, and that only, I should think I had done enough, and could retire from public life with comfort, and the conscious satisfaction, that I had done my duty.*[38]

These were not empty words. Aunts fondly remembered that 'poor Mr Fox (when he found his illness to grow serious) expressed in the warmest manner how contentedly he should die, if he were so happy as to see the Slave Trade abolished.'[39] His nephew recalled how often Fox had told him that peace and relief for the slaves were 'the two objects nearest his heart'.[40] It was a point of family pride that Holland should be asked to play a part in drawing up the appropriate legislation.[41]

Prominent among the figures represented on Fox's monument in Westminster Abbey is that of a weeping Negro looking up to the couch on which the statesman lies dying, thereby suggesting that Fox had established an almost proprietorial claim to the title of patron of the slaves. It was an idea which certainly enters Foxite iconography in the thirty years after his death. Holland repeatedly reminded Parliament that his family had special claims to be consulted on the subject of slavery, because 'not three hours in the day passed without that subject being uppermost in his [Fox's] mind.'[42] Wilberforce continued to solicit his advice and support 'quasi Lord Holland and quasi nephew to Mr Fox'.[43] On many points, the selective nature of memory was kind to Fox. Inconsistencies and equivocations were forgotten in the presentation of an image of a man who never deviated from the advocacy of liberal causes. On the slave question, above all, memory and fact were in step.

*

The questions of religious toleration and slavery were similar, in that both pivoted on the extent to which an individual should be constrained by governmental or societal influences. On this ground, Fox was at his strongest. As someone who from infancy had never accepted any restraints on conduct, he never had any qualms about extending the freedoms he enjoyed to others. If this can be called liberalism, it was a liberalism that came as a natural extension of a certain personality rather from deep reading in political science. This being so, Fox never showed the same open-mindedness when institutional change was in question. In debates of this nature, he spoke with uncertainty and equivocation. Even if brave words were often used in public, they contrasted strongly with the circumspection he used in letters to friends. On the great issues of the constitutional relationship between England and Ireland and the cause of parliamentary reform, it is hard to see any real depth of concern. They were problems which could easily be subordinated to other worries, and which never engaged Fox's deep sympathy. If Fox is to be hailed as a liberal, there were areas where this liberalism was barely visible.

Initially, there was good reason to hope that Fox would prove to be one of Ireland's greatest friends. His Leinster relations were prominent Irish patriots for the whole of the last quarter of the eighteenth century, on top of which Fox had spoken admiringly of those Volunteers who had agitated for Irish home rule in the late 1770s. He bluntly told the Commons that the Irish patriots 'had not done a single act, for which they had not his veneration and respect'.[44] Henry Grattan and the other Irish leaders were delighted that Fox should return to power in 1782, and their confidence was rewarded by the establishment of a Parliament in Dublin and legislative independence for their country. Home rule had materialized to vindicate

Fox's 'intention to do away completely the idea of England legislating for Ireland'.[45]

Between 1782 and 1784, under the Lord-Lieutenancies of Portland and Manchester, the Whigs took Fox's advice to make their harvest in Ireland, which during the dark days of the 1780s was a source of limitless encouragement for the party.[46] Everything seemed to promise well. Fox busied himself on Ireland's behalf,[47] and Grattan paid him the compliment of calling his views 'liberall [*sic*] to Ireland and just to those lately concerned in her redemption'.[48]

Once the 1782 legislation was in place, however, a line was to be drawn. As the Volunteers continued to press claims, Fox's response was clear:

Immense Concessions were made in the D. of Portland's Time, and these Concessions were declared by an almost unanimous House of Commons to be sufficient. The Account must be considered as having been closed on the Day of that Vote, and should never again be opened on any Pretence whatever . . . Volunteers, and soon possibly Volunteers without Property, will be the only Government in Ireland, unless they are faced this year in a manful manner.[49]

Fox was clear that the establishment of a Dublin Parliament did not release Ireland from her commitments to the cost of national defence, or from the necessity of recognizing gratefully the benefits received from being part of the United Kingdom. Even as he voted to give Ireland a measure of home rule, Fox was desirous of 'some clear understanding with respect to what we are to expect from Ireland in return for that protection and assistance which she receives from those fleets which cost us such enormous sums, and her nothing'.[50]

Fox's opposition to Pitt's commercial treaty with Ireland of 1785 was not simply motivated, therefore, by a wish to embarrass the Prime Minister, though that was no doubt an added bonus. It was 'folly',[51] and, as Sheridan's sister rightly noted, Fox 'acts on this occasion from his own feelings, totally independent of any wish his party may have to harass the Minister'.[52] Showing an unusual doggedness and attention to business, Fox attacked the proposals in a series of speeches, between February and July 1785. One, delivered on 12 May at one in the morning, covered thirty pages in the parliamentary record. The arguments brought forward ranged from the plausible to the fantastical. Ireland would become a smugglers' paradise; the navigation acts would be destroyed forever; and to allow the Irish to trade in India would violate the charter of the East India Company.[53] More seriously, if Ireland accepted, as the price of free access to English markets, that her commerce could be regulated from London, the legislative independence granted in 1782 would be rendered meaningless. A double disaster therefore threatened.

Pitt's ideas 'possessed the most extraordinary qualities that ever marked a negotiation: it promised so much to Ireland, that it threatened the existence of many of our most valuable manufactories; it also demanded a surrender from Ireland of her legislative independence.'[54] Not surprisingly perhaps, Fox was ridiculed in these debates 'as being now an English, now an Irish patriot',[55] but the basis of his argument was that the purity of the 1782 settlement should be upheld as a final answer to Irish demands.

The defeat of the 1785 bill was a major blow to Pitt and therefore a matter for Foxite rejoicing. Pittites complained that 'by the considerate and patriotic exertion of Mr Fox and his Friends, it is now become a question, on which depends almost the very continuance of friendly connection and intercourse.'[56] Such concern was unlikely to trouble Fox. His sympathy for American patriots had had real limits,[57] and so had his concern for Ireland. The settlement of 1782 defined his response. In the Irish disturbances of the 1790s, Fox was emotionally involved on behalf of his Leinster cousins,[58] but was strangely unresponsive to the issues raised by the rebellion of 1798 or the Act of Union of 1801. Neither event could tempt him to resume full-time parliamentary life. After 1782, his friendship with Henry Grattan cooled, and he never managed to get on terms with Henry Flood. The Irish dimension to British politics in the 1790s and 1800s is noticeably missing in Fox's papers and speeches, except in so far as it is related to the question of religious toleration. Irish patriots were never sure of Fox, and their doubt was entirely justified.

*

Even more equivocation dominates Fox's response to calls for parliamentary reform. In a sense, this was a determining issue, in that it offers clear evidence of how far Fox was able to think outside the conventional nostrums of eighteenth-century politics. Initially, the omens were good. Fox's early career was peppered with pro-reform votes, on questions as varied as a redistribution of seats and annual parliaments.[59] Between 1780 and 1783, he shared with Pitt the parliamentary leadership of the reform campaign. On public platforms in Westminster, he would assert to his constituents that the constitution was 'defaced' by malpractice, and 'That without a comprehensive and thorough reform of the representation of the people, and duration of Parliament, there can neither be any radical cure of the corruption, which, after the best regulations of office, or partial reforms, may still be employed on the representative body, by bad ministers.' Public virtue depended on a House of Commons that sprang 'effectively from the mass of the people'.[60] At tavern dinners, he pledged himself to support reform 'with all his abilities in the House', and called on Pitt to bring forward a specific plan.[61] Perhaps significantly, Fox had no plan to offer himself.

Even when Fox was most publicly involved in the reform movement between 1780 and 1784, contemporaries frequently doubted his sincerity. It was hard to believe that the son of Henry Fox should be seriously worried about corruption in politics, when the family fortunes had been built upon it. Sir Philip Francis, who knew the family well, was certain that, on the issue of parliamentary reform, Fox was only 'a well-strung instrument that vibrated when it was touched. The vibration was in the nerve, and there it ended.'[62] Nathaniel Wraxall believed that the cry for reform was nothing but a device to be used by those in opposition to cause trouble, and that 'if Fox had been once confirmed in office and acceptable to the sovereign, he would have steadily repressed all democratic innovations.'[63] The best that critics could do for Fox and his friends was to describe them as captives in the victory procession of a conquering people. Never reformers themselves, they followed, or rather scrambled after, the unavoidable: 'The Whigs, in fact, did not so much originate and propose to the people a measure of Reform, as the people, by their clamours, proposed it to them;—they followed, not led, the popular feeling.'[64] To many, Foxite Whigs were never convincing reformers: they achieved reform or had it thrust upon them. As far as they were seriously interested in it at all, it was to reinforce the effectiveness of traditional political forms, rather than to invent new ones.

Had such critics had access to statements made by Fox in private, their suspicions would have been more than justified. In the hearing of Lord Stanhope, one of the most radical reformers, Fox remarked that 'Parliamentary reform was a fit thing to be made use of in argument in the House of Commons, but not to be carried into execution.'[65] As early as 1783 or 1784, at a dinner party, Fox told John Jebb, a leader of the Westminster reform movement, that he 'Never disguised from adherents of this School, his decided aversion to their schemes of parliamentary reform. This is quite according to Fox's characteristic candour.'[66] Little wonder, then, that in the election of 1784 many reformers like Jebb voted for Pitt rather than Fox, as the better bet to ensure movement on the subject of reform. Fox's coalition with Lord North, a noted anti-reformer, hardly inspired confidence. Long before the French Revolution's influence began to complicate the reform question, the differences between Fox's private and public pronouncements on the matter were glaring.

Private doubts were paralleled by a voting record on reform that was unpredictable and erratic. Fox seemed to act on impulse, without any clearly thought-out terms of reference. In June 1782, for example, he opposed a proposal that, at election time, the hustings should be held in more than one place for the convenience of voters, on the rather quaint argument that such a change would undermine the natural 'intimacy' that should exist between candidate and elector.[67] When the same point came up again two years later, Fox was entirely happy to do whatever Fitzwilliam recommended.[68] He was capable of voting for the idea of annual parliaments, while privately pronouncing against it.[69] As chairman of a committee for parliamentary reform in Westminster, Fox spent much of his time and energy counselling caution and delay,[70] blowing hot and cold in a way that was to become painfully familiar to Christopher Wyvill and the other leaders of the reform movement over the next two decades. When the coalition with North was agreed, Wyvill was driven to a public denunciation of Fox:

Do the adherents of Mr Fox think, or does Mr Fox himself think, the People of England are satisfied with an able speech *from him* in behalf of their great business of parliamentary reformation, when it is evident the weight of that Administration, in which he is employed is clearly and decisively against it? If this be the opinion of the once-popular Secretary and his friends, we will venture to affirm, THEY ARE DECEIVED AND THE PEOPLE OF ENGLAND ARE NOT. That the Whig Secretary is a friend to Whig doctrines, provided a strict adherence to them would not be contrary to his political interests, no one doubts. But the man who means to deserve, and to obtain the hearts and affections of the public, must convince them that his political interests are subservient and secondary to theirs.[71]

A working relationship was re-established with Wyvill in 1795, but the two men were never cordial. As for Horne Tooke and Sir Francis Burdett, Fox was careful to keep them at arm's length.

The most extraordinary instance of hesitation and ambiguity concerns Fox's response to the Association of the Friends of the People, set up in April 1792 by a number of his friends to push for reform.[72] He had not been consulted about the project, and wholeheartedly disapproved of it when it was made public. According to Thomas Moore,[73] when Fox was asked why he declined to become a member, his 'reason was, that though he saw great and enormous grievances, he did not see the remedy'.[74] All was lacklustre and unresponsive. In a confessional letter to Fitzwilliam, he tried to articulate his position on reform:

the truth is that I am more bound by former declarations and consistency, than by any strong opinion I entertain in its favour. I am far from being sanguine that any new scheme would produce better parliaments than the present mode of election has furnished; but perhaps the House of Commons in the present reign has been so dragged through the dirt and bespattered, in early times by the Whigs[75] and in later by the King & Pitt & the Tories that one constructed on a new plan might be better from the mere circumstance of its novelty. However this is all speculation & very uncertain, & I much doubt whether the part you have taken on the question be not upon the whole the most manly and judicious.[76]

In spite of these reservations, Fox supported the Associators Bill in the Commons, leaving many of his friends in a state of complete bewilderment. Carlisle, for example, while happy to 'acquite [*sic*] him of any real love of reform of Parliament',[77] not unreasonably asked him for a 'clearing away all doubt'[78] upon the question. Fox would neither use his authority to stop the Association, nor join them. He voted for them in public, and grumbled in private. As far as he had any clear line of policy, it was to plead that the matter should remain an open question within the party,[79] but that, for many, was not good enough.

Equally in need of explanation was Fox's propensity to form coalitions with politicians whose opposition to parliamentary reform was notorious. On each occasion he seemed suspiciously willing to sacrifice the issue to the prejudices of his new associates. In 1783, he assured Lord North that, on the subject of reform, 'he was pledged to try it once but if it failed he would declare that as it was not the sense of parliament it should never be tried again.'[80] Ironically, Pitt was to agree very similar terms with George III. If Wyvill and his friends, in 1800, could rejoice at Fox telling Grey that both men were so committed to the idea of reform 'that it must be an inevitable consequence of power being in either of our hands',[81] their disillusionment must have been the greater as they saw Fox once again retreating from calling up the question, as a condition of his union with the Grenvillites. Wyvill cautioned Fox against 'disabling yourself to serve the Cause of Constitutional Liberty', by allowing a 'dereliction of that Cause'.[82] As the terms of the Fox–Grenville alliance became known, these fears were more than justified. In 1805, Fox bluntly told Wyvill that parliamentary reform was a dead issue for their generation: 'It is with great concern that I have observed for some Years past the growing apathy on the subject of Reform even among those who used to be friendly towards the measure, & much I am afraid that it will be next to impossible in our times to revive any zeal in favour of it.'[83] Again and again, Fox sacrificed reform to the more immediate priority of securing the friendship of men like North and Grenville. That in itself was bad enough. What was worse was the obvious fact that it gave him so little pain to do so.

When the Talents Ministry came into being, in January 1806, Fox's pretensions could finally be tested. Cartwright and Wyvill were anxious to exploit the opportunity by organizing a petitioning movement. Fox grudgingly agreed, making the only condition that nothing should be attempted in London or adjacent counties, on the rather strange argument that 'there should not appear too much either of aristocracy or Democracy.'[84] Presumably, both these elements were found in abundance around the capital. Wyvill, clear that nothing could be achieved without London's participation, saw Fox's answer as a device to frustrate the whole venture. Reluctantly, he agreed that it was 'necessary to drop the measure',[85] adding darkly that 'Parliamentary reform, I see, must be deferred till a change of Opinions and of political Circumstances has taken place.'[86] The veteran reformer Thomas Cartwright persevered with a petitioning movement in Middlesex, well aware that 'Mr Fox and his friends in the highest circles' would not look favourably upon it.[87] There was an argument that slaves and possibly Catholics might benefit if parliamentary reform was temporarily shelved, but to many reformers the failure of the Talents Ministry to act merely crowned a lifetime of equivocation on Fox's part. Bold words on platforms had never been matched by steady voting. His reforming credentials were threadbare.

As the shallowness of Fox's support for reform became obvious, there were real penalties to be paid, not least with his own constituents in Westminster. The constituency was important to him. As representative of one of the largest borough electorates in England, Fox could, and often did, claim to represent the political nation more legitimately than the Members for rotten boroughs massed around Pitt. He gloried in his title of 'Man of the People'.[88] Westminster was also a platform from which Foxite views could be promulgated as effectively as in the House of Commons. On a number of occasions when defeated in the Commons, Fox merely adjourned to Westminster Hall to make the same speech to a cheering throng of electors and admirers.[89] On the anniversary of his first election, a dinner was held annually at the Shakespeare Tavern, which, as the *Morning Chronicle* report for 1787 makes clear, provided a marvellous opportunity to make party points, as Fox and his constituents congratulated themselves on their 'attachment to the genuine principles of the constitution'.[90] In sum, Westminster was a resource for Fox, and possibly a source of power. French Laurence thought that there was 'a force in Westminster fully sufficient to counterbalance the influence of the Crown'.[91] Such a view was too generous, but it underlines the value that Foxites put on holding this one constituency.

Among the many clubs and societies in Westminster was the Westminster Association, founded in 1780 to promote parliamentary reform with a programme that included universal male suffrage and annual parliaments. Fox tried hard to be on terms with the Association's members but, very quickly, influential reformers came to have doubts about his trustworthiness. Lord Mahon, as early as June 1782, had rejected Fox's claims to be considered a reformer, after witnessing his bill for the suppression of bribery at elections being supported by Pitt but opposed by a gaggle of Foxites.[92] A year later, Fox's coalition with North split the Association asunder. John Jebb, for example, charitably but firmly cut his ties with Fox:

I know his virtues, and I know his faults. I know the influence his party has upon him. I see how his conduct has ruined public confidence, and, I trust, I resented it as a citizen ought to do: but I deplore his loss. I do verily believe, that in every point he thinks with us in these matters; but his intimacies, his connections, bind him down to other counsels, and the habits of his life have gotten too much hold of him, and ambition is his ruling passion.[93]

No meetings of the Association were held between April 1783 and January 1784. Controversy about Fox's behaviour had literally brought the reforming effort at Westminster to a halt. When fitful meetings were resumed in 1784–5, the Association represented no one except a rump of Foxites, led by Sheridan and Fitzpatrick, who used it as an increasingly ineffective weapon against Pitt.[94]

Little wonder that, after 1784, Fox could be assaulted as well as cheered by Westminster crowds. In the election of that year, Westminster was keenly contested, and Fox, for much of the campaign, was clear that he would lose.[95] Quite clearly, the constituency was no longer Fox's fief. Horne Tooke's challenges to Fox in the elections of 1790 and 1796 were, therefore, far from silly. In 1790, for example, Lady Palmerston noted that 'Charles wished his friends to poll early in order to be a thousand ahead. He was very ill received on the first day, and would have been worse treated if he had not retired into the Shakespeare.'[96] It must have been with a sense of relief that Fox negotiated with Pitt and Dundas for an agreement by which the representation of Westminster would be shared by Fox and a Pittite.[97] If, after 1790, Fox's security in Westminster depended as much on an arrangement with Pitt as on the support of reformers, contemporaries were not slow to notice the irony in the situation.

Reviewing the evidence, Sir Nathaniel Wraxall was not alone in concluding that parliamentary reform was nothing but a device by which Pitt and Fox sought to embarrass each other. When Fox was in power, Pitt sponsored reform bills that Foxites voted down.[98] When Pitt was Minister, Fox returned the compliment.[99] Most spectacularly, Foxites failed to support Pitt's reform bill of 1785. At least twelve leading Foxites were unaccountably absent from the division, in which the measure failed by only seventy-four votes, leading many to conclude that, rather than allow Pitt a victory on reform, Foxites would prefer no reform at all:

If Pitt had been strong enough in his [Fox's] opinion to have obtained leave for bringing in the bill, I am convinced he would have opposed it *in limine*; but foreseeing

Pitt could not get leave for the bill without his assistance he was in hopes to get the bill in, and then display all its inconsistencies, ill consequences, inadequacies, etc. . . . in committee.[100]

It mattered little whether Foxites wished to kill the measure outright or destroy it in committee. On both counts, the reform idea had been subordinated to the first priority of hurting Pitt. If more evidence were needed, an attempt by Wyvill to congratulate Pitt for his efforts was voted down at a meeting of reformers by 'Mr Fox and his gamesters from Brookes's'.[101]

Certainly, after 1785, Fox took great pleasure in pointing out that Pitt had withdrawn from all interest in parliamentary reform. In 1793, looking back to the Parliament of 1780–4, Fox reminded the Commons that

Thrice had that House of Commons of which he had spoken, and which he should never mention but with honour, resisted the influence of the crown, and nothing then was talked but a reform of parliament. The House of Commons had been now for nine years a complaisant and confiding body, and the cry of reform from those who were formerly the loudest and most active was heard no more.[102]

The issue of parliamentary reform retained some interest for Fox, if only because, whenever it was raised, Pitt's apostasy would be obvious to reformers, while the memory of his minister's vigorous, reforming sympathies, early in his career, could be guaranteed to irritate George III. What was a source of amusement to Foxites, however, was merely further misery for Wyvill and the reform leadership. Somehow, reform had become a victim of the personal rivalry between Pitt and Fox. Both men were to blame, but it was a matter of considerable regret to Wyvill that Fox 'neglected' to occupy 'the strong ground'.[103] It seemed that Fox's attachment to politics was not sufficient to allow him to take even the great question of parliamentary reform seriously.

*

So, what did Fox think of parliamentary reform? Can any points of consistency be found in this record of contradictory speech-making, voting, and epistolary confessions? In fact, such points did exist, and foremost among them was a determination to resist any move towards universal suffrage. Fox assured the Commons, in 1793, that 'however he might have been misrepresented out of doors, there was not in the kingdom a more steady and decided enemy to general and universal representation, than himself.'[104] Even some critics could see that this was a view that separated him at once from 'all the wild class of reformers'.[105] His reasoning was clear. Men defended their liberties against governments if their property was at risk. What was needed, in the late eighteenth century, was a measure to enfranchise more property-holders. Giving the vote to people who had no property was to enfranchise the apathetic, and those who could be bribed or bullied. The Whig historian and jurist Sir James Mackintosh quoted Fox as saying: 'That principle of representation is the best which calls into activity the greatest number of independent votes, and excludes those whose condition takes away from them the powers of deliberation.'[106] Crucially, in considering the nature of the franchise, Fox clung tenaciously to well-worn notions about property and its merits. There was no nodding towards natural rights theories, in either their Painite or French dimensions.

Secondly, he always insisted that the right of the subject of petition was absolute, and that such petitions should always be heard.[107] He held to this idea, even when he disagreed profoundly with a petition's contents.[108] Petitioning was described as the way in which the unenfranchised were allowed to speak in politics. Some such device was needed, lest men noticed 'How absurd was it that because a man had not the good fortune to have a freehold qualification of forty shillings valued rent, he must not be allowed to speak his sentiments on subjects which involve his dearest and most important concerns.'[109] Petitioning was the method employed to avoid 'a fatal distinction between the constituents and non-constituents in the kingdom'.[110] Looking back on a long career, Fox was sure that petitioning had a real impact on Westminster politics,[111] and that it had been particularly useful in the anti-slavery campaigns and in the search for peace after 1793.[112] It followed from this reasoning that Fox might be more receptive to reform initiatives, if a petitioning movement demonstrated a wide base support for the idea in the country as a whole.

Thirdly, in all the debates on reform in which Fox participated, he steadfastly refused to accept that borough-owners should be compensated for the loss of their boroughs. Most of Fox's contemporaries saw a borough as a species of property which could be bought and sold, and which consequently could not be abolished without compensation being offered. Fox disagreed. He told the Commons in 1785 that 'He was uniformly of an opinion, which, though not a popular one, he was ready to aver, that the right of governing was not property, but a trust.'[113] His views were not changed by the French Revolution's more comprehensive attack on property. In 1800, he wrote to Fitzpatrick to say that a proposal to compensate the owners of rotten boroughs was 'one of the most bitter Pills that ever was swallowed'. It was simply no longer tolerable that such people should be able 'to sell directly and avowedly the influence a Man has upon others'.[114]

Along with these technical points went one major preoccupation, which related the issue of parliamentary reform to his personal experiences in politics. Reform had no appeal for Fox in itself, particularly when predicated on theories based on the rights of man, but it could have a value as a solution to a real and pressing problem. As early as 1782, the disaster of the American War had begun to convince him that 'the voice of the people was not to be collected from the votes of that House.'[115] By 'people', he of course referred to the propertied nation. He voted for reform in May 1783 because what he called 'opinion' was no longer represented by the Commons. The theory of the constitution remained valid, but its practice needed to be adjusted to restore the just representation of property. He never looked for the overthrow of the constitution, but what he called its 'relief'.[116] The long exile in the political wilderness of the Marquess of Rockingham and his friends proved that property no longer ruled. A retuning of the system was necessary.

Such worries were compounded by the staggering electoral defeat of 1784. It was clear to Fox that the campaign to make the power of the King and the executive supreme centred on the rotten boroughs. They had been invaded by George and his friends, and through their Members the King determined debates and votes in the Commons. In supporting Henry Flood's reform bill in 1790, Fox was sure that if the measure had passed earlier, 'what happened in 1784 would never, in that case, have taken place.'[117] It was clear, for example, that Cornwall's forty-four seats and Scotland's forty-five were more or less entirely at the King's disposal. Even when Fox was disinclined to agitate the reform question generally, he always maintained a quick interest in the dubious world of Scottish politics,[118] urging Lauderdale to draw up schemes for reform even in the difficult circumstances of 1806.[119] Rotten boroughs no longer performed their allotted task of allowing the property of great men to be represented. Instead, like malignant cells, they had been taken over by the executive, and were now working the destruction of the whole body politic.

Fox, strangely, was a parliamentary reformer, but his motives were different from those of Wyvill, Tooke, and Paine. Most reformers looked down at the unrepresented, and, with varied arguments, pushed for their representation. To do so often involved the stepping outside of customary ways of thinking. By contrast, Fox looked upwards at the ways of a wicked king and his campaign to undermine representative government. Parliamentary reform was to be called in to defeat him. On this basis, no new ideas were wanted or requested. By 1797, Commons and Lords had been transformed into Houses of royal poodles, who endlessly gave 'ministers their confidence and support, upon convicted failure, imposition and incapacity'. To restore their independence and ability to resist the Crown, a reform might be necessary. Rotten boroughs were not wrong in themselves, but unfortunately they had been infiltrated by royal influence. Speaking in favour of Grey's bill of May 1797, Fox asserted that 'it is only by a reform that we can have a chance of rescuing ourselves from a state of extreme peril and distress.'[120] The nature of that distress was plain. Throughout the whole of George III's reign, nothing 'has been gained to the people, while the constant current has run towards the crown; and God knows what is to be the consequence, both to the crown and country! I believe that we are come to the last moment of possible remedy.'[121]

Foxites were so clear about this threat that they assumed that even the most bigoted of their contemporaries and opponents would be brought to acknowledge it. This fact accounts for the otherwise inexplicable insistence among them, even in the darkest days of the 1790s, that reform would prevail. Sheridan, in 1793, gave Fitzpatrick odds of two-to-one that a reform would pass within two years.[122] Fox took the same view in 1797. Writing to Thomas Anson, he observed:

I do not know what your opinion may have formerly been upon reform, but I am sure the conduct of the House of Commons this year must make it appear necessary even to those who before doubted, and indeed in the present state of things it is of great importance that the lead in such a business should be in the hands of persons who mean well, and not of Corresponding Societies etc.[123]

Parliamentary reform, for Fox, was never seen as a concession to pressure from below. Indeed, he was always sceptical about the extent and potential of such pressure. Rather, it was a device to shore up what once had worked well. He told the Commons that his aim was

not to pull down, but to work upon our constitution, to examine it with care and reverence, to repair it where decayed, to amend it where defective, to prop it where it wanted support, to adapt it to the purposes of the present time, as our ancestors had done from generation to generation, and always transmitted it not only unimpaired, but improved, to their posterity.[124]

If liberalism meant securing those institutions through which liberties were believed to be traditionally guaranteed, Fox might be allowed the title. If liberalism, however, is taken to include a wish to remodel those institutions according to the requirements of some new, theoretical plan, then Fox would himself politely have refused the title.

Epilogue

MUCH-LOVED in his lifetime, Fox was deified almost immediately after his death. A cult of Fox was developed that, in its depth and variety, represents an important aspect of Whig party history in the early nineteenth century.[1] Indeed, until the 1830s, Foxite and Whig were interchangeable terms. A Fox Club had been established as early as 1790.[2] From 1808 onwards, the Club held Fox Dinners on the anniversary of their hero's birthday, and by 1820 such convivial gatherings could be found all over the country. The ritual observed at these functions rarely varied. An associate of Fox's from the 1780s or 1790s would be guest of honour and principal speaker. Representations of Magna Carta or the Bill of Rights would be consumed as puddings. Standardized toasts intoned the litany of the Foxite creed. After drinking to Fox's memory his name would then be linked to toasts damning slavery and wishing success to Dissenters, Catholics, and not infrequently parliamentary reformers. Even issues which had only arisen after his death could be incorporated into the Foxite canon, for, as Grey told a Fox dinner at Newcastle, 'What subject is there, whether of foreign or domestic interest, or that in the smallest degree affects our Constitution which does not immediately associate itself with the memory of Mr. Fox?'[3]

These functions had many uses. They were a device 'to beat up for political friends';[4] they were a forum for expressing views that were purely Whig, with no Radical influence; and at moments of crisis they were invaluable in providing platforms for campaigns against particular measures of Lord Liverpool's government, or for collecting funds. But there was more to them than this. Central to each meeting was the notion that there was a Foxite creed, that Fox had in fact believed in certain things. With every year that passed after his death, the facts of Fox's career were lost in myth and nostalgia. Gradually, the Foxite creed took on a shape and definition that it had never really enjoyed before 1806. By 1823, Sir James Mackintosh, who had known Fox well, could confidently tell an audience of Edinburgh diners that 'it is said those who hold the opinions of Mr Fox are the advocates of Catholic Emancipation and Parliamentary Reform. We are the advocates of Catholic Emancipation and Parliamentary Reform.'[5] A career full of ambiguities and hesitations had been smoothed into a tale of undeviating consistency.

Alongside Fox dinners, the cult established a number of other talismen. All the Whig houses proudly displayed the Nollekens bust of Fox in halls and drawing rooms, or, as at Woburn, as the centrepiece of a Temple of Worthies. In 1811, the Prince of Wales took the oaths of office as Regent with the bust at his side. His first meeting of the Privy Council was delayed for half an hour while he and his advisers contemplated it.[6] His precocious daughter, Princess Charlotte, was in the habit of giving the bust as a present to unsuspecting friends, expressing the hope that 'Happy, thrice happy, will the moment be when the plans Mr Fox pursued and planned are put into *full force*.'[7] Clearly, she too was sure that the career of her hero had been guided by plans. Less conclusively, boys were frequently christened Charles James or even Charles James Fox, while locks of hair became such treasured possessions that they could inspire verses:

> Could reliques as at Rome they show
> Work Miracles on Earth below
> This hallowed little lock of Hair
> Might sooth the Patriots' anxious care
> Might to St Stephen's Chapel brought
> Inspire each Noble Virtuous thought.[8]

No Fox miracles are recorded, but the whole phenomenon of the cult was miraculous enough to be in need of explanation. After all, no politician had ever been less successful in exercising power.

Exactly why Fox was so influential during his lifetime and so powerful after his death was a question contemporaries felt compelled to ask themselves. In recording his death, the *Morning Chronicle* put the question: 'To what then is the number, the constancy, the ardour of that body of friends and followers who have so long acted under his standard to be ascribed?' This obituary took refuge in commonplace references to 'superior wisdom and incorruptible integrity',[9] but such phrases hardly meet the case. Apart from the Libel Act and the abolition of the slave trade, it is hard to think of any other major measure with which Fox was successfully associated, or which was, in a narrow sense, specifically his. In opposition for most of his career, influence of any kind, legislative or otherwise, was likely to be denied him. Always bored by financial matters, he could not, like Pitt, look back on a restructuring of tax systems or the management of a major war as achievements that guaranteed a reputation. Further, on a number of crucial issues, notably his assessments of the French Revolution and Napoleon, he was proved wrong, and wrong in a way that led him to be accused of treasonable thoughts. He was loathed by the King, by the prudent, the cautious, and the moral. What then, to return to the enquiry initiated by the *Morning Chronicle*, gave Fox his prominence?

First and foremost, Fox had little or no interest in the exercise of power. He was a politician *malgré lui*. Having influence gave him pleasure, in that it sometimes allowed him to promote or reward his friends, and to pursue single issues like the slave question, but that was the extent of it. He was quite incapable of mastering the detail of a question, as Burke did to harry Warren Hastings or Pitt to finance a great war. Much of the political agenda, notably economic affairs, bored him. He would make no concessions in his personal life in order to win approval. He simply could not be bothered to flatter or cajole. Herculean energies were at his disposal, but they were only rarely concentrated in the political arena. As Fox came to assimilate, and then mould, the values of the Grand Whiggery, hours spent on politics were rationed, as only part of a London day.

This distancing of himself from politics was taken to such extremes that, at times, it seemed that Fox was actually afraid of the exercise of power. His career was marked by spasms of formidable energy interrupting long periods of quiescence. Fox could be fired by a particular injustice, but there was no sustaining the mood. At moments of decision, during the Regency Crisis for example, he was simply absent. At others, he appeared paralysed. Burke, Sheridan, and the Associators, reflecting on the terrible divisions provoked by the French Revolution, all later regretted that Fox had been so unwilling to exert himself. Instead, he refused to console Burke or discipline Sheridan and Grey. After 1797, he hovered uncertainly between political life and full retirement into private life. Little wonder that a secession from Parliament was often talked of and finally accomplished. Few of his friends would have been surprised if he had left politics altogether. All this might have been expected of a man who had gone into politics in order to defend the reputation of an adored father, with no values that had not been bequeathed him by his family. After 1782–4, he discovered the issue of George III's assault on English constitutionalism, in which he had been much involved and very hurt. Its reiteration provided him with the opportunity for some of his finest parliamentary performances. After 1797, however, not even this theme could tie him to Westminster.

Since Fox was not primarily a political man, his politics have to be refracted through other media. Above all, Fox was a sociable man, for whom public life was a function of friendship. Before the mid-1780s, he was happiest at Newmarket and Brooks's. Foxites were called 'the witty and wicked satellites'[10] of their master. By contrast, the House of Commons was hardly worth the effort of preparing a speech or even washing. Fox's papers, unlike Burke's, are not full of speeches in draft. Fox spoke spontaneously and without preparation. Not infrequently he did so after a night spent gambling, or wearing clothes that showed the muddy evidence of a recent journey from Newmarket or Brighton. After 1785, when Mrs Armistead's influence grew stronger and stronger, Parliament still took second place, but this time to the literary and historical pursuits of St Anne's Hill. Unlike his great rival Pitt, whose life was devoted to politics, Fox had a kind of contempt for its workings, and for men who had no other resources.

A biographer of Fox therefore finally comes up against the problem of describing the personality of Fox as it operated in his many deep friendships. That it was compelling was agreed by those who reacted for or against it. As a young man, Fox was the best company in London. He became a kind of standing cabaret. When, infrequently, he found himself in office, subscriptions to Brooks's Club fell away, in testimony to the fact that the main attraction was otherwise engaged. Formidably clever, he had the attraction of one who lived life on his own terms, inside or outside convention, without intending to either ingratiate or shock. Foxite living was hectic, but it was natural. Hypocrisy, a term often levelled against Pitt, was almost the strongest word of abuse in Foxite vocabulary.

A Foxite friendship ran on special terms. Throughout his career, Fox loathed hurting friends or giving them orders. When men like Fitzwilliam and Carlisle parted company with Fox over the French Revolution, it was the loss of their friendship he bemoaned, rather than that of their political influence. Always most comfortable in the company of young people, he encouraged their ideas and projects, however wayward. With some justice, the Burke family accused Fox of being led by Grey and Lauderdale in the 1790s, when he should instead have been leading them. On the other hand, Fox's friends accorded him many privileges. For some, it was nothing less than the surrender of their free will. Men as diverse as Creevey the diarist and Lord John Russell called themselves Foxite, in the sense that they followed his creed without addition or deduction.[11] They all agreed that Fox was a special person, allowed to live his life under special dispensations. They might accuse him of being wrong because he was too easygoing, but never of meaning intentional harm. Even when old friends like Fitzwilliam parted company with Fox politically, they continued to pay over large sums to cover the peccadilloes of Fox's private life. They never criticized them because, somehow, they recognized that Fox had a right to them. He was a man who was always forgiven.

Fox's importance lay in the fact that he was a politician who held power cheap. He knew philosophically what it was worth. He had entered the game without too much relish, and he stayed in it with ever-increasing reluctance. Instead, he truly valued people he liked. He so organized his life that he could give absolute attention to friendship. Successful politicians, at the end of their careers, often find themselves isolated within a sense of once having been powerful. Frequently, too, they find themselves with few friends to offer consolation. By contrast, Fox had lots. Long after Fox's death, Samuel Rogers recorded that elderly Foxites, remembering the loss of their mentor, would 'burst into tears with a vehemence of grief such as I hardly ever saw exhibited by a man'.[12] Quite simply, 'He was their world.'[13]

Notes

NOTES

Chapter 1

1. Lord Ilchester, *Henry Fox, First Lord Holland* (London 1920), i. 174.
2. For the career of Sir Stephen Fox, see C. Clay, *Public Finance and Private Wealth* (Oxford 1978).
3. W. L. Clements Lib., Ann Arbor, Mich., Fox MSS, C. J. Fox to Caroline Fox [1 Apr. 1804]. See also the character of C. J. Fox written by Frederick, Earl of Carlisle, Castle Howard MSS J14/74/10: 'I never abandoned an idea formed in the morning of our friendship, that He was ever in his heart more inclined to Tory, than what in these times are called Whig principles. His nurse & his Parents had done much in his infancy to make his relationship, thro' his mother, to the Rl. House of Stuart, by no means indifferent to him, & if an idle quarrel had not happened between him & Ld. North, we might have seen him a supporter of the American War, a champion for the prerogative of the Crown, & a favorite [*sic*] in the Closet.'
4. See family tree, Fig. 1.
5. H. B. Wheatley (ed.), *The Historical and Posthumous Memoirs of Sir Nathaniel Wraxall* (London 1884), ii. 18.
6. Lord John Russell (ed.), *The Memorials and Correspondence of Charles James Fox* (London 1853–7), i. 76.
7. BL Add. MSS 51416, fo. 196, Holland to Lady Holland, 21 Dec. 1754.
8. *Fox*, i. 25.
9. Ibid.
10. BL Add. MSS 51416, fo. 228, Holland to Lady Holland, 13 Feb. 1756.
11. G. Selwyn to Carlisle, 30 July [1774], HMC, XV Report, Carlisle MSS, 273.
12. B. Fitzgerald, *Emily, Duchess of Leinster* (London 1949), 75–6, Lady Holland to Lady Kildare, n.d. When Charles Fox was 3 years old, he complained to his father about his mother's absences, 'I have said Mama would come ev'ry day, & She comes never a day Papa!' BL Add. MSS 51416, fo. 161, Holland to Lady Holland, 27 Mar. 1752.
13. She admitted to her husband that Charles was her favourite son. See BL Add. MSS 51415, fo. 41, Lady Holland to Holland, 14 Mar. 1750.
14. Reminiscences of Sir G. Colebrooke, *Fox*, i. 7.
15. BL Add. MSS 51415, fo. 94, Holland to Lady Holland, 15 Aug. 1751.
16. Ibid., fo. 235 [19 Feb. 1756].
17. Ibid., fo. 120, 11 Mar. 1752.
18. Henry Fox promised his son that 'I shall make King's Gate very pretty for you . . . I hope you will spend many happy hours after I am dead and gone. I hope to spend a few with you.' Quoted in G. O. Trevelyan, *The Early History of Charles James Fox* (London 1881), 280.
19. Anon., *Les Amours et les Aventures du Lord Fox* (Geneva 1785), 17–18.
20. BL Add. MSS 47570, fo. 6, Fox to Lady Holland [1773].
21. BL Add. MSS 51434, fo. 153, Mme de Geoffrin to Lady Holland, 7 Dec. 1773.
22. BL Add. MSS 51416, fo. 53, Holland to Lady Holland, 28 Nov. 1758.
23. *Fox*, i. 8.
24. Holland to Lord Ilchester, 5 Aug. 1757, *Holland*, ii. 96.
25. BL Add. MSS 51416, fo. 42, Holland to Lady Holland, 30 Sept. 1758.
26. Ibid., fo. 96, 21 Sept. 1761.

27. Ibid., fo. 45, 20 Nov. 1758.
28. L. S. Benjamin, *The Windham Papers* (London 1913), i. 6.
29. B. Connell, *Portrait of a Whig Peer* (London 1957), 88.
30. Ibid. 128.
31. Lady Ilchester and Lord Stavordale, *Life and Letters of Lady Sarah Lennox* (London 1901), i. 114, Lady S. Lennox to Lady S. Fox Strangways, 24 Oct. 1761.
32. Ibid. i. 199, Lady S. Bunbury to Lady S. O'Brien, 3 Sept. 1766.
33. BL Add. MSS 51467, fo. 7, C. J. Fox to Lady S. O'Brien, 29 Nov. 1761.
34. Ibid., fo. 4, C. J. Fox to S. Fox, 1 Feb. 1760. When Lady Susan married, Fox, aged 15, magnanimously promised to try to like her husband, entreating her: 'For God's sake be calm, and hope at least, if it be only to spare those agonies, which the appearance of your happiness must give your C. J. Fox.' BL Add. MSS 51467, fo. 11, C. J. Fox to Lady S. O'Brien, 11 Apr. 1764.
35. Eton College Library, *Musae Etonenses* (n.d.).
36. R. J. Mackintosh (ed.), *Memoirs of the Life of Sir James Mackintosh* (London 1835), i. 325.
37. *Gentleman's Magazine*, Apr. 1835, 352.
38. Edinburgh, Nat. Reg. Arch., Blair Adam MSS, T. Erskine to W. Adam, 23 July 1793.
39. *Blackwood's Magazine*, Aug. 1826, 353.
40. BL Add. MSS 47582, fo. 81, J. Hare to R. Fitzpatrick, 16 May 1782. The 'Bank' referred to here is that found in gambling rooms.
41. E. B. de Fonblanque, *Life and Correspondence of the Rt. Hon. John Burgoyne* (London 1876), 429.
42. PRO, Pitt MSS 30/8 157, fo. 131, H. Dundas to W. Pitt, 5 Aug. 1792, reporting the death of General Burgoyne at Fox's house at St Anne's Hill.
43. BL Add. MSS 51467, fo. 28, C. J. Fox to D. O'Bryen, 23 Jan. [1793].
44. BL Add. MSS 37873, fo. 226, S. Douglas to W. Windham, 22 Oct. 1793.
45. J. Carswell, *The Old Cause* (London 1954), 332.
46. Eton College Library, Dr Barnard's Entrance Book, bb 96–115.
47. *The World*, 3 Feb. 1787.
48. Ibid.
49. BL Add. MSS 47568, fo. 4, C. J. Fox to Sir G. Macartney, 13 Feb. 1765.
50. BL Add. MSS 47561, fo. 35, C. J. Fox to Duke of Portland, 25 June 1782.
51. BL Add. MSS 47568, fo. 12, C. J. Fox to Sir G. Macartney, 6 Aug. 1767.
52. BL Add. MSS 47571, fo. 9, C. J. Fox to Lord Holland, 5 May 1792.
53. Castle Howard MSS J14/65/5, Character of C. J. Fox written by the 5th Earl of Carlisle. See also *Fox*, i. 11–13 and J. Greig, *The Farington Diary* (London 1922), i. 103.
54. BL Add. MSS 51422, fos. 216–17, C. J. Fox to Lord Holland, 18 Oct. 1763.
55. BL Add. MSS 51350, fo. 5, ? to Lord Ilchester [8 Sept. 1763].
56. See *Lennox*, i. 161.
57. BL Add. MSS 51468, fo. 1, W. Newcome to C. J. Fox, 1 May 1765.
58. BL Add. MSS 47568, fo. 7, Lord Holland to Sir G. Macartney, 12 Apr. 1765.
59. C. Upton to Lord Holland, 17 May 1765, *Holland*, ii. 286–7.
60. BL Add. MSS 51422, fo. 226, C. J. Fox to Lord Holland, 29 Apr. 1765.
61. BL Add. MSS 47580, fo. 7, C. J. Fox to R. Fitzpatrick, 10 Oct. 1769. Fluency in French never stood in the way of Fox's idiosyncratic use of the language, which is reproduced from manuscript sources without emendation or comment.
62. Ibid. This maxim might be particularly attractive to Fox since he admitted to suffering from

a dose of venereal disease, or 'chaudepisse', at the time of writing. As a further conceit, he tried always to write in verse, acknowledging the difficulties of this aspiration:

> For the Muses are coy and the more that I woo 'em.
> The more difficult 'tis as I find to get to 'em.
> They are whimsical Bitches but spite of their malice
> I will send you a letter tomorrow from Calais.

BL Add. MSS 47580, fo. 6, C. J. Fox to R. Fitzpatrick [Oct.] 1769.

63. W. S. Lewis, *Horace Walpole's Correspondence* (New Haven, Conn. 1937–80), iv. 322, Mme du Deffand to H. Walpole, 20 Dec. 1769. Fox would have particularly resented being compared to Jean Jacques Rousseau, whose work he detested. See also ibid., v. 10, 13 Jan. 1771.

64. BL Add. MSS 51544, fo. 7, Travel Journal of the 1st Lady Holland.

65. BL Add. MSS 47568, fo. 9, Lord Holland to Sir G. Macartney, 30 June 1766. A *petit maître* was a dandy or man-about-town.

66. BL Add. MSS 47580, fo. 1, C. J. Fox to R. Fitzpatrick, 22 Sept. 1767.

67. Castle Howard MSS J14/65/5, Character of C. J. Fox.

68. *Fox*, i. 46–7; U. Price to S. Rogers, 1767, see also A. Dyce, *Reminiscences and Table Talk of Samuel Rogers* (Edinburgh 1903), 76–7, U. Price to E. H. Barker, 24 Mar. 1827.

69. *Rogers*, 72.

70. Ibid. 73.

71. Castle Howard MSS, J14/65/5, Character of C. J. Fox.

72. Ibid.

73. Anon., *Les Amours et les Aventures du Lord Fox*, 44 ff.

74. BL Add. MSS 47576, fo. 1, C. J. Fox to U. Price, 27 Oct. 1767.

75. Ibid., fo. 3, 24 Feb. 1768.

76. Ibid. See also BL Add. MSS 47580, fo. 4, C. J. Fox to R. Fitzpatrick, 23 Jan. 1768.

77. BL Add. MSS 47580, fos. 11–12, C. J. Fox to R. Fitzpatrick, 12 Nov. 1769.

78. Ibid.

79. BL Add. MSS 47576, fo. 3, C. J. Fox to U. Price, 24 Feb. 1768.

80. Lord Charlemont to T. Beauclerk, July 1774, HMC XII Report, Charlemont MSS, 320.

81. Connell, *Portrait of a Whig Peer*, 64. Fox was elected in 1769.

82. J. Boswell, *Life of Dr Samuel Johnson* (Oxford 1965), 558. Fox was elected in 1774.

83. Ibid. 1196. Fox had first met Burke at dinner in 1764. The precocious 15-year-old had solemnly recorded his opinion that Burke was 'one of the most agreeable Men I have known'. BL Add. MSS 51422, fo. 222, C. J. Fox to Lord Holland, 13 Oct. 1764.

84. *Macaroni and Theatrical Magazine*, Jan. 1773, quoted in *Walpole*, xxxiii. 268.

85. *Fox*, i. 71.

86. BL Add. MSS 51422, fo. 222, C. J. Fox to Lord Holland, 13 Oct. 1764.

87. Ibid., fo. 224, 24 Oct. 1764.

88. BL Add. MSS 47580, fo. 13, C. J. Fox to R. Fitzpatrick, n.d. [*c*.1770].

89. Castle Howard MSS J14/74/10, Character of C. J. Fox. See also A. F. Steuart, *Last Journals of Horace Walpole* (London 1910), i. 270.

90. Castle Howard MSS J14/64/1, Character of C. J. Fox.

91. See Chap. 5.

92. BL Add. MSS 47580, fo. 15, C. J. Fox to R. Fitzpatrick, 19 Aug. [1770].

93. BL Add. MSS 51467, fo. 15.

94. W. Combe, *Letter from a Country Gentleman to a Member of Parliament* (London 1789), 24.

95. [C. J. Fox], *Essay upon Wind* [Dec. 1783]. The authorship cannot be substantiated. It was dedicated to Lord Thurlow who 'farts without reserve when seated on the woolsack'.

96. BL Add. MSS 51359, fo. 90, Journal of Lady Susan O'Brien.

97. Castle Howard MSS J14/65/5, Carlisle Memorandum.

98. Ibid., J14/74/10, Character of C. J. Fox.

99. Ibid. J14/64/1.

100. Ibid.

101. BL Add. MSS 47568, fo. 12, C. J. Fox to Sir G. Macartney, 6 Aug. 1767.

102. BL Add. MSS 51422, fos. 213–14, C. J. Fox to Lord Holland, 9 Sept. 1763.

103. H. Walpole, *Memoirs of the Reign of George III* (London 1894), iv. 205.

104. *Fox*, i. 95, 26 Jan. 1774. The Pelhamite Innocents were those followers of the Duke of Newcastle who lost positions and sinecures after their patron's disgrace. Holland was widely assumed to have managed the operation.

105. J. Wright (ed.), *The Speeches of the Rt. Hon. C. J. Fox in the House of Commons* (London 1815), v. 244, 8 Apr. 1794. See also ibid., i. 370–6, 11 June 1781.

106. Trevelyan, *Early History of Fox*, 277.

107. BL Add. MSS 51416, Lord Holland to Lady Holland, 26 May 1765.

108. BL Add. MSS 47578, fo. 84, 1765.

109. BL Add. MSS 47568, fo. 9, C. J. Fox to Sir G. Macartney, 3 May 1766.

110. Ibid., fo. 12, 6 Aug. 1767.

111. *Fox*, i. 34, C. J. Fox to J. Crauford, 15 Jan. 1767.

112. T. Copeland, *The Correspondence of Edmund Burke* (Cambridge 1958–70), ii. 51, E. Burke to Lord Rockingham, 30 July 1769. The Bedfords were particularly loathed by the Fox family because they were held to have treated Bute badly. See *Holland*, ii. 312–13.

113. Rockingham's nephew.

114. C. J. Fox to Earl Fitzwilliam, 13 Jan. 1767, quoted in D. Johnson, 'Charles James Fox: From Government to Opposition 1771–1774', *Eng. Hist. Rev.*, 89 (1974), 752.

115. Ibid. 754.

116. Ibid.

117. *Fox*, i. 51.

118. BL Add. MSS 51416, fo. 118, Lord Holland to Lady Holland, 18 Nov. 1763.

119. Johnson, 'Fox', 753.

120. *Fox*, i. 60, J. Crauford to Lord Holland, 1813.

121. Ibid. i. 52, 14 Apr. 1769.

122. BL Add. MSS 47568, fo. 14, H. Walpole to ?, 8 May 1769. See also Walpole, *Reign of George III*, iii. 238.

123. *Fox*, i. 54, Lord Holland to J. Campbell, 11 May 1769. None of this parliamentary activity interrupted the flow of social life, however. Nor did it prevent Fox from undertaking yet another visit to France, from Sept. 1769 to Jan. 1770.

124. BL Add. MSS 47568, fo. 1, C. J. Fox to Sir G. Macartney, 25 Dec. 1765.

125. *Fox*, i. 59.

126. Johnson, 'Fox', 757.

127. The accommodating of Fox in office caused Lord North considerable difficulties, entailing a minor reshuffle of government ministers, *Fox*, i. 87–8.

128. *Fox*, i. 68, 11 Feb. 1771.

129. *Correspondence of William Pitt, Earl of Chatham* (London 1839), iv. 332, Lord Chatham to Lord Shelburne, 6 Mar. 1774.

130. *Speeches*, 25 Mar. 1771, i. 13–14.
131. Johnson, 'Fox', 757.
132. Lord Malmesbury, *Diaries and Correspondence of Lord Malmesbury* (London 1844), i. 223–4, Mrs Harris to Sir J. Harris, 29 Mar. 1771.
133. Walpole, *Reign of George III*, iv. 192.
134. *Walpole*, xxiii. 291 n., Journal of Horace Walpole, 1771.
135. Ibid.
136. Johnson, 'Fox', 757.
137. The problem was complicated by the fact that the King had been personally involved in drawing up the measure, telling Lord North that he expected 'every nerve to be strained to carry the bill'. *Fox*, i. 76.
138. *Speeches*, i. 17, 9 Mar. 1772. See also BL Add. MSS 51468, fos. 8–12, for a manuscript of Fox's speech.
139. *Fox*, i. 70.
140. Ibid. i. 87.
141. Johnson, 'Fox', 760.
142. *Malmesbury*, i. 253, Mrs Harris to Sir J. Harris, 25 Feb. 1772. See also Steuart, *Last Journals of Walpole*, i. 6.
143. *Holland*, ii. 347, Lady Holland to H. E. Fox, 24 Feb. 1772.
144. BL Add. MSS 47579, fo. 1, J. Crauford to Lord Upper Ossory, 21 Feb. 1772. According to a contemporary newspaper report, Fox sent North a letter saying, 'You have grossly insulted me, and I will resent it. I am just going to set out for St. James's to resign.' Quoted in Johnson, 'Fox', 764.
145. BL Add. MSS 47579, fo. 1, C. J. Fox to Lord Upper Ossory [*c.* Feb. 1772].
146. Steuart, *Last Journals of Walpole*, i. 22.
147. Ibid. i. 46. It is, however, worth noting that the 3rd Lord Holland vigorously denied this, and insisted that his grandfather had been annoyed by his son's resignation, being a ministerialist by nature and knowing the barrenness of opposition, *Fox*, i. 74–5.
148. Johnson, 'Fox', 765.
149. *Speeches*, i. 16, 9 Mar. 1772.
150. He attended 38 out of 62 Treasury Board meetings, whereas he had attended only 30 out of a possible 390 meetings of the Admiralty Board. See Johnson, 'Fox', 769.
151. In Feb.–Mar. 1773. Interestingly, he also wanted to be more severe on Clive than North wished, ibid. 773.
152. *Fox*, i. 96–8, 14 Feb. 1774.
153. *Fox*, i. 99, George III to Lord North, 15 Feb. 1774.
154. Ibid.
155. Ibid. i. 100, 19 Feb. 1774.
156. *Fox*, i. 101, George III to Lord North, 23 Feb. 1774.
157. Ibid. i. 134, 26 Feb. 1774.
158. Ibid. i. 133.
159. HMC XII Report, Donoughmore MSS, 278, Lord Townshend to J. Hely Hutchinson, 25 Feb. 1774.
160. Steuart, *Last Journals of Walpole*, i. 305. See also ibid. i. 298, for Walpole's account of this rather murky transaction, in which David Garrick was also implicated. According to Johnson the land speculation involved was in the West Indies, Johnson, 'Fox', 778.
161. *Correspondence of William Pitt, Earl of Chatham*, iv. 327, Shelburne to Chatham, 27 Feb. 1774.

162. BL Add. MSS 41579, fos. 20–1, Journal of Lady Elizabeth Foster, 5 Jan. 1789. See also *Walpole*, vi. 24, H. Walpole to Mme du Deffand, 1 Mar. 1774.
163. *Walpole*, vi. 24.
164. HMC, XII Report, Donoughmore MSS, 279, Lord Townshend to J. Hely Hutchinson, 25 Feb. 1774.
165. [J. Trotter], *Circumstantial Details of the Long Illness and last Moments of the Right Hon. Charles James Fox* (London 1806), 29. See also *Fox*, i. 76–7.
166. Castle Howard MSS J14/74/10, Character of C. J. Fox.
167. *Fox*, i. 136.
168. Ibid. i. 134.

Chapter 2

1. W. L. Clements Lib., Ann Arbor, Mich., Fox MSS, W. Jackson to C. J. Fox, 26 Apr. 1800.
2. Lord Albemarle, *Memoirs of the Marquis of Rockingham*, (London 1852), ii. 276.
3. Ibid.
4. V. H. Foster, *Two Duchesses*, (London 1898), 227, A. Foster to Lady E. Foster, 30 June 1805.
5. Bod. Lib. MSS Eng. Lett. c234, fo. 104, Lord Holland to H. E. Fox, 28 Feb. 1838.
6. *Speeches*, i. 157, 8 Mar. 1779.
7. Ibid. i. 397, 12 June 1781.
8. Ibid. i. 70, 17 Feb. 1777. Fox made great capital out of the fact that he knew of the Franco-American Treaty before North. On this occasion, Fox was seen 'pluming himself' and North 'was thunderstruck'. *Fox*, i. 172–4.
9. Burgoyne was to die at Fox's house at St Anne's Hill, whereupon Fox assumed responsibility for his children.
10. W. L. Clements Lib., Ann Arbor, Mich., Fox MSS, R. Fitzpatrick to C. J. Fox, 5 Nov. 1777.
11. *Speeches*, i. 158, 8 Mar. 1779.
12. *Fox*, i. 135, 19 Apr. 1774.
13. Ibid. i. 138, 6 Mar. 1775.
14. Ibid. i. 136, 3 May 1774. See also ibid. i. 135, 22 Apr. 1774.
15. *Speeches*, i. 32, 27 Jan. 1775.
16. *Fox*, i. 137, 2 Feb. 1775. See also *Speeches*, i. 37, 20 Feb. 1775. Fox assured George Selwyn that the American question could not be settled without a change of government: 'there must be a change of Ministry, *quelconque*, no matter what, as a preliminary assurance to the Insurgents.' HMC XV Report, Carlisle MSS, 294, G. Selwyn to Earl of Carlisle, 11 Oct. [1775].
17. HMC XV Report, Carlisle MSS, 313.
18. Betting Book, Brooks's Club.
19. BL Add. MSS 47579, fo. 5, C. J. Fox to Lord Upper Ossory, 24 June 1776.
20. *Speeches*, i. 56, 24 Apr. 1776.
21. Ibid. i. 60, 31 Oct. 1776.
22. M. D. George, *English Political Caricature* (Oxford 1959), i. 153.
23. *Fox*, i. 167, C. J. Fox to R. Fitzpatrick, 3 Feb. 1778.
24. Ibid. i. 171.
25. *Fox*, i. 165, 2 Feb. 1778.
26. *Fox*, i. 161, J. Crauford to Lord Upper Ossory, 4 Dec. 1777.
27. Horace Walpole cited in *Fox*, i. 163.

28. Ibid. Fox was unkind enough to threaten Germain with a second 'trial', the first having been for cowardice allegedly shown at the Battle of Minden. See also *Fox*, i. 172.

29. *Fox*, i. 204, R. Fitzpatrick to Lord Upper Ossory, 12 Dec. 1778.

30. Ibid. i. 206.

31. Two of Keppel's most determined opponents.

32. *Fox*, i. 224.

33. Anon., *Opposition Mornings*, (London 1779). See also Anon., *A Short History of the Opposition*, (London 1779). A mob, acting 'at the instigation of the Court', broke Fox's windows ten days later, *Fox*, i. 226.

34. *Fox*, i. 224–5, 18 Feb. 1779.

35. *The Englishman* (London, Mar.–June 1779).

36. Edinburgh, Nat. Reg. Arch., Dundas of Ochertyre MSS, GD 35/49/9, D. Dundas to J. Dundas, 18 Dec. 1779.

37. *Speeches*, i. 204–6.

38. HMC XIV Report, Emly MSS, 205b, Lord Lucan to Mr Pery, 29 Nov. 1779. A narrative account of the duel by Adam is to be found in the Edinburgh, Nat. Reg. Arch., Blair Adam MSS, Misc. Correspondence and Papers, Bundle 28. See also W. Adam to his father, 11 Dec. 1779, General Correspondence 1769–1779.

39. BL Add. MSS 51352, fo. 37, Lady S. O'Brien to ?, 29 Nov. 1779.

40. Bod. Lib., Bowood MSS, Box 975, R. Fitzpatrick to Lord Shelburne [29 Nov. 1779].

41. *Fox*, i. 165.

42. Lady Granville, *Lord Granville Leveson Gower* (London 1916), ii. 388–9, Lady Bessborough to G. Leveson Gower [July 1811].

43. *Fox*, i. 146, C. J. Fox to E. Burke, 13 Oct. 1776. The serious appeal of the letter may have been undermined by the fact that it was written in Newmarket. See also *Burke*, iii. 294, C. J. Fox to E. Burke, 13 Oct. 1776.

44. *Fox*, i. 154. See also BL Add. MSS 47579, fo. 9, C. J. Fox to Lord Upper Ossory, 29 Nov. 1777.

45. *Fox*, i. 136.

46. *Speeches*, i. 44, 26 Oct. 1775.

47. *Fox*, i. 139. This speech was described as 'very abusive but able, and full of those quick turns he inherited from his father', Lord George Sackville to General Irwin, 27 Oct. 1775, HMC IX Report, 31.

48. W. R. Anson, *Memoirs of Augustus Hervey, Third Duke of Grafton* (London 1898), 297, C. J. Fox to Duke of Grafton, 12 Dec. 1777. See also *Fox*, i. 163 and 174–5.

49. BL Add. MSS 47580, fo. 68, C. J. Fox to R. Fitzpatrick, 9 Sept. 1781.

50. Ibid., fo. 57, 27 Sept. 1779.

51. *Fox*, i. 176.

52. *Speeches*, i. 134, 26 Nov. 1778.

53. Ibid. i. 242–3, 8 Mar. 1780.

54. *Fox*, i. 243.

55. Ibid. i. 203.

56. Ibid. i. 164.

57. *Speeches*, i. 363, 30 May 1781.

58. Ibid. i. 79, 16 Apr. 1777.

59. Ibid. i. 338, 8 May 1781.

60. BL Add. MSS 51467, fo. 20, C. J. Fox to Mr O'Brien, 15 Dec. 1777.

61. *Speeches*, i. 265, 24 Apr. 1780.
62. Ibid. i. 261.
63. Ibid. i. 275–6, 8 May 1780.
64. *Fox*, i. 269–70. George III publicly insisted that the Prince of Wales would no longer talk to him because he was so 'governed' by Fox and his friends.
65. *Burke*, iii. 390, E. Burke to G. Nagle, 26 Oct. 1777.
66. Ibid. iii. 385, E. Burke to C. J. Fox, 8 Oct. 1777. According to one source, Fox had made a commitment to the Rockingham Whigs by 1777, *Fox*, i. 157. In view of later events, however, this report must be treated warily.
67. *Speeches*, vi. 19, 17 Nov. 1795.
68. Ibid. i. 221, 219, 6 Dec. 1779.
69. Ibid. i. 309, 23 Feb. 1781.
70. HMC XII Report, Charlemont MSS, 370, C. J. Fox to Duke of Leinster, 4 Jan. 1780.
71. BL Add. MSS 51467, fo. 22, C. J. Fox to Mr O'Brien, 29 July 1779.
72. *Walpole*, xxv. 10–11, H. Walpole to Sir H. Mann, 6 Feb. 1780. See also *Fox*, i. 241, where Walpole reflected that 'It was curious to see Charles Fox, lately so unpopular a character, become the idol of the people.'
73. BL Add. MSS 51354, fo. 106, Lady S. Lennox to Lady S. O'Brien, 5 Mar. 1780.
74. BL Add. MSS 47579, fo. 15, C. J. Fox to Lord Upper Ossory, Sept. 1780.
75. *Fox*, i. 258, R. Fitzpatrick to Lord Upper Ossory, Oct. 1780.
76. Ibid. The figures were Sir G. Rodney, 5,298, C. J. Fox, 4,878, Lord Lincoln, 4,157.
77. *Speech of the Hon. Charles James Fox* (London 1781).
78. *Fox*, i. 270.
79. See Chap. 11.
80. Bod. Lib. MS Autograph d38, fos. 7–10, C. J. Fox to C. Wyvill, 8 Feb. 1780.
81. Bod. Lib., Bowood MSS, Box 975, C. J. Fox to Lord Shelburne, 10 Feb. 1780.
82. *Speeches*, i. 290, 13 Nov. 1780. Fox believed that he had been elected 'in direct defiance of the avowed . . . influence of the crown', ibid. i. 291.
83. For Fox's support of annual parliaments and 100 more county members, see *Fox*, i. 247, for his voting for triennial parliaments, see ibid. i. 249–50. See also ibid. i. 243–4.
84. *Speeches*, i. 347–8, 8 May 1781.
85. BL Add. MSS 47580, fo. 22, C. J. Fox to R. Fitzpatrick, 3 Feb. 1778.
86. *Fox*, i. 142.
87. Quoted in M. D. George, *Hogarth to Cruickshank* (London 1967), 136.
88. Anon., *Life of the Right Honourable Charles James Fox* (London 1807), 55–6.
89. *Fox*, i. 148, George III to Lord North, 15 Nov. 1776.
90. *Fox*, i. 149, Mme du Deffand to H. Walpole, 13 Jan. 1777. To be fair she also reported Fox to be dining with Necker, where no doubt the company was a little more sober, *Walpole*, vi. 381.
91. HMC XV Report, Carlisle MSS, 583–4, G. Selwyn to Lord Carlisle, 25 Feb. 1782.
92. See Chap. 5.
93. BL Add. MSS 47580, fo. 35, C. J. Fox to R. Fitzpatrick, 11 Nov. 1778.
94. BL Add. MSS 61867, fo. 39, C. J. Fox to Lord North, 13 Apr. [1780]. For a more charitable account, see HMC X Report, Abergavenny MSS, 24, J. Robinson to Lord North, 31 Jan. 1779. This letter makes the point that the American question potentially divided Fox from Rockingham as much as it did from North and the King.
95. *Fox*, i. 155–6.

96. Ibid. i. 177.
97. *Speeches*, i. 224–5, 15 Dec. 1779.
98. BL Add. MSS 47568, fo. 72, Duke of Richmond to C. J. Fox, 7 Feb. 1779.
99. Ibid.
100. *Speeches*, i. 195, 22 June 1779.
101. W. Eden, *Secret Negotiation for a New Arrangement in March 1778, which failed; Fox*, i. 181.
102. Albemarle, *Rockingham*, ii. 353, Duke of Portland to Lord Rockingham, 29 May 1778.
103. *Burke*, iv. 39, C. J. Fox to E. Burke, 24 Jan. 1779.
104. *Fox*, i. 210, George III to Lord North, 29 Jan. 1779.
105. Sir J. Fortescue, *The Correspondence of George III, 1760–1783* (London 1927–8), iv. 264 and 353, Lord North to George III, 1 Feb. 1779.
106. *Fox*, i. 226–7, R. Fitzpatrick to Lord Upper Ossory, 15 Feb. 1779.
107. Fortescue, *Correspondence of George III*, iv. 368, Lord Sandwich to George III, 22 June 1779.
108. Albemarle, *Rockingham*, ii. 385, Lord Rockingham to A. Keppel, Nov. 1779. Burke was also sceptical, see *Burke*, iv. 154, E. Burke to Duke of Portland, 16 Oct. 1779.
109. Ibid. 156, E. Burke to Lord Rockingham, 17 Oct. 1779.
110. *Fox*, i. 237, George III to Lord Thurlow, 8 Dec. 1779.
111. Ibid. 253, George III to Lord North, June 1780.
112. Ibid.
113. J. Parkes and H. Merivale, *Memoirs of Sir Philip Francis* (London 1867), ii. 172, J. Bristow to Sir P. Francis, 4 Feb. 1779.
114. *Fox*, i. 254, R. Fitzpatrick to Lord Upper Ossory, July 1780. Fitzpatrick himself doubted the King's sincerity in this as in other negotiations.
115. Horace Walpole quoted in I. R. Christie, 'The Marquis of Rockingham and Lord North's Offer of a Coalition, June–July 1780', *Eng. Hist. Rev.*, 64 (1954), 390. See also Bod. Lib., Bowood MSS, C. J. Fox to Lord Shelburne, 1780.
116. *Fox*, i. 156–7.
117. Ibid. i. 275, C. J. Fox to Sir G. Macartney, 26 Jan. 1782.
118. Ibid.
119. BL Add. MSS 47580, fo. 22, C. J. Fox to R. Fitzpatrick, 3 Feb. 1778.
120. *Fox*, i. 207, C. J. Fox to Lord Rockingham, 24 Jan. 1779. In this long and important letter, the distance that Fox sets between himself and the Rockinghams is impressive.
121. *Fox*, i. 219, Duke of Richmond C. J. Fox, 7 Feb. 1779.

Chapter 3

1. For a detailed account of the politics of these years, see J. Cannon, *The Fox–North Coalition, 1782–1784* (Cambridge 1969); and L. G. Mitchell, *Charles James Fox and the Disintegration of the Whig Party, 1782–1794* (Oxford 1971).
2. HMC XV Report, Carlisle MSS, 599, G. Selwyn to Lord Carlisle, 19 Mar. [1782]. See also ibid. 591, 12 Mar. 1782.
3. *Speeches*, ii. 35, 4 Mar. 1782. He argued that if government contractors had been excluded from the Commons, North would have been in a minority of 'upwards of a hundred', ibid. ii. 40.
4. Ibid. ii. 47, 20 Mar. 1782.
5. C. Wyvill, *Political Tracts and Papers* (York 1779–1804), i. 402.
6. *Morning Chronicle*, 4 Apr. 1782. In his victory procession, he was chaired as 'the man of the people', HMC XIV Report, Emly MSS, 165, Lord Lucan to Mr Pery, 3 Apr. 1782.

7. A. I. M. Duncan, 'A Study of the Life and Public Career of Frederick Howard, Fifth Earl of Carlisle' (Oxford D.Phil. 1981), 134.

8. F. Hardy, *Memoirs of the Political and Private Life of James Caulfield, Earl of Charlemont* (London 1812), ii. 13, C. J. Fox to Lord Charlemont, 4 Apr. 1782.

9. BL Add. MSS 47561, fo. 27, C. J. Fox to Duke of Portland, 20 Apr. 1782.

10. BL Add. MSS 47585, fo. 113, George III to Lord North, 27 Mar. 1782.

11. *Memoirs of Sir Samuel Romilly* (London 1840), i. 217, S. Romilly to Rev. J. Roget, 12 Apr. 1782.

12. See Lord Shelburne to George III, 1 May and 1 June 1782, Sir J. Fortescue, *The Correspondence of George III, 1760–1783*, vi. 1 and 51–2; Wentworth Woodhouse Muniments, Rlq., C. J. Fox to Lord Rockingham, May 1782; BL Add. MSS 47579, fo. 85, Lord Upper Ossory to R. Fitzpatrick, 3 May 1782.

13. Wentworth Woodhouse Muniments, Rlq., C. J. Fox to Lord Rockingham, May 1782.

14. Bod. Lib., Bowood MSS, Shelburne Memorandum, 21 Mar. 1782. See also ibid., George III to Lord Shelburne, Mar. 1782.

15. See family tree (Fig. 1).

16. BL Add. MSS 51732, fos. 170–1, Caroline Fox to Lord Holland, 5 Feb. 1795.

17. BL Add. MSS 27918, fo. 70, Duke of Leeds Memorandum, 18 Apr. 1782. See also BL Add. MSS 47580, fo. 93; *Morning Herald*, 6 Apr. and 17 June 1782.

18. Christopher Wyvill had expectations of both. See Bod. Lib., Bowood MSS, *Short Account of the Interviews between Lord Shelburne & Lord Rockingham, separately, with Mr Wyvill in June 1782.*

19. BL Add. MSS 47580, fo. 77, C. J. Fox to R. Fitzpatrick, 15 Apr. 1782. The same subject had produced 'a very warm debate' three days earlier, ibid., fo. 71.

20. BL Add. MSS 47579, fo. 85, Lord Upper Ossory to R. Fitzpatrick, 3 May 1782. For a kinder reading of Shelburne's behaviour, see D. L. Keir, 'Economical Reform 1779–1787', *Law Quarterly Review*, 1934; and J. Norris, *Shelburne and Reform* (London 1963).

21. BL Add. MSS 47568, fo. 92, Lord Charlemont to C. J. Fox, Apr. 1782 and ibid., fo. 95, H. Grattan to C. J. Fox, 18 Apr. 1782.

22. BL Add. MSS 47580, fo. 105, C. J. Fox to H. Grattan, 27 Apr. 1782.

23. Bod. Lib., Bowood MSS, C. J. Fox to Lord Shelburne, 2 Apr. 1782.

24. C. Price, *The Letters of R. B. Sheridan* (Oxford 1966), i. 64, R. Sheridan to R. Fitzpatrick, 20 May 1782.

25. BL Add. MSS 47562, fo. 107, C. J. Fox to Frederick II, 1782.

26. Bod. Lib., Bland Burges MSS, fo. 38, C. J. Fox to Count Lusi, 16 June 1782. A Prussian–English–Russian alliance remained one of Fox's favourite projects for much of his life.

27. *Morning Herald*, 2 and 20 Apr. 1782.

28. Norris, *Shelburne and Reform*, 165.

29. HMC V Report, Lansdowne MSS, 253, Sir R. Keith to C. J. Fox, 4 May 1782.

30. BL Add. MSS 47559, fo. 9, Cabinet Minutes, 23 Apr. 1782, and ibid., fo. 15, 18 May 1782. The nature of England's proposal was also communicated to other powers, Bod. Lib., Bland Burges MSS, fos. 35–7, C. J. Fox to Count Lusi, 9 May 1782. The only area of ambiguity lay in Fox telling Grenville to use his discretion about stating whether these were simply his own views or those of the British government. Bargaining advantages could be in question, PRO FO 27/2, fo. 85, C. J. Fox to T. Grenville, 30 Apr. 1782.

31. BL Add. MSS 47559, fo. 21, Cabinet Minutes, 23 May 1782.

32. PRO FO 27/2, fo. 144, T. Grenville to C. J. Fox, 14 May 1782.

33. Ibid., fo. 108, C. J. Fox to T. Grenville, 26 May 1782.

34. BL Add. MSS Northumberland MSS, Microfilm 370, fo. 30, Lord Shelburne to Sir G. Carleton, 5 June 1782.
35. Norris, *Shelburne and Reform*, 168, 23 May 1782.
36. T. Grenville to C. J. Fox, 4 June 1782, Duke of Buckingham, *Memoirs of the Court and Cabinets of George III* (London 1853–5), i. 39. See also BL Add. MSS 47563, fo. 22, T. Grenville to R. Sheridan, 8 June 1782. Grenville told Sheridan that 'an unequivocal undivided ambassador is the person that Charles must find, and without whom he will lose ground.'
37. C. J. Fox to T. Grenville, 10 June 1782, Buckingham, *Court and Cabinets of George III*, i. 39.
38. Lord E. Fitzmaurice, *Life of William, Earl of Shelburne* (London 1912), ii. 148.
39. Fortescue, *Correspondence of George III*, vi. 69, Lord Shelburne to George III, 30 June 1782.
40. BL Add. MSS 34418, fo. 484, Lord Shelburne to Duke of Marlborough, 8 July 1782.
41. W. Suffolk PRO, Grafton MSS, fo. 759, Lord Shelburne to Duke of Grafton, 3 July 1782. See also B. Connell, *Portrait of a Whig Peer* (London 1957), 132.
42. Bod. Lib., Bowood MSS, George III to Lord Shelburne, 1 July 1782.
43. For details, see Mitchell, *Fox and Disintegration of Whig Party*, 35–6.
44. BL Add. MSS 47579, fo. 19, C. J. Fox to Lord Upper Ossory, 3 July 1782.
45. Ibid., fo. 90, R. Fitzpatrick to Lord Upper Ossory, 3 July 1782.
46. Journals of Richard Fitzpatrick, quoted in *Fox*, i. 435.
47. Durham Univ. Lib., Grey MSS, Lord F. Cavendish to Lady Ponsonby, 8 July 1782: 'It is pretty clear that the game in the year 66 is play'd over again.'
48. See BL Add. MSS 27918, fo. 75, Duke of Leeds Memorandum, 2 July 1782; Sheffield Pub. Lib., Wentworth Woodhouse Muniments, F636, C. J. Fox to Earl Fitzwilliam, 1 July 1782; A. M. W. Stirling, *Coke of Norfolk and His Friends* (London 1912), 127, C. J. Fox to T. W. Coke, 2 July 1782.
49. *Morning Herald*, 1 and 2 July 1782.
50. BL Add. MSS 47561, fo. 42, Duke of Portland to C. J. Fox, 6 July 1782. See also ibid., fo. 41, C. J. Fox to Duke of Portland, 5 July 1782.
51. BL Add. MSS 47568, fo. 106, E. Burke to C. J. Fox, 3 July 1782.
52. I. Leveson Gower, *The Face Without a Frown* (London 1944), 82, BL Add. MSS 47568, fo. 104, J. Burgoyne to C. J. Fox, 5 July 1782.
53. Others doubted whether all the Whigs would submit 'to become the mere creatures of Mr Fox, however highly they might think of his abilities', O. Browning, *Political Memoranda of the Fifth Duke of Leeds* (London 1884), 69–70.
54. BL Add. MSS 27918, fo. 79, Duke of Leeds Memorandum, 4 July 1782. See also Bod. Lib., Bowood MSS, George III to Lord Shelburne, 3 July 1782; and BL Add. MSS 47582, fo. 162, Memorandum of R. Fitzpatrick.
55. BL Add. MSS 34418, fo. 477, Lord Loughborough to W. Eden, 4 July 1782. See also HMC V Report, Sutherland MSS, 210, Lord Thurlow to Lord Gower, 6 July 1782.
56. *Walpole*, xxxv. 520.
57. *Sheridan*, i. 152, R. Sheridan to T. Grenville, 4 July 1782.
58. BL Add. MSS 27918, fo. 79, Duke of Leeds Memorandum, 7 July 1782. See also BL Add. MSS 47579, fo. 92, R. Fitzpatrick to Lord Upper Ossory, 5 July 1782.
59. W. Suffolk PRO, Grafton MSS, fo. 137, General Conway to Duke of Grafton, 5 July 1782.
60. Bod. Lib., Bowood MSS, George III to Lord Shelburne, 4 July 1782.
61. A. Gilbert, 'Political Correspondence of Charles Lennox, Third Duke of Richmond' (Oxford D.Phil. 1956), 627, Duke of Richmond to Lord George Lennox, 8 July 1782. See also Nottingham Univ. Lib., Portland MSS PWF 9190, Duke of Portland to Lady

Rockingham, 1 July 1782. Richmond's defection was particularly damaging, in that he shared with Fox the leadership of the Reform party within Whig circles. His continuing belief in Shelburne's reforming intentions undermined one of Fox's principal arguments. His dislike of Fox has been variously attributed to a dispute with the Fox family in 1768 and to the conviction that his own claims to the leadership of the Whigs had been ignored, see A. Olson, *The Radical Duke* (Oxford 1961), 64 ff. and *Edinburgh Review*, 99: 22 (1854).

62. Bod. Lib., Bowood MSS, Duke of Grafton to Lord Shelburne, 5 July 1782.

63. W. Suffolk PRO, Bunbury MSS E18/750/2, fo. 57, Lady L. Connolly to Lady S. Napier, 10 July 1782.

64. *Lennox*, ii. 19, Lady S. Napier to Lady S. O'Brien, 9 July 1782.

65. Buckingham, *Court and Cabinets of George III*, i. 51, Lord Temple to T. Grenville, 4 July 1782.

66. *Walpole*, xxix. 261, H. Walpole to W. Mason, 8 July 1782.

67. H. Walpole, *Letters Addressed to the Countess of Upper Ossory* (London 1848), ii. 97, H. Walpole to Lady Upper Ossory, 7 July 1782.

68. T. Wright, *The Works of James Gillray, the Caricaturist* (London 1873), 41.

69. HMC XIV Report, Emly MSS, 169, Lord Shelburne to Mr Pery, 9 July 1782.

70. Lord Herbert, *The Pembroke Papers* (London 1950), 202, Lord Pembroke to W. Coxe, 12 July 1782.

71. W. Suffolk PRO, Grafton MSS, fo. 757, Bishop of Peterborough to Duke of Grafton, 8 July 1782.

72. HMC Var. Coll., vi. 185, Lord Sackville to W. Knox, 9 July 1782.

73. Edinburgh N.R.O. GD10/1421/351, P. Johnston to ?, 6 July 1782. See also 41851, fo. 12, Duke of Buckingham to T. Grenville, July 1782.

74. E. B. de Fonblanque, *Life and Correspondence of the Rt. Hon. John Burgoyne* (London 1876), 413, Duke of Portland to J. Burgoyne, n.d.

75. Bod. Lib., Bowood MSS, George III to Lord Shelburne, 9 July 1782.

76. HMC XV Report, Stopford-Sackville MSS, 78–9, W. Knox to Lord Sackville, 6 July 1782.

77. *Parl. Hist.* xxiii. 138, 2 July 1782; see also *Morning Herald*, 13 July 1782; BL Add. MSS 27018, fo. 81, Duke of Leeds Memorandum, 8 July 1782.

78. HMC V Report, Sutherland MSS, 211, Lord Thurlow to Lord Gower, n.d. See also *Morning Herald*, 8 July 1782: 'The contest was merely a trial of political *power*, the dependence or independence of America being totally out of the question.'

79. BL Add. MSS 47580, fo. 122, C. J. Fox to R. Fitzpatrick, 4 July 1782.

80. HMC XV Report, Carlisle MSS, 632, Lord Carlisle to Lord Gower, 8 July 1782.

81. Durham Univ. Lib., Grey MSS, Lord F. Cavendish to Lady Ponsonby, 6 July 1782. For more hostile accounts, see Fortescue, *Correspondence of George III*, vi. 76–7, Lord Shelburne to George III, 9 July 1782; W. Suffolk PRO, Grafton MSS, fo. 761, Lord Shelburne to Duke of Grafton, 7 July 1782.

82. BL Add. MSS 47563, fo. 33, T. Grenville to C. J. Fox, 9 July 1782.

83. HMC XV Report, Carlisle MSS, 632, Lord Carlisle to Lord Gower, 8 July 1782.

84. *Speeches*, ii. 74, 9 July 1782.

85. Ibid. ii. 75.

86. Ibid. ii. 73.

87. Not all could. General Conway, a Cabinet colleague, declared himself mystified, whereupon Fox observed that 'it was the fate of his right honourable friend to be the last to discover those things that struck every man alive', ibid. ii. 79.

88. *Memoirs of Sir Samuel Romilly*, 235–7, Sir S. Romilly to J. Roget, 11 July 1782.

89. F. D. Cartwright, *The Life and Correspondence of Major Cartwright* (London 1826), 145–6.
90. *Speech of the Rt. Hon. C. J. Fox at a Meeting of the Electors of Westminster* (London 1782), 19.
91. *Morning Post*, 14 Oct. 1782. See also [J. Moir], *History of the Political Life and Public Services of the Rt. Hon. Charles James Fox* (London 1783), 513–15.
92. BL Add. MSS 47561, fo. 43, C. J. Fox to Duke of Portland, 12 July 1782. See also Buckingham, *Court and Cabinets of George III*, i. 63, C. J. Fox to T. Grenville, 13 July 1782; and BL Add. MSS 47582, fo. 124, L. O'Beirne to Mrs Crewe, 16 July 1782.
93. *Morning Post*, 23 Nov. 1782.
94. BL Althorp MSS, Lord Althorp to Lady Spencer, 22 Nov. 1782.
95. H. Walpole, *Letters Addressed to the Countess of Upper Ossory*, ii. 109, H. Walpole to Lady Upper Ossory, 31 Aug. 1782.
96. BL Add. MSS 51354, fo. 151, Lady S. Lennox to Lady S. O'Brien, 11 Sept. 1782. The lady in question was Perdita Robinson, the well-known actress.
97. *Morning Herald*, 6 Nov. 1782.
98. Edinburgh, Nat. Reg. Arch., Blair Adam MSS, R. Rigby to W. Adam, 14 July 1782.
99. *Journal and Correspondence of William Eden, First Lord Auckland* (London 1861), i. 9, Lord Loughborough to W. Eden, 14 July 1782. See also W. Beresford, *Correspondence of the Rt. Hon. John Beresford* (London 1854), i. 214, W. Eden to J. Beresford, 10 July 1782; L. V. Harcourt, *Diaries and Correspondence of the Rt. Hon. George Rose* (London 1860), i. 27.
100. BL Add. MSS 34418, fo. 513, W. Eden to Lord Loughborough, 24 July 1782. See also *Auckland*, i. 32, Lord Loughborough to W. Eden, 25 Aug. 1782. At this stage, North rejected the proposals 'with great derision'.
101. *Morning Post*, 24 Sept. 1782.
102. BL Add. MSS 34419, fo. 4, Lord Loughborough to W. Eden, 2 Aug. 1782.
103. *Morning Herald*, 14 Sept. 1782.
104. Edinburgh, Nat. Reg. Arch., Blair Adam MSS, W. Adam to C. J. Fox, 11 Jan. 1783.
105. W. Anson, *Memoirs of Augustus Henry, Third Duke of Grafton* (London 1898), 353.
106. Fitzmaurice, *Life of Earl of Shelburne*, ii. 231.
107. BL Althorp MSS, Earl Spencer to Lord Althorp, 14 Dec. 1782. See also *Morning Chronicle*, 23 Dec. 1782.
108. *Parl. Hist.* xxiii. 707, 31 Mar. 1783. According to his secretary, not always a reliable source, Fox never spoke of North without 'a strain of eulogy', Trotter, 29.
109. *Speeches*, ii. 110 ff., 18 Dec. 1782.
110. *Auckland*, i. 41, Lord Loughborough to W. Eden, 20 Jan. 1783.
111. Bod. Lib., Bowood MSS, B. Vaughan to Lord Shelburne, 15 Dec. 1782. See also *Morning Herald*, 23 Dec. 1782 and H. B. Wheatley, *Wraxall*, ii. 408.
112. Durham Univ. Lib., Grey MSS, Duchess of Portland to Mrs Ponsonby, 20 Jan. 1783.
113. *Burke*, v. 57, E. Burke to J. Burgoyne, 24 Dec. 1782.
114. Fox had put Pitt up for Brooks's Club.
115. *Wraxall*, iii. 6.
116. Buckingham, *Court and Cabinets of George III*, i. 149, W. Grenville to Lord Temple, 11 Feb. 1783. See also Bod. Lib., Bowood MSS, George III to Lord Shelburne, 11 Feb. 1783.
117. Details of the hurried formation of the Fox–North Coalition may be found in two important memoranda in the Edinburgh, Nat. Reg. Arch., Blair Adam MSS, both written by William Adam: 'The Coalition of 1783', and 'Contemporary Version'.
118. *Speeches*, ii. 121, 17 Feb. 1783.

119. Ibid. ii. 130, 21 Feb. 1783.

120. HMC X Report, Abergavenny MSS, 59, R. Atkinson to J. Robinson, 25 Mar. 1783.

121. Lord Guilford's Memorandum, quoted in I. R. Christie, *Wilkes, Wyvill and Reform* (London 1962), 177.

122. *Fox*, ii. 19.

123. BL Add. MSS 37835, fo. 199, R. Atkinson to J. Robinson, 18 Mar. 1783.

124. PRO, Pitt MSS, 30/8, 103, fo. 7, George III to W. Pitt, 24 Mar. 1783. For details of the Coalition's negotiations with the King, see BL Add. MSS 47582, fo. 164, R. Fitzpatrick's Memorandum.

125. PRO, Pitt MSS, 30/8, 103, fo. 9, George III to W. Pitt, 25 Mar. 1783.

126. A. Aspinall, *Correspondence of George, Prince of Wales* (London 1963–71), i. 104, George III to Prince of Wales, Mar. 1780.

127. Fortescue, *Correspondence of George III*, vi. 316–17, George III Memorandum.

128. Buckingham, *Court and Cabinets of George III*, i. 219, George III to Lord Temple, 1 Apr. 1783.

129. *Speeches*, ii. 148–9, 6 Mar. 1783.

130. Castle Howard MSS J 14/74/12, Lord Carlisle's Memorandum.

131. BL Add. MSS 47580, fo. 124, C. J. Fox to R. Fitzpatrick [Mar. 1783].

132. BL Add. MSS 27918, fo. 67, Memorandum of the Duke of Leeds, 26 Mar. 1783.

133. *Gentleman's Magazine*, Sept. 1806, 885.

134. Sir Samuel Romilly called it 'scandalous', *Memoirs of Sir Samuel Romilly*, i. 269 and 273, Sir S. Romilly to J. Roget, 21 Mar. and 1 Apr. 1783. See also A. M. W. Stirling, *Annals of a Yorkshire House* (London 1911), 39, W. S. Stanhope to his son [1783], and Durham PRO, Lee MSS D/80, fo. 40, W. Bush to J. Lee, 14 Mar. 1783.

135. *Speeches*, ii. 253, 1 Dec. 1783. As Fox's cousin put it, 'Why should it be a crying sin in Charles to do what every Politician does for ever?', W. Suffolk PRO, Bunbury MSS E18/750/2, fo. 21, Lady S. Napier to Mr Connolly [Mar.] 1783.

136. Though in Westminster the making of the Coalition was much debated, particularly on the point that an association with North would neuter reform initiatives. *Morning Herald*, 8 Mar. and 8 Apr. 1783; J. Disney, *The Works of John Jebb* (London 1787), i. 180.

137. W. Suffolk PRO, Bunbury MSS E18/750/2, fo. 21, Lady S. Napier to Mr Connolly [Mar.] 1783.

138. BL Add. MSS 34419, fo. 13, W. Eden to Lord North, 25 Feb. 1783.

139. *Parl. Hist.* xxxiii. 795, 25 Apr. 1783.

140. BL Add. MSS 47559, fo. 45, C. J. Fox to George III, 16 Apr. 1783; G. Martelli, *Life of John Montagu, Fourth Earl of Sandwich* (London 1962), 282, Lord North to Lord Sandwich, *c.*14 Apr. 1783; Fonblanque, *Burgoyne*, 429, C. J. Fox to J. Burgoyne, 1783.

141. BL Add. MSS 47579, fo. 21, C. J. Fox to Lord Upper Ossory, 18 Apr. 1783.

142. *Morning Herald*, 24 May 1783.

143. BL Add. MSS 47562, fo. 45, C. J. Fox to Sir J. Stepney, 20 May 1783, *Wraxall*, iii. 86. The matter was made more embarrassing by the fact of Powell being heavily involved in the management of Fox's debts.

144. Edinburgh, Nat. Lib. of Scotland, Minto MSS 13021, fo. 1518, C. J. Fox to H. Elliot, 12 Aug. 1783.

145. BL Add. MSS 47559, fo. 91, George III to C. J. Fox, 19 July 1783. For Fox's correspondence with Madrid, see the MSS of Sir Robert Liston in the Nat. Lib. of Scotland.

146. BL Add. MSS 47563, fo. 106, Duke of Manchester to C. J. Fox, 31 July 1783. See also

Fox–Manchester correspondence in HMC VIII Report, Appendix 128*a*–129*a*, and Fox–Portland letters in BL Add. MSS 47561, fo. 53 and 57.

147. See correspondence between C. J. Fox, the Prince of Wales, and the Duchess of Devonshire in *Prince of Wales*, i. 120–8; and Chatsworth MSS, 508, Duchess of Devonshire to Lady E. Foster, 20 June 1783.

148. Fox was twice declared bankrupt in this period.

149. Wright, *Works of James Gillray*, 48.

150. BL Add. MSS 47567, fo. 1, C. J. Fox to Lord Northington, 17 June 1783.

151. A. F. Steuart, *Last Journals of Horace Walpole* (London 1910), ii. 525; and *Prince of Wales*, i. 126–8, correspondence between C. J. Fox, the Prince of Wales, and the Duke of Portland.

152. BL Add. MSS 47567, fo. 9, C. J. Fox to Lord Northington, July 1783.

153. BL Add. MSS 47579, fo. 27, C. J. Fox to Lord Upper Ossory, 9 Sept. 1783. See also ibid., fo. 23, 12 Aug. 1783.

154. BL Add. MSS 34149, fo. 253, W. Eden to Lord Loughborough, 25 Aug. 1783.

155. Using his nickname of 'the Eyebrow', the Duchess reported that he had 'made a general rout amongst my lovers', Lord Bessborough, *Georgiana, Duchess of Devonshire* (London 1955), 98, Duchess of Devonshire to Lady E. Foster, 18 Oct. 1783.

156. *Morning Herald*, 15 Aug. 1783.

157. HMC VIII Report, Appendix 131*b*, Duke of Portland to Duke of Manchester, 4 Sept. 1783.

158. HMC X Report, Abergavenny MSS, 54, George III to J. Robinson, 7 Aug. 1783.

159. BL Add. MSS 47567, fo. 21, C. J. Fox to Lord Northington, 1 Nov. 1783.

160. BL Add. MSS 47568, fo. 205, C. J. Fox to J. Burgoyne, 17 Nov. 1783.

161. BL Add. MSS 33100, fo. 401, W. Eden to Lord Northington, 25 Nov. 1783.

162. HMC VIII Report, Appendix 133*a*, Duke of Portland to Duke of Manchester, 20 Sept. 1783.

163. P. J. Marshall, *The Impeachment of Warren Hastings* (Oxford 1965), 20, Sir G. Elliot to Lady Elliot, 20 Aug. 1783. See also 'The Secret History of the India Bill', in Edinburgh, Nat. Reg. Arch., Blair Adam MSS.

164. Marshall, *Hastings*, 21, J. Scott to A. Halhead, 9 Sept. 1787. See also Fortescue, *Correspondence of George III*, vi. 466, Lord Temple to George III.

165. BL Add. MSS 47567, fo. 49, C. J. Fox to Lord Northington, 14 Nov. 1783 and ibid., 47568, fo. 195, G. Berkeley to C. J. Fox, 13 Oct. 1783.

166. Bod. Lib., Bowood MSS, Sir F. Baring to Lord Shelburne, 20 Nov. 1783.

167. W. L. Clements Lib., Ann Arbor, Mich., Fox MSS, C. J. Fox to ?, 22 Nov. 1783.

168. BL Add. MSS 47579, fo. 35, C. J. Fox to Lord Upper Ossory, 21 Nov. 1783.

169. *Speeches*, ii. 199, 18 Nov. 1783.

170. Ibid. ii. 238, 1 Dec. 1783.

171. Ibid. ii. 245.

172. Commissioners drawn from great Whig families would not be corrupt because they were 'renowned for their ancestry, important for their possessions, distinguished for their personal worth, with all that is valuable to men at stake, hereditary fortunes and hereditary honours', ibid. ii. 258–9.

173. BL Add. MSS 47579, fo. 35, 21 Nov. 1783.

174. *Auckland*, i. 63, C. J. Fox to W. Eden, 28 Nov. 1783.

175. HMC VIII Report, 138*b*, C. J. Fox to Duke of Manchester, 2 Dec. 1783.

176. As early as 3 December, the King's political managers were ready: 'Every thing stands

prepared for the blow if a certain person has courage to strike it', HMC X Report, Abergavenny MSS, 61, R. Atkinson to J. Robinson, 3 Dec. 1783.

177. BL Add. MSS 33100, fo. 450, J. Burgoyne to Lord Northington, 6 Dec. 1.783.

178. BL Add. MSS 47570, fo. 153, C. J. Fox to Mrs Armistead, *c.* 10 Dec. 1783.

179. Bod. Lib. MSS Eng. Lett. c144, fo. 66, C. J. Fox to Duke of Portland, 13 Dec. 1783.

180. BL Add. MSS 47579, fo. 145, St A. St John to Lord Upper Ossory, 15 Dec. 1783. See also ibid. 33100, fo. 522, W. Windham to Lord Northington, 13 Dec. 1783, and ibid., fo. 464, J. Burgoyne to Lord Northington, 15 Dec. 1783.

181. Bod. Lib., Bowood MSS, T. Orde to Lord Shelburne, 16 Dec. 1783.

182. J. Hutton, *Letters and Correspondence of Sir James Bland Burges* (London 1885), 65.

183. *Windham*, i. 55, W. Windham to Lord Northington, 18 Dec. 1783.

184. BL Add. MSS 47570, fo. 156, C. J. Fox to Mrs Armistead, *c.* 17 Dec. 1783.

185. Blenheim MSS E62, George III to Duke of Marlborough, 29 Dec. 1783.

186. W. L. Clements Lib., Ann Arbor, Mich., Fox MSS, C. J. Fox to ?, 16 Dec. 1783.

187. Stirling, *Coke*, 135, C. J. Fox to T. W. Coke, 16 Dec. 1783.

188. Bod. Lib., Bowood MSS, T. Orde to Lord Shelburne, 22 Dec. 1783.

189. *Speeches*, ii. 267, 17 Dec. 1783.

190. Ibid. ii. 275.

191. *Morning Chronicle*, 7 Jan. 1784.

192. Durham PRO, Lee MSS D/BO, fo. 26, Duchess of Devonshire to Lady Spencer, 3 Jan. 1784.

193. Bod. Lib., Bowood MSS, T. Orde to Lord Shelburne, 22 Dec. 1783.

194. BL Add. MSS 47567, fo. 73, C. J. Fox to Lord Northington, 22 Dec. 1783.

195. *Lennox*, ii. 44, Lady S. Napier to Lady S. O'Brien, 22 Dec. 1783.

196. PRO, Pitt MSS, 30/8 103, fo. 15, George III to W. Pitt, 23 Dec. 1783.

197. Bod. Lib., Bowood MSS, T. Orde to Lord Shelburne, 22 Dec. 1783.

198. See BL Althorp MSS, W. Pitt to Lord Spencer, 21 Dec. 1783; D. Barnes, *George III and William Pitt* (London 1939), Lord Temple to George III, 21 Dec. 1783; *Malmesbury*, ii. 59, Sir G. Elliot to Sir G. Harris, 1 Jan. 1784; and *Morning Herald*, 7 Jan. 1784.

199. *Speeches*, ii. 313, 24 Dec. 1783. See also Lady Minto, *Life and Letters of Sir Gilbert Elliot, First Earl of Minto* (London 1874), i. 89, Sir G. Elliot to H. Elliot, Dec. 1783.

200. BL Add. MSS 47570, fo. 154, C. J. Fox to Mrs Armistead, 30 Dec. 1783.

201. BL Add. MSS 47567, fo. 75, C. J. Fox to Lord Northington, 26 Dec. 1783.

202. The Betting Book of Brooks's Club, 27 Dec. 1783.

203. Anson, *Grafton*, 385, C. J. Fox to Duke of Grafton, 18 Dec. 1783; and BL Add. MSS 47579, fo. 127, R. Fitzpatrick to Lord Upper Ossory, 1783.

204. *Speeches*, ii. 305, 19 Dec. 1783. See also ibid. ii. 309 ff., 22 Dec. 1783.

205. Ibid. ii. 306, 19 Dec. 1783.

206. *The Fox and the Badger Dismissed* (London 1784); M. D. George, *English Political Caricature*, i. 182.

207. For the collapse in Fox's parliamentary vote, see G. Tomline, *Memoirs of the Life of the Rt. Hon. William Pitt* (London 1821), i. 464–5.

208. Northants PRO, Milton MSS, xxxviii., fo. 19.

209. Edinburgh, Nat. Reg. Arch., Blair Adam MSS, General Correspondence 1784–5, W. Adam to C. J. Fox, 11 Jan. 1784. See also *Wraxall*, iii. 236.

210. *Malmesbury*, ii. 60, Sir G. Elliot to Sir J. Harris, 26 Feb. 1784.

211. N. C. Phillips, *Yorkshire and National Politics* (Christchurch, New Zealand 1961), 60, C. Wyvill to Sir W. Horton, 30 Apr. 1784.

212. Wyvill, *Political Tracts and Papers*, iv. 352, W. Mason to C. Wyvill, 22 Jan. 1784.

213. Ibid. ii. 328, *Debate among Yorkshire Members on Recent Occurrences*. See also Phillips, *Yorkshire and National Politics*, Sir C. Turner to C. Wyvill, 25 Mar. 1784; and BL Add. MSS 35641, fo. 77, J. Beldam to P. Yorke, 28 Feb. 1784.

214. Anon., *Life of the Right Honourable Charles James Fox* (London 1807), 104–5. See also HMC X Report, Abergavenny MSS, 66, Duchess of Portland to Mrs Ponsonby, 15 Feb. 1784; and *Morning Herald*, 14 Feb. 1784.

215. One of the most devastating pamphlets of the period was *Beauties and Deformities of Fox, North and Burke* (London 1784), which simply set out in parallel columns what each man had said of the others.

216. *Morning Chronicle*, 29 Jan. 1784. See also BL Add. MSS 47561, fo. 66, C. J. Fox to Duke of Portland, 29 Jan. 1784; *Speeches*, ii. 365, 2 Feb. 1784; and C. Ross, *Correspondence of the First Marquis Cornwallis* (London 1859), i. 156–7, Lord Cornwallis to Lt. Col. Ross, 26 Jan. 1784.

217. BL Althorp MSS, Lord J. Cavendish to Lord Spencer, 27 Jan. 1784.

218. For a list of the unseated Coalitionists, see Anon., *Fox's Martyrs or a New Book of the Sufferings of the Faithful* (London 1784), and Mitchell, *Fox and Disintegration of the Whig Party*, 92–6.

219. J. Marchand, *A Frenchman in England, 1784*, (Cambridge 1933), 112.

220. Durham Univ. Lib., Grey MSS, Lord J. Cavendish to Mrs Ponsonby, 6 May 1784.

221. George III to W. Pitt, 13 Apr. 1784, PRO, Pitt MSS, 30/8 103, fo. 93.

222. In addition to standard accounts of this election, see BL Add. MSS 51466, fo. 4, Fox to ?, 14 Apr. 1784.

223. Merton Coll. Malmesbury MSS, Box 1, Sir J. Harris to Mrs Robinson, 29 Mar. 1784; Edinburgh, Nat. Reg. Arch., Blair Adam MSS, General Correspondence 1784–5, Sir T. Dundas to W. Adam, 18 Apr. 1784.

224. Nottingham Univ. Lib., Portland MSS, PwF 9193, Duke of Portland to Lady Rockingham, 8 Apr. 1784; Edinburgh, Nat. Reg. Arch., Blair Adam MSS, C. J. Fox to J. Anstruther, 8 Apr. 1784.

225. After being reseated for Westminster after the scrutiny, Fox sued Thomas Corbet, the bailiff of Westminster, for £100,000 in damages. He was awarded £2,000.

226. BL Add. MSS 37843, fo. 5, E. Burke to W. Windham, 14 Oct. 1784.

227. *Speeches*, v. 316, 16 June 1794.

228. BL Add. MSS 47573, fo. 121, 8 Feb. 1779.

229. BL Add. MSS 47570, fo. 159, C. J. Fox to Mrs Armistead, 8 Apr. 1794.

Chapter 4

1. BL Add. MSS 34149, fo. 35, C. J. Fox to W. Eden, 1785.

2. PRO, Pitt MSS, 30/8 103, fo. 119, George III to W. Pitt, 29 July 1784.

3. Nottingham Univ. Lib., Portland MSS, PwF 3971, Duke of Portland to W. Eden, 24 Apr. 1785.

4. Sheffield Pub. Lib., Wentworth Woodhouse Muniments, Burke 1, D. Long to E. Burke, 1784.

5. BL Add. MSS 47561, fo. 84, C. J. Fox to Duke of Portland, 1 Aug. 1784.

6. *Morning Herald*, 30 July 1784.

7. *Burke*, v. 166, E. Burke to G. Elliot, 3 Aug. 1784.

8. BL Add. MSS 47581, fo. 81; C. J. Fox to Duke of Portland, 27 July 1784.

9. W. Suffolk PRO, Grafton MSS, fo. 100, Lord Camden to Duke of Grafton, 27 Jan. 1785.

See also HMC XIV Report, Rutland III MSS, 97–8, D. Pulteney to Duke of Rutland, 27 May 1784.

10. W. Suffolk PRO, Grafton MSS, fo. 97, Lord Camden to Duke of Grafton, 6 Jan. 1786.

11. Bod. Lib., Bowood MSS, R. Price to Lord Shelburne, 24 Nov. 1784. See also Bod. Lib., Bowood MSS, Sir F. Baring to Lord Shelburne, 28 July 1784; and Edinburgh, Nat. Reg. Arch., Blair Adam MSS, G. Wilson to W. Adam, 24 Sept. 1784.

12. M. D. George, *English Political Caricature*, i. 165.

13. For example, *The Last Dying Words of Reynard the Fox* (London 1784), which begins

> Beneath this Turf poor REYNARD lies,
> By some believed no more to rise;
> A true-born Subject of OLD NICK,
> Who's serv'd him now a hellish Trick.

14. W. T. Laprade, 'William Pitt and the Westminster Elections', *American Historical Review*, 23 (1912), 263.

15. *Speeches*, ii. 344, 16 Jan. 1784.

16. Ibid. ii. 345. See also ibid. ii. 348 ff., 20 Jan. 1784.

17. Ibid. ii. 417, 1 Mar. 1784.

18. PRO, Pitt MSS 30/8 103, fo. 42, George III to W. Pitt, 26 Jan. 1784.

19. Ibid., fo. 48, 14 Feb. 1784.

20. Ibid., fo. 31, 13 Jan. 1784.

21. See Chap. 5.

22. J. Boswell, *The Life of Dr Samuel Johnson* (Oxford 1965), 1292.

23. Between 1780 and 1782, the two men seemed to have enjoyed some sort of friendship. Fox stood as sponsor for Pitt's candidature for Brooks's.

24. Such conversations were certainly held in Feb. 1783, Dec. 1783, Mar. 1791, May–June 1792, Nov. 1792, Feb. 1793, Aug. 1796, Apr.–May 1804, and July 1805. Unsubstantiated rumour would add other dates to this list.

25. Sir N. Wraxall, *A Short Review of the Political State of Great Britain* (London 1787), 28–9.

26. *Parl. Hist.* xxiv. 312, 12 Jan. 1784.

27. *Speeches*, iii. 201, 27 Feb. 1786.

28. Referring to Pitt, it was reported that 'a work abt. the *royal recommendation* seemed to call up more blood than usual into the cheeks. I suspect, that the Allusions to Back Stairs etc continue to agitate and distress.' T. Orde to Lord Shelburne, Bod. Lib., Bowood MSS, 17 June 1784.

29. Lord Bessborough, *Georgiana, Duchess of Devonshire* (London 1955), 75, Duchess of Devonshire to Lady Spencer, 8 Feb. 1784.

30. See D. Ginter, 'The Financing of the Whig Party Organisation 1783–1793', *American Historical Review* (1966), and *Whig Organisation in the General Election of 1790* (Berkeley 1966). See also *The Whig Club Rule Book* (London 1784).

31. BL Add. MSS 47570, fo. 171, C. J. Fox to Mrs Armistead, 10 Sept. 1785.

32. *Walpole*, xxiii. 490–1, H. Walpole to Sir H. Mann, 15 June 1773.

33. Edinburgh, Nat. Reg. Arch., Buccleuch MSS GD224/628/7, C. J. Fox to Duke of Buccleuch, 25 May [1773].

34. Quoted in P. J. Marshall, *The Impeachment of Warren Hastings* (Oxford 1965), 19.

35. PRO, Pitt MSS 30/8 103, fo. 165, George III to W. Pitt, 6 May 1785.

36. *Parl. Hist.* xxv. 151, 16 Feb. 1784.

37. *Burke*, v. 154, E. Burke to W. Baker, 22 June 1784. See also ibid. v. 340, E. Burke to T. Burgh, 1 July 1787: 'Perhaps we may consider it as some addition to the success we have had, that this House of Commons, chosen for the express purpose of discrediting the last, has acquitted its predecessor with honour.'

38. *Speeches*, iii. 348, 11 Dec. 1787.

39. B. Fitzgerald, *Emily, Duchess of Leinster* (London 1949), 183, Journal of Lady Sophia Fitzgerald, Feb. 1788.

40. Indian money had been in evidence to support anti-Coalition candidates in the 1784 election.

41. *Wraxall*, iv. 8, 4 Aug. 1784.

42. Ibid. iv. 302.

43. Ibid. iv. 147-8.

44. HMC XIV Report, Rutland III MSS, 370, D. Pulteney to Duke of Rutland, 8 Feb. 1787.

45. For details of the impeachment, see Marshall, *Impeachment of Warren Hastings*.

46. *Morning Chronicle*, 23 Feb. 1788.

47. *Speeches*, iii. 220. See also J. Owen, *Letter to Mr Fox on the Duration of the Trial of Mr Hastings* (London 1794).

48. BL Add. MSS 24266. The renewed interest shown in 1791 is interesting. Possibly, as party divisions widened under the impact of the French Revolution, the Managers' Box was one of the few places where competing factions could still meet.

49. Fitzgerald, *Emily, Duchess of Leinster*, 184, Journal of Lady S. Fitzgerald, Feb. 1788.

50. E. B. de Fonblanque, *Life and Correspondence of the Rt. Hon. John Burgoyne* (London 1876), 448, E. Burke to J. Burgoyne, 4 May 1788.

51. *Burke*, v. 472, E. Burke to C. J. Fox, 11 May 1789.

52. Edinburgh, Nat. Reg. Arch., Blair Adam MSS Gen. Correspondence 1792, C. J. Fox to W. Adam, 26 May 1792. See also Durham Univ. Lib., Grey MSS, Lord J. Cavendish to Miss Ponsonby [1794].

53. *Parl. Hist.* xxvii. 539 and xxviii. 545-6, 20 May 1788 and 10 Mar. 1790. See also *Speeches*, iii. 478 and iv. 92, 1 and 27 May 1790.

54. Lord Bessborough, *Lady Bessborough and her Family Circle* (London 1940), 89, Lord Bessborough to Lady Bessborough, 31 May 1793.

55. *Parl. Hist.* xxxi. 946, 20 June 1794.

56. *Burke*, v. 304, E. Burke to Sir P. Francis, *c*.2 Jan. 1787. See also Windsor Castle, Palmerston MSS, Lord Palmerston to Lady Palmerston, 20 Dec. 1790.

57. *Burke*, v. 241-4, E. Burke to Sir P. Francis, 10 Dec. 1785.

58. *Morning Chronicle*, 7 May 1788.

59. *Burke*, vi. 58, E. Burke to Sir P. Francis, 17 Dec. 1789.

60. J. Grieg, *The Farington Diary* (London 1922), i. 51.

61. For a detailed account of the Regency Crisis, see J. W. Derry, *The Regency Crisis and the Whigs, 1788-1789* (Cambridge 1963).

62. E. M. Bell, *The Hamwood Papers* (London 1930), 156.

63. F. M. Bladon, *The Diaries of Robert Fulke Greville* (London 1930), 128.

64. Bell, *Hamwood Papers*, 156.

65. *Prince of Wales*, i. 384, C. J. Fox to Prince of Wales, *c*.25 Nov. 1788.

66. BL Add. MSS 47561, fo. 95, C. J. Fox to Duke of Portland, 21 Jan. 1789. See also *Minto*, i. 260, Sir G. Elliot to Lady Elliot, 10 Jan. 1789.

67. *Minto*, i. 238, Sir G. Elliot to Lady Elliot, 25 Nov. 1788.

68. Windsor Castle, Palmerston MSS, Lord Palmerston to Lady Palmerston, 4 Nov. 1788.

69. *Minto*, i. 244–8.

70. Windsor Castle, Palmerston MSS, Lady Palmerston to Lord Palmerston, 18 Nov. 1788.

71. Durham Univ. Lib., Grey MSS, Lord F. Cavendish to Mrs Ponsonby, 4 Dec. 1788, W. Sichel, *Sheridan* (London 1909), ii. 412. Diary of the Duchess of Devonshire, 5 Dec. 1788; Bell, *Hamwood Papers*, 174–5.

72. BL Add. MSS 41579, fo. 14, Lady E. Foster's Journal, 17 Dec. 1788; Windsor Castle, Palmerston MSS, Lord Palmerston to Lady Palmerston, 18 Dec. 1788; *Wraxall*, v. 207.

73. Derry, *Regency Crisis*, 174–5, Archbishop of Canterbury to W. Eden, 13 Feb. 1789; E. S. Roscoe and H. Clergue, *George Selwyn, his Letters and his Life* (London 1899), 245, G. Selwyn to Lady Carlisle, 4 Dec. 1788.

74. *Prince of Wales*, i. 484–5, C. J. Fox to Prince of Wales, 4 Feb. 1789; BL Add. MSS 47561, fo. 111, C. J. Fox to Duke of Portland, 21 Feb. 1789.

75. Windsor Castle, Palmerston MSS, Lord Palmerston to Lady Palmerston, 31 Jan. 1789.

76. HMC XIV Report, Kenyon MSS, 527, W. Wilberforce to M. Kenyon, 12 Feb. 1789.

77. Edinburgh, Nat. Reg. Arch., Blair Adam MSS, C. J. Fox to W. Adam, 8 and 15 Feb. 1789.

78. BL Add. MSS 47580, fo. 137, C. J. Fox to R. Fitzpatrick, 8 Feb. 1789.

79. BL Add. MSS 37873, fo. 159, W. Windham to ?, 26 Nov. 1788.

80. Broughton MSS GD22/1/315, F. Laurence to R. Graham, 2 Jan. 1789.

81. C. J. Fox, *A History of the Early Part of the Reign of James II* (London 1808), 38–9.

82. *A Letter to the Rt. Hon. C. J. Fox on the Late Conduct of his Party* (London 1789), 8–9. Since the two men remained rivals, a change of front by Fox necessarily was complemented by a change of front by Pitt. Curiously though, charges of duplicity are almost always levelled at Fox and only rarely at Pitt.

83. BL Add. MSS 47560, fos. 86–94.

84. Sichel, *Sheridan*, ii. 412, Diary of the Duchess of Devonshire, 5 Dec. 1788.

85. Derry, *Regency Crisis*, 78–9.

86. *Speeches*, iii. 401, 10 Dec. 1788.

87. Ibid. iii. 400.

88. W. Suffolk PRO, Grafton MSS, fo. 746, R. Hopkins to Duke of Grafton, 11 Dec. 1788.

89. B. Connell, *Portrait of a Whig Peer* (London 1957), 188, Lord Palmerston to Lady Palmerston, 12 Dec. 1788. See also W. Suffolk PRO, Grafton MSS, fo. 958, Bishop of Peterborough to Duke of Grafton, 11 Dec. 1788; *Auckland*, ii. 253, Sir J. Eden to W. Eden, 12 Dec. 1788.

90. Althorp MSS, Earl Spencer to Dowager Countess Spencer, 12 Dec. 1788.

91. Derry, *Regency Crisis*, 70. See also *Speeches*, iii. 402.

92. Sir W. Blackstone, *Commentaries on the Laws of England* (London 1765–9), i. 241–2.

93. Anon., *Fox Against Fox: Or Political Blossoms of the Rt. Hon. C. J. Fox* (London 1788).

94. BL Add. MSS 41579, fo. 20, Lady E. Foster's Journal, c. 4 Jan. 1789.

95. *Speeches*, iii. 422, 16 Dec. 1788.

96. Ibid. iii. 425. See also ibid. iii. 405, 12 Dec. 1788; ibid. iii. 429; 22 Dec. 1788; and ibid. iii. 442, 6 Jan. 1789.

97. J. Johnstone, *The Works of Dr Samuel Parr* (London 1828), viii. 468, Mrs Sheridan to Dr Parr, 13 Dec. [1788].

98. *Minto*, i. 249, Sir G. Elliot to Lady Elliot, 27 Dec. 1788. See also Lord Campbell, *Lives of the Lord Chancellors and Keepers of the Great Seal of England* (London 1856), viii. 98, C. J. Fox to Lord Loughborough, 26 Dec. 1788.

99. BL Add. MSS 47570, fo. 178, C. J. Fox to Mrs Armistead, 15 Dec. 1788.

100. Durham Univ. Lib., Grey MSS, Lord G. Cavendish to Lady Ponsonby, 25 Dec. 1788.

101. Windsor Castle, Palmerston MSS, Lord Palmerston to Lady Palmerston, 26 Dec. 1788.

102. *Minto*, i. 257, Sir G. Elliot to Lady Elliot, 6 Jan. 1789.

103. BL Add. MSS 47590, fo. 40, The Commonplace Book of Samuel Rogers, fo. 40.

104. Sichel, *Sheridan*, ii. 400, Diary of the Duchess of Devonshire, 1802.

105. *Burke*, v. 428–9, E. Burke to W. Windham, 1788.

106. BL Add. MSS 37843, fo. 13, E. Burke to W. Windham, 25 Dec. 1788.

107. *Burke*, v. 439, E. Burke to W. Windham, c.24 Jan. 1789.

108. L. J. Jennings, *The Croker Papers* (London 1884), i. 291, George IV to J. W. Croker, 1789.

109. In terms of the number of speeches made in the House of Commons, the prosecution of Hastings was as important to Burke as the French Revolution itself.

110. *Prince of Wales*, i. 364–5, R. B. Sheridan to Prince of Wales and vice versa, 6–7 Nov. 1788; BL Add. MSS 41579, fo. 4, Journal of Lady E. Foster, 23 Nov. 1788; *Sheridan*, i. 199, R. B. Sheridan to J. Payne, 24 Nov. 1788. The incident is incorrectly remembered by W. Adam in BL Add. MSS 47591, fo. 88.

111. Althorp MSS, R. Bingham to Earl Spencer, 12 Nov. 1788.

112. HMC XIII Report, Dropmore MSS, Fortescue I, 374, Duke of Buckingham to W. Grenville, 23 Nov. 1788.

113. W. Sichel, *Sheridan*, ii. 404, Diary of Duchess of Devonshire, 20 Nov. 1788.

114. G. Selwyn to Lady Carlisle, 26 Nov. 1788, Roscoe and Clergue, *Selwyn*, 242.

115. *Sheridan*, ii. 31, C. J. Fox to R. B. Sheridan, c.30 Nov. 1788.

116. Campbell, *Lives of the Lord Chancellors*, viii. 93, C. J. Fox to Lord Loughborough, Dec. 1788.

117. Chatsworth MSS, Journal of Lady E. Foster, 20 Jan. 1789.

118. Ibid. 11 Jan. 1789.

119. Ibid.

120. Anon., *A Letter to the Rt. Hon. C. J. Fox on the Late Conduct of his Party*, 29.

121. Chatsworth MSS, Journal of Lady E. Foster, 20 Dec. 1788; ibid. ii. 418.

122. BL Add. MSS 41579, fo. 19, Journal of Lady E. Foster, 2 Jan. 1789.

123. Ibid., fo. 20, ibid. 4 Jan. 1789.

124. J. Parkes and H. Merivale, *Memoirs of Sir Philip Francis* (London 1867), ii. 451. Francis, a hostile witness who blamed Fox for the frustration of his own career in politics, always suggested that Fox '*hated* very little, because in general he loved nobody'.

125. Chatsworth MSS, Journal of Lady E. Foster, 28 Jan. 1794.

126. E. Burke to Lord Charlemont, 10 July 1789, F. Hardy, *Memoirs of Charlemont* (London 1812), ii. 218.

127. Chatsworth MSS, Journal of Lady E. Foster, 5 Mar. 1789.

128. *Fox*, ii. 308 ff.

129. Chatsworth MSS, Journal of Lady E. Foster, 10 Mar. 1789.

130. BL Add. MSS 47568, fo. 256, C. J. Fox to W. Adam, 15 Mar. 1789.

131. Chatsworth MSS, Journal of Lady E. Foster, 12 Mar. 1789.

132. T. Moore, *Memoirs of R. B. Sheridan* (London 1825), i. 470.

133. BL Add. MSS 51705, fo. 69, T. Pelham to Lady Webster, Dec. 1791. The Prince had won a substantial sum of money on a race which, it was suspected, had been fixed. Sheridan was sent to Newmarket to prove that the race had been fairly run. Fox bluntly told the Prince that 'he could not think it much to his credit to have such a Jockey as Shiffney.'

134. A. Aspinall, *The Later Correspondence of George III* (Cambridge 1963–70), i. 149–51.

135. W. Combe, *A Letter from a Country Gentleman to a Member of Parliament* (London 1789), 73.

136. Aspinall, *Later Correspondence of George III*, i. 150, Conversation between C. J. Fox and Lord Southampton, 28 Mar. 1785.

137. G. M. Trevelyan, *Lord Grey of the Reform Bill* (London 1929), 18.

138. *Speeches*, iii. 325, 30 Apr. 1787.

139. *The Croker Papers*, i. 292, George IV to J. W. Croker, n.d. Mrs Fitzherbert remained one of Fox's most determined enemies for the rest of his life.

140. Lord J. Russell, *Memoirs, Journal and Correspondence of Thomas Moore* (London 1853), iv. 227.

141. *The Croker Papers*, i. 293.

142. *Minto*, i. 162, Sir G. Elliot to Lady Elliot, 5 May 1787.

143. Connell, *Portrait of a Whig Peer*, 186, Sir G. Elliot to Lord Palmerston, 1 Dec. 1788.

144. BL Egerton MSS 3260, W. Eden to Lord Hertford, 17 May 1787.

145. Lord Buckingham to W. W. Grenville, 11 Nov. 1788, HMC XIII Report, Dropmore MSS, Fortescue I, 362.

146. H. Minchin to Lord Spencer, 29 Apr. 1787, Althorp MSS.

147. Bell, *Hamwood Papers*, 206. See also *Auckland*, ii. 266, Archbishop of Canterbury to W. Eden, 16 Jan. 1789.

148. Nottingham Univ. Lib., Portland MSS PwF 9217, Duke of Portland to Lord Loughborough, 3 May 1787.

149. *Sheridan*, i. 190 n. 3.

150. Derry, *Regency Crisis*, 127, Diary of the Duchess of Devonshire, 13 Jan. 1789.

151. BL Add. MSS 41579, fo. 5, Journal of Lady E. Foster, 24 Nov. 1788.

152. *Prince of Wales*, ii. 20–2, C. J. Fox to Prince of Wales, 18 July 1789.

153. BL Egerton MSS 3260, W. Eden to Lord Hertford, 17 May 1787.

Chapter 5

1. C. Pigott, *The Whig Club* (London 1794), 10 n. 1.

2. Ibid. 16.

3. W. Combe, *The Diaboliad* (London 1777), 10.

4. Anon., *A Collection of Odes, Songs and Epigrams against the Whigs alias the Buff and Blue* (London 1790), 5.

5. *The Diary of Thomas Campbell* (Cambridge 1947), 103.

6. HMC XV Report, Carlisle MSS, 591, G. Selwyn to Lord Carlisle, 12 Mar. 1782.

7. Ibid. 551, 13 Dec. 1781.

8. F. Bickley, *The Diaries of Sylvester Douglas, Lord Glenbervie* (London 1928), ii. 320.

9. To jockey was to swindle or deceive.

10. See C. Pigott, *The Jockey Club* (London 1792), and *The Female Jockey Club* (London 1794).

11. 'Fox's Dinner' in *A Collection of Odes, Songs and Epigrams . . .*, 30–1.

12. HMC XV Report, Carlisle MSS, 277, G. Selwyn to Lord Carlisle, 13 Aug. 1774.

13. In Foxite writings, the words 'le monde' are used exclusively in this sense.

14. *The True Briton*, 18 Mar. 1797.

15. BL Add. MSS 47566, fo. 75, C. J. Fox to D. O'Bryen, 19 Feb. 1801.

16. Anon., *Life of the Right Honourable Charles James Fox* (London 1807), 363. Although the authorship of these lines may be in doubt, the sentiments expressed are authentically Foxite.

17. H. Wyndham, *The Correspondence of Sarah Spencer, Lady Lyttelton* (London 1912), 175, Diary of Lady S. Lyttelton, 5 Dec. 1813.
18. G. O. Trevelyan, *The Life and Letters of Lord Macaulay* (London 1959), 137, Journal of Lord Macaulay, 3 Jan. 1832.
19. He refused to harry Pitt on points of financial irregularity. See H. Maxwell, *The Creevey Papers* (London 1903), i. 37, T. Creevey to Dr Currie, 28 July 1805.
20. HMC XV Report, Lothian MSS, 428, Sir T. Durrant to Lord Buckinghamshire, 25 Feb. 1784.
21. *Speeches*, i. 264, 24 Apr. 1780.
22. G. Berkeley, *My Life and Recollections* (London 1866), iv. 2.
23. Leics. PRO, the Papers and Correspondence of Sir Henry Halford. It was also reported that the heart and lungs were whole.
24. HMC XV Report, Carlisle MSS, 512, G. Selwyn to Lord Carlisle, June 1781.
25. A. Steuart, *The Last Journals of Horace Walpole* (London 1910), ii. 248.
26. Bickley, *Glenbervie*, ii. 321.
27. Brooks's Betting Book.
28. BL Add. MSS 60487B, unfoliated, Fox memorandum.
29. BL Add. MSS 47568, fo. 143, W. Windham to C. J. Fox, 28 July 1783.
30. BL Add. MSS 47582, fo. 131, J. Hare to R. Fitzpatrick, 31 July 1782. Tarleton and Lord John Townshend remained loyal to Fox, as MPs, all through the 1790s.
31. Lord Bessborough, *Georgiana, Duchess of Devonshire* (London 1955), 68, Duchess of Devonshire to Lady E. Foster, 18 Oct. 1783. See also Chatsworh MSS, fo. 679, Same to Same, June 1785.
32. Bod. Lib. MSS Eng. Misc. 169, fo. 33, C. J. Fox, *Verses to Mrs Crewe*.
33. Lady Granville, *Lord Granville Leveson Gower* (London 1916), i. 344, Lady Bessborough to G. Leveson Gower [July 1802]. For Fox's relationship with Mrs Armistead, see Chap. 9.
34. Essay by R. Porter in P. G. Boucé, *Sexuality in Eighteenth Century Britain* (Manchester 1982), 13.
35. BL Add. MSS 60487B, unfoliated, R. Fitzpatrick to Mrs Benwell, 10 Apr. 1783.
36. J. Parkes and H. Merivale, *Memoirs of Sir Philip Francis* (London 1867), ii. 446.
37. *Malmesbury*, ii. 279, Mrs Harris to Sir J. Harris, 14 Jan. 1774.
38. Anon., *Life of the Right Honourable Charles James Fox*, 193–7.
39. For example, *Lloyd's Evening Post*, 16 July 1772. 'Fox's "Sober" beat Mr Vernon's "Swiss"—500 gns. Bolingbroke's "Gnawpost" beat Fox's "Mittimus" 300 gns. Mr Pigott's "Lycurgus" beat Fox's "Pantaloon" 1,000 gns to 600 gns.'
40. J. Marchand, *A Frenchman in England*, 1784 (Cambridge 1933), 69.
41. *Fox*, i. 70.
42. A card game resembling *vingt-et-un*.
43. HMC XV Report, Carlisle MSS, 511, G. Selwyn to Lord Carlisle, 30 June 1781.
44. Ibid. 554. The sight of Fox in a clean shirt was obviously a matter for comment, ibid. 483.
45. M. D. George, *English Political Caricature* (Oxford 1959), i. 164.
46. *Rogers*, 73.
47. *Fox*, i. 264, H. Walpole to Sir H. Mann, 17 May 1781.
48. Bod. Lib., Bowood MSS, *Verses on Fox written by Colonel Fitzpatrick*. Its tone may be gauged from the lines

> At Almac's of pigeons they say there are flocks.
> But 'tis thought the completest is one Mr Fox;

If he touches a card, if he rattles a Box
Away fly the guineas of this Mr Fox.

.   .   .   .   .

He's a Member of Parliament too (with a Pox),
Or he'd soon be in prison would this Mr Fox.

A 'pigeon' was an amateur who could be 'plucked' by cardsharps.

49. HMC XV Report, Carlisle MSS, 266, G. Selwyn to Lord Carlisle, 5 Feb. [1774].

50. *Walpole*, xxiv. 25, H. Walpole to Sir H. Mann, 3 Aug. 1774. For some reason, the balance on the sale of Kingsgate did not reach Fox until 1790; Coutts MSS, Ledgers, fo. 562. See also A. I. M. Duncan, 'A Study of the Life and Public Career of Frederick Howard, Fifth Earl of Carlisle' (Oxford D.Phil. 1981), 8.

51. BL Add. MSS 47568, fo. 68, C. J. Fox to ?, 27 June [1774].

52. HMC XV Report, Carlisle MSS, 489, G. Selwyn to Lord Carlisle, 31 May 1781.

53. Ibid. 491, 1 June [1781]. Henry Fox nicknamed his son the 'Second Messiah', born for the destruction of Jewish moneylenders. Fox himself called the antechamber to his bedroom, where creditors waited, his 'Jerusalem Chamber'.

54. Foxites stood surety for one another and arranged loans. For example, see BL Add. MSS 47566, fos. 52 and 111, C. J. Fox to D. O'Bryen, 2 Nov. 1800 and 12 May 1802.

55. HMC XV Report, Carlisle MSS, 264–5, G. Selwyn to Lord Carlisle, 5 Feb. [1774].

56. BL Add. MSS 47568, fo. 14, H. Walpole memorandum, *c*. Feb. 1772.

57. BL Add. MSS 35068, fo. 12, Lord Holland to J. Powell, 26 Nov. 1773.

58. He would commit suicide in 1782 when irregularities in the Pay Office were under investigation.

59. Castle Howard MSS, J/14/1, fo. 151, G. Selwyn to Lord Carlisle, 15 Jan. [1774].

60. BL Add. MSS 47570, fo. 8, C. J. Fox to Lady Holland, n.d.

61. *Walpole*, xxiii. 542, H. Walpole to Sir H. Mann, 11 Jan. 1774.

62. Castle Howard MSS, J/14/1, fo. 142, G. Selwyn to Lord Carlisle, 1773.

63. BL Add. MSS 47570, fo. 10, C. J. Fox to S. Fox, 1773.

64. Anon., *The Life of the Right Honourable Charles James Fox*, 58.

65. For details, see Duncan, 'The Life and Public Career of Frederick Howard, Fifth Earl of Carlisle', 8 ff. See also Castle Howard MSS, J/14/1, fo. 541, 'The State of the Case between Mr Charles Fox and Lord Carlisle'.

66. Castle Howard MSS, J/14/1, fo. 540, Lord Carlisle to Lady Holland, 5 Dec. 1773.

67. Ibid., fo. 538, S. Fox to Lord Carlisle, 9 Mar. [1774].

68. G. Selwyn to Lord Carlisle, 12 Aug. 1775. Ibid., fo. 169.

69. HMC XV Report, Carlisle MSS, 250, Same to Same, 27 Nov. 1773.

70. Castle Howard MSS, J/14/1, fo. 169, Same to Same, 12 Aug. [1775]. Selwyn predictably became one of Fox's major detractors. Typical of his comments was the following: 'I heard a friend of Charles say yesterday, "I shall be damned angry with Charles if he engages any more at Newmarket till his father dies." I am tempted to give him some credit for that, because the first meeting at Newmarket will not be till April, and Lord Holland will not live in all probability till January.'

71. HMC XV Report, Carlisle MSS, 261–2, G. Selwyn to Lord Carlisle, 18 Jan. [1774].

72. Ibid. 282, 17 Sept. [1775].

73. Castle Howard MSS, J/14/1, fo. 552, C. J. Fox to Lord Carlisle, 12 Oct. 1780.

74. HMC XV Report, Carlisle MSS, 492, G. Selwyn to Lord Carlisle, 2 June [1781].

75. *Walpole*, xxxii. 170.

292 *Notes to Chap. 5*

76. BL Add. MSS 51466, fo. 17, T. Coutts to C. J. Fox, 30 July 1787.

77. J. Carswell, *The Old Cause* (London 1954), 291, T. Coutts to Duchess of Devonshire, *c*.1787.

78. Coutts MSS, document 466, T. Coutts Memorandum Book.

79. Ibid., fo. 1003, C. J. Fox to T. Coutts, 1 Aug. 1787.

80. Ibid.

81. E. Coleridge, *The Life of Thomas Coutts* (London 1920), i. 243–6, C. J. Fox to T. Coutts, 15 June 1788.

82. W. L. Clements Lib., Ann Arbor, Mich., Fox MSS, C. J. Fox to T. Coutts, Apr. 1800.

83. BL Add. MSS 51466, fo. 11, T. Coutts to C. J. Fox, 30 July 1787.

84. Bickley, *Glenbervie*, i. 340.

85. BL Add. MSS 47571, fo. 169, C. J. Fox to Lord Holland, 5 Oct. 1794. It is worth noting that Fox's French debts were managed by the banker Perregaux from 1794 until his death.

86. BL Add. MSS 47564, fo. 49, C. J. Fox to Lord Lauderdale, 1798.

87. BL Add. MSS 47569, fo. 120, C. J. Fox to W. Adam, 20 May 1802; Durham Univ. Lib., Grey MSS, R. Fitzpatrick to Lord Lauderdale, Mar. 1802; BL Add. MSS 47565, fo. 207, C. J. Fox to R. Adair, 19 Apr. 1802.

88. BL Add. MSS 47580, fo. 133, C. J. Fox to R. Fitzpatrick, Aug. 1787.

89. BL Add. MSS 47564, fo. 260, C. J. Fox to Lord Lauderdale, [1806].

90. Durham Univ. Lib., Grey MSS, C. J. Fox to D. O'Bryen, 20 Nov. 1800.

91. BL Add. MSS 51466, fo. 34, C. J. Fox to J. B. Church, 26 Mar. 1789.

92. Ibid., fo. 43, *c*. Aug. 1791.

93. Edinburgh, Nat. Reg. Arch., Blair Adam MSS Misc. Correspondence & Papers *c*.1800–19, Bundle 70, Lord Robert Spencer to W. Adam, 1807.

94. Nottingham Univ. Lib., Portland MSS, PwF 20, Sjt. Adair to Duke of Portland, 4 June 1793.

95. BL Add. MSS 51468, fos. 26–8. The Committee consisted of Lord J. Russell, Lord G. H. Cavendish, Mr Francis, Mr Crewe, Mr Vyner, Mr Wrightson, Mr Alderman Skinner, Mr Alderman Coombe, and Adair himself.

96. Lord Bessborough, *Lady Bessborough and Her Family Circle* (London 1940), 90, Lord Bessborough to Lady Bessborough, 11 June 1793.

97. Nottingham Univ. Lib., Portland MSS, PwG 131, Mrs Crewe to Duchess of Portland, July 1793.

98. Edinburgh, Nat. Reg. Arch., McKenzie of Seaforth MSS, GD 46/4/119, H. Erskine to McKenzie of Seaforth, 29 July 1793. A list of the 'Independent Friends' may be found in GD 214/769.

99. Edinburgh, Nat. Reg. Arch., Blair Adam MSS, C. Dundas to W. Adam, 30 June 1793.

100. BL Add. MSS 51845, fo. 54, Lord Sheffield to Lady Webster, 14 June 1793; Coutts MSS, Ledgers, fo. 584; BL Add. MSS 47569, fo. 63, 'State of the Receipts and Payments by Mr Fox's Trustees'.

101. Northants PRO, Milton MSS, Box 45, Duke of Bedford to Earl Fitzwilliam, 13 Dec. 1793. See also BL Add. MSS 47569, fo. 3, C. J. Fox to W. Adam, 20 June 1793.

102. Ibid., fo. 32 [Dec. 1793].

103. C. Grosvenor, *The First Lady Wharncliffe and Her Family* (London 1927), i. 33, Archbishop of Aix to Lady Wharncliffe, 29 June 1793.

104. BL Add. MSS 51845, fo. 54, Lord Sheffield to Lady Webster, 14 June 1793.

105. BL Add. MSS 47571, fo. 29, C. J. Fox to Lord Holland, 14 June 1793.

106. BL Add. MSS 51472, fo. 46. William Adam once again acted as treasurer.

107. A significant loss of Dissenting votes in 1784 might be cited as a case in point.

108. Lady Granville, *Lord Granville Leveson Gower*, i. 119–20, Lady Bessborough to G. Leveson Gower, 29 Jan. 1796.

Chapter 6

1. For a detailed account of these years, see F. O'Gorman, *The Whig Party and the French Revolution* (London 1967); and L. G. Mitchell, *Charles James Fox and the Disintegration of the Whig Party* (Oxford 1971).

2. *Speeches*, iii. 273, 12 Feb. 1787.

3. Ibid. Such containment was usually to be found by allying with Prussia and Russia.

4. Ibid. iii. 272 ff. and 286 ff., 12–16 Feb. 1787.

5. BL Add. MSS 47570, fo. 175, C. J. Fox to Mrs Armistead, 1787.

6. *Speeches*, iii. 337, 27 Nov. 1787.

7. Ibid. iii. 255, 23 Jan. 1787.

8. C. Fox to H. Fox, 31 Oct. 1831, Lord Ilchester, *Chronicles of Holland House* (London 1937), 146.

9. BL Add. MSS 51635, fo. 111, Talleyrand to Lord Holland, 30 Jan. [1831?].

10. Cornell Univ. Lib., Dean Collection, Lafayette to Lord Holland, 15 Dec. 1815.

11. BL Add. MSS 51635, fos. 198–9, Lafayette to Lord Holland, 14 Apr. 1830.

12. BL Add. MSS 47582, fo. 168, Noailles to R. Fitzpatrick, Apr. 1783.

13. BL Althorp MSS, Lord Althorp to Lady Spencer, 10 May 1783. See also BL Add. MSS 47583, fo. 11, Lafayette to R. Fitzpatrick, 6 Jan. 1788.

14. The Duc d'Orléans was a cousin of Louis XVI. His daughter, Pamela, married Lord Edward Fitzgerald, who was Fox's cousin.

15. BL Althorp MSS, Duchess of Devonshire to Lady Spencer, 5 July 1789. See also *Minto*, i. 349, T. Pelham to Sir G. Elliot, 21 Aug. 1790.

16. Chatsworth MSS, Journal of Lady E. Foster, 2 July 1791. See also Windsor Castle, Palmerston MSS, T. Pelham to Lord Palmerston, 22 July 1791.

17. HMC XIV Report, Fortescue MSS, 144, Lord Grenville to Lord Auckland, 29 July 1791.

18. Chatsworth MSS, Journal of Lady E. Foster, 9 Aug. 1791.

19. HMC XIV Report, Fortescue MSS, 154, F. Moore to T. Bland Burges, 4 Aug. 1791.

20. Coutts MSS, fo. 1013, C. J. Fox to T. Coutts, 21 Aug. 1789.

21. BL Add. MSS 60487B, unfol., C. J. Fox to T. Grenville, Aug. 1789.

22. Northants PRO, Milton MSS, Box 40, F. Wentworth to Lady Fitzwilliam, 11 Oct. 1789.

23. BL Add. MSS 47580, fo. 139, C. J. Fox to R. Fitzpatrick, 30 July 1789.

24. *Speeches*, iv. 41, 9 Feb. 1790. Interestingly, Fox admitted that he had failed to predict the events of 1789, adding that if anyone had made such a prediction in 1786 or 1787, it would have been taken 'as a corroboration of his insanity', ibid.

25. Ibid. iv. 53.

26. The plausibility of Fox's views was so real that it is dark forebodings of France that were widely rejected, even beyond the ranks of the Foxites, see L. G. Mitchell, *The Writings and Speeches of Edmund Burke* (Oxford 1990), vol. viii, Introduction.

27. *Speeches*, iv. 199 and 198, 15 Apr. 1791.

28. See Chap. 4.

29. BL Add. MSS 60487B, unfol., R. Fitzpatrick to Mrs Benwell, 29 Feb. 1790.

30. Chatsworth MSS, fo. 1045, J. Hare to Duchess of Devonshire, 23 Feb. 1790.

31. Lord J. Russell, *Memoirs, Journal and Correspondence of Thomas Moore* (London 1853), iv. 265. A peace conference called at Burlington House to reconcile the two men came to nothing, 'The D. will tell you of Burke & Sheridan's reconciliation which was perfectly irish, for they are now upon worse terms than ever.' Chatsworth MSS, fo. 1037, Lady Jersey to Duchess of Devonshire, 12 Feb. 1790.

32. In the press and in cartoons, he was referred to as 'Sherry' as a compliment to his drinking, and as Joseph Surface as a reference to unscrupulousness.

33. BL Add. MSS 47571, fo. 1, C. J. Fox to Lord Holland, May 1791. See also Nottingham Univ. Lib., Portland MSS, PwG 130, Mrs Crewe to Duchess of Portland, *c.* July 1791; BL Add. MSS 51705, fo. 4, T. Pelham to Lady Webster, 13 June 1791.

34. *Speeches*, iv. 221, 6 May 1791.

35. Ibid. iv. 72, 2 Mar. 1790.

36. *Rogers*, 79–80.

37. BL Add. MSS 47590, fo. 24, Commonplace Book of Samuel Rogers.

38. W. Suffolk PRO, Grafton MSS, fo. 741, Bishop of Peterborough to Duke of Grafton, 7 Dec. 1790.

39. *Minto*, i. 369–70, Sir G. to Lady Elliot, 5 Dec. 1790.

40. Northants PRO, Milton MSS, A IV, fo. 71b, E. Burke to Lord Fitzwilliam, 29 July 1790. In the same letter Burke reported, in a sinister manner, that 'Sheridan . . . knows what he is about.'

41. Sheffield Pub. Lib., Wentworth Woodhouse Muniments, F115d, T. Grenville to Lord Fitzwilliam, 19 Apr. 1791.

42. *Public Advertizer*, 29 Apr. 1791.

43. Sheffield Pub. Lib., Wentworth Woodhouse Muniments, F115d, T. Grenville to Lord Fitzwilliam, 22 Apr. 1791.

44. Ibid., Duke of Portland to Lord Fitzwilliam, 21 Apr. 1791.

45. Ibid., T. Grenville to Lord Fitzwilliam, 22 Apr. 1791.

46. As T. W. Blanning has recently pointed out, the diplomatic incapacity of France allowed for the possibility of a reordering of relations between Austria, Prussia, Russia, Turkey, and Poland.

47. *Walpole*, xi. 263, H. Walpole to M. Berry, 12 May 1791.

48. Sheffield Pub. Lib., Wentworth Woodhouse Muniments, Burke I, E. Burke to Lord Fitzwilliam, 5 June 1791.

49. A. Le Blond, *Charlotte Sophie, Countess Bentinck* (London 1912), i. 162–4.

50. For example, see *Minto*, i. 376–8.

51. *Speeches*, iv. 225, 6 May 1791.

52. *Burke*, viii. 335, E. Burke to Lord Auckland, 30 Oct. 1795.

53. W. Derry, *Dr Parr* (Oxford 1966), 226, C. J. Fox to Dr Parr, 1800.

54. *Memoirs of Sir Samuel Romilly*, i. 426, Sir S. Romilly to Mme G., 20 May 1791.

55. Chatsworth MSS, Journal of Lady E. Foster, 6 May 1791.

56. Anon., *Parallel Between the Conduct of Mr Burke and that of Mr Fox* (London 1791), 5.

57. *Morning Chronicle*, 12 May 1791.

58. The Foxite poet William Roscoe, caught the mood in his poem 'The Life, Death and Wonderful Achievements of Edmund Burke', of which the first two verses give the general quality:

> Full tilt he ran at all he met,
> And round he dealt his knocks,

Till with a backward stroke at last,
He hit poor CHARLEY FOX.

Now CHARLEY was of all his friends
The warmest friend he had;
So when he dealt this graceless blow
He deemed the man was mad.

The representation of Burke as an enfeebled Don Quixote, tilting at imaginary enemies, is commonly found in the cartoons of 1790–1.

59. *Speeches*, iv. 235, 11 May 1791.
60. Ibid. iv. 296–7, 31 Jan. 1792.
61. *Parl. Hist.* xxix. 1338, 30 Apr. 1792.
62. *Minto*, ii. 2, Sir G. to Lady Elliot, 24 Mar. 1792.
63. R. J. Mackintosh, *Memoirs of the Life of Sir James Mackintosh* (London 1835), i. 61.
64. *Public Advertizer*, 18 Feb. 1791. There seems to be some basis to the rumour, see P. Jupp, *Lord Grenville 1759–1834* (Oxford 1985), 123–4.
65. Sheffield Pub. Lib., Wentworth Woodhouse Muniments, Burke I, E. Burke to R. Burke Jnr., 5 Aug. 1791.
66. BL Add. MSS 60487B, unfol., Lord Fitzwilliam to T. Grenville [*c*. May 1791].
67. Bod. Lib. Curzon MSS b25, fo. 16, C. J. Fox to J. Lee, 1 Apr. 1791. See also BL Add. MSS 47570, fo. 183, C. J. Fox to Mrs Armistead, 14 Apr. 1791; *Speeches*, iv. 178, 29 Mar. 1791.
68. *Morning Chronicle*, 5 Apr. 1791.
69. Once again, the constitutional propriety of an opposition politician complicating the expression of British policy abroad by actions of this kind was much in doubt. Pitt's envoy in Russia was not amused: HMC XIV Report, Fortescue MSS, 114, W. Fawkener to Lord Grenville, 1 July 1791. See also Castle Howard MSS, J14/65/2.
70. *Minto*, i. 392, Lady Malmesbury to her sister, 8 Aug. 1791.
71. This particularly related to the freedom of the press, which Fox believed had been endangered by 'a series of judgments and a series of punishments on free writings'. *Speeches*, iv. 247, 20 May 1791.
72. *Morning Chronicle*, 7 June 1791.
73. Sheffield Pub. Lib., Wentworth Woodhouse Muniments, Burke I, L. O'Beirne to R. Burke Jnr., 25 July 1791.
74. *Morning Chronicle*, 11 July 1791.
75. Nottingham Univ. Lib., Portland MSS, PwF 6239, Duke of Portland to Dr Laurence, 23 Aug. 1791.
76. BL Add. MSS 51843, fo. 3, A. Storer to Lady Webster, 12 July 1791.
77. *Morning Post*, 19 July 1791.
78. *Sheffield Advertizer*, 16 Aug. 1791.
79. Edinburgh, Nat. Reg. Arch., Blair Adam MSS, Lord Fitzwilliam to W. Adam, 8 Sept. 1791.
80. *Burke*, vii. 52, E. Burke to W. Weddel, 31 Jan. 1792.
81. Sheffield Pub. Lib., Wentworth Woodhouse Muniments, Burke I, E. Burke to R. Burke Jnr., 1 Sept. 1791.
82. Ibid.
83. Northants PRO, Milton MSS, Box 44, C. J. Fox to Lord Fitzwilliam, 16 Mar. 1792. By Apr. 1792, Fox is already being shown in cartoons as a thoroughgoing sympathizer of the Revolution. For example, in Gillray's *Patriots Amusing Themselves*, Fox and Sheridan,

wearing French cockades bearing the words 'Ça Ira' are shown firing at a post modelled as the head of George III.

84. For a detailed account of the Association, see E. A. Smith, *Lord Grey* (Oxford 1990), 36–51.

85. For a list of members, see F. D. Cartwright, *Life and Correspondence of Major Cartwright*, Appendix VII.

86. Lord Holland, *Memoirs of the Whig Party During My Time* (London 1852), i. 13–14.

87. C. Grey, *The Life and Opinions of the Second Earl Grey* (London 1861), 11–12. See also R. Adair, *A Whig's Apology for His Consistency* (London 1795), 34.

88. J. Hutton, *Letters and Correspondence of Sir James Bland Burges*, 220, J. B. Burges to Col. Simcoe, 4 May 1792. See also *Morning Herald*, 30 Apr. 1792.

89. BL Add. MSS 51705, fo. 134, T. Pelham to Lady Webster, 15 June 1792. See also Holland, *Memoirs*, i. 13.

90. *Morning Herald*, 7 June 1792.

91. BL Add. MSS 51705, fo. 117, T. Pelham to Lady Webster, 29 Apr. 1792. The increasing hysteria may be measured by an incident that occurred in May, when a pair of fustian breeches burning in a cupboard led to panic in the House of Commons, which feared an incendiary attack. Windsor Castle, Palmerston MSS, Lady Palmerston to Lord Palmerston, 10 May 1792.

92. *Speeches*, iv. 411, 30 Apr. 1792.

93. D. Barnes, *George III and William Pitt* (London 1939), 220, George III to W. Pitt, *c.* 30 Apr. 1792. See also *Minto*, ii. 17, Sir G. to Lady Elliot, 1 May 1792.

94. C. Wyvill, *Political Tracts and Papers* (York 1779–1804), iii. appendix 159.

95. BL Add. MSS 47580, fo. 143, C. J. Fox to R. Fitzpatrick, 25 Apr. 1792.

96. Durham Univ. Lib., Gen. Charles Grey MSS, D8, Preface to a Life of Earl Grey.

97. Sheffield Pub. Lib., Wentworth Woodhouse Muniments, R164, Lord Fitzwilliam to Lady Rockingham, 23 Feb. 1793.

98. T. Green, *Extracts from the Diary of a Lover of Literature* (Ipswich 1810), 57.

99. Chatsworth MSS, fo. 1126, J. Hare to Duchess of Devonshire, 1 May 1792. See also BL Althorp MSS, Lord Spencer to Lady Spencer, 3 May 1792.

100. BL Add. MSS 51731, fo. 68, Caroline Fox to Lord Holland, 7 May 1792.

101. Preface to a Life of Earl Grey, Durham Univ. Lib., Gen. Charles Grey MSS, D8.

102. Northants PRO, Milton MSS, Burke A IV, fo. 34, E. Burke to W. Burke, 3 Sept. 1792.

103. J. Johnstone, *The Works of Dr Samuel Parr* (London 1828), i. 444, J. Tweddell to Dr Parr, May 1792.

104. BL Add. MSS 51705, fo. 131, T. Pelham to Lady Webster, 28 May 1792; *Minto*, ii. 24; and Holland, *Memoirs*, i. 15 ff.

105. *Minto*, ii. 30, Sir G. to Lady Elliot, 24 May 1792. See also H. Butterfield, 'Charles James Fox and the Whig Opposition in 1792', *Camb. Hist. Journal*, 9 (1949).

106. *Speeches*, iv. 441, 25 May 1792.

107. Ironically, Pitt privately rather shared Fox's assessment of domestic troubles.

108. *Auckland*, ii. 402, W. Pitt to Lord Auckland, 1 May 1792; PRO, Pitt MSS, 30/8 153, fo. 83. Lord Loughborough to W. Pitt, 4 May 1792; O. Browning, *Political Memoranda of the Fifth Duke of Leeds* (London 1884), 191–3.

109. *Malmesbury*, ii. 459, Diary of Lord Malmesbury, 13 June 1792. See also Sheffield Pub. Lib., Wentworth Woodhouse Muniments, Burke I, Lord Loughborough to E. Burke, 13 June 1792.

110. *Minto*, ii. 43, Elliot of Wells to Sir G. Elliot, 19 June 1792.

111. BL Add. MSS 47561, fo. 121, C. J. Fox to Duke of Portland, 26 July 1792. See also BL Add. MSS 27918, fo. 261, Duke of Leeds Memorandum, 3 Aug. 1792.

112. *Malmesbury*, ii. 472, Diary of Lord Malmesbury, 30 July 1792.

113. BL Add. MSS 51845, fo. 40, Ann Pelham to Lady Webster, 31 Oct. 1792.

114. Ibid., fo. 35, Lord Sheffield to Lady Webster, 21 July 1792.

115. Nottingham Univ. Lib., Portland MSS, PwF 9224, Duke of Portland to Duke of Leeds, 29 July 1792.

116. Browning, *Political Memoranda of the Fifth Duke of Leeds*, 190; A. Aspinall, *The Later Correspondence of George III* (Cambridge 1963–70), i. 607, W. Pitt to George III, 18 Aug. 1792; BL Add. MSS 47561, fo. 135, Duke of Portland to C. J. Fox, 21 Aug. 1792.

117. BL Add. MSS 47561, fo. 117, C. J. Fox to Duke of Portland, 21 July 1792.

118. Sheffield Pub. Lib., Wentworth Woodhouse Muniments, F31a, Duke of Portland to Earl Fitzwilliam, 27 June 1792. See also Chatsworth MSS, fo. 1129, J. Hare to Duchess of Devonshire, 17 July 1792.

119. BL Add. MSS 47571, fo. 13, C. J. Fox to Lord Holland, 3 Sept. 1792.

120. BL Add. MSS 47570, fo. 11, Same to Same, 20 Aug. 1792. The Duke had threatened Paris with total destruction if the French royal family were harmed.

121. BL Add. MSS 47571, fo. 16, Same to Same [Sept. 1792]. War had broken out between France and Austria in Apr. 1792. By Aug., the Austrians were approaching Paris itself.

122. *Speeches*, vi. 41, 25 Nov. 1795.

123. BL Add. MSS 51731, fo. 88, Lord Holland to Caroline Fox, 23 Oct. 1792.

124. BL Add. MSS 47571, fo. 17, C. J. Fox to Lord Holland, 12 Oct. 1792.

125. BL Add. MSS 47570, fo. 11, Same to Same, 20 Aug. 1792.

126. BL Add. MSS 47571, fo. 13, Same to Same, 3 Sept. 1792. No doubt these views were influenced by Fox's contacts with the Marquis de Chauvelin, the envoy of the new Republic, in the autumn and winter of 1792. See Archives Nationales F[7] 4434, Chauvelin to Committee of General Security, 22 Pluviôse, an II.

127. BL Add. MSS 47570, fo. 189, C. J. Fox to Mrs Armistead, 7 Oct. 1792. See also T. Moore, *Life of Lord Edward Fitzgerald* (London 1831), 169, Lord E. Fitzgerald to Duchess of Leinster, Oct. 1792.

128. BL Add. MSS 47571, fo. 20, C. J. Fox to Lord Holland, Nov. 1792.

129. So powerful was this point that the Fox family, though deeply deploring Lafayette's imprisonment by Austria, criticized him and the Feuillants for making the mistake of allowing Louis XVI a veto. BL Add. MSS 51731, fo. 88, Lord Holland to Caroline Fox, 23 Oct. 1792.

130. HMC XV Report, Carlisle MSS, 696, C. J. Fox to Lord Carlisle, 25 July 1792.

131. Durham Univ. Lib., Grey MSS, G. Tierney to C. Grey, 15 Nov. 1792. Tierney asserted that 'Fox must ruin that cabal at Burlington House [Portland's London house], or that cabal will ruin him.' See also T. Moore, *Memoirs of R. B. Sheridan* (London 1825), ii. 184, R. Sheridan to ?, 1792. Fox was a second in a duel on Lauderdale's behalf in June. BL Add. MSS 51705, fo. 143, T. Pelham to Lady Webster, 1 July 1792. A further ambiguity lay in Fox's very genuine concern for Louis XVI and Marie Antoinette as people coexisting with his strictures on their behaviour as king and queen.

132. Northants PRO, Milton MSS, Box 44, Lord Fitzwilliam to Lord Carlisle, 31 Oct. 1792. See also BL Add. MSS 60487B, unfol., Lord Fitzwilliam to T. Grenville, 15 Nov. 1792; Northants PRO, Milton MSS, Box 44, Duke of Portland to Lord Fitzwilliam, 26 Sept. 1792.

133. Durham Univ. Lib., Grey MSS, Lord J. Cavendish to Mrs Ponsonby, 26 Jan. [1793].

134. BL Add. MSS 51731, fo. 100, Lord Holland to Caroline Fox, 25 Dec. 1792.

135. Castle Howard MSS, J14/74/7, 'Refutation of the Accusation of deserting the party of Opposition. 1793'.

136. BL Add. MSS 60487B, unfol., C.J. Fox to T. Grenville, 27 Nov. 1792. See also ibid., 18 Nov. 1792; Northants PRO, Milton MSS, Box 44, T. Grenville to Lord Fitzwilliam, 24 Nov. 1792.

137. BL Althorp MSS, Lord Spencer to Lady Spencer, 21 Nov. 1792.

138. BL Add. MSS 60487B, unfol., C.J. Fox to T. Grenville, 6 Dec. 1792.

139. Ibid. 1 Dec. 1792. See also BL Add. MSS 47568, fo. 276, C.J. Fox to W. Adam, 1 Dec. 1792.

140. BL Add. MSS 47561, fo. 134, C.J. Fox to Duke of Portland, 1 Dec. 1792. See also *A Letter from the Rt. Hon. C.J. Fox to the Worthy and Independent Electors of Westminster* (London 1793).

141. HMC XIII Report, Charlemont MSS, 203, T. Malone to Lord Charlemont, 3 Dec. 1792. See also *Malmesbury*, ii. 473.

142. *Speech of the Rt. Hon. C.J. Fox . . . Spoken at the Whig Club* (London 1792).

143. Northants PRO, Milton MSS, Box 45, Earl Fitzwilliam to Lady Fitzwilliam, 6 Dec. 1792. See also Sheffield Pub. Lib., Wentworth Woodhouse Muniments, Burke I, Dr Laurence to E. Burke, 8 Dec. 1792. Little wonder that Carlisle should call the Whig Club Fox's 'Theatre', where he could say anything 'without the pain of weighing the consequence of uttering it', Castle Howard MSS, J14/74/10.

144. To a fearful public, the idea that George III was a greater danger than the French was barely credible. Fox begins to be compared to Lafayette or called 'the Marat of England', Le Blond, *Countess Bentinck*, i. 291–2. At the Literary Club, bishops could 'hardly look at him without horror', *Diaries and Letters of Mme D'Arblay*, v. 168, Dr Burney to Miss Burney, 31 Jan. 1793.

145. BL Add. MSS 47570, fo. 193, C.J. Fox to Mrs Armistead, 13 Dec. 1792.

146. *Speeches*, iv. 462 and 451, 13 Dec. 1792.

147. A result that was partly produced by Fox missing party meetings. See *Malmesbury*, ii. 475 and *Minto*, ii. 79–80; also *Observations on the Conduct of Mr Fox by a Suffolk Freeholder* (Bury St Edmunds 1794), 12.

148. For example, *Speeches*, iv. 473 and v. 6, 15 Dec. 1792 and 4 Jan. 1793.

149. *Malmesbury*, ii. 476–8, and *Minto*, ii. 80–2.

150. BL Add. MSS 47570, fo. 195, C.J. Fox to Mrs Armistead, 15 Dec. 1792.

151. BL Add. MSS 47580, fo. 150, C.J. Fox to R. Fitzpatrick, 1 Jan. 1794.

152. Johnstone, *Works of Dr Samuel Parr*, vii. 285.

153. BL Add. MSS 47571, fo. 97, C.J. Fox to Lord Holland, 28 Dec. 1793. See also ibid., fo. 58, 17 Sept. 1793.

154. F. Bickley, *The Diaries of Sylvester Douglas, Lord Glenbervie* (London 1928), i. 21. See also BL Add. MSS 47568, fo. 28, C.J. Fox to W. Adam, 17 Dec. 1793; *Parl. Hist.* xxx. 1450, 24 Feb. 1793.

155. BL Add. MSS 47569, fo. 34, T. Palmer to C.J. Fox, 8 Mar. 1794.

156. Ibid., fo. 18, 22 Oct. 1793.

157. *Speeches*, v. 206, 10 Mar. 1794.

158. He told Fitzpatrick that war would simply bring 'dangers innumerable & no chance of good.' BL Add. MSS 47580, fo. 145, C.J. Fox to R. Fitzpatrick, 5 Dec. 1792.

159. *Speeches*, iv. 477, 15 Dec. 1792. The argument was elaborated in 1793 in *A Letter from the Rt. Hon. C.J. Fox to the Worthy and Independent Electors of Westminster*. This pamphlet became, for

a time, 'quite the *political GO*'. N. Roe, *Wordsworth and Coleridge: The Radical Years* (Oxford 1988), 99, S. T. Coleridge to M. Evans, 1793.

160. R. Adair, *The Letter of the Rt. Hon. C. J. Fox to the Electors of Westminster, With an Application of its Principles to Subsequent Events* (London 1802), 80–5. See also Bod. Lib. 22871 c12, fo. 16, Marquis de Chauvelin to Lord Grenville, 27 Dec. 1792.

161. BL Add. MSS 47571, fo. 23, C. J. Fox to Lord Holland, 23 Nov. 1792.

162. *Speeches*, v. 17, 1 Feb. 1793.

163. Ibid. v. 20.

164. Ibid. v. 143, 17 June 1793.

165. Ibid. v. 35, 12 Feb. 1793.

166. He saw the destruction of Poland as 'ten thousand times more reprehensible than the conduct of France towards any other nations.' Ibid. v. 88, 25 Apr. 1793.

167. Sheffield Pub. Lib., Wentworth Woodhouse Muniments, F31a, Duke of Portland to Lord Fitzwilliam, 30 Nov. 1792.

168. BL Add. MSS 47571, fo. 97, C. J. Fox to Lord Holland, 28 Dec. 1793.

169. Bod. Lib. North MSS c12, fo. 8, C. J. Fox to T. Coutts, 1 Jan. 1806.

170. BL Add. MSS 47571, fo. 87, C. J. Fox to Lord Holland, 21 Nov. 1793.

171. BL Add. MSS 51467, fo. 29, C. J. Fox to D. O'Bryen, 23 Jan. [1793].

172. BL Add. MSS 47571, fo. 78, C. J. Fox to Lord Holland, 3 Nov. 1793. The concern expressed for the French royal family as individuals was very genuine. See Chatsworth MSS, Journal of Lady E. Foster, 20 Oct. 1793; *Speeches*, iv. 481, 20 Dec. 1792.

173. BL Add. MSS 47571, fo. 85, C. J. Fox to Lord Holland, 7 Nov. 1793.

174. Ibid., fo. 28, 14 June 1792.

175. C. J. Fox to Lord Holland, 22 Aug. 1792; *Fox*, iii. 47.

176. Lady Granville, *Lord Granville Leveson Gower*, i. 77, Lady Stafford to G. Leveson Gower, 22 Jan. 1794.

177. BL Add. MSS 47571, fo. 136, Lord Holland to C. J. Fox, July 1794.

178. *Speeches*, v. 60, 4 Mar. 1793.

179. BL Add. MSS 47569, fo. 1, Dumouriez to C. J. Fox, 3 May 1793. He also asked that Fox should open up a subscription list for his forthcoming *Mémoires*.

180. G. D. Elliott, *Journal of My Life during the French Revolution* (London 1859), 146.

181. BL Add. MSS 42058, fo. 120, Lord Fitzwilliam to T. Grenville, 7 Nov. 1793.

182. Lady Granville, *Lord Granville Leveson Gower* (London 1916), i. 79, Lady Stafford to G. Leveson Gower, 5 Feb. 1794.

183. H. Walpole, *Letters Addressed to the Countess of Upper Ossory*, ii. 97.

184. Nottingham Univ. Lib., Portland MSS, PwF 3174, Mrs Crewe to Duke of Portland, 19 May 1793.

185. *Remarks on a Pamphlet Published as Mr Fox's Speech at the Opening of Parliament* (London 1793).

186. Lord Malmesbury to Lady Palmerston, 3 May 1793, Merton Coll., Malmesbury MSS, Box 3.

187. BL Add. MSS 28067, fo. 98, Lord Malmesbury to Duke of Leeds, 29 Dec. 1792.

188. BL Add. MSS 47570, fo. 199, C. J. Fox to Mrs Armistead, 28 Dec. 1792.

189. Holland, *Memoirs*, i. 85.

190. BL Add. MSS 47571, fo. 97, C. J. Fox to Lord Holland, *c*.28 Dec. 1793.

191. BL Add. MSS 37845, fo. 18, Duke of Portland to W. Windham, 11 Jan. 1794. See also Sheffield Pub. Lib., Wentworth Woodhouse Muniments, R164, Lord Fitzwilliam to Lady Rockingham, 28 Feb. 1793.

192. Durham Univ. Lib., Grey MSS, Lord J. Cavendish to Lady Ponsonby, 4 Apr. [1793].
193. *Parl. Hist.* xxx. 940, 24 May 1793.
194. *Speeches*, v. 319, 16 June 1794.
195. Ibid. v. 153, 21 Jan. 1794.
196. BL Add. MSS 47571, fo. 120, C. J. Fox to Lord Holland, 25 Apr. 1794.
197. *Speeches*, v. 189, 10 Feb. 1794.
198. Ibid. v. 281, 17 May 1794. See also ibid. v. 228, 245, 260, major speeches on 28 Mar., 17 Apr., 30 Apr. 1794.
199. BL Add. MSS 42058, fo. 135, C. J. Fox to T. Grenville, 6 Jan. 1794.
200. BL Add. MSS 47569, fo. 30, T. Grenville to C. J. Fox, 29 Dec. 1793.
201. Chatsworth MSS, Journal of Lady E. Foster, 22 Jan. 1794. See also BL Add. MSS 51705, fo. 108, T. Pelham to Lady Webster, 18 Jan. 1794.
202. Hickleton MSS, A1.2.1., fo. 88, Lady E. Ponsonby to Lady L. Ponsonby, 6 Feb. 1794.
203. BL Add. MSS 47571, fo. 111, C. J. Fox to Lord Holland, 18 Mar. 1794.
204. Ibid., fo. 106, 9 Mar. 1794.
205. BL Add. MSS 47569, fo. 14, C. J. Fox to W. Adam, 18 Sept. 1793.
206. BL Add. MSS 51732, fo. 24, Caroline Fox to Lord Holland, 19 June 1794.

Chapter 7

1. R. Adair, *A Whig's Apology for His Consistency* (London 1795), 15. See also *Morning Chronicle*, 8 July 1794.
2. Sheffield Pub. Lib., Wentworth Woodhouse Muniments, F115a, C. J. Fox to Lord Fitzwilliam, July 1794.
3. BL Add. MSS 47571, fo. 143, C. J. Fox to Lord Holland, 18 Aug. 1794.
4. C. J. Fox to G. Wakefield [1798], *Correspondence of Gilbert Wakefield with the Right Honourable Charles James Fox* (London 1813), 16.
5. For details of these men, see L. G. Mitchell, *Charles James Fox and the Disintegration of the Whig Party* (Oxford 1971), 247 ff.
6. W. Suffolk PRO, Grafton MSS 423/160, C. J. Fox to Duke of Grafton, Dec. 1794.
7. BL Add. MSS 47569, fo. 61, Earl Fitzwilliam to C. J. Fox, 5 Apr. 1795.
8. Ibid., fo. 58, W. Dickson to C. J. Fox, 9 Mar. 1795. See also BL Add. MSS 47572, fo. 22, C. J. Fox to Lord Holland, 6 Mar. 1795. Fox went out of his way to defend Fitzwilliam's performance in Ireland, *Speeches*, v. 459–60, 27 Feb. 1795.
9. BL Add. MSS 51732, fos. 141, 159, 192, Lord Holland to Caroline Fox, 2 Dec. 1794, 24 Jan. 1795 and 22 Mar. 1795. Bod. Lib., Bowood MSS, Lord Lansdowne to Lady Ossory, 1794; BL Add. MSS 47572, fo. 30, Lord Holland to C. J. Fox, 30 Mar. 1795.
10. H. Brougham, *The Life and Times of Henry, Lord Brougham* (Edinburgh 1871), iii. 465.
11. *Memoirs of Sir Samuel Romilly* (London 1840), i. 455, Sir S. Romilly to Mme G, 6 Dec. 1791.
12. *Speeches*, iii. 201, 27 Feb. 1786.
13. BL Add. MSS 47573, fo. 229, notes for a speech, c.1800.
14. BL Add. MSS 47566, fo. 56, C. J. Fox to D. O'Bryen, 28 Nov. 1800.
15. Ibid., fo. 58, 11 Dec. 1800.
16. *Speeches*, vi. 227, 18 Oct. 1796.
17. BL Add. MSS 47573, fo. 28, C. J. Fox to Lord Holland, 20 Apr. 1798.
18. BL Add. MSS 47564, fo. 31, C. J. Fox to Lord Lauderdale, c.1797.
19. BL Add. MSS 47565, fo. 3, C. J. Fox to Lord Grey, 1799.

20. BL Add. MSS 47573, fo. 13, C. J. Fox to Lord Holland, Feb. 1798.
21. BL Add. MSS 47571, fo. 165, Same to Same, 5 Oct. 1794. See also ibid., fo. 189, 15 Dec. 1794.
22. *Speeches*, vi. 191, 10 May 1796.
23. Ibid. vi. 199.
24. Ibid. vi. 193.
25. Ibid. v. 397, 25 Mar. 1795.
26. Ibid. vi. 78, 10 Dec. 1795.
27. BL Add. MSS 47572, fo. 93, C. J. Fox to Lord Holland, 15 Nov. 1795.
28. *Speeches*, vi. 8, 10 Nov. 1795. The proposals represented 'a total annihilation of their liberty', ibid. vi. 6.
29. *Fox*, iii. 268, C. J. Fox to R. Fitzpatrick, 9 Nov. 1795.
30. BL Add. MSS 47572, fo. 100, C. J. Fox to Lord Holland, 24 Dec. 1795. See also BL Add. MSS 47569, fo. 68, C. J. Fox to ?, 28 Dec. 1795.
31. Lord Colchester, *The Diary and Correspondence of Charles Abbot, Lord Colchester* (London 1861), i. 7.
32. The absence of powder and the cutting off of the pigtail were thought to be hairstyles that symbolically rejected the *ancien régime*. The style was known as a Bedford level.
33. N. Roe, *Wordsworth and Coleridge* (Oxford 1988), 153–4.
34. BL Add. MSS 47572, fo. 98, C. J. Fox to Lord Holland, 17 Nov. 1795. In the Commons and in the Lords, Fox gathered a few more votes, but nowhere near enough to threaten Pitt.
35. *Speeches*, v. 390, 24 Mar. 1795.
36. *Diary and Correspondence of Lord Colchester*, i. 14.
37. *Speeches*, vi. 150, 8 Apr. 1796.
38. *Windham*, i. 321, E. Malone to W. Windham, 18 Nov. 1795.
39. *Burke*, ix. 79, E. Burke to Lord Fitzwilliam, 2 Sept. 1796.
40. S. R. Keppel, *Sovereign Lady* (London 1974), 99, Lady Holland's Journal, 14 Oct. 1797.
41. *Speeches*, v. 292, 17 May 1794.
42. BL Add. MSS 51732, fo. 10, Caroline Fox to Lord Holland, 19 May 1794.
43. BL Add. MSS 47571, fo. 122, C. J. Fox to Lord Holland, 29 Apr. 1794.
44. BL Add. MSS 47581, fo. 15, C. J. Fox to R. Fitzpatrick, 11 Mar. 1798.
45. Castle Howard MSS, LB1, Lord Holland to Lord Morpeth, n.d.
46. Durham Univ. Lib., Grey MSS, Box 7, C. Grey to T. Bigge, 3 June 1797.
47. *Fox*, iv. 383, G. Wakefield to C. J. Fox, 13 Mar. 1800.
48. BL Add. MSS 47574, fo. 41, C. J. Fox to Lord Holland, Dec. 1799.
49. BL Add. MSS 47564, fo. 50, C. J. Fox to Lord Lauderdale, 13 May 1799.
50. BL Add. MSS 47566, fo. 26, C. J. Fox to D. O'Bryen, 14 Jan. 1799.
51. Ibid., fo. 67, 23 Jan. 1801.
52. BL Add. MSS 47581, fo. 12, C. J. Fox to R. Fitzpatrick, 9 Mar. 1798. The house in question was in South St.
53. BL Add. MSS 51467, fo. 32, C. J. Fox to D. O'Bryen, 19 Mar. 1798.
54. *Correspondence of Gilbert Wakefield with the Right Honourable Charles James Fox*, 133–4, C. J. Fox to G. Wakefield, 12 Mar. 1800. This quotation has been translated from the Greek which Fox uses in this letter. I am grateful to Dr C. Souvinou-Inwood for assistance in this matter.
55. For example, *Morning Herald*, 11 Oct. 1794.
56. Bod. Lib., Bowood MSS, J. Jekyll to Lord Lansdowne, n.d.
57. *Fox*, iii. 281, C. J. Fox to Lord Lauderdale, 31 May 1798.

58. BL Add. MSS 47574, fo. 64, C. J. Fox to Lord Holland, Jan. 1800.

59. BL Add. MSS 47566, fo. 45, C. J. Fox to D. O'Bryen, 13 Apr. 1800.

60. *Fox*, iii. 282, C. J. Fox to R. Fitzpatrick, Dec. 1798. See also BL Add. MSS 47573, fo. 87, C. J. Fox to Lord Holland, 5 Jan. 1799.

61. *Speeches*, vi. 308, 23 Mar. 1797.

62. BL Add. MSS 51799, fo. 17, R. Fitzpatrick to Lord Holland, 26 Jan. 1799.

63. BL Add. MSS 47569, fo. 98, C. J. Fox to H. Grattan [*c.* Feb. 1799].

64. BL Add. MSS 47573, fos. 150, 158, C. J. Fox to Lord Holland, 23 and 26 Feb. 1799.

65. See Chap. 12.

66. BL Add. MSS 47566, fo. 22, C. J. Fox to D. O'Bryen, Sept. 1798.

67. BL Add. MSS 47581, fo. 55, C. J. Fox to R. Fitzpatrick, 8 Mar. 1799.

68. Durham Univ. Lib., Grey MSS, Box 35, C. Grey to Lord Holland, 1799. See also Lord Holland, *Memoirs of the Whig Party During My Time* (London 1852), 143.

69. BL Add. MSS 47565, fo. 23, C. J. Fox to C. Grey, 1800.

70. *Speeches*, vi. 20, 17 Nov. 1795.

71. BL Add. MSS 47569, fo. 71, C. J. Fox to ? [15 Jan. 1797]. See also *Fox*, iii. 274, C. J. Fox to Lord Lauderdale, 26 Nov. 1797.

72. BL Add. MSS 47564, fo. 28, C. J. Fox to Lord Lauderdale, 11 Jan. 1798.

73. Ibid., fo. 30, 12 Jan. 1798.

74. *Fox*, iii. 306–7, C. J. Fox to C. Grey, 1800.

75. BL Add. MSS 47581, fo. 61, C. J. Fox to R. Fitzpatrick, 1799.

76. BL Add. MSS 51468, fo. 45, C. Wyvill to C. J. Fox, 25 Oct. 1799.

77. BL Add. MSS 47564, fo. 24, C. J. Fox to Lord Lauderdale, 1797.

78. BL Add. MSS 47572, fo. 179, C. J. Fox to Lord Holland, 7 Aug. 1797.

79. BL Add. MSS 47573, fo. 67, Same to Same, 21 Oct. 1798.

80. BL Add. MSS 47574, fo. 74, Same to Same, 24 Jan. 1800.

81. BL Add. MSS 47566, fo. 16, C. J. Fox to D. O'Bryen, 6 July 1800.

82. BL Add. MSS 47572, fo. 191, C. J. Fox to Lord Holland, 19 Nov. 1797. See also BL Add. MSS 47573, fo. 23, Mar. 1798.

83. *Memoirs of Sir Philip Francis* (London 1867), ii. 304–5, C. J. Fox to C. Grey, 8 Apr. 1798.

84. BL Add. MSS 47572, fo. 189, C. J. Fox to Lord Holland, 1797.

85. BL Add. MSS 51741, fo. 233, Lord Holland to Caroline Fox, 4 Dec. 1825.

86. Holland, *Memoirs*, i. 3–4.

87. BL Add. MSS 51732, fo. 132, Lord Holland to Caroline Fox, Dec. 1794. See also BL Add. MSS 51733, fo. 161, Same to Same, 5 Jan. 1796.

88. *Fox*, iii. 139, C. J. Fox to Lord Holland, 14 Dec. 1797; ibid. iii. 140, 21 Dec. 1797.

89. BL Add. MSS 47573, fo. 134, C. J. Fox to Lord Holland, 18 Feb. 1799.

90. Ibid., fo. 95, 19 Jan. 1799.

91. BL Add. MSS 51749, fo. 169, Lord Holland to H. Fox, 28 Jan. 1826.

92. See L. G. Mitchell, *Holland House* (London 1980).

93. Bod. Lib., Bowood MSS, G. Tierney to Lord Lansdowne, 19 Nov. [1799?].

94. BL Add. MSS 47566, fo. 5, C. J. Fox to D. O'Bryen, 24 Oct. 1797.

95. BL Add. MSS 51592, fo. 1, Lord Holland to D. O'Bryen, 30 Dec. 1798.

96. Durham Univ. Lib., Grey MSS, Box 7, C. Grey to T. Bigge, 7 Dec. 1797.

97. BL Add. MSS 40763, fo. 12, Sir P. Francis to C. J. Fox, 16 Nov. 1797.

98. Parkes and Merivale, *Memoirs of Sir Philip Francis*, ii. Appendix, 451.

99. Durham Univ. Lib., Grey MSS, Box 7, C. Grey to T. Bigge, 15 June 1797.

100. BL Add. MSS 47564, fo. 14, C. J. Fox to Lord Lauderdale, 2 June 1797.

101. *Minto*, ii. 397, Sir G. Elliot to Lady Elliot, 25 May 1797.

102. See p. 153.

103. C. Edmonds, *The Poetry of the Anti-Jacobin* (London 1890), 91–4. It echoed a toast given by the Duke of Norfolk a few days earlier.

104. Ibid. 79–81.

105. Ibid. 119; see also J. R. Dinwiddy, *History*, 55 (1970).

106. Edmonds, *Poetry of the Anti-Jacobin*, 114.

107. Anon., *A Letter to the Hon. Charles James Fox Shewing how Appearances May Deceive* (London 1798), 7–8.

108. HMC XIII Report, Fortescue MSS, 187, W. Pitt to Lord Grenville, 5 May 1798.

109. P. H. Marshall, *William Godwin* (London 1984), 122.

110. *Address and Speeches of the Right Honourable Charles James Fox at the late Westminster Election* (London 1796), 19, 11.

111. BL Althorp MSS, Duchess of Devonshire to Lord Spencer, 26 June 1796.

112. BL Add. MSS 47572, fo. 128, C. J. Fox to Lord Holland, 1796.

113. BL Add. MSS 47581, fo. 23, C. J. Fox to R. Fitzpatrick, 11 May 1798. See also Lady Granville, *Lord Granville Leveson Gower* (London 1916), i. 193–4, G. Leveson Gower to Lady Stafford, 5 Jan. 1798.

114. Norfolk, too, had been struck off the Privy Council and deprived of his Lord-Lieutenancies.

115. BL Add. MSS 47569, fo. 75, C. J. Fox to Duke of Norfolk, 4 July 1798.

116. BL Add. MSS 47564, fo. 33, C. J. Fox to Lord Lauderdale, 4 Feb. 1798. See also Holland, *Memoirs*, 133.

117. T. Spence, *Pig's Meat* (London 1793), iii. 56.

118. W. E. S. Thomas, *The Philosophic Radicals* (Oxford 1979), 71.

119. W. L. Clements Lib., Ann Arbor, Mich., Fox MSS, C. J. Fox to T. Coutts [1794].

120. *Speeches*, vi. 333, 23 May 1797.

121. *Fox*, iii. 95, C. J. Fox to Lord Holland, 15 Dec. 1794.

122. *Speeches*, v. 344, 5 Jan. 1795. See also W. L. Clements Lib., Ann Arbor, Mich., Fox MSS, C. J. Fox to T. Coutts, 17 Nov. 1794.

123. BL Add. MSS 47581, fo. 12, C. J. Fox to R. Fitzpatrick, 9 Mar. 1798.

124. BL Add. MSS 47573, fo. 21, C. J. Fox to Lord Holland, 4 Mar. 1798.

125. Ibid., fo. 36, 22 May 1798.

126. Anon., *Mr Fox's Title to Patriot and Man of the People Disputed* (London 1806), 60.

127. BL Add. MSS 47566, fo. 30, C. J. Fox to D. O'Bryen, 25 Apr. 1799. See also BL Add. MSS 47569, fo. 88, A. O'Connor to C. J. Fox [1798] and R. Fulford, *Samuel Whitbread* (London 1967), 63.

128. Durham Univ. Lib., Grey MSS, Box 7, C. Grey to T. Bigge, 5 Mar. 1798.

129. BL Add. MSS 47564, fo. 39, C. J. Fox to Lord Lauderdale, 8 May 1798.

130. BL Add. MSS 47566, fo. 32, C. J. Fox to D. O'Bryen, 26 Apr. 1799.

131. G. Wakefield, *A Reply to some Parts of the Bishop of Llandaff's Address to the People of Great Britain* (London 1798).

132. BL Add. MSS 47566, fo. 19, C. J. Fox to D. O'Bryen, 20 July 1798.

133. *Correspondence of Gilbert Wakefield with the Right Honourable Charles James Fox*. See Chap. 9.

134. BL Add. MSS 47576, fo. 94, C. J. Fox to G. Wakefield, 2 Mar. 1799.

135. BL Add. MSS 47573, fo. 218, C. J. Fox to Lord Holland, 1 June 1799.

136. BL Add. MSS 47576, fo. 85, C. J. Fox to G. Wakefield, n.d.
137. *Fox*, iv. 389, C. J. Fox to G. Wakefield, 20 Apr. 1800.
138. Fox's mother, Caroline, and Emily, Duchess of Leinster, Fitzgerald's mother, were sisters.
139. BL Add. MSS 47566, fo. 12, C. J. Fox to D. O'Bryen, 8 June 1798.
140. BL Add. MSS 30990, fo. 45, C. J. Fox to Duchess of Leinster, 21 Oct. 1798.
141. B. Fitzgerald, *Emily, Duchess of Leinster* (London 1949), 249, C. J. Fox to Lord Henry Fitzgerald. See also *Lennox*, ii. Appendix E.
142. BL Add. MSS 47581, fo. 19, C. J. Fox to R. Fitzpatrick, 1 Apr. 1798.
143. BL Add. MSS 47573, fo. 61, C. J. Fox to Lord Holland, Sept. 1798.
144. BL Add. MSS 47565, fo. 170, C. J. Fox to R. Adair, 6 Aug. 1798. See also BL Add. MSS 47573, fos. 41, 48, C. J. Fox to Lord Holland, June and 22 Aug. 1798.
145. See Chap. 9.

Chapter 8

1. BL Add. MSS 47570, fo. 210, C. J. Fox to Mrs Fox, 1 Oct. 1797.
2. BL Add. MSS 47581, fo. 78, C. J. Fox to R. Fitzpatrick, 6 June 1800.
3. Ibid., fo. 16, 16 Aug. 1797.
4. BL Add. MSS 51468, fo. 49, Lafayette to C. J. Fox, 6 Nivôse 1800.
5. Ibid., fo. 38, 26 Oct. 1797.
6. Ibid.
7. BL Add. MSS 51635, fo. 156, Lafayette to Lord Holland, 1 Nivôse 1801.
8. W. A. S. Hewins, *The Whitefoord Papers* (Oxford 1898), 262, Sir G. Colebrook to C. Whitefoord, Jan. 1806.
9. *Morning Post*, 4 Nov. 1802.
10. *The Palmerston–Sulivan Letters, 1804–1863*, Camden Fourth Series (London 1979), xxiii. 38, Lord Palmerston to L. Sulivan, 11 Apr. 1805.
11. E. A. Smith, *Whig Principles and Party Politics* (Manchester 1975), 242, Lord Fitzwilliam to S. Croft, Jan. 1798.
12. HMC XIII Report, Fortescue MSS, iv. 69, M. de Luc to Lord Grenville, Jan. 1798.
13. *Speeches*, v. 505, 29 Oct. 1795.
14. BL Add. MSS 51733, fo. 120, Lord Holland to Caroline Fox, 24 Nov. 1795.
15. Ibid., fo. 161, 5 Jan. 1796.
16. Lord Holland to C. Vaughan, Aug. 1808, All Souls Coll., Vaughan MSS c 55/1, see also BL Add. MSS 47571, fo. 193, C. J. Fox to Lord Holland, 25 Dec. 1794; and BL Add. MSS 47572, fo. 81, Same to Same, 10 Sept. 1795.
17. BL Add. MSS 47572, fo. 77, C. J. Fox to Lord Holland, 7 Aug. 1795.
18. *Fox*, iii. 116, C. J. Fox to Lord Holland, 28 July 1795.
19. Ibid. iii. 112, 16 June 1795.
20. BL Add. MSS 47580, fo. 158, C. J. Fox to R. Fitzpatrick, 26 Aug. 1796.
21. *Speeches*, v. 339–40, 30 Dec. 1794.
22. Ibid. vi. 386, 3 Feb. 1800.
23. Betting Book, Brooks's Club.
24. BL Add. MSS 47572, fo. 77, C. J. Fox to Lord Holland, 7 Aug. 1795.
25. BL Add. MSS 47580, fo. 156, C. J. Fox to R. Fitzpatrick, 24 Aug. 1795.
26. W. L. Clements Lib., Ann Arbor, Mich., Fox MSS, C. J. Fox to T. Coutts, 28 Sept. [1794].
27. BL Add. MSS 47572, fo. 81, C. J. Fox to Lord Holland, 10 Sept. 1795.
28. Ibid., fo. 74, 28 July 1795. See also ibid., fo. 14, 24 Feb. 1795.

29. Ibid., fo. 50, 17 May 1795.
30. *Speeches*, vi. 98, 14 Dec. 1795.
31. Ibid. vi. 99.
32. BL Add. MSS 47571, fo. 147, C. J. Fox to Lord Holland, 21 Aug. 1794. See also ibid., fo. 168, 5 Oct. 1794.
33. BL Add. MSS 51468, fo. 32, C. J. Fox to R. B. Sheridan, 21 Sept. 1794.
34. BL Add. MSS 47572, fo. 36, C. J. Fox to Lord Holland, 12 Apr. 1795.
35. Ibid., fo. 108, 18 Feb. 1796.
36. Ibid., fo. 56, 14 June 1795.
37. Ibid., fo. 125, 16 Sept. 1796.
38. BL Add. MSS 47581, fo. 3, C. J. Fox to R. Fitzpatrick, 2 Sept. 1796.
39. *Speeches*, vi. 211, 6 Oct. 1796.
40. BL Add. MSS 47565, fo. 1, C. J. Fox to C. Grey, n.d.
41. *Speeches*, vi. 273, 30 Dec. 1796. In private correspondence, Fox was prepared to admit that the Directory too had been maladroit, *Fox*, iii. 268 C. J. Fox to Lauderdale.
42. B. Connell, *Portrait of a Whig Peer (London 1957)*, 394.
43. *Speeches*, vi. 321, 10 Apr. 1797.
44. *Burke*, ix. 294, F. Laurence to E. Burke, 28 Mar. 1797.
45. *Speeches*, v. 472, 27 May 1795.
46. Ibid. v. 383, 379, 5 Feb. 1895.
47. BL Add. MSS 47581, fo. 31, C. J. Fox to R. Fitzpatrick, 6 June 1799. Fox was receiving direct information about Naples from Hugh Elliot, see Edinburgh, Nat. Lib. of Scotland, Minto MSS 13025, fo. 187.
48. *Speeches*, v. 369 ff. and vi. 109 ff., 26 Jan. 1795 and 15 Feb. 1796.
49. *Windham*, ii. 31, E. Burke to W. Windham, 18 Dec. 1796.
50. BL Add. MSS 47565, fo. 11, C. J. Fox to C. Grey, 1800.
51. BL Add. MSS 47574, fo. 36, C. J. Fox to Lord Holland, 23 Nov. 1799.
52. Ibid., fo. 65, Jan. 1800.
53. Ibid., fo. 67, Jan. 1800. See also BL Add. MSS 47565, fo. 41, C. J. Fox to D. O'Bryen, 30 Dec. 1799.
54. N. Yorks. PRO, Wyvill MSS 7/2/129, fo. 17, C. J. Fox to C. Wyvill, 8 Jan. 1800.
55. BL Add. MSS 51735, fo. 165, Lord Holland to Caroline Fox, 21 Jan. 1800.
56. BL Add. MSS 47574, fo. 50, Lord Holland to C. J. Fox, 30 Dec. 1799.
57. Ibid., fo. 72, C. J. Fox to Lord Holland, 21 Jan. 1800.
58. *Speeches*, vi. 386 ff., 3 Feb. 1800.
59. N. Yorks. PRO, Wyvill MSS 7/2/150, fo. 1, C. J. Fox to C. Wyvill, 26 Jan. 1800.
60. Ibid. 7/2/129, fo. 23, 17 Feb. 1800.
61. BL Add. MSS 47574, fo. 78, C. J. Fox to Lord Holland, 24 Mar. 1800.
62. BL Add. MSS 47566, fo. 49, C. J. Fox to D. O'Bryen, 16 July 1800.
63. BL Add. MSS 47574, fo. 100, C. J. Fox to Lord Holland, 4 July 1800.
64. BL Add. MSS 47581, fo. 97, C. J. Fox to R. Fitzpatrick, 1801.
65. BL Add. MSS 47566, fo. 60, C. J. Fox to D. O'Bryen, 29 Dec. 1800.
66. BL Add. MSS 47574, fo. 124, C. J. Fox to Lord Holland, Oct. 1800.
67. C. J. Fox to H. E. Fox, 15 May 1801, Bod. Lib., Curzon MSS b18, fo. 69.
68. BL Add. MSS 47566, fo. 65, C. J. Fox to D. O'Bryen, 7 Jan. 1801.
69. Ibid., fo. 56, 28 Nov. 1800.
70. BL Add. MSS 47581, fo. 82, C. J. Fox to R. Fitzpatrick, 10 Sept. 1800.

71. Sir J. Walsh, *On the Present Balance of Parties in the State* (London 1832), 23–4.
72. *The Creevey Papers* (London 1903), i. 9, T. Creevey to Dr Currie, 25 Nov. 1802. See also Castle Howard MSS, J/4/64/1.
73. BL Add. MSS 47564, fo. 106, C. J. Fox to Lord Lauderdale, 17 June 1801.
74. N. Yorks. PRO, Wyvill MSS, 7/2/32/2, C. J. Fox to C. Wyvill, 28 Oct. 1800.
75. *Fox*, iii. 345, C. J. Fox to T. Maitland, 1801.
76. BL Add. MSS 47566, fo. 98, C. J. Fox to D. O'Bryen, 4 Oct. 1801.
77. *Mr Fox's Speech on the Glorious Anniversary of his Election* (London 1801), 5.
78. H. Sandford, *Thomas Poole and His Friends* (London 1888), ii. 74–5.
79. Ibid. 75.
80. Smith, *Whig Principles*, 265.
81. Durham Univ. Lib., Grey MSS, Box 55, G. Tierney to C. Grey, Oct. 1801.
82. BL Add. MSS 47565, fo. 50, C. J. Fox to C. Grey, 22 Oct. 1801.
83. Ibid., fo. 48, 12 Oct. 1801.
84. Lady Granville, *Granville Leveson Gower* (London 1916), i. 305, Lady Bessborough to G. Leveson Gower [Nov.] 1801.
85. *Speeches*, vi. 459, 3 Nov. 1801.
86. Connell, *Portrait of a Whig Peer*, 448–9.
87. BL Add. MSS 51475A, fo. 2, Journal of C. J. Fox, 30 July 1802.
88. BL Add. MSS 51468, fo. 56, Mrs Fox to H. Willoughby, 1 Aug. 1802.
89. Ibid., fo. 58.
90. Perrégaux and de Grave had both been well-known figures in Orleanist circles. De Grave fled with Lafayette from France in the summer of 1792.
91. BL Add. MSS 51475A, fo. 19, Journal of C. J. Fox, 19 Aug. 1802.
92. Sandford, *Thomas Poole and His Friends*, ii. 88–9.
93. BL Add. MSS 51475A, fo. 21, Journal of C. J. Fox, 21 Aug. 1802. Interestingly, Fox dates his letters from Paris according to both the old and the revolutionary calendars. See Hertford Coll. MSS, C. J. Fox to H. E. Fox, 17 Oct. 1802.
94. BL Add. MSS 51468, fo. 59, A. Merry to C. J. Fox, 4 Sept. 1802.
95. Trotter, 49, 51.
96. Ibid.
97. A. M. W. Stirling, *Coke of Norfolk and His Friends* (London 1912), 525. Lafayette described himself as a 'Worshipper' of Fox's memory, ibid., 526. See also BL Add. MSS 51635, fo. 162, Lafayette to Lord Holland, 15 Jan. 1816.
98. Bibliothèque Nationale, n.a.fr 14073, fo. 471, R. Adair to Mme Récamier, 6 May 1836.
99. BL Add. MSS 47566, fo. 120, C. J. Fox to D. O'Bryen, 24 Sept. 1802.
100. BL Add. MSS 51460, fo. 23, A. Merry to G. Hammond, 25 Sept. 1802.
101. Ibid., fo. 20, 20 Sept. 1802.
102. *Prince of Wales*, iv. 354, McMahon to Duke of Northumberland, 1 Jan. 1803.
103. Lady Airlie, *In Whig Society*, 47, R. Adair to Lady Melbourne, 27 Sept. 1802.
104. BL Add. MSS 51460, fo. 26, A. Merry to G. Hammond, 11 Nov. 1802.
105. C. L. Brightwell, *Memorials of the Life of Amelia Opie* (London 1854), 103.
106. BL Add. MSS 51475A, fo. 21, Journal of C. J. Fox, 21 Aug. 1802.
107. BL Add. MSS 51455, fo. 9, Journal of R. Fitzpatrick, 2 Sept. 1802.
108. BL Add. MSS 51475A, fo. 25, Journal of C. J. Fox, 2 Sept. 1802.
109. Lady Bessborough to G. Leveson Gower, 1802, Lady Granville, *Granville Leveson Gower*, i. 353.

110. BL Add. MSS 51455, fo. 9, Journal of R. Fitzpatrick, 2 Sept. 1802.

111. Lady Granville, *Lord Granville Leveson Gower*, i. 354, Lady Bessborough to G. Leveson Gower [1802].

112. Ibid. i. 355, 13 Sept. 1802.

113. BL Add. MSS 51455, fo. 19, Journal of Richard Fitzpatrick, 7 Oct. 1802.

114. Hertford Coll. MSS, C. J. Fox to H. E. Fox, 17 Oct. 1802.

115. J. Greig, *The Farington Diary* (London 1922), ii. 104.

116. BL Add. MSS 51746, fo. 20, Gen. O'Meara to Mrs Fox, 22 Aug. 1822.

117. BL Add. MSS 51475B, fo. 17, Journal of C. J. Fox, 17 Nov. 1802.

118. D. V. Erdman, *The Collected Works of Samuel Taylor Coleridge* (Princeton 1978), iii. 393, 396, Letter to Mr Fox, 9 Nov. 1802.

119. Quoted in Smith, *Whig Principles*, 267–8.

120. *The Windham Papers*, ii. 199, W. Windham to Mrs Crewe, 25 Sept. 1802.

121. HMC XIII Report, Fortescue MSS, vii. 111, Lord Buckingham to Lord Grenville, 26 Sept. 1802.

122. M. D. George, *English Political Caricature* (Oxford 1959), ii. 60.

123. BL Add. MSS 47564, fo. 153, C. J. Fox to Lord Lauderdale, 18 Nov. 1802.

124. Lord Bessborough, *Georgiana, Duchess of Devonshire* (London 1955), 254, C. J. Fox to Duchess of Devonshire, 1 Nov. 1802.

125. BL Add. MSS 47574, fo. 213, C. J. Fox to Lord Holland, 21 Nov. 1802. See also BL Add. MSS 47565, fo. 209, C. J. Fox to R. Adair, 20 Nov. 1802.

Chapter 9

1. BL Add. MSS 51732, fo. 66, Caroline Fox to Lord Holland, 14 Aug. 1794.

2. BL Add. MSS 47574, fo. 146, C. J. Fox to Lord Holland, 19 Apr. 1801.

3. HMC XV Report, Carlisle MSS, 555, J. Hare to Lord Carlisle, 29 Dec. 1781.

4. P. W. Clayden, *The Early Life of Samuel Rogers* (London 1887), 245.

5. BL Add. MSS 47531, fo. 30, C. J. Fox to Mrs Armistead, 17 July 1793.

6. BL Add. MSS 47570, fo. 83, Mrs Armistead to C. J. Fox, 10 Sept. 1795; ibid., fo. 110, 10 Feb. 1796.

7. Ibid., fo. 170, 7 May 1784.

8. Ibid., fo. 175, 1787.

9. *Minto*, iii. 361, Lord Minto to Lady Minto, 24 Aug. 1805.

10. BL Add. MSS 47569, fo. 71, C. J. Fox to ? [15 Jan. 1797].

11. BL Add. MSS 47570, fo. 215, C. J. Fox to Mrs Armistead, n.d.

12. Anon., *A Life of the Right Honourable Charles James Fox* (London 1807), 365.

13. BL Add. MSS 47570, fo. 204, C. J. Fox to Mrs Armistead, 25 Sept. 1795.

14. Ibid.

15. BL Add. MSS 51467, fo. 71, C. J. Fox to Caroline Fox, 12 Aug. 1802.

16. Lord Bessborough, *Georgiana, Duchess of Devonshire* (London 1955), 250.

17. BL Add. MSS 51736, fo. 78, Lord Holland to Caroline Fox, 3 Sept. 1802.

18. A. M. W. Stirling, *The Letter Bag of Lady Elizabeth Spencer Stanhope* (London 1913), i. 51–2, Mrs Stanhope to J. S. Stanhope, 6 June 1806.

19. Merton Coll. Malmesbury MSS, Box 3, Lord Malmesbury to Lady Palmerston, 2 Aug. 1792.

20. Lord Ilchester, *Elizabeth, Lady Holland to her Son* (London 1946), 45, Lady Holland to Henry Fox, 17 July 1826.

21. BL Add. MSS 47569, fo. 122, C. J. Fox to W. Adam, 30 May 1802. Harriet Willoughby's papers may be found in BL Add. MSS 62899–62904.
22. J. Greig, *The Farington Diary* (London 1922), i. 12.
23. Ibid., ii. 191; *Rogers*, 80–1.
24. BL Add. MSS 47571, fo. 81, C. J. Fox to Lord Holland, 3 Nov. 1793. See Chap. 8.
25. Anon., *Life of the Right Honourable Charles James Fox*, 354–5.
26. Edinburgh, Nat. Lib. of Scotland, Liston MSS 5542, fo. 138, C. J. Fox to Sir R. Liston [1786].
27. Coutts Ledgers, 1789, fo. 562, 25 Jan. 1789.
28. Ibid. 22 Oct. 1802.
29. Edinburgh, Nat. Reg. Arch., Blair Adam MSS, Gen. Corresp. 1797, A–J, C. J. Fox to W. Adam, 1797.
30. Lord Albemarle, *Fifty Years of My Life* (London 1876), i. 242–3.
31. BL Add. MSS 51734, fo. 25, Lord Holland to Caroline Fox, 20 July 1796. On his death, the following verse was found on Holland's desk,

> Nephew of Fox and Friend of Grey
> Enough my Need of Fame
> If those who deigned t'observe me say
> I've tarnished neither name.

(Bod. Lib. MS Eng. Lett. c234, fo. 113)

32. Bod. Lib., Curzon MSS 618, fo. 70, C. J. Fox to H. E. Fox, 15 May 1801.
33. BL Add. MSS 47572, fo. 160, C. J. Fox to Lord Holland, 20 June 1797.
34. P. Mandler, *Aristocratic Government in the Age of Reform* (Oxford 1990), 64.
35. BL Add. MSS 47564, fo. 140, C. J. Fox to Lord Lauderdale, 22 Apr. 1802.
36. Albemarle, *Fifty Years of My Life*, i. 243–4.
37. *Speeches*, vi. 141, 4 Mar. 1796.
38. Durham Univ. Lib., Grey MSS, C. Grey to Mrs Grey, 26 Mar. 1803.
39. Ibid. 23 July 1800.
40. Lady Granville, *Lord Granville Leveson Gower* (London 1916), ii. 44, Lady Bessborough to G. Leveson Gower, 31 Mar. 1805.
41. Examples of his verses may be found in Nat. Lib. of Scotland 5758, fo. 1 and 14258, fo. 23.
42. Trotter's book was highly controversial. Many of its points were contested by the Hollands.
43. Trotter, 68–9.
44. *Speeches*, v. 115, 7 May 1793.
45. BL Add. MSS 47576, fo. 54, C. J. Fox to U. Price, 6 June 1802.
46. W. E. S. Thomas, *The Philosophic Radicals* (Oxford 1979), 53.
47. Sir A. West, *Recollections 1832–1866* (London 1899), ii. 297–8.
48. BL Add. MSS 47575, fo. 114, C. J. Fox to Lord Holland, 29 Mar. 1804.
49. Ibid., fo. 22, 23 Feb. 1803.
50. Trotter, *Circumstantial Details . . .* , 36.
51. Lord Colchester, *The Diary and Correspondence of Charles Abbot, Lord Colchester* (London 1861), ii. 71.
52. G. O. Trevelyan, *The Early History of Charles James Fox* (London 1881), 284.
53. BL Add. MSS 47571, fo. 30, C. J. Fox to Lord Holland, 17 July 1793.
54. Edinburgh, Nat. Reg. Arch., Blair Adam MSS, Gen. Corresp. 1798 A–I, J. Hare to W. Adam, 26 Jan. 1798.

55. BL Add. MSS 47572, fo. 110, Mrs Fox to Lord Holland, 18 Feb. 1796.

56. C. Fendall and E. Critchley, *The Diary of Benjamin Newton* (Cambridge 1933), 60–1.

57. Hertford Coll. MSS, C. J. Fox to J. Trotter, 1801.

58. BL Add. MSS 47576, fos. 73–150, Fox–Wakefield MSS.

59. See S. R. West, *Journal of Hellenic Studies*, 104 (1984), 127–51.

60. BL Add. MSS 47566, fo. 246, C. J. Fox to D. O'Bryen, 2 Dec. 1805.

61. BL Add. MSS 47581, fo. 116, C. J. Fox to R. Fitzpatrick, 19 Jan. 1803.

62. BL Add. MSS 47571, fo. 34, C. J. Fox to Lord Holland, n.d.

63. Ibid., fo. 108, 9 Mar. 1794.

64. Ibid., fo. 60, 17 Sept. 1793.

65. BL Add. MSS 47572, fo. 76, ibid. 28 July 1795.

66. Ibid., fo. 59, 16 June 1795. The Fox–Buonaiuti letters may be found in BL Add. MSS 47578, fos. 1–81.

67. BL Add. MSS 47578, fos. 86–9.

68. P. W. Clayden, *Samuel Rogers and his Contemporaries* (London 1889), ii. 264.

69. *Fox*, iii. 182, C. J. Fox to Lord Holland, 28 Sept. 1800. See also *Minto*, iii. 285, Lord Minto to Lady Minto, 28 Apr. 1803.

70. S. Coleridge to T. Poole, H. Sandford, *Thomas Poole and His Friends* (London 1888), ii. 27.

71. Dyce, *Rogers*, 88.

72. Ibid. 90–2.

73. L. G. Mitchell, 'The *Edinburgh Review* and the Lake Poets', in H. Lloyd-Jones (ed.), *Essays presented to C. M. Bowra* (Oxford 1970), 33.

74. BL Add. MSS 51653, fos. 23–4, Lord Holland to Sir J. Mackintosh, 1807.

75. Lord J. Russell, *The Life of William, Lord Russell* (London 1820), i. Preface xiii.

76. *Edinburgh Review*, xii. 273, July 1808.

77. D. Hume, *The History of England from the invasion of Julius Caesar to the Revolution of 1688* (London 1763).

78. BL Add. MSS 47578, fo. 3, C. J. Fox to M. Laing, 24 Sept. 1800.

79. BL Add. MSS 47564, fo. 56, C. J. Fox to Lord Lauderdale [1799 or 1800].

80. BL Add. MSS 47566, fo. 40, C. J. Fox to D. O'Bryen, 22 Jan. 1800.

81. W. L. Clements Lib., Ann Arbor, Mich., Fox MSS, C. J. Fox to W. Belsham, 1800; Nat. Lib. of Scotland 8294, fo. 238, C. J. Fox to A. Stuart, 12 Dec. 1799.

82. BL Add. MSS 47564, fos. 56–60, C. J. Fox to Lord Lauderdale, 1800.

83. BL Add. MSS 47578, fo. 14. For more details see J. R. Dinwiddy, 'Charles James Fox as Historian', *Historical Journal*, 12 (1969).

84. BL Add. MSS 47574, fo. 98, C. J. Fox to Lord Holland, June 1800.

85. BL Add. MSS 47578, fos. 93 and 96. Miller ultimately won the battle to publish.

86. BL Add. MSS 47565, fo. 194, C. J. Fox to R. Adair, 3 Jan. 1803.

87. BL Add. MSS 47574, fo. 98, C. J. Fox to Lord Holland, June 1800.

88. BL Add. MSS 47566, fo. 106, C. J. Fox to D. O'Bryen, 10 Jan. 1802.

89. Chatsworth MSS, Journal of Lady E. Foster, 17 July 1802.

90. C. J. Fox, *A History of the Early Part of the Reign of James II* (London 1808), 6.

91. Ibid. 9–10.

92. Ibid. 17. He was compared to Caesar, and unfavourably to Washington.

93. Ibid. 20–2.

94. Ibid. 103.

95. Ibid., p. vi.

96. C. J. Fox, *A History of the Early Part of the Reign of James II* (London 1808), 44.
97. Ibid. 54.
98. Edinburgh, Nat. Reg. Arch., Blair Adam MSS, Gen. Corresp. 1801 D–G, C. J. Fox to W. Adam, 20 Dec. 1801.
99. N. Yorks. PRO, Wyvill MSS 7/2/164, fo. 2, 'Memorandum of what passed this morning in Conversation with Mr Fox', 27 Apr. 1804.

Chapter 10

1. For example BL Add. MSS 47564, fo. 109, C. J. Fox to Lord Lauderdale, 7 Jan. 1802.
2. BL Add. MSS 47565, fo. 40, C. J. Fox to C. Grey, 1801.
3. BL Add. MSS 47575, fo. 91, C. J. Fox to Lord Holland, 9 Jan. 1804.
4. BL Add. MSS 47565, fo. 42, C. J. Fox to C. Grey, 1801.
5. BL Add. MSS 47575, fo. 46, C. J. Fox to Lord Holland, 6 June 1803.
6. BL Add. MSS 47574, fo. 7, 24 Jan. 1803.
7. BL Add. MSS 47565, fo. 59, C. J. Fox to C. Grey, May 1802.
8. BL Add. MSS 47566, fo. 126, C. J. Fox to D. O'Bryen, 19 Nov. 1802.
9. BL Add. MSS 47565, fo. 106, C. J. Fox to C. Grey, 17 Dec. 1803.
10. *Fox*, iii. 366, C. J. Fox to Lord Lauderdale, 26 Mar. 1802.
11. BL Add. MSS 47566, fo. 118, C. J. Fox to D. O'Bryen, 24 June 1802.
12. Durham Univ. Lib., Grey MSS, Box 55, G. Tierney to C. Grey, 6 Mar. 1802.
13. Ibid., Dec. 1802.
14. Ibid. 19 Feb. 1802.
15. Ibid. 11 Feb. 1802.
16. BL Add. MSS 47565, fo. 73, C. J. Fox to C. Grey, 28 Feb. 1803.
17. N. Yorks. PRO, Wyvill MSS 7/2/160, fo. 2, C. Wyvill to C. J. Fox, 31 July 1803.
18. BL Add. MSS 47565, fo. 78, C. J. Fox to C. Grey, Mar. 1803.
19. BL Add. MSS 47566, fo. 70, C. J. Fox to D. O'Bryen, 2 Feb. 1801.
20. BL Add. MSS 47574, fo. 134, C. J. Fox to Lord Holland, 8 Feb. 1801.
21. BL Add. MSS 47565, fos. 27–9, C. J. Fox to C. Grey, 1801.
22. BL Add. MSS 47574, fo. 144, Lord Holland to C. J. Fox, 17 Apr. 1801; see also ibid., fo. 132, C. J. Fox to Lord Holland, 8 Feb. 1801.
23. Ibid., fo. 132, C. J. Fox to Lord Holland, 8 Feb. 1801.
24. N. Yorks. PRO, Wyvill MSS 7/2/32, fo. 19, C. J. Fox to C. Wyvill, 12 Feb. 1801.
25. BL Add. MSS 47566, fo. 72, C. J. Fox to D. O'Bryen, 16 Feb. 1801.
26. BL Add. MSS 47581, fo. 87, C. J. Fox to R. Fitzpatrick, 9 Feb. 1801.
27. BL Add. MSS 47564, fo. 81, C. J. Fox to Lord Lauderdale, 19 Feb. 1801. See also Castle Howard MSS J14/64/1, Carlisle Memorandum.
28. BL Add. MSS 47564, fo. 132, C. J. Fox to Lord Holland, 8 Feb. 1801.
29. BL Add. MSS 47574, fo. 178, Same to Same, Feb. 1802.
30. BL Add. MSS 47565, fo. 36, C. J. Fox to C. Grey [1801].
31. *Speeches*, vi. 444, 25 Mar. 1801.
32. BL Add. MSS 47565, fo. 38, C. J. Fox to C. Grey [June] 1801, see also BL Add. MSS 47574, fo. 148, C. J. Fox to Lord Holland, 1 June 1801.
33. BL Add. MSS 47565, fo. 44, C. J. Fox to C. Grey, 5 Oct. 1801.
34. Ibid., fo. 103, C. J. Fox to R. Adair, 1 Dec. 1801.
35. N. Yorks. PRO, Wyvill MSS 7/2/150, fo. 13, C. J. Fox to C. Wyvill, 18 June 1801.
36. BL Add. MSS 47566, fo. 96, C. J. Fox to D. O'Bryen, 17 Sept. 1801.

37. BL Add. MSS 47574, fo. 174, C. J. Fox to Lord Holland, 26 Jan. 1802.
38. BL Add. MSS 47565, fos. 52, 54, 56, 58, C. J. Fox to C. Grey, 14 Jan., 31 Jan., 9 Feb., and 21 Feb. 1802.
39. BL Add. MSS 47574, fo. 165, C. J. Fox to Lord Holland, 22 Oct. 1801. See also Durham Univ. Lib., Grey MSS, Box 55, G. Tierney to C. Grey, 22 Oct. 1801.
40. BL Add. MSS 47569, fo. 111, C. J. Fox to W. Smith, 15 Nov. 1801.
41. BL Add. MSS 51577, fo. 99, Lord Morpeth to Lord Holland, 17 Apr. 1803.
42. BL Add. MSS 47566, fo. 134, C. J. Fox to D. O'Bryen, 24 Dec. 1802. See also N. Yorks. PRO, Wyvill MSS 7/2/150, fo. 7, C. J. Fox to C. Wyvill, 18 Mar. 1802.
43. Durham Univ. Lib., Grey MSS, Box 16, C. J. Fox to C. Grey, 29 Dec. 1802.
44. Fox and his friends continued to visit and correspond with France in 1803. In Jan. 1803, Erskine and Lauderdale went to Paris, carrying letters to Lafayette, the contents of which were so confidential that, if they could not be delivered personally, they were to be brought back to England. BL Add. MSS 47564, fo. 164, C. J. Fox to Lord Lauderdale, Jan. 1803; and Durham Univ. Lib., Grey MSS, Box 44, T. Erskine to C. Grey, 14 Jan. 1803.
45. BL Add. MSS 47574, fo. 1, C. J. Fox to Lord Holland, 1 Jan. 1803.
46. *Fox*, iii. 205–6, C. J. Fox to Lord Holland, 19 Dec. 1802.
47. BL Add. MSS 47565, fo. 62, C. J. Fox to C. Grey, 29 Nov. 1802.
48. Ibid.
49. Ibid., fo. 80, 18 Mar. 1803.
50. Durham Univ. Lib., Grey MSS, Box 16, C. J. Fox to C. Grey [12 Dec. 1802].
51. *Fox*, iii. 218–19, C. J. Fox to Lord Holland, 29 Mar. 1803.
52. Durham Univ. Lib., Grey MSS, Box 16, C. J. Fox to C. Grey, 17 Jan. 1803.
53. BL Add. MSS 47581, fo. 120, C. J. Fox to R. Fitzpatrick, 10 Jan. 1803.
54. BL Add. MSS 47565, fo. 83, C. J. Fox to C. Grey [Mar. 1803].
55. BL Add. MSS 47565, fo. 228, C. J. Fox to R. Adair, Jan. 1803.
56. Ibid.
57. Lord Bessborough, *Georgiana, Duchess of Devonshire* (London 1955), 258–9, C. J. Fox to Duchess of Devonshire [Dec. 1802].
58. BL Add. MSS 47569, fo. 127, C. J. Fox to W. Adam, 28 Dec. 1802.
59. BL Add. MSS 47565, fo. 68, C. J. Fox to C. Grey, 12 Dec. 1802.
60. BL Add. MSS 47566, fo. 131, C. J. Fox to D. O'Bryen, 14 Dec. 1802.
61. BL Add. MSS 47575, fo. 29, C. J. Fox to Lord Holland, 23 Mar. 1803.
62. Durham Univ. Lib., Grey MSS, Box 16, C. J. Fox to C. Grey, 15 Mar. 1803.
63. BL Add. MSS 47565, fo. 85, C. J. Fox to C. Grey, 21 May 1803.
64. BL Add. MSS 47564, fo. 197, C. J. Fox to Lord Lauderdale, 24 Feb. 1804.
65. BL Add. MSS 47566, fo. 165, C. J. Fox to D. O'Bryen, 13 Nov. 1803.
66. Lady Granville, *Lord Granville Leveson Gower* (London 1916), iv. 441–2, Lady Bessborough to G. Leveson Gower [1803].
67. G. Pellew, *The Life and Correspondence of the Right Hon. Henry Addington, First Viscount Sidmouth* (London 1847), ii. 257, T. Erskine to Mr Bond, 10 Sept. 1803.
68. *Fox*, iii. 398, C. J. Fox to C. Grey, 12 Mar. 1803.
69. Ibid. iii. 398–9.
70. Durham Univ. Lib., Grey MSS, Box 16, C. Grey to C. J. Fox, 15 Mar. 1803.
71. BL Add. MSS 47565, fo. 87, C. J. Fox to C. Grey, July 1803.
72. Durham Univ. Lib., Grey MSS, Box 16, C. J. Fox to C. Grey, 9 Aug. 1803.
73. BL Add. MSS 47565, fo. 225, C. J. Fox to R. Adair, 1803.

74. BL Add. MSS 47565, fo. 225, C. J. Fox to R. Adair, 1803.
75. BL Add. MSS 47581, fo. 132, C. J. Fox to R. Fitzgerald, 6 June 1803.
76. BL Add. MSS 34079, fo. 81, C. J. Fox to D. O'Bryen, 22 June 1803.
77. BL Add. MSS 47566, fo. 141, 26 June 1803.
78. Ibid., fo. 162, 14 Oct. 1803.
79. Ibid. 140, 17 June 1803.
80. BL Add. MSS 47581, fo. 236, C. J. Fox to R. Fitzpatrick, 25 Sept. 1803.
81. BL Add. MSS 47564, fo. 169, C. J. Fox to Lord Lauderdale, 7 July 1803; BL Add. MSS 47566, fo. 172, C. J. Fox to D. O'Bryen, 31 Dec. 1803; Hertford Coll. MSS, C. J. Fox to H. E. Fox [1803].
82. BL Add. MSS 47564, fo. 177, C. J. Fox to Lord Lauderdale, 21 Aug. 1803. See also similar letters between these men in the same volume, fos. 170, 175, 179.
83. BL Add. MSS 47565, fo. 108, C. J. Fox to C. Grey, 6 Jan. 1804.
84. Ibid., fo. 101, 27 Nov. 1803.
85. Ibid., fo. 230, C. J. Fox to R. Adair, 31 July 1803.
86. Ibid., fo. 90, 8 Aug. 1803.
87. Ibid., fo. 96, 19 Oct. 1803.
88. Ibid., fo. 92, 18 Aug. 1803. See also *Prince of Wales*, iv. 402–5, C. J. Fox to Prince of Wales, 18 Aug. 1803.
89. BL Add. MSS 47581, fo. 136, C. J. Fox to R. Fitzpatrick, 30 Nov. 1803.
90. BL Add. MSS 41856, fo. 122, C. J. Fox to T. Grenville, 20 Dec. 1803. See also ibid., fos. 234, 236, C. J. Fox to R. Adair, 5 and 6 Jan. 1804; and BL Add. MSS 47581, fo. 145, C. J. Fox to R. Fitzpatrick, 6 Jan. 1804.
91. BL Add. MSS 47575, fo. 87, C. J. Fox to Lord Holland, 17 Dec. 1803.
92. BL Add. MSS 47564, fo. 184, C. J. Fox to Lord Lauderdale [1804].
93. BL Add. MSS 47575, fo. 97, C. J. Fox to Lord Holland, 18 Jan. 1804.
94. BL Add. MSS 41852, fo. 194, Lord Grenville to W. Pitt, 31 Jan. 1804. See also ibid., fo. 190, Lord Grenville to ?, 11 Jan. 1804.
95. *Windham*, ii. 228–9, W. Windham to T. Amyot, 5 Jan. 1804.
96. Ibid. ii. 230, W. Windham to C. J. Fox, 2 Feb. 1804. A Grenville alliance would, Fox hoped, renew his friendships with Spencer, Carlisle, and Fitzwilliam.
97. J. J. Sack, *The Grenvillites, 1801–1829 (Chicago 1979)*, 73.
98. BL Add. MSS 47581, fo. 147, C. J. Fox to R. Fitzpatrick, 27 Jan. 1804.
99. BL Add. MSS 47565, fo. 110, C. J. Fox to C. Grey, 29 Jan. 1804.
100. HMC XV Report, Bathurst MSS, 32, Lord Camden to Lord Bathurst, 14 Feb. 1804. See also *Minto*, iii. 305, Lord Minto to Lady Minto, 24 Feb. 1804.
101. H. Maxwell, *The Creevey Papers*, i. 20, T. Creevey to Dr Currie, 21 Dec. 1803. See also BL Add. MSS 47581, fo. 156, C. J. Fox to R. Fitzpatrick, 25 Feb. 1804.
102. Durham Univ. Lib., Grey MSS, C. Grey to Mrs Grey, 4 Mar. 1804. Edinburgh, Nat. Ref. Arch., Hope of Lufness MSS GD364/1154, Journal of Sir A. Hope, 1 Mar. 1804.
103. Edinburgh, Nat. Ref. Arch., Hope of Lufness MSS GD364/1154, Journal of Sir A. Hope, c.20 Feb. 1804.
104. BL Add. MSS 47566, fo. 182, C. J. Fox to D. O'Bryen, 29 Jan. 1804.
105. BL Add. MSS 47581, fo. 150, C. J. Fox to R. Fitzpatrick, 29 Jan. 1804.
106. Ibid., fo. 152, 24 Feb. 1804.
107. Edinburgh, Nat. Ref. Arch., Hope of Lufness MSS GD364/1154, Journal of Sir A. Hope, 1 Mar. 1804.

108. BL Add. MSS 47569, fo. 168, C.J. Fox to W. Smith, 12 Mar. 1804.

109. Castle Howard MSS J14/65/3, Carlisle Memorandum, Feb. 1804.

110. BL Add. MSS 41856, fo. 169, C.J. Fox to T. Grenville, 6 May 1804.

111. BL Add. MSS 47569, fo. 173, T. Grenville to C.J. Fox, 6 May 1804.

112. *Fox*, iv. 35, C.J. Fox to Lord Lauderdale, 30 Mar. 1804.

113. BL Add. MSS 47564, fo. 217, C.J. Fox to Lord Lauderdale, 9 Apr. 1804.

114. H. K. Olphin, *George Tierney* (London 1934), 86–7, T. Creevey to Dr Currie, 21 Jan. 1804.

115. BL Add. MSS 47575, fo. 111, C.J. Fox to Lord Holland, 20 Mar. 1804. See also Lord Colchester, *The Diary and Correspondence of Charles Abbot, Lord Colchester* (London 1861), i. 481.

116. Edinburgh, Nat. Ref. Arch., Hope of Lufness MSS GD364/1154, Journal of Sir A. Hope, 24 Mar. 1804.

117. D. V. Erdman, *The Collected Works of S. T. Coleridge* (Princeton 1978), iii. 81–4. Even Grey was unenthusiastic, Durham Univ. Lib., Grey MSS, Box 16, C. Grey to C.J. Fox, 24 Dec. 1803.

118. BL Add. MSS 58884, fo. 27, T. Grenville to Lord Grenville, 30 Nov. 1803.

119. *Sheridan*, ii. 216, R. B. Sheridan to Mrs Sheridan, 27 Feb. 1804.

120. BL Add. MSS 47566, fo. 153, C.J. Fox to D. O'Bryen, 18 Aug. 1803.

121. Edinburgh, Nat. Ref. Arch., Hope of Lufness MSS GD364/1154, Journal of Sir A. Hope, Feb.–Mar. 1804. See also BL Add. MSS 47565, fo. 100, C. J. Fox to C. Grey, 27 Nov. 1803.

122. Durham Univ. Lib., Grey MSS, Box 11, Duchess of Devonshire to C. Grey, 10 Nov. 1804. The Duchess had been the Prince's mistress, and remained one of his closest friends.

123. BL Add. MSS 47564, fo. 181, C.J. Fox to Lord Lauderdale, 4 Dec. 1803.

124. HMC III Report, 221, Grenville Memorandum, 1804. See also Edinburgh, Nat. Ref. Arch., Hope of Lufness MSS GD364/1154, Journal of Sir A. Hope, 25 Mar. 1804; and Edinburgh, Nat. Reg. Arch., Buccleuch MSS GD224/689/2, Lord Melville to Duke of Buccleuch, 1 May 1804.

125. *The Creevey Papers*, i. 27, T. Creevey to Dr Currie, 3 May 1804.

126. HMC XV Report, Bathurst MSS, 37, George III to W. Pitt, 5 May 1804.

127. *The Diary and Correspondence of Charles Abbot, Lord Colchester*, i. 506. See also Durham Univ. Lib., Grey MSS, C. Grey to Mrs Grey, 9 May 1804.

128. Edinburgh, Nat. Reg. Arch., Buccleuch MSS GD224/689/2, Lord Melville to Duke of Buccleuch, 8 May 1804. See also Castle Howard MSS J14/64/1, Carlisle Memorandum, May 1804.

129. *The Creevey Papers*, i. 27, T. Creevey to Dr Currie, 8 May 1804.

130. *Fox*, iv. 55, Lord Grenville to W. Pitt, 8 May 1804. See also *Minto*, iii. 331, Lord Minto to G. Elliot, 9 May 1804.

131. BL Add. MSS 51737, fo. 41, Caroline Fox to Lord Holland, 14 May 1804.

132. Durham Univ. Lib., Grey MSS, Box 16, C. Grey to C.J. Fox, 8 Apr. 1804.

133. Ibid., C.J. Fox to C. Grey, 19 Apr. 1804.

134. Castle Howard MSS J14/1/773, Lord Carlisle to T. Grenville, 28 Nov. 1804. See also Edinburgh, Nat. Reg. Arch., Melville MSS GD51/111/1, Lord Eldon to Lord Melville, n.d.

135. Durham Univ. Lib., Grey MSS, Box 16, C.J. Fox to C. Grey, 28 Mar. 1804.

136. *The Windham Papers*, ii. 264, C.J. Fox to W. Windham, 12 July 1805.

137. Durham Univ. Lib., Grey MSS, Box 16, C. J. Fox to C. Grey, 12 July 1805. See also BL Add. MSS 58884, fo. 134, T. Grenville to Lord Grenville, 18 July 1805.

138. BL Add. MSS 47565, fo. 268, R. Adair to C. J. Fox, 9 July 1805. See also Edinburgh, Nat. Lib. of Scotland, Ellice MSS 15016, fo. 3, Memorandum on Fox's Conduct, 12 July 1805.

139. BL Add. MSS 47564, fos. 240, 246, C. J. Fox to Lord Lauderdale, 30 Sept., 27 Aug. 1805.

140. Durham Univ. Lib., Grey MSS, Box 16, C. J. Fox to C. Grey, 28 Aug. 1805; Castle Howard MSS J14/65/3, Carlisle Memorandum; BL Add. MSS 58884, fo. 147, T. Grenville to Lord Grenville, 26 Sept. 1805.

141. HMC XV Report, Bathurst MSS, 50, W. Pitt to Lord Bathurst, 27 Sept. 1805; Durham Univ. Lib., Gen. Charles Grey MSS M15 IX/10, Sir G. Cornewall Lewis to Gen. C. Grey, 27 Apr. 1858.

142. BL Add. MSS 47565, fo. 261, C. J. Fox to R. Adair, 5 July [1805].

143. BL Add. MSS 47564, fo. 237, C. J. Fox to Lord Lauderdale, 12 July 1805.

144. *The Windham Papers*, ii. 259, C. J. Fox to W. Windham, 5 July 1805.

145. BL Add. MSS 47569, fo. 192, W. Windham to C. J. Fox, 29 Nov. 1804.

146. *The Windham Papers*, ii. 244, C. J. Fox to Windham, 24 Nov. 1804.

147. BL Add. MSS 47565, fo. 258, C. J. Fox to R. Adair [*c*. Dec. 1804]. See also BL Add. MSS 47566, fo. 202, C. J. Fox to D. O'Bryen, 25 Dec. 1804.

148. BL Add. MSS 47575, fo. 123, C. J. Fox to Lord Holland, 24 July 1804.

149. *Fox*, iv. 125–6, C. J. Fox to Lord Lauderdale, 17 Dec. 1805.

150. BL Add. MSS 47575, fo. 148, C. J. Fox to Lord Holland, 19 Mar. 1805.

151. H. Brougham, *The Life and Times of Henry, Lord Brougham* (Edinburgh 1871), ii. 297, H. Brougham to C. Grey, 5 Dec. 1815.

152. *Speeches*, vi. 571, 18 June 1804.

153. Bod. Lib., North MSS c12, fo. 8, C. J. Fox to T. Coutts, 31 Dec. 1805.

154. Durham Univ. Lib., Grey MSS, Box 16, C. J. Fox to C. Grey, 13 Apr. 1804.

155. BL Add. MSS 47569, fo. 187, W. Windham to C. J. Fox, 15 Mar. 1804.

156. *The Windham Papers*, ii. 239–40, C. J. Fox to W. Windham, 18 Nov. 1804.

157. BL Add. MSS 47575, fo. 114, C. J. Fox to Lord Holland, 29 Mar. 1804.

158. BL Add. MSS 47565, fo. 126, C. J. Fox to C. Grey, 17 Apr. 1804.

159. Durham Univ. Lib., Grey MSS, Box 16, C. Grey to C. J. Fox, 20 Apr. 1804.

160. BL Add. MSS 47575, fo. 131, C. J. Fox to Lord Holland, 17 Dec. 1804.

161. *The Windham Papers*, ii. 254, C. J. Fox to W. Windham, 1 May 1805.

162. BL Add. MSS 47565, fo. 128, C. J. Fox to Lord Grenville, 20 Apr. 1804.

163. Ibid., fo. 135, C. J. Fox to C. Grey, 18 Nov. 1804. See also Durham Univ. Lib., Grey MSS, C. J. Fox to W. Ponsonby, 27 Nov. 1804.

164. BL Add. MSS 47575, fo. 156, C. J. Fox to Lord Holland, 26 Apr. 1805.

165. Ibid., fo. 160, 2 May 1805.

166. BL Add. MSS 47569, fo. 228, Irish Roman Catholic Bishops to C. J. Fox, 5 July 1805.

167. *Speeches*, vi. 523, 24 May 1803.

168. Durham Univ. Lib., Grey MSS, Box 16, C. J. Fox to C. Grey, 19 Sept. 1804.

169. *The Windham Papers*, ii. 246, C. J. Fox to W. Windham, 25 Dec. 1804.

170. *Minto*, iii. 362, Lord Minto to Lady Minto, 24 Aug. 1805.

171. Lady Granville, *Granville Leveson Gower*, ii. 103–4, Lady Bessborough to G. Leveson Gower [14 Aug. 1805].

172. *The Windham Papers*, ii. 265, C. J. Fox to W. Windham, 30 Aug. 1805.

173. BL Add. MSS 47575, fo. 193, C. J. Fox to Lord Holland, 7 Nov. 1805.

174. Durham Univ. Lib., Grey MSS, Box 16, C. J. Fox to C. Grey, 29 Sept. 1805.

175. BL Add. MSS 47575, fo. 186, C. J. Fox to Lord Holland, 21 Sept. 1805.

176. Nat. Lib. of Scotland 14527, fo. 250, C. J. Fox to Prince Talleyrand, 16 June 1804.

177. Durham Univ. Lib., Grey MSS, C. Grey to Mrs Grey, 4 June 1804.

178. BL Add. MSS 47569, fo. 196, Novosiltsov to C. J. Fox, 30 Oct. 1804. See also ibid., fo. 197, C. J. Fox to ?, n.d.; and ibid., fo. 223, Czartoryski to C. J. Fox, 15 Apr. 1805.

179. P. Clayden, *The Early Life of Samuel Rogers* (London 1887), 378. See also Lady Granville, *Granville Leveson Gower*, ii. 11, Lady Stafford to G. Leveson Gower, 3 Feb. [1805].

180. *The Windham Papers*, ii. 268, C. J. Fox to W. Windham, 11 Sept. 1805. See also BL Add. MSS 47565, fo. 272, C. J. Fox to R. Adair, n.d.

181. BL Add. MSS 47566, fo. 240, C. J. Fox to D. O'Bryen, 6 Nov. 1805.

182. Bessborough, *Georgiana, Duchess of Devonshire*, 274, C. J. Fox to Duchess of Devonshire [*c.* Dec. 1805].

183. BL Add. MSS 47565, fo. 155, C. J. Fox to C. Grey, 3 Dec. 1805.

184. Ibid.

Chapter 11

1. BL Add. MSS 47575, fo. 217, C. J. Fox to Lord Holland, 2 Jan. 1806. See also BL Add. MSS 47564, fo. 254, C. J. Fox to Lord Lauderdale, 2 Jan. 1806.

2. A. Aspinall, *The Later Correspondence of George III* (Cambridge 1963–70), iv. 379, C. Yorke to ?, 21 Jan. 1806.

3. Lady Granville, *Lord Granville Leveson Gower* (London 1916), ii. 162–3, Lady Bessborough to G. Leveson Gower, 23 Jan. 1806. See also Lord Bessborough, *Georgiana, Duchess of Devonshire* (London 1955), 276–7, Duchess of Devonshire to Lord Hartington, 23 Jan. 1806.

4. *Speeches*, vi. 626, 629, 630, 27 Jan. 1806.

5. Lord Colchester, *The Diary and Correspondence of Charles Abbot, Lord Colchester* (London 1861), ii. 31. See also Lady Granville, *Granville Leveson Gower*, ii. 162, Lady Bessborough to G. Leveson Gower, 22 Jan. [1806].

6. BL Add. MSS 47566, fo. 262, C. J. Fox to D. O'Bryen, Jan. 1806.

7. BL Add. MSS 47575, fo. 217, C. J. Fox to Lord Holland, 2 Jan. 1806.

8. BL Add. MSS 51467, fo. 59, C. J. Fox to Lady S. O'Brien, 1806.

9. *Lennox*, ii. 207, Lady S. Napier to Lady S. O'Brien, 1 June 1806.

10. BL Add. MSS 47569, fo. 275, C. J. Fox to Duke of Bedford, 9 June 1806.

11. T. Wright, *The Works of James Gillray the Caricaturist* (London 1873), 328–9.

12. A. M. W. Stirling, *Annals of a Yorkshire House* (London 1911), 293, Mrs Stanhope to J. S. Stanhope, 29 Jan. 1806; Edinburgh, Nat. Ref. Arch., Hope of Lufness MSS GD364/1165/3, Sir A. Hope to Lord Hopetoun, 29 Feb. 1806.

13. L. G. Mitchell, *Holland House* (London 1980), 127, Duchess of Devonshire to Sir A. Clifford [Jan. 1806].

14. H. Maxwell, *The Creevey Papers* (London 1903), ii. 119, T. Creevey to Lord Sefton, 31 May 1827.

15. L. Horner, *Memoirs and Correspondence of Francis Horner, M.P.* (London 1843), i. 343, F. Horner to J. Murray, 7 Feb. 1806.

16. *Quarterly Review*, 5 (Feb. 1811), 101.

17. BL Add. MSS 58885, fo. 1, T. Grenville to Lord Grenville, 23 Jan. 1806.

18. G. Pellew, *The Life and Correspondence of the Right Honourable Henry Addington, First Viscount Sidmouth* (London 1847), ii. 405.

19. *Prince of Wales*, v. 316, R. Dundas to Lord Melville, 4 Feb. 1806.
20. Pellew, *Addington*, ii. 412–15.
21. Lord Holland, *Memoirs of the Whig Party During My Time* (London 1852), i. 232.
22. Durham Univ. Lib., Grey MSS, Box 42, Gen. H. Fox to C. Grey, 10 Nov. 1806.
23. *Lennox*, ii. 202, Lady S. Napier to Lady S. O'Brien, 23 Mar. 1806.
24. Nat. Lib. of Scotland 580, fo. 241, C.J. Fox to D. O'Bryen [Mar. 1806].
25. BL Add. MSS 47569, fo. 263, C.J. Fox to Duke of Bedford, 13 May 1806.
26. BL Add. MSS 41856, fo. 198, C.J. Fox to T. Grenville [1806].
27. Ibid., fo. 204.
28. For details, see P. Jupp, *Lord Grenville 1759–1834* (Oxford 1985), 346–7.
29. HMC XIII Report, Fortescue MSS, x. 362, Lord Grenville to C. Grey, 24 Nov. 1813.
30. Ibid. viii. 108, Lord Grenville to C.J. Fox, 19 Apr. 1806.
31. BL Add. MSS 58953, fo. 37, C.J. Fox to Lord Grenville, 28 Feb. 1806.
32. HMC XIII Report, Fortescue MSS, vii. 338, Lord Buckingham to Lord Grenville, 25 Jan. 1806.
33. BL Add. MSS 58953, fo. 14, C.J. Fox to Lord Grenville, 6 Feb. 1806.
34. B. Fitzgerald, *Emily, Duchess of Leinster* (London 1949), 276, Duke of Leinster to Duchess of Leinster, 1806.
35. HMC XIII Report, Fortescue MSS, viii. 376, Prince of Wales to Lord Grenville, 7 Oct. 1806.
36. BL Add. MSS 47569, fo. 242, W. Fawkener to C.J. Fox, 4 Feb. 1806.
37. Holland, *Memoirs*, i. 197.
38. Ibid. ii. 159. See also BL Add. MSS 51661, fo. 72, Duke of Bedford to Lord Holland, 28 Feb. 1807.
39. Pellew, *Addington*, ii. 435.
40. BL Add. MSS 47569, fo. 244, C.J. Fox to E. Hay, 20 Feb. 1806.
41. J. Greig, *The Farington Diary* (London 1922), iii. 158.
42. HMC XIII Report, Fortescue MSS, x. 211, T. Grenville to Lord Grenville, 13 Feb. 1812.
43. Holland, *Memoirs*, i. 213.
44. BL Add. MSS 51544, fo. 197, Lord Holland to C. Grey, 13 Jan. 1810.
45. Ibid.
46. Horner, *Francis Horner*, i. 323.
47. BL Add. MSS 47576, fo. 71, C.J. Fox to U. Price, n.d.
48. BL Add. MSS 51468, fo. 62, Lafayette to C.J. Fox, 7 Feb. 1803.
49. Ibid., fo. 66, 16 Apr. 1803.
50. Coutts MSS, fo. 1017, C.J. Fox to T. Coutts, 22 July 1803.
51. Anon., *The State of the Negotiation* (London 1806), 59. See also HMC Var. Coll., vi. 418, Mrs S. Nugent to W. Cornwallis, 23 Jan. 1806.
52. HMC XIII Report, Lonsdale MSS, 166, Lord Westmorland to Lord Lowther, 14 Feb. 1806. Westmorland had been irritated by a recent meeting of the Whig Club, at which Fox had offered the toast of 'The cause of liberty all over the world'.
53. HMC XIII Report, Fortescue MSS, x. 371, T. Grenville to Lord Grenville, 24 Jan. 1814.
54. Durham Univ. Lib., Grey MSS, Box 16, C.J. Fox to C. Grey, 10 Jan. 1806.
55. BL Add. MSS 47575, fo. 214, C.J. Fox to Lord Holland, 1 Jan. 1806.
56. Lord Palmerston to L. Sulivan, 26 June 1806, *The Palmerston–Sulivan Letters, 1804–1863*, Camden Fourth Series (London 1979), xxiii. 57.
57. Duc de Broglie, *Mémoires du Prince de Talleyrand* (Paris 1891), i. 227.
58. Durham Univ. Lib., Grey MSS, Talleyrand to C.J. Fox, 5 Mar. 1806.

59. *Fox*, iv. 150, Talleyrand to C. J. Fox, 1 Apr. 1806.
60. Durham Univ. Lib., Grey MSS, C. J. Fox to Talleyrand, 26 Mar. 1806.
61. Ibid.
62. BL Add. MSS 51457, fo. 61, C. J. Fox to Talleyrand, 18 Feb. 1806.
63. *Fox*, iv. 148, Talleyrand to C. J. Fox, 5 Mar. 1800.
64. Ibid. iv. 150, C. J. Fox to Talleyrand, 26 Mar. 1806.
65. T. Wright, *Rowlandson, the Caricaturist*, ii. 61.
66. *Moniteur*, 8 June 1806.
67. Durham Univ. Lib., Grey MSS, C. J. Fox to Talleyrand, 9 Apr. 1806.
68. BL Add. MSS 51457, fo. 8, Cabinet Memorandum, 12 Mar. 1806.
69. *Speeches*, vi. 643–4, 23 Apr. 1806.
70. BL Add. MSS 58953, fo. 75, C. J. Fox to Lord Grenville, 20 Apr. 1806.
71. BL Add. MSS 47569, fo. 249, C. J. Fox to Duke of Bedford, 13 Apr. 1806.
72. Durham Univ. Lib., Grey MSS, Box 41, Comte Munster to C. J. Fox, 11 Mar. 1806.
73. BL Add. MSS 51457, fo. 1, Cabinet Memorandum to George III, 2 Mar. 1806. See also Aspinall, *Later Correspondence of George III*, iv. 403, C. J. Fox to George III, 2 Mar. 1806.
74. Durham Univ. Lib., Grey MSS, Box 42, C. J. Fox to Gen. H. Fox, 9 May 1806.
75. Ibid., Gen. H. Fox to C. J. Fox, 9 Sept. 1806.
76. BL Add. MSS 47570, fo. 107, Gen. H. Fox to Lord Holland, Sept. 1806.
77. Ibid. For Gen. Fox's reports, see also BL Add. MSS 51459, fos. 1–58.
78. Edinburgh, Nat. Lib. of Scotland, Minto MSS, 13023, fo. 87, C. J. Fox to H. Elliot, 3 Mar. 1806.
79. Ibid., fo. 149, C. J. Fox to Prince Castelcicala, 9 May 1806.
80. BL Add. MSS 51460, fo. 131, C. J. Fox to G. Leveson Gower, 8 Apr. 1806.
81. BL Add. MSS 51461, fo. 79, C. J. Fox to Prince Czartoryski [June] 1806.
82. Alexander's father, Paul I, had taken up the quixotic notion that Russia might have a claim to Malta, with himself as the heir of the Knights of St John.
83. Bod. Lib., Curzon MS b21, fo. 232, Prince Czartoryski to C. J. Fox, 10 July 1806.
84. Durham Univ. Lib., Grey MSS, Box 7, Sir B. Boothby to C. J. Fox, 30 June 1806.
85. Durham Univ. Lib., Grey MSS, Talleyrand to C. J. Fox, 1 Apr. 1806.
86. BL Add. MSS 51457, fo. 30, George III to C. J. Fox, 9 Apr. 1806; ibid., fo. 33, C. J. Fox to George III, 19 Apr. 1806. See also BL Add. MSS 58953, fo. 66, C. J. Fox to Lord Grenville, 9 Apr. 1806.
87. *Fox*, iv. 156–7, C. J. Fox to Prince Talleyrand, 8 Apr. 1806.
88. Durham Univ. Lib., Grey MSS, Prince Talleyrand to C. J. Fox, 16 Apr. 1806.
89. Ibid., C. J. Fox to Prince Talleyrand, 22 Apr. 1806.
90. See *Fox*, iv. 168–73, letters between Fox and Talleyrand, 2 and 14 June 1806.
91. BL Add. MSS 47569, fo. 254, C. J. Fox to Duke of Bedford, 26 Apr. 1806.
92. BL Add. MSS 58953, fo. 71, C. J. Fox to Lord Grenville, 19 Apr. 1806.
93. Ibid.
94. Ibid., fo. 73, Lord Grenville to C. J. Fox, 19 Apr. 1806.
95. Ibid., fo. 99, C. J. Fox to Lord Grenville, 21 June 1806.
96. BL Add. MSS 51457, fo. 47, Cabinet Memorandum to the King, 13 June 1806.
97. BL Add. MSS 51458, fo. 9, C. J. Fox to Lord Yarmouth, 26 June 1806.
98. Ibid., fo. 7.
99. Ibid.
100. Ibid., fo. 55, Lord Yarmouth to C. J. Fox, 20 July 1806.

101. BL Add. MSS 51458, fo. 81, C. J. Fox to Lord Yarmouth, 26 July 1806.
102. See Chap. 12.
103. BL Add. MSS 51458, fo. 81, C. J. Fox to Lord Yarmouth, 26 July 1806.
104. Ibid., fo. 173, Lord Lauderdale to C. J. Fox, 7 Sept. 1806.
105. *The Palmerston–Sulivan Letters*, 60–1, Lord Palmerston to L. Sulivan, 8 Aug. 1806.
106. H. Sandford, *Thomas Poole and His Friends* (London 1888), ii. 160, J. Rickman to T. Poole, 30 Apr. 1806.
107. Ibid., 29 June 1806.
108. Trotter, 58–9, 64.
109. *Lennox*, ii. 204–5, Lady S. Napier to Lady S. O'Brien, 21 May 1806.
110. BL Add. MSS 51459, fo. 85, ? to R. Adair, 1 July 1806.
111. *Lennox*, ii. 212, Lady S. Napier to Lady S. O'Brien, 17 July 1806.
112. N. Yorks. PRO, Wyvill MSS 7/2/188, fo. 12, C. Wyvill to C. J. Fox, 22 July 1806. Wyvill wrote to recommend a particular type of treatment.
113. BL Add. MSS 41859, fo. 127, Lord Carlisle to T. Grenville, 3 Aug. 1806. See also Durham Univ. Lib., Grey MSS, Box 47, G. Ponsonby to C. Grey, 5 Aug. 1806.
114. [Trotter], *Circumstantial Details . . .* , 66–7.
115. Ibid. 72.
116. Holland, *Memoirs*, i. 245–75.
117. Journal of Mrs Fox, quoted in *Lennox*, ii Appendix G.
118. Pellew, *Addington*, ii. 434, H. Addington to H. Bathurst, 14 Sept. 1806.
119. Ibid., H. Addington to H. Bathurst, 14 Sept. 1806.
120. Journal of Mrs Fox, quoted in Lennox, ii Appendix G. See also Edinburgh, Nat. Reg. Arch., Blair Adam MSS, Misc. Corresp. and Papers 1800–1819, Mrs Fox to W. Adam, 25 Sept. 1806.
121. Leics. PRO, Halford MSS, DG 24/809/21.
122. HMC XIII Report, Fortescue MSS, viii. 332, Lord Grenville to Lord Lauderdale, 14 Sept. 1806.
123. Ibid. 358, Lord Lauderdale to Lord Grenville, 26 Sept. 1806.
124. BL Add. MSS 51470, fo. 78, Lafayette to Mrs Fox, 5 Oct. 1806.
125. BL Add. MSS 51520, fo. 12, Prince of Wales to Lord Holland, 12 Sept. 1806.
126. Philopatris Varvicensis, *Characters of the late Charles James Fox* (London 1809). See also BL Add. MSS 47570, fo. 115, and BL Add. MSS 51661, fos. 33–4.
127. BL Add. MSS 27937, fo. 25, Will of C. J. Fox.
128. See Chap. 9.
129. *Morning Chronicle*, 8 Oct. 1806.
130. Ibid., 11 Oct. 1806.
131. Ibid.
132. BL Add. MSS 51472, fo. 39, S. Rogers to J. Allen, Sept. 1806.
133. Ibid., fo. 54.
134. For details of this fund-raising, see BL Add. MSS 51474.
135. See Chap. 5.
136. See Chap. 12.

Chapter 12

1. Prominent among these are G. O. Trevelyan, *The Early History of Charles James Fox* (London 1881), and the biographies written by J. L. Hammond and J. Drinkwater.

2. D. Johnson, 'Charles James Fox: From Government to Opposition, 1771–1774', *Eng. Hist. Rev.* 89 (1974), 770–1.

3. *Gentleman's Magazine,* July 1834, 14–5.

4. Bod. Lib. MS Eng. Misc. 162, fo. 225.

5. BL Add. MSS 47590, fo. 16, Commonplace Book of Samuel Rogers.

6. BL Add. MSS 47591, fo. 13, J. Trotter to Lord Holland, 1806.

7. *The Gazetteer*, 19 Feb. 1790.

8. *Speeches*, vi. 601, 14 May 1805.

9. BL Add. MSS 47565, fo. 163, C. J. Fox to R. Adair, 29 Nov. 1792.

10. *Speeches*, iv. 147, 1 Mar. 1791.

11. Ibid. iv. 419, 11 May 1792.

12. For Fox's view of Paine, see Chap. 7.

13. *Speeches*, iv. 2, 8 May 1789.

14. Ibid.

15. BL Add. MSS 47578, fo. 109, C. Butler to Lord Holland, 12 Apr. 1808.

16. *Speeches*, vi. 447–8, 25 Mar. 1801.

17. Ibid. i. 18–19, 23 Feb. 1773.

18. *The General Gazetteer*, 14 Sept. 1780.

19. *Burke*, iv. 283, C. J. Fox to E. Burke, 15 Sept. 1780.

20. W. L. Clements Lib., Ann Arbor, Mich., Fox MSS, C. J. Fox to W. Hanbury, 3 Dec. 1789. Other addresses may be found in the Edinburgh, Nat. Reg. Arch., Blair Adam MSS.

21. Sheffield Pub. Lib., Wentworth Woodhouse Muniments, Burke I, R. Bright to E. Burke, 13 Feb. 1790.

22. J. Johnstone, *The Works of Dr Samuel Parr* (London 1828), i. 355, Lord J. Townshend to Dr Parr, 1 Mar. 1790.

23. Ibid. i. 346, Dr Parr to H. Homer, 1790.

24. Ibid. i. 355, 16 Feb. 1790.

25. Sheffield Pub. Lib., Wentworth Woodhouse Muniments, F115a, C. J. Fox to Earl Fitzwilliam, 13 Nov. 1789.

26. See Chap. 11.

27. Lord Ilchester, *Elizabeth, Lady Holland to her Son* (London 1946), 101, Lady Holland to H. Fox, 10 Apr. 1829.

28. BL Add. MSS 47570, fo. 182, C. J. Fox to Mrs Armistead [Apr. 1791].

29. *Speeches*, iii. 390, 9 May 1788.

30. Ibid. iv. 16, 12 May 1789.

31. BL Add. MSS 51820, fo. 45, W. Wilberforce to Lord Holland, 4 Jan. 1832.

32. Northants PRO, Milton MSS, Box 44, C. J. Fox to Earl Fitzwilliam, 16 Mar. 1792.

33. BL Add. MSS 47572, fo. 100, C. J. Fox to Lord Holland, 19 Feb. 1796.

34. BL Add. MSS 47569, fo. 99, C. J. Fox to W. Wilberforce, 21 Feb. 1799.

35. Ibid.

36. *Speeches*, iv. 192, 183, 19 Apr. 1791. A rider was added to the effect that 'men inured to slavery all their lives felt certainly less degraded by it than those who were born to independence'; ibid. iv. 191.

37. Ibid. iv. 385, 2 Apr. 1792.

38. Ibid. vi. 659, 10 June 1806.

39. Lady L. Connolly to ?, 11 Dec. 1806, R. W. Bond, *The Marlay Letters* (London 1937), 100.

40. *Parl. Hist.* xliv. 672, 5 Feb. 1807.

41. Lord Holland, *Memoirs of the Whig Party During My Time* (London 1852), ii. 157–8.
42. *Parl. Hist.* lxiv. 356, 27 June 1814.
43. BL Add. MSS 51820, fo. 38, W. Wilberforce to Lord Holland, 23 Feb. 1823.
44. *Speeches*, ii. 66, 17 May 1782.
45. Ibid.
46. J. C. Beckett, 'Anglo-Irish Constitutional Relations in the Later Eighteenth Century', *Irish Hist. Stud.* 14 (1964), 20–38.
47. BL Add. MSS 47582, fo. 73, J. Burgoyne to R. Fitzpatrick, 6 May 1782.
48. Ibid., fo. 149, H. Grattan to R. Fitzpatrick, 5 Jan. 1783.
49. BL Add. MSS 38716, fo. 22, C. J. Fox to Lord Northington, 1 Nov. 1783.
50. BL Add. MSS 47580, fo. 94, C. J. Fox to R. Fitzpatrick, 28 Apr. 1782.
51. BL Add. MSS 47579, fo. 37, C. J. Fox to Lord Upper Ossory, 22 July 1785.
52. B. Sheridan to Miss Sheridan, 20 June 1785, W. Lefanu, *Betsy Sheridan's Journal* (London 1960), 58.
53. *Speeches*, iii. 94, 12 May 1785; ibid. iii. 90; ibid. iii. 112, 23 May 1785.
54. Ibid. iii. 113, 23 May 1785.
55. Ibid. iii. 131, 30 May 1785.
56. Bod. Lib., Bowood MSS, T. Orde to Lord Lansdowne, 26 June 1785.
57. See Chap. 2.
58. See Chap. 7.
59. *Parl. Hist.* xxiii. 17 May 1782. Significantly, Fox added that he 'should vote for the present motion, as he believed it to be the wish of the people, but whether it would produce the desired effect, he had his doubts.'
60. *Speech of the Rt. Hon. C. J. Fox at a Meeting of the Electors of Westminster* (London 1782), 5–6. No definition of the word 'mass' is offered.
61. *Morning Chronicle*, 12 Mar. 1784.
62. J. Carswell, *The Old Cause* (London 1954), 305.
63. *Wraxall*, ii. 316. This writer also questioned Pitt's sincerity on the issue.
64. Anon., *What Have the Whigs Done?* (London 1835), 3.
65. F. D. Cartwright, *The Life and Correspondence of Major Cartwright* (London 1826), 132 n.
66. T. Green, *Extracts from the Diary of a Lover of Literature* (Ipswich 1810), 174–5.
67. *Parl. Hist.* xxiii. 103–4, 19 June 1782.
68. Sheffield Pub. Lib., Wentworth Woodhouse Muniments, F63c, Duke of Portland to Earl Fitzwilliam, 21 Aug. 1784.
69. BL Althorp MSS, Lord Althorp to Lady Spencer, 17 May 1783.
70. C. Wyvill, *Political Tracts and Papers* (York 1779–1804), ii. 104–5, C. J. Fox to C. Wyvill, 4 Dec. 1782.
71. *York Chronicle*, 22 Aug. 1783, quoted in I. R. Christie, *Wilkes, Wyvill and Reform* (London 1962), 192.
72. For the origins of this Association, see Chap. 6.
73. Significantly, Moore himself doubted 'whether Mr Fox ever fully admitted the principle upon which the demand for a Reform is founded. When he afterwards espoused the question so warmly, it seems to have been merely as one of those weapons caught up in the heat of a warfare, in which Liberty itself appeared to him too imminently endangered, to admit of the consideration of an abstract principle', T. Moore, *Memoirs of R. B. Sheridan* (London 1825), ii. 182–3.
74. Ibid. ii. 182.

75. Interestingly, Fox even in 1792 clung to family criticism of Whig behaviour in the 1760s. See Chap. 1.

76. Northants PRO, Milton MSS, Box 44, C. J. Fox to Earl Fitzwilliam, 16 Mar. 1792.

77. Castle Howard MSS, J14/1/f722, Earl of Carlisle to Earl Fitzwilliam, 17 Oct. 1792.

78. BL Add. MSS 47568, fo. 277, Earl of Carlisle to C. J. Fox, 23 July 1792.

79. BL Add. MSS 47565, fo. 163, C. J. Fox to R. Adair, 29 Nov. 1792.

80. Lord Guilford's Memorandum, 1783, quoted in Christie, *Wilkes, Wyvill and Reform*, 177.

81. Durham Univ. Lib., Grey MSS, Box 16, fo. 8, C. J. Fox to C. Grey, 1800.

82. N. Yorks. PRO, Wyvill MSS 7/2/182, fo. 8, C. Wyvill to C. J. Fox, 27 Apr. 1804.

83. Ibid. 7/2/183, fo. 3, C. J. Fox to C. Wyvill [Dec. 1805].

84. Ibid.

85. Ibid. 7/2/182, fo. 11, C. Wyvill to C. J. Fox, 24 Dec. 1805.

86. Ibid. 7/2/188, fo. 7, 5 Feb. 1806.

87. BL Add. MSS 51468, fo. 94, Major Cartwright to C. J. Fox, 5 Jan. 1806.

88. When, during the Westminster scrutiny of 1784–5, Fox had to sit as representative for the twelve electors of Orkney and Shetland, this title came to have an ironic quality that was not missed by wags and rhymsters.

89. BL Add. MSS 38594, fos. 29, 39, Minutes of the Westminster Association, 23 Mar., 15 May 1782; *Gentleman's Magazine*, July 1782, 355.

90. *Morning Chronicle*, 12 Oct. 1787.

91. *The Epistolary Correspondence of the Rt. Hon. Edmund Burke and Dr French Laurence* (London 1827), 6–7, F. Laurence to E. Burke, Aug. 1788.

92. Lord Mahon to C. Wyvill, 22 June 1782, quoted in Christie, *Wilkes, Wyvill and Reform*, 149.

93. J. Disney, *The Works of John Jebb* (London 1787), i. 199 n., J. Jebb to ? [c. Apr. 1783].

94. Christie, *Wilkes, Wyvill and Reform*, 198; BL Add. MSS 38595, fos. 20, 34, Minutes of the Westminster Association.

95. See Chap. 3.

96. *Minto*, i. 363, Lady Palmerston to Sir G. Elliot, 19 June 1790.

97. PRO, Pitt MSS 30/8 157, fo. 106, Dundas Memorandum, 15 Mar. 1790.

98. *Wraxall*, iii. 102.

99. *Speeches*, ii. 491, 16 June 1784.

100. D. Pulteney to Duke of Rutland, 19 Apr. 1785, quoted in Christie, *Wilkes, Wyvill and Reform*, 218.

101. Ibid., 221, C. Wyvill to W. Gray, 24 May 1785.

102. *Speeches*, v. 113–14, 7 May 1793.

103. Bod. Lib., Bowood MSS, C. Wyvill to Lord Lansdowne, 31 Dec. 1795.

104. *Speeches*, v. 97, 2 May 1793.

105. *Prince of Wales*, iii. 341, Memorandum on C. J. Fox, 22 May 1797.

106. *The Miscellaneous Works of the Rt. Hon. Sir James Mackintosh* (London 1846), iii. 227.

107. *Parl. Hist.* xxvi. 1307, 12 Dec. 1787.

108. Ibid. xxx. 461, 21 Feb. 1793. Fox insisted that a petition from Nottingham be heard, while at the same time disavowing its call for universal suffrage.

109. *Speeches*, vi. 24, 17 Nov. 1795.

110. Ibid.

111. *Windham*, ii. 253, C. J. Fox to W. Windham, 17 Apr. 1805.

112. BL Add. MSS 47576, fo. 143, C. J. Fox to G. Wakefield, 28 Apr. 1801.

113. *Speeches*, iii. 151, 18 Apr. 1785.

114. BL Add. MSS 47581, fo. 69, C. J. Fox to R. Fitzpatrick, 3 Apr. 1800.

115. *Speeches*, ii. 68, 7 May 1782.

116. Ibid. ii. 174, 7 May 1783.

117. Ibid. iv. 77, 4 Mar. 1790. See also ibid. iv. 410, 30 Apr. 1792.

118. BL Add. MSS 47565, fo. 163, C. J. Fox to R. Adair, 29 Nov. 1792.

119. BL Add. MSS 58941, fo. 41, Earl of Lauderdale to Lord Grenville, 21 Feb. 1806.

120. *Speeches*, vi. 340, 26 May 1797.

121. Ibid. 369. On this occasion, Fox supported the idea of household suffrage.

122. Brooks's Club Betting Book, 25 May 1793.

123. A. Aspinall, *The Later Correspondence of George III* (Cambridge 1963–70), ii. 581, C. J. Fox to T. Anson, 20 May 1797.

124. *Speeches*, v. 109, 7 May 1793.

Epilogue

1. For a full discussion of this cult, see L. G. Mitchell, *Holland House* (London 1980), chaps. 2 and 3; and N. B. Penny, 'The Whig Cult in Nineteenth-Century Sculpture', *Past and Present*, 70 (1976).

2. BL Add. MSS 51516, Membership list of the Whig Club.

3. *The Times*, 7 Jan. 1819.

4. H. Maxwell, *The Creevey Papers* (London 1903), i. 187, H. G. Bennet to T. Creevey, 24 Sept. 1813.

5. *Morning Chronicle*, 18 Jan. 1823.

6. Penny, 'The Whig Cult', 96.

7. Lord Albemarle, *Fifty Years of My Life* (London 1876), i. 331. Princess Charlotte to Lord Albemarle, 17 Jan. 1812.

8. Anon., *Written Impromptu on receiving . . . a lock of the late Mr Fox's Hair*, Bod. Lib. MS Eng. Misc. e 888, fo. 2.

9. *Morning Chronicle*, 15 Sept. 1806.

10. F. Bickley, *The Diaries of Sylvester Douglas, Lord Glenbervie* (London 1928), ii. 321.

11. Lord J. Russell, *An Essay on the History of the English Government and Constitution* (London 1823), 270–1.

12. *Rogers*, 97.

13. Lord Bessborough, *Lady Bessborough and her Family Circle* (London 1940), 147, Mrs G. Lamb to Lady C. Lamb, 9 Sept. 1806.

SELECT BIBLIOGRAPHY

I. Manuscript Sources

BODLEIAN LIBRARY, OXFORD

A. I. M. Duncan, 'A Study of the Life and Public Career of Frederick Howard, Fifth Earl of Carlisle' (Oxford D.Phil. 1981).

A. Gilbert, 'The Political Correspondence of Charles Lennox, Third Duke of Richmond, 1765–1784' (Oxford D.Phil. 1956).

P. J. Marshall, 'The Impeachment of Warren Hastings' (Oxford D.Phil. 1963).

Bod. Lib., Bowood MSS. Correspondence of William, First Marquess of Lansdowne.

Bland Burges MSS. Papers and Correspondence of Sir J. Bland Burges.

North MSS. Papers and Correspondence of Frederick, Second Earl of Guilford.

BRITISH LIBRARY

Abergavenny MSS, facs 340. Papers and Memoranda of John Robinson MP.

Adair MSS, Add. MSS 50829. Papers and Correspondence of James Adair.

Althorp MSS, unfol. Papers and Correspondence of John, Second Earl Spencer.

Auckland MSS, Add. MSS 34418–19. Papers and Correspondence of William Eden, First Baron Auckland.

Foster MSS, Add. MSS 41579. Journal of Lady Elizabeth Foster.

Fox MSS, Add. MSS 47559–81 and 51468–75. Papers and Correspondence of Charles James Fox.

Francis MSS, Add. MSS 40763. Correspondence of Sir Philip Francis.

Grenville MSS, Add. MSS 41856, 42058, 58884–5, 60487. Papers and Correspondence of Thomas Grenville.

Grenville MSS, Add. MSS 58941, 58953. Papers of William Grenville, First Baron Grenville.

Hardwicke MSS, Add. MSS 35641. Correspondence of Philip Yorke, Third Earl of Hardwicke.

Hastings MSS, Add. MSS 29196, 24266. Papers and Correspondence of Warren Hastings.

Holland House MSS, Add. MSS 51414–16, 51422, 51434, 51444–5. Correspondence of the First Lord and Lady Holland.

Holland House MSS, Add. MSS 51544. Travel Journal of the First Lady Holland.

Holland House MSS, Add. MSS 51550, 51592, 51799, 51731–8. Correspondence of the Third Lord Holland.

Holland House MSS, Add. MSS 51350. Papers of Second Earl of Ilchester.

Holland House MSS, Add. MSS 51352, 51354, 51359. Correspondence of Lady Susan O'Brien.

Holland House MSS, Add. MSS 51455. Journal of Richard Fitzpatrick.

Leeds MSS, Add. MSS 27918, 28061, 28067. Memoranda and Correspondence of the Fifth Duke of Leeds.

Leinster MSS, Add. MSS 30990. Papers of Emily, Duchess of Leinster.

North MSS, Add. MSS 61867. Papers of Second Earl of Guilford.
Northington MSS, Add. MSS 38716. Letter Book of the Second Earl of Northington.
Pelham MSS, Add. MSS 33100–1, 41852, 41854. Papers of the Second Earl of Chichester.
Westminster Association MSS, Add. MSS 38594–5.
Willoughby MSS, Add. MSS 62899–902. Papers of Harriet Willoughby.
Windham MSS, Add. MSS 37843–5, 37847–8, 37853, 37873, 37909. Papers of William Windham.

BROOKS'S CLUB, LONDON

The Betting Book of Brooks's Club.

CASTLE HOWARD, YORKSHIRE

Papers and Correspondence of the Fifth Earl of Carlisle.

CHATSWORTH, DERBYSHIRE

Correspondence of Georgiana, Fifth Duchess of Devonshire and of Lady Elizabeth Foster.

CORNELL UNIVERSITY LIBRARY

Dean Collection. Papers and Correspondence of C. J. Fox and the Marquis de Lafayette.

COUTTS BANK, LONDON

Papers and Correspondence of Thomas Coutts.

DURHAM PUBLIC RECORD OFFICE

Papers and Correspondence of John Lee.

DURHAM UNIVERSITY LIBRARY

Papers and Correspondence of Charles, Second Earl Grey.

EDINBURGH, NATIONAL LIBRARY OF SCOTLAND

Edinburgh, Nat. Lib. of Scotland, Ellice MSS. Papers of Edward Ellice.
Edinburgh, Nat. Lib. of Scotland, Liston MSS. Papers of Sir Robert Liston.
Edinburgh, Nat. Lib. of Scotland, Minto MSS. Papers of Sir Hugh Elliot.

EDINBURGH, NATIONAL REGISTRY OF ARCHIVES

Edinburgh, Nat. Reg. Arch., Blair Adam MSS. Papers and Correspondence of William Adam (unfol.).
Edinburgh, Nat. Reg. Arch., Buccleuch MSS. Papers of the Duke of Buccleuch.

Edinburgh, Nat. Reg. Arch., Dundas of Ochtertyre MSS. Papers of Henry Dundas.
Edinburgh, Nat. Ref. Arch., Hope of Lufness MSS. Papers of John and Alexander Hope.
Edinburgh, Nat. Reg. Arch., McKenzie of Seaforth MSS.
Edinburgh, Nat. Reg. Arch., Melville MSS. Papers of the Dundas family.

ETON COLLEGE, BERKSHIRE

Dr Barnard's Admissions Book.

HAMPSHIRE PUBLIC RECORD OFFICE

Papers and Correspondence of the Second Viscount Palmerston. These manuscripts have since been moved to Windsor Castle.

HERTFORD COLLEGE, OXFORD

Correspondence of Charles James Fox.

HICKLETON CASTLE, YORKSHIRE

Correspondence and Papers of the Ponsonby Family.

LEICESTERSHIRE PUBLIC RECORD OFFICE

Papers and Correspondence of Sir Henry Halford.

MERTON COLLEGE, OXFORD

Malmesbury MSS.

NORTHAMPTONSHIRE PUBLIC RECORD OFFICE

Northants PRO, Milton MSS. Papers and Correspondence of (i) Edmund Burke and (ii) the Second Earl Fitzwilliam.

NOTTINGHAM UNIVERSITY LIBRARY

Nottingham Univ. Lib., Portland MSS. Papers and Correspondence of the Third Duke of Portland.

PUBLIC RECORD OFFICE, LONDON

Chatham MSS. Papers and Correspondence of William Pitt.

SHEFFIELD PUBLIC LIBRARY

Sheffield Pub. Lib., Wentworth Woodhouse Muniments. Correspondence and Papers of (i) Edmund Burke and (ii) the Second Marquess of Rockingham.

WEST SUFFOLK PUBLIC RECORD OFFICE

W. Suffolk PRO, Bunbury MSS. Correspondence and Papers of Sir Charles Bunbury.

W. Suffolk PRO, Grafton MSS. Correspondence and Papers of the Third Duke of
   Grafton.

NORTH YORKSHIRE PUBLIC RECORD OFFICE

N. Yorks. PRO, Wyvill MSS. Correspondence and Papers of the Rev. C. Wyvill.

W. L. CLEMENTS LIBRARY, ANN ARBOR, MICH.

Fox MSS.

II. Printed Sources

A. *Primary Sources*

1. *Historical Manuscripts Commission*

V Report	*Manuscripts of the Duke of Sutherland.*
VIII Report	*Manuscripts of the Duke of Manchester.*
IX Report	*Manuscripts of A. Morrison, Esq.*
X Report	*Manuscripts of the Marquess of Abergavenny.*
XII Report	*Manuscripts of the Earl of Charlemont.*
	Manuscripts of the Earl of Donoughmore.
	Manuscripts of P. V. Smith, Esq.
XIII Report	*Manuscripts of the Earl of Charlemont.*
	Manuscripts of J. B. Fortescue, Esq.
	Manuscripts of the Earl of Lonsdale.
XIV Report	*Manuscripts of Lord Kenyon.*
	Manuscripts of the Duke of Rutland.
	Manuscripts of Lord Emly.
XV Report	*Manuscripts of the Earl of Bathurst.*
	Manuscripts of the Earl of Carlisle.
	Manuscripts of W. Knox, Esq.
	Manuscripts of the Earl of Lothian.
	Manuscripts of Mrs Stopford-Sackville.

2. *Newspapers and Periodicals*

London Chronicle
Morning Chronicle
Morning Herald
Morning Post
Public Advertizer
Sheffield Advertizer
The Times

Blackwood's Magazine
Edinburgh Review
Gentleman's Magazine
The Englishman

3. *Books*

Adair	R. Adair, *A Sketch of the Character of the Late Duke of Devonshire* (London 1811).
Addington	G. Pellew, *The Life and Correspondence of the Right Hon. Henry Addington, First Viscount Sidmouth* (London 1847).

Albemarle	Earl of Albemarle, *Fifty Years of My Life* (London 1876).
Anon.	Anon., *Les Amours et les Aventures du Lord Fox* (Geneva 1785).
————	Anon. *Life of the Right Honourable Charles James Fox* (London 1807).
d'Arblay	A. Dobson, *Diary and Letters of Madame d'Arblay* (London 1905).
Auckland	Lord Auckland, *Journal and Correspondence of William Eden, First Lord Auckland* (London 1861).
Bentinck	Mrs A. Le Blond, *Charlotte Sophie, Countess Bentinck* (London 1912).
Beresford	W. Beresford, *Correspondence of the Rt. Hon. John Beresford* (London 1854).
Bessborough	Lord Bessborough, *Lady Bessborough and her Family Circle* (London 1940).
Boswell	J. Boswell, *The Life of Dr Samuel Johnson* (Oxford 1965).
Buckingham	Duke of Buckingham and Chandos, *Memoirs of the Court and Cabinets of George III* (London 1853–5).
Burges	J. Hutton, *Letters and Correspondence of Sir James Bland Burges* (London 1885).
Burgoyne	E. B. de Fonblanque, *Life and Correspondence of the Rt. Hon. John Burgoyne* (London 1876).
Burke	T. Copeland, *The Correspondence of Edmund Burke* (Cambridge 1958–70).
Campbell	Lord Campbell, *Lives of the Lord Chancellors and Keepers of the Great Seal of England* (London 1856).
————	*The Diary of Thomas Campbell* (Cambridge 1947).
Cartwright	F. D. Cartwright, *The Life and Correspondence of Major Cartwright* (London 1826).
Chatham	*Correspondence of William Pitt, Earl of Chatham* (London 1839).
Cockburn	Lord Cockburn, *Memorials of His Time* (Edinburgh 1909).
Colchester	Lord Colchester, *The Diary and Correspondence of Charles Abbot, Lord Colchester* (London 1861).
Coleridge	D. V. Erdman, *The Collected Works of S. T. Coleridge* (Princeton 1978).
Connell	B. Connell, *Portrait of a Whig Peer* (London 1957).
Cornwallis	C. Ross, *Correspondence of the First Marquis Cornwallis* (London 1859).
Creevey	H. Maxwell, *The Creevey Papers* (London 1903).
Croker	L. J. Jennings, *The Croker Papers* (London 1884).
Devonshire	Lord Bessborough, *Georgiana, Duchess of Devonshire* (London 1955).
Farington	J. Greig, *The Farington Diary* (London 1922).
Fitzgerald	T. Moore, *The Life of Lord Edward Fitzgerald* (London 1831).
Fitzmaurice	Lord E. Fitzmaurice, *Life of William, Earl of Shelburne* (London 1912).
Fox	[C. J. Fox], *An Essay upon Wind* (London n.d.).
————	[C. J. Fox], *To Mrs Crewe* (n.p., n.d.).

—— [J. Moir], *History of the Political Life and Public Services . . . of the Right Honourable Charles James Fox* (London 1783).

—— *Correspondence between M. Bertrand de Moleville and the Honourable Charles James Fox* (London 1800).

—— C. J. Fox, *A History of the Early Part of the Reign of James II* (London 1808).

—— *Proceedings in an Action for Debt between the Rt. Hon. Charles J. Fox and John Horne Tooke* (London 1812).

—— *The Correspondence of Gilbert Wakefield with the Right Honourable Charles James Fox* (London 1813).

—— J. Wright, *The Speeches of the Rt. Hon. C. J. Fox in the House of Commons* (London 1815).

—— [J. Trotter], *Circumstantial Details of the Long Illness and last Moments of the Right Hon. Charles James Fox* (London 1806).

—— J. Trotter, *Memoirs of the Later Years of the Rt. Hon. C. J. Fox* (London 1811).

—— R. Fell, *Memoirs of the Public Life of the late right honourable Charles James Fox* (London 1808).

—— Dr S. Parr, *Characters of Charles James Fox* (London 1809).

—— Philopatris Varvicensis, *Characters of the late Charles James Fox* (London 1809).

—— Lord J. Russell, *Memorials and Correspondence of C. J. Fox* (London 1853–7).

Francis   J. Parkes and H. Merivale, *Memoirs of Sir Philip Francis* (London 1867).

——   B. Francis and E. Keary, *The Francis Papers* (London 1901).

George P. of W.   A. Aspinall, *Correspondence of George, Prince of Wales* (London 1963–71).

George III   Sir J. Fortescue, *The Correspondence of George III, 1760–1783* (London 1927–8).

——   A. Aspinall, *The Later Correspondence of George III* (Cambridge 1963–70).

Glenbervie   F. Bickley, *The Diaries of Sylvester Douglas, Lord Glenbervie* (London 1928).

Grafton   W. Anson, *Memoirs of Augustus Henry, Third Duke of Grafton* (London 1898).

Granville   Lady Granville, *Lord Granville Leveson Gower* (London 1916).

Green   T. Green, *Extracts from the Diary of a Lover of Literature* (Ipswich 1810).

Greville   F. M. Bladon, *The Diaries of Robert Fulke Greville* (London 1930).

Hamwood   E. M. Bell, *The Hamwood Papers* (London 1930).

Hardy   F. Hardy, *Memoirs of the Political and Private Life of James Caulfield, Earl of Charlemont* (London 1812).

Herbert	Lord Herbert, *The Pembroke Papers* (London 1824–6).
Holland, Lady	Lord Ilchester, *Elizabeth, Lady Holland to her Son* (London 1946).
Holland, Lord	Lord Ilchester, *Henry Fox, First Lord Holland* (London 1920).
——	Lord Holland, *Memoirs of the Whig Party During My Time* (London 1852).
Horner	L. Horner, *Memoirs and Correspondence of Francis Horner, M.P.* (London 1843).
Jebb	J. Disney, *The Works of John Jebb* (London 1787).
Laurence	Dr F. Laurence, *History of the Political Life and Public Services of the Rt. Hon. C. J. Fox* (London 1783).
——	*The Epistolary Correspondence of the Rt. Hon. Edmund Burke and Dr French Laurence* (London 1827).
Leeds	O. Browning, *The Political Memoranda of the Fifth Duke of Leeds* (London 1884).
Leinster	B. Fitzgerald, *Emily, Duchess of Leinster* (London 1949).
Lennox	Lady Ilchester and Lord Stavordale, *Life and Letters of Lady Sarah Lennox* (London 1901).
Lyttleton	H. Wyndham, *The Correspondence of Sarah Spencer, Lady Lyttelton* (London 1912).
Macaulay	G. O. Trevelyan, *Life and Letters of Lord Macaulay* (London 1959).
Mackintosh	R. J. Mackintosh, *Memoirs of the Life of Sir James Mackintosh* (London 1835).
Malmesbury	Lord Malmesbury, *Diaries and Correspondence of Lord Malmesbury* (London 1844).
Marchand	J. Marchand, *A Frenchman in England, 1784* (Cambridge 1933).
Marlay	R. W. Bond, *The Marlay Letters* (London 1937).
Minto	Lady Minto, *Life and Letters of Sir Gilbert Elliot, First Earl of Minto* (London 1874).
——	Lady Minto, *A Memoir of the Rt. Hon. Hugh Elliot* (Edinburgh 1868).
Montagu	G. Martelli, *Life of John Montagu, Fourth Earl of Sandwich* (London 1962).
Moore	Lord J. Russell, *Memoirs, Journal and Correspondence of Thomas Moore* (London 1853).
Newton	C. Fendall and E. Critchley, *The Diary of Benjamin Newton* (Cambridge 1933).
O'Connell	M. R. O'Connell, *The Correspondence of D. O'Connell* (Dublin 1972–80).
Opie	C. L. Brightwell, *Memorials of the Life of Amelia Opie* (London 1854).
Palmerston	*The Palmerston–Sulivan Letters, 1804–1863*, Camden Society Fourth Series (London 1979).
Parliament	*Papers Presented to Parliament 1789–1796.*
	The Parliamentary History.
Parr	J. Johnstone, *The Works of Dr Samuel Parr* (London 1828).
Robinson	W. T. Laprade, *The Parliamentary Papers of John Robinson, 1774–1784* (London 1922).

Rockingham Lord Albemarle, *Memoirs of the Marquis of Rockingham* (London 1852).

Rogers *Recollections of the Table talk of Samuel Rogers* (London 1856).
——— Rev. A. Dyce, *Reminiscences and Table Talk of Samuel Rogers* (Edinburgh 1903).

Romilly *Memoirs of Sir Samuel Romilly* (London 1840).
Rose L. V. Harcourt, *Diaries and Correspondence of the Rt. Hon. George Rose* (London 1860).

Russell Lord J. Russell, *Recollections and Suggestions, 1813–1873* (London 1875).

Selwyn E. S. Roscoe and H. Clergue, *George Selwyn, his Letters and his Life* (London 1899).

Shelley R. Edgecumbe, *The Diary of Lady Frances Shelley, 1787–1813* (London 1913).

Sheridan J. Watkins, *Memoirs of the Rt. Hon. R. B. Sheridan* (London 1817).
——— T. Moore, *Memoirs of R. B. Sheridan* (London 1825).
——— C. Price, *The Letters of R. B. Sheridan* (Oxford 1966).
——— W. Lefanu, *Betsy Sheridan's Journal* (London 1960).

Sinclair *The Correspondence of Sir John Sinclair* (London 1831).
Stirling A. M. W. Stirling, *Annals of a Yorkshire House* (London 1911).
——— A. M. W. Stirling, *Coke of Norfolk and His Friends* (London 1912).
——— A. M. W. Stirling, *The Letter Bag of Lady Elizabeth Spencer Stanhope* (London 1913).

Talleyrand Duc de Broglie, *Mémoires du Prince de Talleyrand* (Paris 1891).
Tomline G. Tomline, *Memoirs of the Life of the Rt. Hon. William Pitt* (London 1821).

Walpole *Letters Addressed to the Countess of Upper Ossory by Horace Walpole* (London 1848).
——— H. Walpole, *Memoirs of the Reign of George III* (London 1894).
——— A. F. Steuart, *The Last Journals of Horace Walpole* (London 1910).
——— W. S. Lewis, *Horace Walpole's Correspondence* (New Haven, Conn. 1937–80).

West Sir A. West, *Recollections 1832–1866* (London 1899).
Whig Club *The Whig Club Rule Book* (London 1784).
Whiteefoord W. A. S. Hewins, *The Whiteefoord Papers* (Oxford 1898).
Windham Mrs H. Baring, *The Diary of the Right Hon. William Windham* (London 1866).
——— L. S. Benjamin, *The Windham Papers* (London 1913).
Wraxall H. B. Wheatley, *The Historical and Posthumous Memoirs of Sir Nathaniel Wraxall* (London 1884).
Wyvill C. Wyvill, *Political Tracts and Papers* (York 1779–1804).

4. *Pamphlets*

W. Combe, *The Diaboliad* (London 1777).
A Short History of the Opposition (London 1779).
Opposition Mornings (London 1779).
Speech of the Hon. Charles James Fox (London 1781).

Speech of the Rt. Hon. C. J. Fox at a Meeting of the Electors of Westminster (London 1782).

A Letter from a Liveryman on Mr Fox's Introduction of a Bill for Depriving the East India Company of Their Charter (London 1783).

Fox's Martyrs or a New Book of the Sufferings of the Faithful (London 1784).

The Beauties and Deformities of Fox, North and Burke (London 1784).

The Last Dying Words of Reynard the Fox (London 1784).

The Fox and the Badger Dismissed (London 1784).

Fox against Fox: Or Political Blossoms of the Rt. Hon. C. J. Fox (London 1788).

A Letter to the Rt. Hon. C. J. Fox on the Late Conduct of his Party (London 1789).

W. Combe, *A Letter from a Country Gentleman to a Member of Parliament* (London 1789).

A Collection of Odes, Songs and Epigrams against the Whigs alias the Buff and Blue (London 1790).

Parallel Between the Conduct of Mr Burke and that of Mr Fox, in their Late Parliamentary Contest (London 1791).

C. Pigott, *The Jockey Club* (London 1792).

Speech of the Rt. Hon. C. J. Fox Containing the Declaration of his Principles Respecting the Present Crisis of Public Affairs (London 1792).

Speech of the Rt. Hon. C. J. Fox . . . Spoken at the Whig Club (London 1792).

A Letter from the Rt. Hon. C. J. Fox to the Worthy and Independent Electors of Westminster (London 1793).

The Letter of the Rt. Hon. C. J. Fox to the Electors of Westminster Anatomized (London 1793).

A Letter to the Rt. Hon. C. J. Fox in Which Is Proved the Absolute Necessity of an Immediate Declaration of War Against France (London 1793).

A Letter to the Rt. Hon. C. J. Fox Upon the Dangerous and Inflammatory Tendency of His late Conduct in Parliament (London 1793).

Remarks on a Pamphlet Published as Mr Fox's Speech at the Opening of Parliament (London 1793).

C. Pigott, *The Whig Club* (London 1794).

Observations on the Conduct of Mr Fox by a Suffolk Freeholder (Bury St Edmunds 1794).

J. Owen, *Letter to Mr Fox on the Duration of the Trial of Mr Hastings* (London 1794).

R. Adair, *A Whig's Apology for His Consistency* (London 1795).

Address and Speeches of the Right Honourable Charles James Fox at the late Westminster Election (London 1796).

A Letter to the Right Honourable Charles James Fox from a Yeoman of England (London 1797).

A Letter to the Hon. Charles James Fox Shewing how Appearances May Deceive (London 1798).

Mr Fox's Speech on the Glorious Anniversary of his Election (London 1801).

R. Adair, *The Letter of the Rt. Hon. C. J. Fox to the Electors of Westminster, With an Application of its Principles to Subsequent Events* (London 1802).

Mr Fox's Title to Patriot and Man of the People Disputed (London 1806).

The State of the Negotiation (London 1806).

A View of the Negotiation (London 1806).

An Elegy on the Death of the Right Honourable Charles James Fox (London 1806).

B. *Secondary Sources*

1. *Books*

D. Barnes, *George III and William Pitt* (London 1939).

P. Boucé, *Sexuality in Eighteenth Century Britain* (Manchester 1982).

J. Cannon, *The Fox–North Coalition, 1782–1784* (Cambridge 1969).

J. Carswell, *The Old Cause* (London 1954).

I. R. Christie, *The End of North's Ministry, 1780–1782* (London 1958).

I. R. Christie, *Wilkes, Wyvill and Reform* (London 1962).

E. Coleridge, *The Life of Thomas Coutts* (London 1920).

J. W. Derry, *The Regency Crisis and the Whigs* (Cambridge 1963).

J. W. Derry, *Charles James Fox* (London 1972).

W. Derry, *Dr Parr* (Oxford 1966).

J. Drinkwater, *Charles James Fox* (London 1928).

J. Ehrman, *The Younger Pitt* (London 1969, 1982).

D. V. Erdman, *Commerce des Lumières* (Columbia 1986).

V. H. Foster, *Two Duchesses* (London 1898).

R. Fulford, *Samuel Whitbread* (London 1967).

M. D. George, *English Political Caricature* (Oxford 1959).

M. D. George, *Hogarth to Cruikshank* (London 1967).

I. Leveson Gower, *The Face without a Frown* (London 1944).

J. Greig, *The Diary of a Duchess* (London 1926).

C. Grey, *The Life and Opinions of the Second Earl Grey* (London 1861).

C. Hobhouse, *Fox* (London 1947).

P. Jupp, *Lord Grenville 1759–1835* (Oxford 1985).

E. Lascelles, *The Life of Charles James Fox* (Oxford 1936).

P. J. Marshall, *The Impeachment of Warren Hastings* (Oxford 1965).

P. Mandler, *Aristocratic Government in the Age of Reform* (Oxford 1990).

A. Mitchell, *The Whigs in Opposition, 1815–1830* (Oxford 1967).

L. G. Mitchell, *Charles James Fox and the Disintegration of the Whig Party, 1782–1794* (Oxford 1971).

L. G. Mitchell, *Holland House* (London 1980).

J. Norris, *Shelburne and Reform* (London 1963).

F. O'Gorman, *The Whig Party and the French Revolution* (London 1967).

H. K. Olphin, *George Tierney* (London 1934).

N. C. Phillips, *Yorkshire and National Politics, 1783–1784* (Christchurch, New Zealand 1961).

D. Powell, *Charles James Fox* (London 1989).

W. F. Rae, *Wilkes, Sheridan and Fox* (London 1874).

L. Reid, *Charles James Fox* (London 1969).

N. Roe, *Wordsworth and Coleridge* (Oxford 1988).

Lord J. Russell, *The Life and Times of Charles James Fox* (London 1859–66).

J. J. Sack, *The Grenvillites, 1801–1829* (Chicago 1979).

L. Sanders, *The Holland House Circle* (London 1908).

H. Sandford, *Thomas Poole and His Friends* (London 1888).

W. Sichel, *Sheridan* (London 1909).

E. A. Smith, *Whig Principles and Party Politics* (Manchester 1975).

E. A. Smith, *Lord Grey* (Oxford 1990).

L. S. Sutherland, *The East India Company in Eighteenth- Century Politics* (Oxford 1952).

P. G. Thomas, *Lord North* (London 1976).

G. O. Trevelyan, *The Early History of Charles James Fox* (London 1881).

G. M. Trevelyan, *Lord Grey of the Reform Bill* (London 1929).

T. Wright, *The Works of James Gillray, the Caricaturist* (London 1873).

2. *Articles*

J. C. Beckett, 'Anglo-Irish Constitutional Relations in the late Eighteenth Century', *Irish Historical Studies*, xiv 1964.

H. Butterfield, 'Charles James Fox and the Whig Opposition in 1792', *Cambridge Historical Journal*, 9 (1949).

I. R. Christie, 'The Marquis of Rockingham and Lord North's Offer of a Coalition, June–July 1780', *English Historical Review*, 64 (1954).

J. R. Dinwiddy, 'Charles James Fox as Historian', *Historical Journal*, 12 (1969).

J. R. Dinwiddy, 'Charles James Fox and the People', *History*, 55 (1970).

C. E. Fryer, 'The General Election of 1784', *History*, 11 (1925).

E. George, 'Fox's Martyrs: The General Election of 1784', *Transactions of the Royal Historical Society*, 21 (1937).

D. Ginter, 'The Financing of the Whig Party Organisation, 1783–1793', *American Historical Review*, 71 (1966).

B. W. Hill, 'Fox and Burke: the Whig party and the Question of Principles', *English Historical Review*, 39 (1974).

E. Hughes, 'The Scottish Reform Movement and Charles Grey 1792–1794', *Scottish Historical Review*, 35 (1956).

D. Johnson, 'Charles James Fox: From Government to Opposition 1771–1774', *English Historical Review*, 89 (1974).

W. T. Laprade, 'William Pitt and the Westminster Election', *American Historical Review*, 23 (1912).

W. T. Laprade, 'Public Opinion and the General Election of 1784', *English Historical Review*, 31 (1916).

A. Mitchell, 'The Association Movement 1792–1793', *Historical Journal*, 4 (1961).

N. B. Penny, 'The Whig Cult of Fox in Nineteenth Century Sculpture', *Past and Present*, 70 (1976).

C. H. Philips, 'The East India Company Interest and English Government', *Transactions of the Royal Historical Society*, 20 (1937).

Index